Frommer's®

Jamaica

4th Edition

by Darwin Porter & Danforth Prince

Here's what the critics say about Frommer's:

"Amazingly easy to use. Very portable, very complete."

—*Booklist*

"Detailed, accurate, and easy-to-read information for all price ranges."
—*Glamour Magazine*

"Hotel information is close to encyclopedic."

—*Des Moines Sunday Register*

"Frommer's Guides have a way of giving you a real feel for a place."
—*Knight Ridder Newspapers*

WILEY

Wiley Publishing, Inc.

About the Authors

As a team of veteran travel writers, **Darwin Porter** and **Danforth Prince** have produced numerous titles for Frommer's including best-selling guides to Italy, France, the Caribbean, England, and Germany. Porter, a former bureau chief of *The Miami Herald*, is also a noted Hollywood biographer. His most recent release is entitled *Brando Unzipped*, a close-up of the private life of the late Marlon Brando. Prince was formerly employed by the Paris bureau of the *New York Times*, and is today the president of Blood Moon Productions and other media-related firms.

Published by:

Wiley Publishing, Inc.

111 River St.
Hoboken, NJ 07030-5774

ISBN-13: 978-0-471-94614-4
ISBN-10: 0-471-94614-1

Editor: Michael Kelly
Production Editor: M. Faunette Johnston
Cartographer: Anton Crane
Photo Editor: Richard Fox
Production by Wiley Indianapolis Composition Services

For information on our other products and services or to obtain technical support, please contact our Customer Care Department within the U.S. at 800/762-2974, outside the U.S. at 317/572-3993 or fax 317/572-4002.

Wiley also publishes its books in a variety of electronic formats. Some content that appears in print may not be available in electronic formats.

Manufactured in the United States of America

5   4   3   2   1

Contents

8   Port Antonio

190

9   Kingston & the Blue Mountains

223

Appendix: Jamaica in Depth

250

Index

267

List of Maps

An Invitation to the Reader

In researching this book, we discovered many wonderful places—hotels, restaurants, shops, and more. We're sure you'll find others. Please tell us about them, so we can share the information with your fellow travelers in upcoming editions. If you were disappointed with a recommendation, we'd love to know that, too. Please write to:

Frommer's Jamaica, 4th Edition
Wiley Publishing, Inc. • 111 River St. • Hoboken, NJ 07030-5774

An Additional Note

Please be advised that travel information is subject to change at any time—and this is especially true of prices. We therefore suggest that you write or call ahead for confirmation when making your travel plans. The authors, editors, and publisher cannot be held responsible for the experiences of readers while traveling. Your safety is important to us, however, so we encourage you to stay alert and be aware of your surroundings. Keep a close eye on cameras, purses, and wallets, all favorite targets of thieves and pickpockets.

Frommer's Star Ratings, Icons & Abbreviations

Every hotel, restaurant, and attraction listing in this guide has been ranked for quality, value, service, amenities, and special features using a **star-rating system.** In country, state, and regional guides, we also rate towns and regions to help you narrow down your choices and budget your time accordingly. Hotels and restaurants are rated on a scale of zero (recommended) to three stars (exceptional). Attractions, shopping, nightlife, towns, and regions are rated according to the following scale: zero stars (recommended), one star (highly recommended), two stars (very highly recommended), and three stars (must-see).

In addition to the star-rating system, we also use **eight feature icons** that point you to the great deals, in-the-know advice, and unique experiences that separate travelers from tourists. Throughout the book, look for:

Finds	Special finds—those places only insiders know about
Fun Fact	Fun facts—details that make travelers more informed and their trips more fun
Kids	Best bets for kids and advice for the whole family
Moments	Special moments—those experiences that memories are made of
Overrated	Places or experiences not worth your time or money
Tips	Insider tips—great ways to save time and money
Value	Great values—where to get the best deals
Warning	Warning—traveler's advisories are usually in effect

The following **abbreviations** are used for credit cards:

AE	American Express	DISC	Discover	V	Visa
DC	Diners Club	MC	MasterCard		

Frommers.com

Now that you have the guidebook to a great trip, visit our website at **www.frommers.com** for travel information on more than 3,000 destinations. With features updated regularly, we give you instant access to the most current trip-planning information available. At Frommers.com, you'll also find the best prices on airfares, accommodations, and car rentals—and you can even book travel online through our travel booking partners. At Frommers.com, you'll also find the following:

- Online updates to our most popular guidebooks
- Vacation sweepstakes and contest giveaways
- Newsletter highlighting the hottest travel trends
- Online travel message boards with featured travel discussions

What's New in Jamaica

The most volatile country in the Caribbean continues to explode with change. Here is a preview of just some of the latest developments.

MONTEGO BAY For those who want to escape the all-inclusives, two affordable hotels have been upgraded and offer desirable accommodations to the frugal traveler. **Gloriana,** 1-21 Sunset Blvd. (✆ 876/979-0669; www.hotelgloriana. com), is just a 10-minute walk from Doctors Cave Beach. Bedrooms are compact but comfortably furnished. Another choice, **The Gloustershire Hotel,** Gloucester Ave. (✆ 877/574-8497 or 876/952-4420), opens right onto Doctors Cave Beach. Attractively and comfortably furnished rooms at moderate tariffs are the attraction, along with the resort's Waterfront Restaurant, known mainly for its Jamaican dishes.

New restaurants have continued to open, hoping to lure diners away from their hotels at night. Among the best is **Jasmine,** in the Ritz-Carlton at Rose Hall (✆ 876/953-2800). Its international cuisine lures diners from outside the hotel, who dine by candlelight from an impeccable menu at intricately laid tables. Its chief rival is **Nikkita's,** Gloucester Ave. (✆ 876/979-6373), with a skilled kitchen staff offering one of the best modern Jamaican cuisines on the island. First-rate ingredients and finely honed dishes await you.

NEGRIL At Jamaica's most hedonistic resort, the latest hotel development centers around two choices from a Spanish chain, **Riu Tropical Bay** and **Club Riu Negril,** Norman Manley Blvd. (✆ 876/957-5900; www.riu.com). Opening onto a beachfront in the town center, the sprawling resort is painted in fiesta-inspired colors and offers cost-conscious all-inclusive deals. The resort has eight restaurants and a dozen bars.

SOUTH COAST Sandals, the all-inclusive Jamaican chain of couples-only retreats, has now invaded the south coast of Jamaica. The largest and best resort along the coast is at Whitehouse in Westmoreland province. **Sandals Whitehouse European Village & Spa** (✆ 800/SANDALS or 876/640-3000; www.sandals.com) is the most massive hotel development the South Coast has ever seen. It occupies a 3.2km (2-mile) stretch of beachfront in a lush setting of 18 tropical hectares (45 acres). A 90-minute drive from Montego Bay airport, the resort features the usual high-quality bedrooms typical of Sandals properties, and seven different restaurants with a varied cuisine.

OCHO RIOS At this coastal resort, so beloved by cruise-ship passengers, **Shaw Park Beach Hotel,** Cutlass Bay (✆ 800/377-1126 or 876/974-2552; www.shawparkbeachhotel.com), has made a dramatic comeback. The original hotel opened in 1955 but had grown tired over the years. Completely restored and redesigned, it is back with better rooms than ever, each well appointed, and the location on a private white sandy beach remains the same. Frugal travelers are discovering the 99-unit **Rooms on the Beach,** Main Street (© **888/467-8737** or 876/974-6632; www.roomsresorts. com), originally constructed in the 1970s but now restored. With simple but tasteful rooms offering practical comfort, it opens onto a desirable stretch of Mallard's Beach.

Making its debut is a Spanish chain hotel, **Riu Clubhotel Ocho Rios,** Mammee Bay (© **888/666-8816** or 876/972-2200; www.riu.com). Accommodations are quite *luxe* with private balconies and verandas and marble floors. The mammoth **Sunset Jamaica Grande Resort & Spa,** Main Street (© **800/243-1707** or 876/974-2200; www. sunsetjamaicagrande.com), has seen yet another reincarnation. Still one of the largest hotels on the islands, it is now an all-inclusive. Millions of dollars have been poured into its rejuvenation, and the money was well spent. A lot of Disney-inspired theatrics entice today's visitors, including lagoon-shaped swimming pools and waterfalls.

The most discerning foodies in Ocho Rios are heading for **The Dinner Terrace at The Jamaica Inn,** Main Street (© **876/974-2514**), drawn by its deluxe setting and its sublime continental and Caribbean cuisine, including Jamaican specialties. The menu changes nightly and has been vastly improved since its initial opening, with the recent hiring of new chefs. Come here for a night of Jamaican posh. Equally grand but more pretentious is **Le Papillon Restaurant and the Caviar Bar at the Royal Plantation,** Main Street (© **876/974-5601**), featuring a refined continental cuisine and the best caviar on the island. Small jars of caviar are opened like holy relics, but you can also feast on such delights as Caribbean lobster soup with black pepper rum.

PORT ANTONIO   At long last a new marina has opened in this remote resort, and the best chef in Jamaica, Norma Shirley, has already invaded. She calls her place **Norma's at the Marina** (© **876/993-9510**), and her take on Jamaican specialties and a refined continental cuisine is one of the best—if not the best—offered along the island's north coast. You can sit on the terrace checking out the arriving yachts, or retreat inside the mahogany-trimmed dining room open to the breezes. From the reggae salad studded with sautéed shrimp to several different versions of grilled fish, Norma will feed you well.

The Best of Jamaica

Most visitors already have a mental picture of Jamaica before they arrive: its boisterous culture of reggae and Rastafarianism; its white-sand beaches; and its lush foliage, rivers, mountains, and clear waterfalls. Jamaica's art and cuisine are also remarkable.

Yet Jamaica's appealing aspects have to be weighed against its poverty, crime, and racial tensions, the legacy of colonial rule and subsequent political upheavals.

So, should you go? By all means. Just be prudent and cautious. The island has fine hotels and savory food. It's well geared to couples who come to tie the knot or celebrate a honeymoon. And Jamaica boasts the best golf courses in the West Indies, some of the finest diving waters in the world, and good river rafting. In this chapter we lay out our favorite places and experiences.

1 The Best Beaches

- **Doctors Cave Beach** (Montego Bay): This 8km (5-mile) stretch of white sand made "Mo Bay" a tourist destination. Waters are placid and crystal clear, and there are changing rooms and a beach bar. This one is a family favorite. See p. 88.
- **Cornwall Beach** (Montego Bay): Although it's often crowded, this beach is covered with soft, white, sugary sand. The water is clean and warm, and it's a good spot to take the family. But "higglers"—vendors—will aggressively hawk anything from jewelry to drugs. See p. 88.
- **Seven Mile Beach** (Negril): This beach stretches 11km (7 miles) along the west coast. These golden sands are

fine for families, though there are several (sectioned-off) nudist patches where guests bare all. See p. 131.
- **Treasure Beach** (South Coast): Tired of fighting the crowds? Head for this beach on the dry, sunny South Coast. The undertow can be dangerous, so swimming is tricky. But crashing waves make it one of the most dramatic beachscapes in Jamaica. See p. 147.
- **Boston Bay Beach** (Port Antonio): It's known not only for its white sands and clear waters, but also for the great jerk-pork stands. This beach has the biggest waves in Jamaica, and you can rent surfboards and even get a lesson. See p. 208.

2 The Best Watersports Outfitters

- **North Coast Marine Sports** (Montego Bay; ✆ 876/953-2211): Offering the best scuba diving in Montego Bay, this staff of instructors knows some great spots to dive among coral reefs. See p. 90.
- **Negril Scuba Centre** (Negril; ✆ 800/818-2963 in the U.S., or 876/957-9641): This is the best-equipped dive facility in Negril, with a very professional staff. See p. 133.

Jamaica

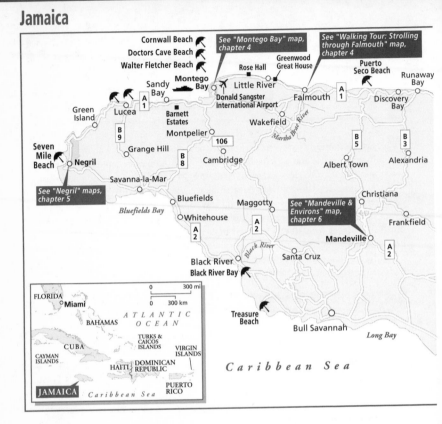

- **Jamaica Dive Center** (Runaway Bay; ☏ **876/973-4845**): Its slogan is "We Be Divin'," and this outfitter takes you to some of the best dive sites along the northern coast. Equipment can be rented on-site, and offerings range from one-tank dives to six-boat packages. See p. 188.

3 The Best Golf Courses

- **White Witch of Rose Hall Golf Course** (Montego Bay; (☏ **876/518-0174**): This is the newest Jamaican golf course and one of the most spectacular, set on 80 hectares (200 acres) of lush greenery. See p. 90.
- **Cinnamon Hill course at Rose Hall Resort & Country Club** (Montego Bay; ☏ **876/953-2650**): This has been called one of the top courses in the world. It's a challenging seaside

and mountain course. The 14th hole passes a waterfall. See p. 90.
- **Tryall Club Jamaica** (Montego Bay; ☏ **876/956-5660**): Jamaica's finest course, this site has hosted prestigious tournaments such as the Johnnie Walker Classic. Wind direction can change suddenly, making the challenging course even harder. See p. 90.

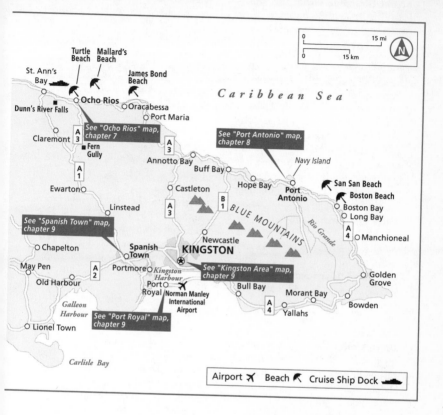

- **Half Moon** (Montego Bay; ✆ **876/953-2211**): A top island course, Half Moon features well-manicured and interestingly shaped greens, but it's not as challenging as the one at Tryall. See p. 91.

- **Sandals Golf & Country Club** (Ocho Rios; ✆ **876/975-0119**): This course is known for panoramic vistas, rolling terrain, and lush vegetation. Sandals guests play for free. See p. 175.

4 The Best Tennis Facilities

- **Half Moon** (Montego Bay; ✆ **876/953-2211**): This is Jamaica's best tennis—13 state-of-the-art courts, 7 of which are lit for night games. See p. 91.

- **Rose Hall Resort & Country Club** (Montego Bay; ✆ **876/953-2650**):

This resort has six hard-surface courts, all lit at night. Hotel guests play free. See p. 92.

- **Tryall Club Jamaica** (Montego Bay; ✆ **876/956-5660**): Tryall has nine superb hard-surface courts, three of which are lit for night play. See p. 91.

- **Sandals Grande Ocho Rios Beach & Villa Resort** (Ocho Rios; ℂ 876/974-1027): This resort offers both clay and hard-surface courts, all lit at night. Twice-a-day clinics are offered for beginners as well as advanced players. See p. 175.

5 The Best Natural Attractions

- **Martha Brae's Rafters Village** (Montego Bay; ℂ 876/952-0889): Martha Brae's Rafters Village offers the best river-rafting experience in and around this popular resort. You sit on a raised dais on bamboo logs and watch the river scenery unfold. See "Beaches, Golf & Other Outdoor Pursuits" in chapter 4.

- **The Black River** (South Coast): You can explore what feels like real Tarzan country, with mangrove trees and crocodiles in the wild, on an outing with **South Coast Safaris** (ℂ 876/965-2513). Lots of wild things grow in these swamps, and birders delight in the bird life. See "The South Coast," in chapter 6.

- **Green Grotto Caves** (Discovery Bay; ℂ 876/973-2841). These limestone caves were once used to hide runaway slaves. They're a world of stalagmites and stalactites, with seemingly endless chambers and eerie Grotto Lake, which you can visit in a boat. See p. 178.

- **Somerset Falls** (Port Antonio): Waters from the Daniels River race down a deep gorge through a rainforest. Flowering vines, waterfalls, and foaming cascades form a lush backdrop. You can swim in the deep rock pools. See "Exploring the Area," in chapter 8.

- **Rafting on the Rio Grande** (Port Antonio; ℂ 876/993-5778): Shades of Errol Flynn, this is the grandest rafting experience in Jamaica. The rafts are propelled by bamboo poles. See "Beaches & Outdoor Pursuits," in chapter 8.

- **Exploring the Blue Mountains** (outside Kingston; ℂ 876/960-6685): This is one of the biggest, wildest, and greenest parks in the Caribbean, ideal for exploring. You must hike 5 to 6 hours through thick vegetation (hearing amazing birdsong on the way) to reach the summit. See "Exploring the Blue Mountains," in chapter 9.

6 The Best Honeymoon Resorts

- **Sandals** (Montego Bay, Negril, and Ocho Rios; ℂ 800/SANDALS in the U.S.): These three resorts pride themselves on fun, food, and drink, laid out in abundance and all paid for in advance—no tips or bills here. Staff members bring heroic amounts of community spirit and enthusiasm to weddings. All the properties are high quality, but Sandals Royal Caribbean at Montego Bay and Sandals Dunn's River at Ocho Rios are probably the best in the chain. See p. 79, 124, and 166.

- **Half Moon** (Montego Bay; ℂ 800/626-0592 or 876/953-2211): This resort offers honeymooners deluxe oceanview rooms and cottages fronting a near-perfect crescent-shaped beach. The resort offers lots of activities, too, such as aerobics, tennis, swimming, and, most definitely, golf. See p. 71.

- **Jake's** (Treasure Beach; ℂ 800/OUTPOST or 876/965-0635): Funky and idiosyncratic, this is a really offbeat choice for a honeymoon where no one will find you. Set on a remote rocky beach, the place is small and personal. See p. 148.

- **Jamaica Inn** (Ocho Rios; ✆ **800/834-4608** in the U.S., or 876/974-2514): Winston Churchill slept in a suite here; if you can't afford that suite, plenty of other classy rooms are just fine for honeymooners. The resort opens onto a private cove with powdery champagne-colored sand and maintains a British colonial aura of formality. See p. 158.

- **Couples Sans Souci** (Ocho Rios; ✆ **800/268-7537** in the U.S., or 876/994-1206): Sink into one of the whirlpool tubs in the elegant marble bathrooms here—with your newly acquired spouse, of course—and the day is yours. This is a far classier joint than the Sandals properties. An on-site spa and clothing-optional beach are also alluring for many couples. See p. 164.

- **Sandals Grande Ocho Rios Beach & Villa Resort** (Ocho Rios; ✆ **800/SANDALS** or 876/974-5691): The honeymoon villas at this stately, plantation-style spa and resort are perfect private retreats for newlyweds. Each has a private attendant and pool. Guests are pampered with massages, pedicures, and manicures. The resort is all-inclusive, with a range of sports facilities. See p. 167.

- **Breezes Runaway Bay** (Runaway Bay; ✆ **800/GO-SUPER** or 876/973-4820): Ten kilometers (6 miles) west of Ocho Rios, this all-inclusive hotel re-creates the South Seas on Jamaican soil. It's stylish, with luxurious accommodations and good food. Activities include reggae classes. See p. 186.

- **Blue Lagoon Villas** (Port Antonio; ✆ **800/237-3237** or 876/993-8491): A favorite with movie stars visiting "off the record," this pocket of posh is pure luxury: Each plush villa comes with a dedicated chef, housekeeper, and butler. Break out your wallet. See p. 196.

7 The Best Family-Friendly Resorts

- **Coyaba** (Mahoe Bay, Little River, Montego Bay; ✆ **877/232-3224** in the U.S., or 876/953-9150): With a graceful British colonial atmosphere, this small all-inclusive resort offers children 11 and under a 50% discount. The oceanfront location is intimate and inviting, with a lovely strip of sandy beach. A nanny service keeps little ones fed and entertained. See p. 74.

- **FDR Pebbles** (Trelawny, near Montego Bay; ✆ **888/FDR-KIDS** or 876/617-2500): This new hotel caters mainly to families with one or two children, though larger groups can be accommodated. The resort offers a host of activities, and you're even assigned a staff member to assist with housekeeping and babysitting. See p. 79.

- **Beaches Negril** (Negril; ✆ **800/BEACHES** in the U.S., or 876/957-9270): Opened in 1997, this is the family-oriented wing of the Sandals chain. A roster of child and teen activities awaits youngsters on grounds studded with palms and sea grapes, adjacent to a sandy beach. The resort even has a restaurant for "children only." See p. 118.

- **Beaches Boscobel Resort & Golf Club** (Boscobel Beach; ✆ **888/BEACHES** or 876/975-7777): On a sandy beach 16km (10 miles) east of Ocho Rios, this property is geared to families more than any other hotel on the north shore. See p. 163.

- **Franklyn D. Resort** (Runaway Bay; ✆ **888/FDR-KIDS** in the U.S., or 876/973-4592): At this family favorite on the North Coast, all meals and activities are included in the price; you're housed in Mediterranean-style villas; and a personal attendant takes care of cooking, cleaning, and child care. Lots of programs keep the kids entertained. A Kiddies' Centre features everything from computers to arts and crafts. See p. 186.

8 The Best Places to Get Away from It All

- **Rockhouse** (Negril; ✆ **876/957-4373**): It's like living on the west coast of Africa. You stay in a thatch-roofed villa in Negril's West End and sleep in an old-fashioned bed under mosquito netting. It's a splendid getaway if you don't mind climbing down ladders carved into the sea cliffs. Open-air showers cool you off—and let you put on a show for the fish. See p. 117.
- **Treasure Beach Hotel** (South Coast; ✆ **800/526-2422** or 876/965-0110): On a lush hillside above a sandy South Coast beach, no one will ever find you at this place. It hardly competes with Jamaica's megaresorts, but it does offer tranquillity and a laid-back feel. Bedrooms are in a series of outlying cottages, all offering complete privacy. It's cheap, too. See p. 149.
- **Noël Coward's Blue Harbour** (Port Maria; ✆ **876/725-0289** or 505/586-1244): This 1950s retreat is where the playwright and composer entertained the rich and famous of his day. Today it's rented whole or in part to paying guests who appreciate its funky nostalgia. See p. 161.
- **Hotel Mocking Bird Hill** (Port Antonio; ✆ **876/993-7267**): One of our favorite retreats in all of Jamaica lies outside this resort, a comfortable and well-maintained inn that offers the epitome of Jamaican hospitality, and at an affordable price. The retreat is both artsy and ecologically sensitive. See p 198.
- **Strawberry Hill** (Blue Mountains; ✆ **800/OUTPOST** or 876/944-8400): This highland retreat has been called "a home-away-from-home for five-star Robinson Crusoes." Perched 930m (3,100 ft.) above the sea, it's our favorite lodging in eastern Jamaica. Set in a well-planted garden, the cottage complex is a memorable and lush retreat. See p. 246.

9 The Best All-Inclusives

- **Sandals Montego Bay** (Montego Bay; ✆ **800/SANDALS** in the U.S., or 876/952-5510): This is a honeymoon haven despite a nearby airport of zooming jets. Everything's included, even the notorious toga parties; this place is for couples who want to have a good time. Guests tend to be extroverted and gregarious, and eat and drink their money's worth. We think it's outclassed by better resorts at Ocho Rios, but many vacationers seem to prefer this location. See p. 79.
- **Breezes Montego Bay** (Montego Bay; ✆ **877/467-8737** or 876/940-1150): This five-story SuperClub complex calls itself "a sandbox for your inner child" and is the only major hotel built on Doctors Cave Beach. From intimate cabins to lavish suites, you can live it up in various styles and price ranges. See p. 78.
- **Royal Plantation Spa & Golf Resort** (Ocho Rios; ✆ **888/48-ROYAL** or 876/974-5601): Less than 3km (2 miles) east of Ocho Rios, the

main house of this recently renovated all-inclusive resort evokes an antebellum Southern mansion. Among its luxurious touches is the finest hotel spa on the North Coast. See p. 165.

- **Couples Ocho Rios** (Ocho Rios; ✆ **800/268-7537** in the U.S., or 876/975-4271): "Any man and woman in love" are pampered and coddled here; the resort even offers its own private island where couples can bask in the buff. It's more upscale and, we think, classier than either of the Sandals resorts in the Ocho Rios area. Accommodations are top quality, and the food is among the best in the area: Four restaurants serve widely varied cuisine. See p. 163.

- **Sandals Grande Ocho Rios Beach & Villa Resort** (Ocho Rios; ✆ **800/**

SANDALS in the U.S., or 876/974-5691): This 18-hectare (45-acre) resort is one of the top all-inclusives in the Ocho Rios area. The lodgings consist of one-, two-, and three-bedroom villas, each with its own pool and fully equipped kitchen. The dining choices are the best of any of the competing resorts. It's not directly on the beach, but it offers a beauty spa and a health-and-fitness center. See p. 166.

- **Hedonism III** (Runaway Bay; ✆ **877/GO-SUPER** or 876/973-4100): Serene and isolated, this all-inclusive is the most fun-oriented hotel on the North Coast. It rents rooms to both singles and couples over age 15. There are two good beaches: one where you can wear your suit, and another that's au naturel. See p. 187.

10 The Best Restaurants

- **Day-O Plantation Restaurant** (Montego Bay; ✆ **876/952-1825**): On the site of the 19th-century Barnett Plantation—a house that sugar built—this fine restaurant, serving a refined international and Jamaican cuisine, is often a venue for singing and other entertainment. Jamaican spices and herbs permeate all dishes. See p. 82.

- **Sugar Mill Restaurant** (Montego Bay; ✆ **876/953-2314**): Located at Half Moon, this is the top restaurant in Montego Bay. The chef's smoked marlin is without equal, and he makes the island's best Jamaican-style bouillabaisse. Guests dine by candlelight indoors or on an open terrace. See p.85

- **Norma's on the Beach at Sea Splash** (Negril; ✆ **876/957-4041**): Widely acclaimed as Jamaica's finest woman chef, Kingston's Norma Shirley has brought her recipes to Negril's Sea

Splash Resort. The Jamaican and international food here is the finest on Seven Mile Beach, and Norma gets the best produce from local vendors. See p. 125.

- **Rockhouse Restaurant** (Negril; ✆ **876/957-4373**): Perched above a rocky inlet, this restaurant serves terrific cuisine, such as smoked marlin and peppered pork with yams. See p. 126.

- **Bloomfield Great House** (Mandeville; ✆ **876/962-7130**): Once part of a coffee plantation, this restaurant today serves one of the island's best-orchestrated menus—everything from smoked marlin with black caviar to the best pasta dishes in this part of Jamaica. See p. 154.

- **Evita's Italian Restaurant** (Ocho Rios; ✆ **876/974-2333**): Evita (actually Eva Myers) is a local culinary star, devoting at least half her menu to pastas. Her recipes range from the north to the south of Italy. Try snapper stuffed with crabmeat or lobster and scampi in buttery white-cream sauce—all washed down with a good Italian wine. See p. 170.

- **Mille Fleurs** (Port Antonio; ✆ **876/993-7267**): In the Hotel Mocking Bird Hill, this restaurant is terraced and perched 180m (600 ft.) above sea level with panoramic views. People come here for the delectable food, which has been praised by *Gourmet* magazine. Opt for coconut-and-garlic soup or the fish with a spicy mango-and-shrimp sauce. See p. 205.
- **Redbones the Blues Café** (Kingston; ✆ **876/978-6091**): In a former Spanish colonial house, one of the most elegant restaurants on the island is the setting for a refined Jamaican cuisine of artful preparation and unexpected flavors. Ever had shrimp, lobster, and salmon in a creamy coconut sauce? See p. 230.
- **Norma's on the Terrace** (Kingston; ✆ **876/968-5488**): Kingston's Norma Shirley, the island's foremost female restaurateur, serves up a nouvelle Jamaican cuisine without equal in the area. Try such Jamaican specialties as chowder with crabmeat, shrimp, conch, and lobster, or grilled smoked pork loin in a teriyaki-and-ginger sauce. See p. 230.
- **Strawberry Hill** (Kingston; ✆ **876/944-8400**): This is one of the best modern Jamaican restaurants, tucked in the Blue Mountains. Even if you don't stay at this exclusive resort, try grilled fish with jerk mango or grilled shrimp with fresh cilantro in its restaurant. See p. 246.

11 The Best Romantic Experiences

- **YS Falls** (Black River): The best place to escape for a romantic picnic is along the coast east of Negril. Three kilometers (2 miles) north of the port of Black River, in a "Me Tarzan, You Jane" setting, you can actually swing from an overhead vine or a jungle rope into cooling ponds made by the waterfall. See p. 145.
- **Bloomfield Great House** (Mandeville; ✆ **876/962-7130**): If you should ever grow nostalgic for the Jamaica that used to be, plan a dinner at this historic house set on 2 hectares (5 acres) of beautiful landscaping. After a drink on the old-fashioned veranda, enjoy an elegantly presented and good-tasting meal in a colonial setting of long ago. See p. 154.
- **Goldeneye** (Oracabessa; ✆ **800/688-7678** or 876/975-3354): An intimate and romantic retreat east of Ocho Rios, this is our favorite spot in Jamaica for a tryst with your own "secret agent." This is where then-owner Ian Fleming created the character 007, James Bond. Rock stars and other celebs often seek it out. See p. 164.
- **The Blue Lagoon** (Port Antonio; ✆ **876/993-7791**): Another beauty spot, this is where teenage Brooke Shields swam nude in the film of the same name. You can have the same experience in an enchanted pool fed by a natural amphitheater. The water, 56m (186 ft.) deep at its deepest point, is said to have aphrodisiac powers—which you'll have to determine for yourself. See p. 196.
- **Reach Falls** (Manchioneal): East of Port Antonio, this is one of the oft-photographed beauty spots of the Caribbean. Visitors enter a virgin rainforest for a cooling dip and perhaps some nude intimacy under the watery cascades. See p. 216.

12 The Best Shopping Buys

- **Art:** Its paintings may never rival those of the finest Haitian artists, but Jamaica is at least the second-best center for art in the Caribbean. Prices are still reasonable, too, even when the artist has a certain renown. Although paintings are sold all over the island, the finest art is found in Kingston at either the **Frame Centre Gallery** or the **Mutual Life Gallery,** the two leading display showcases for the best of the island's artistic talent. See "Shopping," in chapter 9.

- **Handicrafts:** Crafts come in many forms, ranging from alabaster and woodcarvings to weavings. But quality is highly variable. The finest assortment of crafts is at **Harmony Hall** outside Ocho Rios on the North Coast. See p. 178.

- **Fashions:** Many artisans in Jamaica produce quality resort wear; Jamaican women are known as good seamstresses, and they often make quite passable copies of the works of top designers at a fraction of the original's price.

- **Jewelry and Watches:** Some watches at various outlets in Jamaica sell for 20% to 40% off stateside prices. Be sure to buy from a reliable dealer, not vendors hustling gold so-called Rolex watches. Jamaican gemstones include coral agate and black coral, and many fashionable pieces are made from these stones; quality handmade necklaces are sold nearly everywhere.

13 The Best After-Dark Fun

- **Margueritaville Sports Bar & Grill** (Montego Bay; ✆ **876/952-4777**): If you're macho, or at least grow hair on your chest, head for the most popular sports bar in Jamaica. Overlooking the sea, across from the Coral Cliff Hotel, this hangout also serves the best margaritas on the island and features the best sports broadcasts on satellite TV. See p. 86.

- **Time 'n' Place** (Falmouth, east of Montego Bay; ✆ **876/954-4371**): A raffish beach bar built of driftwood, this place looks as though it might blow away in the next storm. The setting is so authentic that many fashion magazines, including *Vogue,* have used it for background shots. The bartender makes the island's best daiquiris. See p. 99.

- **Hedonism II** (Negril; ✆ **876/957-5200**): For the hottest night at this resort, don your toga and head for the most notorious all-inclusive resort in Jamaica, a place known for its wild and raunchy parties. If you aren't already a guest, you'll have to purchase a night pass for $75, entitling you to all the food and drink you can consume. See p. 122.

- **Roof Club** (Port Antonio; no phone). On the north coast of Jamaica you'll find no more authentic and animated local dive than this raunchy joint. Visitors come to see "the real" Jamaica after dark. It's for locals, not tourists. The secondhand *ganga* smoke alone will make you high, and the sounds of reggae blasting at ear-splitting levels. It's not for everyone, and not for the faint-of-heart, but a lot of fun for some adventurous visitors. See p 221.

- **Mingles** (Kingston; ✆ **876/929-9000**): In the Courtleigh Hotel, this is one of the best places—and the safest—to be after dark in the capital of Jamaica. Filled with Jamaican youth, it is both a bar and a dance club, with uniformed bartenders and the constant beat of reggae, pop, and soca. See p. 238.

2

Planning Your Trip to Jamaica

This chapter gives you the nuts-and-bolts information about your trip to Jamaica—specifically, what you need to do before leaving home. We'll answer questions such as when to go, how to get the best airfare or package deal, what to take along, and what documents you'll need. In case you're not sure where in Jamaica you want to go, we begin with a rundown of the various options.

1 Jamaica in Brief

Most casual visitors to Jamaica pick a resort without paying much attention to its location on the island. That is particularly true for guests who prefer to spend most of their time at an all-inclusive resort, venturing out only occasionally to shop or to see some of the local sights. Even so, knowing a bit about the different areas of Jamaica can help you find the perfect resort for you.

Most travelers who visit Kingston do so for business reasons. But for the true Jamaican culture buff, the island's largest city offers the most museums, the best galleries, and some great historic sights. It also has more nightlife than most of the top resorts, ranging from jazz and reggae clubs to upscale supper clubs and English theater. But you don't come here for beaches.

Port Antonio is for the elite traveler who wants to escape the mass package tours of Ocho Rios or Montego Bay. Come here for some good beaches, plus great river rafting, scuba diving, and snorkeling.

To the west, Ocho Rios features some of the grandest and most traditional resorts in Jamaica, as well as some of the leading Sandals properties. But it doesn't have the best beaches, shops, or scenic attractions. Nonetheless, if you're resort-oriented, this might be your choice.

The grande dame of Jamaica is Montego Bay, which boasts four of the poshest resorts in the Caribbean. Although we prefer the beaches of Negril, those of Montego Bay are equally fine (if crowded in winter). Shopping here is superb for Jamaica; nightlife is surprisingly lackluster.

Negril's great beaches are for hedonists and families.

The South Coast is for back-road adventurers. Chances are you'll overlook the inland city of Mandeville, although it's a good day trip from Negril or the South Coast.

MONTEGO BAY

This is the number-one destination for all of Jamaica, appealing to the widest possible range of visitors. "Mo Bay," as it's known, has the best golf in the West Indies, and four of the grandest resorts on the island; the duty-free shopping here is great. This is about as far from rural Jamaica as you can get: The tourist dollar drives its economy. But it also boasts several attractions in its environs, including former great houses of plantations, decaying old towns such as Falmouth, and daylong adventures into remote Maroon Country.

NEGRIL

Situated near Jamaica's relatively arid western tip, Negril enjoys a reputation as the nudist center of the West Indies, with a kind of gently provocative do-as-you-please attitude. Its **Seven Mile Beach** is one of the longest uninterrupted stretches of sand in the Caribbean. Other than that beach, its laidback lifestyle, and wild parties, there isn't much here. Outside the megaresorts, restaurants here tend to be locally run dives; amusing, but rarely the place for first-class cuisine.

THE SOUTH COAST

The little-visited South Coast, lying east of Negril along the A2 (the road to Kingston), is undiscovered Jamaica—although it's becoming better known all the time. Contrary to the island's lush, tropical image, this area is dry and arid. Hotels are few and far between, and they are frequently of the mom-and-pop persuasion. The chief draw here is **Treasure Beach,** tucked away on the secluded coast.

MANDEVILLE

Located in south-central Jamaica, Mandeville is the country's highest-altitude town and is built in a style strongly influenced by the British. It is now the center of the island's noted coffee cultivation; a sense of slow-paced colonial charm remains a trademark of the town.

THE NORTH COAST

This region's primary natural attractions include its steeply sloping terrain, the setting for panoramic public gardens and dramatic waterfalls.

Set on a deep-water harbor easily able to accommodate cruise ships, **Ocho Rios** boasts a dense concentration of resort hotels and other vacation spots. It runs a very distant second to Montego Bay in its appeal, although its hinterlands do contain a number of Jamaica's premier attractions, including the overrun Dunn's River Falls. It also can't compete with Montego Bay in beaches or nightlife. What it does offer, however, are some of the grandest resorts in the Caribbean.

Directly west of Ocho Rios is the satellite town of **Runaway Bay,** which boasts a handful of resorts opening onto some good beaches and has the distinct advantage of not being as overrun with tourists as Ocho Rios.

The hub of verdant eastern Jamaica, **Port Antonio** still basks in nostalgia. Frequently photographed for its Victorian/Caribbean architecture, it is a refreshing change of pace from touristy Negril, Ocho Rios, and Montego Bay. Beaches such as San San are among the most alluring in the country, and this is also a base for exploring some of the major attractions in Jamaica's hinterlands, including rafting on the Rio Grande River.

KINGSTON & SPANISH TOWN

Located on the southeast coast, **Kingston** is Jamaica's capital, largest city, and principal port. It's a cosmopolitan city with approximately 750,000 residents in its metropolitan area and serves as the country's economic, cultural, and government center. Residents proudly call it the world's reggae capital as well. The city's northern district, New Kingston, consists mostly of high-rises, modern buildings, business hotels, and upscale homes. There are, however, extensive poverty-stricken areas as well, and it's not the safest city to visit.

Nevertheless, Kingston could make for a fascinating 1-day visit; it has more cultural attractions, including the National Gallery, than anywhere else on the island.

Nearby are the remains of **Port Royal,** once an infamous lair of pirates and renegades. Twenty minutes west of Kingston by car is **Spanish Town,** a slow-paced village containing the Cathedral of St. James.

THE BLUE MOUNTAINS

A land of soaring peaks and deep valleys with luxuriant vegetation, the Blue Mountain range rises to the north of Kingston. Mountain roads wind and dip, and they are in bad repair, so don't try to visit on your own: It's easy to get lost. However, travel agents in Kingston can book you into tours throughout this region of coffee plantations and rum factories. Maintained by the government, the prime part of the mountain range is the 192-acre Blue Mountain–John Crow Mountain National Park.

2 Visitor Information

TOURIST OFFICES

Before you go, you can get information from the **Jamaica Tourist Board** at 5201 Blue Lagoon Dr., Suite 670, Miami, FL 33126 (℃ **800/233-4582** or 305/665-0557).

In Canada contact the office in **Toronto** at 303 Eglinton Ave. E., Suite 200, Toronto, ON M4P IL3 (℃ **800/465-2624** or 416/482-7850). Brits can contact the **London** office: 1–2 Prince Consort Rd., London SW7 2BZ (℃ **020/7225-9090;** www.visitjamaica.com).

INFO ON THE WEB

The Internet is a great source of travel information. Jamaica is on the Internet at www.visitjamaica.com; www.jamaican.com; www.jamaicatravelnet.com; www.jamaica-guide.info. In addition, **Yahoo** (www.yahoo.com), **Excite** (www.excite.com), **Lycos** (www.lycos.com), and the other major Internet indexing sites all have subcategories for travel, country/regional information, and culture—click on all three for links to travel-related websites.

Other good clearinghouse sites for information are **Microsoft Expedia** (www.expedia.com) and **Travelocity** (www.travelocity.com).

You might also check out "The Unofficial Website on Jamaica" (**www.jamaicans.com**), the best all-around site, with some good pointers, cultural tidbits, a patois primer, and plenty of humor. This is one of the few Jamaica Web pages that isn't either a blatant ad or just somebody's home page with a few vacation pictures.

TRAVEL AGENTS

Travel agents can save you plenty of time and money by steering you toward the best package deals, hunting down the best airfare for your route, and arranging for cruises and rental cars. Airlines have cut commissions, though, and most agents have to charge a service fee to hold the bottom line. Agents don't get the same rates from all hotels—many have special deals with particular hotels that they do a lot of business with. So if one agent turns you down on a hotel, another may still be able to get you a room, and at a different price. In the worst instances, unscrupulous agents will offer you only travel options that bag them the juiciest commissions. Shop around and ask hard questions—use this book to become an informed consumer.

If you decide to use a travel agent, make sure the agent is a member of the **American Society of Travel Agents (ASTA),** 1101 King St., Alexandria, VA 22314 (℃ **703/739-8739;** www.astanet.com). If you send a self-addressed stamped envelope, ASTA will mail you the free booklet *Avoiding Travel Problems.* If you get poor service from an ASTA agent, you can write to the **ASTA Consumer Affairs Department** at the address and phone number above.

You may also want to contact the U.S. State Department for background bulletins, which supply up-to-date information on crime, health concerns, import restrictions, and other travel matters. Write the **Superintendent of Documents, U.S. Government Printing Office,** Washington, DC 20402 (www.gpo.gov).

3 Entry Requirements & Customs

ENTRY REQUIREMENTS

DOCUMENTS   U.S. and Canada residents do not need passports but must have proof of citizenship (or permanent residency) and a return or ongoing ticket. A passport is the best bet, but an original birth certificate (or a certified copy) plus photo ID will usually suffice. Do check on the latest entry requirements before you travel, as the rules can change. Our advice is to always bring a passport when you're going to another country.

Other visitors, including British citizens, need passports that are good for a maximum stay of 6 months.

Immigration cards are given to visitors at the airport arrivals desks. Hold on to yours because you will need to surrender the document to Jamaican Customs when you leave the country.

For information on how to get a passport, go to the "Fast Facts" section of this chapter—the websites listed provide downloadable passport applications as well as the current fees for processing passport applications. For an up-to-date country-by-country listing of passport requirements around the world, go to the "Foreign Entry Requirement" Web page of the U.S. State Department at **http://travel.state.gov/foreignentry reqs.html**.

CUSTOMS

WHAT YOU CAN BRING INTO JAMAICA   Many small island nations in the Caribbean let you go through Customs without a thorough check: Jamaica is an exception. The Jamaican government is concerned about drug running and smuggling more than most other island nations. Therefore, your luggage may get a more thorough check in Jamaica than it would elsewhere.

You can bring in 2 liters of alcohol, plus two cartons of cigarettes. You're allowed to bring in some duty-free goods, but there's potential confusion here. You're not supposed to bring in an "inordinate" amount of such goods; local

---

Tips Passport Alert

Under new Homeland Security regulations, starting December 31, 2006 Americans traveling to Jamaica must show passports upon their return to the United States. A driver's license or a birth certificate will no longer be acceptable identification to re-enter the United States.

Allow plenty of time before your trip to apply for a passport; processing normally takes 3 weeks but can take longer during busy periods (especially spring). And keep in mind that if you need a passport in a hurry, you'll pay a higher processing fee. When traveling, safeguard your passport in an inconspicuous, inaccessible place like a money belt, and keep a copy of the critical pages with your passport number in a separate place. If you lose your passport, visit the nearest consulate of your native country as soon as possible for a replacement.

Traveling with Minors

It's always wise to have plenty of documentation when traveling in today's world with children. For changing details on entry requirements for children traveling abroad, keep up to date by going to the U.S. State Department website: http://travel.state.gov/foreignentryreqs.html.

To prevent international child abduction, governments have initiated procedures at entry and exit points. These often (but not always) include requiring documentary evidence of relationship and permission for the child's travel from the parent or legal guardian not present. Having such documentation on hand, even if not required, facilitates entries and exits. All children must have their own passport. To obtain a passport, the child *must* be present—that is, in person—at the center issuing the passport. Both parents must be present as well. If not, then a notarized statement from the parents is required.

All questions parents or guardians might have can be answered by calling the **National Passport Information Center** at © **877/487-6868** Monday to Friday 8am to 8pm Eastern Standard Time.

Customs officials have great leeway to interpret what's meant by "inordinate." So limit your import of duty-free goods to avoid paying a big import tax.

WHAT YOU CAN TAKE HOME U.S. Customs Returning U.S. citizens who have been away for 48 hours or more are allowed to bring back, once every 30 days, $800 worth of merchandise duty-free. You'll be charged a flat rate of 10% duty on the next $1,000 worth of purchases. Be sure to have your receipts handy. On gifts, the duty-free limit is $100. You cannot bring fresh foodstuffs into the United States; canned foods, however, are allowed.

Joint Customs declarations are possible for members of a family traveling together.

Collect receipts for all purchases made abroad. You must also declare on your Customs form the nature and value of all gifts received during your stay abroad. It's prudent to carry proof that you purchased expensive cameras or jewelry on the U.S. mainland. If you purchased such an item during an earlier trip abroad, you should carry proof that you have previously paid Customs duty on the item.

Sometimes merchants suggest a false receipt to undervalue your purchase. *Be warned:* You could be involved in a sting operation—the merchant might be an informer for U.S. Customs.

If you use any medication that contains controlled substances or requires injection, carry an original prescription or a note from your doctor.

For more specifics, write to the **U.S. Customs & Border Protection (CBP)**, 1300 Pennsylvania Ave. NW, Washington, DC 20229 (© **877/287-8667**; www.customs.ustreas.gov), and request the free pamphlet *Know Before You Go*.

U.K. Customs U.K. citizens returning from a non-E.U. country such as one of the Caribbean nations have a Customs allowance of 200 cigarettes, or 50 cigars, or 250 grams of smoking tobacco; 2 liters of still table wine; 1 liter of spirits or strong liqueurs (over 22% alcohol volume); 2 liters of fortified wine, sparkling wine, or other liqueurs; 60 cubic centimeters (ml) perfume; 250 cubic centimeters (ml) toilet water; and £145 worth of all other goods, including gifts and souvenirs. People under 17 cannot have the tobacco or alcohol allowance. For more information, contact **HM Revenue Customs,** Passenger Enquiry Point, Second Floor Wayfarer House, Great South West Road, Feltham, Middlesex, TW14 8NP (© **0845/010-9000** or 020/8929-0152 from outside the U.K.; www.hmrc.gov.uk).

Canada Customs For a clear summary of Canadian rules, write for the booklet *I Declare,* issued by the **Canada Border Services Agency,** 2265 St. Laurent Blvd., Ottawa, ON K1G 4KE (© **800/461-9999** or 204/983-3500; www.cbsa-asfc.gc.ca). Canada allows its residents of legal age a C$750 exemption, and you're allowed to bring back duty-free 200 cigarettes, 2.2 pounds of tobacco, 40 imperial ounces of liquor, and 50 cigars. In addition, you're allowed to mail gifts to Canada from abroad at the rate of C$60 a day, provided they're unsolicited and don't contain alcohol or tobacco (write on the package "Unsolicited gift, under $60 value"). All valuables should be declared on the Y-38 form before departure from Canada, including serial numbers of valuables you already own, such as expensive foreign cameras. ***Note:*** The C$750 exemption can be used only once a year and only after an absence of 7 days.

Australia Customs The duty-free allowance in Australia is A$900 or, for those under 18, A$450. Citizens 18 and older can bring in 250 cigarettes or 250 grams of loose tobacco, and 2.25 liters of alcohol. If you're returning with valuables you already own, such as foreign-made cameras, you should file form B263. A helpful brochure available from Australian consulates or Customs offices is *Know Before You Go.* For more information, call the **Australian Customs Service** at © **1300/363-263,** or log on to www.customs.gov.au.

New Zealand Customs The duty-free allowance for New Zealand is NZ$700. Citizens over 17 can bring in 200 cigarettes, or 50 cigars, or 250 grams of tobacco (or a mixture of all three if their combined weight does not exceed 250g); plus 4.5 liters of wine and beer, or 1.125 liters of liquor. New Zealand currency does not carry import or export restrictions. When you leave New Zealand, you should fill out a certificate of export, listing the valuables you are taking out of the country; that way, you can bring them back without paying duty. Most questions are answered in a free pamphlet available at New Zealand consulates and Customs offices: *New Zealand Customs Guide for Travellers, Notice no. 4.* For more information, contact **New Zealand Customs Service,** 17–21 Whitmore St., Box 2218, Wellington (© **04/473-6099** or 0800/428-786; www.customs.govt.nz).

4 Money

Jamaica has its own dollar, far less valuable than the U.S. dollar. In all exchanges, ***determine which dollar unit is being quoted in the price.*** Otherwise, it's possible you could get cheated— badly—in a financial transaction.

All the major resorts and first-class restaurants quote prices in U.S. dollars, so many visitors can go through their entire trip without the bother of converting their currency into Jamaican dollars. But it's still prudent to carry some Jamaican dollars: For some transactions, such as a drink of coconut water from a roadside vendor, prices are only quoted in Jamaican dollars.

If you have Jamaican dollars left over at the end of your trip, you'll need to show exchange receipts from a bank or other official bureau for the local dollars you purchased. This is a rather cumbersome process. Exchange only the amount of Jamaican money you think you'll actually need.

You can live in Jamaica on $50 a day or $1,000 a day. It's up to you. In general costs are lower than in urban cities in the United States and a lot lower than London and continental cities such as Paris or Rome. Guests usually book into hotels, especially all-inclusives, on package deals, which considerably cut costs. Restaurants charging more than $30 for a meal are considered expensive by Jamaican standards. Many native restaurants, catering to a local clientele, charge less than $15 for a complete dinner.

Note: Prices in this guide quoted in Jamaican dollars are for *general guidance.* The Jamaican dollar sometimes fluctuates wildly. In general, it has been in a long decline against the Yankee dollar since the early 1990s.

All Jamaican cities and most large towns on the island have banks with a **foreign exchange bureau.** If you're heading into the remote countryside, make sure you have solved your cash problem before setting out. Banks give far better exchange rates than your hotel will.

Because of inadequate ATMs, **traveler's checks** are still a popular means of currency to take to Jamaica. They are widely accepted, but you should always inquire about the fee before cashing them. Sometimes there's a high surcharge, which can vary from place to place.

Relying on **ATMs** is a bit risky in Jamaica. Most banks in cities such as Kingston and Montego Bay have 24-hour ATMs in secure booths. You are, however, given Jamaican dollars—not U.S. dollars—at these machines. *Always try to use ATMs during regular business hours.* There are frequent muggings of visitors who use ATMs at night in Jamaica.

Be aware that many Frommer's readers have written to describe their frustration with the island's ATMs. It's best to ask your local bank how effective your ATM card will be in Jamaica before you depart. Failing all else, we've found that branches of **Scotiabank** work best with North American ATM cards.

CURRENCY

The unit of currency in Jamaica is the Jamaican dollar, with the same symbol as the U.S. dollar, "$." There is no fixed rate of exchange for the Jamaican dollar; it is traded publicly and is subject to market fluctuations.

Visitors to Jamaica can pay for any goods in U.S. dollars, *but be careful.* Always insist on knowing whether a price is quoted in Jamaican or U.S. dollars.

In this guide we quote some prices in both Jamaican and U.S. dollars, though for the most part U.S. dollars are listed alone because the Jamaican dollar tends to fluctuate. U.S. dollar values give a better indication of costs. Prices given in Jamaican dollars are indicated by "J$"; all other prices are in U.S. dollars.

There are Bank of Jamaica **exchange bureaus** at both international airports (Montego Bay and Kingston), at cruise ship piers, and in most hotels. Also, there is no limit to the amount of **foreign currency** you can bring into or out of Jamaica.

Finally, whenever you leave your hotel, take along some **small bills** and coins. They will come in handy, as tips are generally expected for even the smallest service.

ATMs The easiest and best way to get cash away from home is from an ATM (automated teller machine)—bearing in mind the concerns about them in Jamaica that we note above—sometimes referred to as a "cash machine" or a

Currency Exchange Rates

Jamaica$	US$	UK£	Canada$	Jamaica$	US$	UK£	Canada$
1	0.02	0.01	0.02	1,000	16.00	9.50	21.70
5	0.08	0.05	0.11	2,000	32.00	19.00	43.40
10	0.16	0.10	0.22	3,000	48.00	28.50	65.10
50	0.80	0.48	1.09	4,000	64.00	38.00	86.80
75	1.20	0.71	1.63	5,000	80.00	47.50	108.50
100	1.60	0.95	2.17	6,000	96.00	57.00	130.20
200	3.20	1.90	4.34	7,000	112.00	66.50	151.90
300	4.80	2.85	6.51	8,000	128.00	76.00	173.60
400	6.40	3.80	8.68	9,000	144.00	85.50	195.30
500	8.00	4.75	10.85	10,000	160.00	95.00	217.00
600	9.60	5.70	13.02	25,000	400.00	237.50	542.50
700	11.20	6.65	15.19	50,000	800.00	475.00	1,085.00
800	12.80	7.60	17.36	75,000	1,200.00	712.50	1,627.50
900	14.40	8.55	19.53	100,000	1,600.00	950.00	2,170.00

This chart assumes the following conversion rates, each of which was valid at the time of its compilation: J$:US$=.016; J$:£=.0095; J$:CAN$=.0217.

"cashpoint." The **Cirrus** (© 800/424-7787; www.mastercard.com) and **PLUS** (© 800/843-7587; www.visa.com) networks span the globe; look at the back of your bank card to see which network you're on, and then call or check online for ATM locations at your destination. Be sure you know your personal identification number (PIN) and daily withdrawal limit before you depart. *Note:* Remember that many banks impose a fee every time you use a card at another bank's ATM, and that fee can be higher for international transactions (up to $5 or more) than for domestic ones (where they're rarely more than $2). In addition, the bank from which you withdraw cash may charge its own fee. For international withdrawal fees, ask your bank.

CREDIT CARDS Plastic is invaluable when traveling in Jamaica. Credit cards are another safe way to carry money. They also provide a convenient record of all your expenses, and they generally offer relatively good exchange rates. You can withdraw cash advances from your credit cards at banks or ATMs, provided you know your PIN. (If you've forgotten your PIN or didn't even know you had one, call the phone number on the back of your credit card and ask the bank to send it to you. It usually takes 5 to 7 business days, though some banks will provide the number over the phone if you tell them your mother's maiden name or pass some other security clearance. Keep in mind that you'll pay interest from the moment of your withdrawal, even if you pay your monthly bills on time. Also, note that many banks now assess a 1% to 3% "transaction fee" on *all* charges you incur abroad (whether you're using the local currency or your native currency).

What Things Cost in Jamaica (Montego Bay)	U.S.$	U.K. £
Taxi from the airport	25.00	17.75
Local phone calls	0.25	0.14
Double room at Half Moon Resort (expensive)	410.00	225.50
Double room at Coral Cliff Hotel and Entertainment Resort (moderate)	110.00	60.50
Double room at Blue Harbour Hotel (inexpensive)	68.00	37.40
Lunch for one (without wine) at Day-O Plantation Restaurant	15.00	8.25
Lunch for one (without wine) at Pork Pit	6.00	3.30
Dinner for one (without wine) at Jasmine (expensive)	60.00	33.00
Dinner for one (without wine) at The Houseboat Grill (moderate)	32.00	17.60
Dinner for one (without wine) at Glistening Waters	52.00	28.60
Bottle of Red Stripe beer	1.30	0.72
Roll of ASA 100 color film (36 exposures)	6.50	3.58
Movie ticket	6.50	3.58
Admission to Cornwall Beach	3.50	1.93
Greens fees for White Witch of Rose Hall Golf Course (non-guests)	159.00	87.45
Admission to Rose Hall Great House	15.00	8.25

TRAVELER'S CHECKS Traveler's checks are something of an anachronism at many destinations. They are still widely used, however, in Jamaica because of inadequate ATM machines. Traveler's checks are also good if you want the security of knowing you can get a refund if your wallet is stolen in Jamaica. You can buy traveler's checks at most banks. They are offered in denominations of $20, $50, $100, $500, and sometimes $1,000. Generally, you'll pay a service charge ranging from 1% to 4%.

The most popular traveler's checks are offered by **American Express** (© 800/807-6233 or 800/221-7282 for card holders—this number accepts collect calls and offers service in several foreign languages), **Visa** (© 800/732-1322), and **MasterCard** (© 800/223-9920). American Express exempts gold and platinum cardholders from its 1% fee. AAA members can obtain Visa checks for a $9.95 fee (for checks up to $1,500) at most AAA offices or by calling © 866/339-3378.

American Express, Thomas Cook, Visa, and **MasterCard** offer **foreign currency traveler's checks,** which are useful if you're traveling to one country, or to the Euro zone; they're accepted at locations where dollar checks may not be.

If you carry traveler's checks, keep a record of their serial numbers separate from your checks in the event that they are stolen or lost. You'll get a refund faster if you know the numbers.

WHAT TO DO IF YOUR WALLET IS STOLEN Be sure to block charges against your account the minute you discover a credit card has been lost or stolen. Then be sure to file a report at the nearest Jamaican police station.

Every credit card company has an emergency 800-number to call if your card is stolen. They may be able to wire you a cash advance off your credit card immediately, and in many places they can deliver an emergency credit card in a day or two. The issuing bank's 800-number is usually on the back of your credit card—although, of course, if your card has been stolen, that won't help you unless you recorded the number elsewhere.

Citicorp **Visa's** U.S. emergency number is ✆ **800/336-8742. American Express** cardholders and traveler's-check holders should call ✆ **800/221-7282. MasterCard** holders should call ✆ **800/307-7309.** Otherwise, call the toll-free number directory at ✆ **800/555-1212.**

Odds are that if your wallet is gone, the Jamaican police won't be able to recover it for you. However, it's still worth informing them. Your credit card company or insurer may require a police report number or record of the theft. Likewise, if you carry traveler's checks, be sure to keep a record of their serial numbers separate from the checks. You'll get a refund faster if you do.

MONEYGRAMS Sponsored by American Express, **Moneygram** (✆ **800/926-9400;** www.moneygram.com) is the fastest-growing money-wiring service in the world. Funds can be transferred from one individual to another in less than 10 minutes between thousands of locations throughout the world. An American Express phone representative will give you the names of four or five offices near you. (You don't have to go to an American Express office; some locations in Jamaica are pharmacies or convenience stores in small communities.) Acceptable forms of payment include cash, Visa, MasterCard, and Discover, and occasionally, a personal check. Service charges collected by American Express are $40 for the first $500 sent, with a sliding scale of commissions for larger sums. Included in the transfer is a 10-word telex-style message. The deal also includes a free 3-minute phone call to the recipient. Funds are transferred within 10 minutes, and they can then be retrieved by the beneficiary at the most convenient location when proper photo ID, and in some cases, a security code established by whomever provides the funds, is presented.

⟨Tips⟩ Dear Visa: I'm Off to Kingston!

Some credit card companies recommend that you notify them of any impending trip abroad so that they don't become suspicious of foreign transactions and block your charges. Even if you don't call your credit card company in advance, you can always call the card's toll-free emergency number (go to "Lost & Found" in the "Fast Facts" section later in this chapter) if a charge is refused—a good reason to carry the phone number with you. But perhaps the most important lesson here is to carry more than one card with you on your trip; a card might not work for any number of reasons, so having a backup is the smart way to go.

Tips **Easy Money**

You'll avoid lines at airport ATMs by exchanging at least some money—just enough to cover airport incidentals and transportation to your hotel—before you leave home. When you change money, ask for some small bills or loose change. Petty cash will come in handy for tipping and public transportation. Consider keeping the change separate from your larger bills, so that it's readily accessible and you'll be less of a target for theft.

5 When to Go

HIGH SEASON VS. LOW SEASON: SOME PROS & CONS

With its fabled weather balmy all year, Jamaica is more and more a year-round destination. Nevertheless, it has a distinct **high season** running roughly from mid-December through mid-April. Hotels charge their highest prices during this peak winter period, when visitors fleeing cold north winds crowd the island. (We've quoted each hotel's rack rates throughout this guide, but you don't have to pay that much, even in high season, if you book a package instead of calling the hotel directly.)

Reservations should be made 2 to 3 months in advance for trips during the winter. At certain hotels, think about booking a year ahead for Christmas holidays or February.

The **off season** in Jamaica (roughly mid-Apr to mid-Dec) amounts to a summer sale. In most cases, hotel rates are slashed a startling 20% to 60%. Some package-tour charges are as much as 20% lower, and individual excursion airfares are reduced from 5% to 10%. In addition, airline seats and hotel rooms are much easier to come by. It's a bonanza for cost-conscious travelers, especially families.

ANNUAL TEMPERATURE & RAINFALL CHART

	Jan	Feb	Mar	Apr	May	June	July	Aug	Sept	Oct	Nov	Dec
Temp. (°F)	86	85	86	87	88	90	90	90	89	89	87	87
Temp. (°C)	30	29	30	31	31	32	32	32	32	32	31	31
Rainfall (in.)	1.2	0.9	0.9	1.5	4.1	3.8	1.8	4.2	5.0	6.8	3.8	1.6

OFF-SEASON ADVANTAGES

Although Jamaica may appear inviting in the winter to those who live in northern climates, we suggest many reasons why your trip may be much more enjoyable if you go in the off season:

- A less-hurried way of life prevails. You'll have a better chance to appreciate food, culture, and customs.
- Swimming pools and beaches are less crowded—perhaps not crowded at all.
- Year-round resort facilities are offered, often at reduced rates, which

may include snorkeling, boating, and scuba diving.
- To survive, resort boutiques often feature summer sales, hoping to clear excess merchandise.
- You can often appear without a reservation at a top restaurant in, say, Montego Bay and get a table.
- The endless waiting game is over: no waiting for a rented car, tee time, or tennis court.
- Some package-tour fares are as much as 20% lower, and individual excursion

fares are also reduced between 5% and 10%.

- Accommodations and flights are easier to book.
- Finally, the very best of Jamaica attractions remain undiminished in the off season—sea, sand, and surf, with lots of sunshine.

OFF-SEASON DISADVANTAGES

Let's not paint too rosy a picture, though. Although the advantages of off-season travel outweigh the disadvantages, summer travel has its drawbacks:

- You might be staying at a construction site. Jamaican hoteliers save their serious repairs and their major renovations until the off season.
- Services are often reduced.
- Not all restaurants and bars will be fully operational at resorts.
- Hotels and resorts may be operating with reduced staff.

CLIMATE

Jamaica has one of the most varied climates of any Caribbean island. Along the seashore, where most visitors congregate, the island is air-conditioned by northeasterly trade winds, and temperature variations are surprisingly slight. Coastal readings average between 71°F (22°C) and 88°F (31°C) year-round. The Jamaican winter is similar to May in the United States or northern Europe; there can be chilly times in the early morning or at night. Winter is generally the driest season, but can be wet in mountain areas; expect showers, especially in northeastern Jamaica.

Inland, temperatures decrease by approximately 1°F for every 300-ft. (about.55°C for every 91m) increase in elevation.

Rainfall is heaviest along the eastern edge of the island's North Coast, with Port Antonio receiving the most intense downpours. The island has two rainy seasons: May, and October through November.

THE HURRICANE SEASON The curse of Jamaican weather, the hurricane season, officially lasts from June 1 to November 30—but there's no need for panic. Satellite weather forecasts generally give adequate warning so that precautions can be taken. If you're heading to Jamaica during the hurricane season, you can call your local branch of the **National Weather Service** (listed in your phone directory under the U.S. Department of Commerce) for a weather forecast.

Another easy way to receive the weather forecast in the city you plan to visit is by contacting the information service associated with The Weather Channel. On the Internet you can check www.weather.com to get the forecasts.

HOLIDAYS

Jamaica observes the following public holidays: New Year's Day, Ash Wednesday, Good Friday, Easter Sunday and Monday, National Labour Day (late May), Independence Day (a Monday in early Aug), National Heroes Day (3rd Monday in Oct), Christmas Day, and Boxing Day (Dec 26).

JAMAICA CALENDAR OF EVENTS

January

Accompong Maroon Festival, St. Elizabeth. Annual celebration of Maroons of Western Jamaica, with traditional singing and dancing, feasts, ceremonies, blowing of the *abeng* (cow's horn), and playing of Maroon drums. ℂ **876/952-4546.** January 6.

Jamaica Sprint Triathlon, Negril. Hundreds participate in a three-part competition joining swimming, cycling, and running in one sweat-inducing endurance test. Contact the

Jamaica Tourist Board (see "Visitor Information," earlier in this chapter). Late January.

Air Jamaica Jazz & Blues Festival, Montego Bay. Series of concerts at Rose Hall Great House. ℂ **876/952-4425.** www.airjamaicajazzandblues.com. Late January.

February

Bob Marley Week, Kingston. From reggae concerts to movies, this week-long celebration honors the king of reggae. Activities also include arts and crafts booths and food festivals. For more information, contact The Robert Marley Foundation at 56 Hope Rd., Kingston (ℂ **876/978-2991** or 876/978-2929; www.bobmarley.com). Early February.

Bob Marley Birthday Bash, Montego Bay. An annual concert that celebrates a local star. ℂ **876/978-2991.** February 6.

Reggae Summerfest, Ocho Rios. Annual reggae bash, featuring top reggae stars. Call ℂ **876/960-1904** for dates.

April

Montego Bay Yacht Club's Easter Regatta. Annual sailing event of several races staged along the North Coast over a 6-day period around Easter. ℂ **876/979-8038.** Easter weekend.

Carnival in Jamaica, Kingston, Ocho Rios, and Montego Bay. Weeklong series of fetes, concerts, and street parades. Contact local tourist offices. First week of April.

June

Ocho Rios Jazz Festival, Ocho Rios and Montego Bay. International performers play alongside Jamaican jazz artists; other events include barbecues. ℂ **866/649-2137** or 876/927-3544 (www.ochoriosjazz.com). Second week in June.

July

National Dance Theatre Company's Season of Dance, Kingston. Traditional and modern dance, as well as notable singers. ℂ **876/926-6129.** July through August.

Reggae Sumfest, Catherine Hall, Montego Bay. Annual 5-day music festival. ℂ **876/952-0889** (www.reggaesumfest.com). Late July. See "Moving to the Beat at Jamaica's Music Festivals," on p. 81.

September

Falmouth Blue Marlin Tournament, Montego Bay. A big deal locally. ℂ **876/927-0145.** Late September.

October

Port Antonio International Fishing Tournament. One of the oldest and most prestigious sportfishing events in the Caribbean, with participants from Europe and North America. ℂ **876/927-0145.** Mid-October.

December

Motor Sports Championship Series, Dover Raceway, St. Ann. Prestigious championship event. ℂ **876/960-3860.** Early December.

6 Travel Insurance

It's wise to visit the troubled land of Jamaica with full insurance coverage, protecting you against loss of property, theft, or any medical problem that might arise. With medical insurance it's best to secure, if possible, a policy that offers immediate payment—not one where you must shell out in Jamaica, then wait for reimbursement.

If you're an adventure tourist who likes to indulge in scuba diving, hiking in the Blue Mountains, or motorcycling along Jamaica's potholed roads, try to get a policy that does not exclude what most insurers call "hazardous activities." Some motorized watersports also fall under hazardous activities.

Before going, check your existing policies before you buy additional coverage covering trip cancellation, lost luggage, medical expenses, or car-rental insurance. You're likely to have partial coverage, though it may be inadequate. U.S. medical insurance plans seldom cover health costs incurred outside the United States, unless supplemental coverage is purchased. Further, most U.S. Medicare and Medicaid programs do not provide payment for medical services outside the country.

The cost of travel insurance varies widely, depending on the cost and length of your trip, your age and health, and the type of trip you're taking, but expect to pay between 5% and 8% of the vacation itself. You can get estimates from various providers through **InsureMyTrip.com**. Enter your trip cost and dates, your age, and other information for prices from more than a dozen companies.

TRIP-CANCELLATION INSURANCE (TCI)

There are three major types of trip-cancellation insurance: one for when you prepay a Jamaican cruise or tour that gets canceled, and you can't get your money back; a second for when you or someone in your family gets sick or dies, and you can't travel (but beware that you may not be covered for a preexisting condition); and a third for when bad weather, such as a Jamaica hurricane, makes travel impossible. Some insurers provide coverage for events such as jury duty; natural disasters close to home, like floods or fire; even the loss of a job. A few have added provisions for cancellations because of terrorist activities. Always check the fine print before signing on, and don't buy this insurance from a tour operator that may later be responsible for cancellation; buy only from a reputable travel insurance agency. Finally, don't overbuy: You won't be reimbursed more than the cost of your trip.

Trip-cancellation insurance will help retrieve your money if you have to back out of a trip or depart early, or if your travel supplier goes bankrupt. Permissable reasons for trip cancellation can range from sickness to natural disasters to the State Department declaring a destination unsafe for travel.

For more information, contact one of the following recommended insurers: **Access America** (© 866/807-3982; www.accessamerica.com); **Travel Guard International** (© 800/826-4919; www.travelguard.com); **Travel Insured International** (© 800/243-3174; www.travelinsured.com); and **Travelex Insurance Services** (© 888/457-4602; www.travelex-insurance.com).

Travel in the Age of Bankruptcy

Airlines go bankrupt, so protect yourself by **buying your tickets with a credit card**. The Fair Credit Billing Act guarantees that you can get your money back from the credit card company if a travel supplier goes under (and if you request the refund within 60 days of the bankruptcy). **Travel insurance** can also help, but make sure it covers against "carrier default" for your specific travel provider. And be aware that if a U.S. airline goes bust mid-trip, a 2001 federal law requires other carriers to take you to your destination (albeit on a space-available basis) for a fee of no more than $25, provided you rebook within 60 days of the cancellation.

MEDICAL INSURANCE

With the exception of certain HMOs and Medicare/Medicaid, your medical insurance will seldom cover medical treatment—even hospital care—in Jamaica, so you may need to pay the bill up front, and then be reimbursed only after you return home. As a safety net, you may want to buy travel medical insurance, particularly if you're traveling to a remote or high-risk area where emergency evacuation might be necessary. If you require additional medical insurance, try **MEDEX Assistance** (© 410/453-6300; www.medexassist.com), **Travel Assistance International** (© 800/821-2828; www.travelassistance.com; for general information on services, call the company's Worldwide Assistance Services, Inc., at © 800/777-8710), or the **Divers Alert Network (DAN)** (© 800/446-2671 or 919/684-2948; www.diversalert network.org).

CAR-RENTAL INSURANCE

If you hold a private auto insurance policy in the U.S., check to see if you are covered in Jamaica for loss or damage to the car, and liability in case a passenger is injured. The credit card you use to rent the car also may provide some coverage. Policies vary widely from holder to holder. Most American Express cardholders, for example, don't need a damage waiver option, as most Jamaican car-rental agencies recognize Amex's policy, especially if you're dealing with a U.S.-affiliated firm such as Hertz or Avis. However, many local car-rental companies in Jamaica don't recognize the policy; therefore, you may feel safer dealing with a U.S. affiliate rather than a domestic car-rental agency.

Car-rental insurance (about $20 to $25 a day) probably does not cover liability if you caused the accident. Check your own auto insurance policy, the rental company policy, and your credit card coverage for the extent of coverage: Is Jamaica covered? Are other drivers covered? How much liability is covered if a passenger is injured? (If you rely on your credit card for coverage, you may want to bring a second card with you, as damages may be charged to the card.)

LOST-LUGGAGE INSURANCE

On flights within the U.S., checked baggage is covered up to $2,500 per ticketed passenger. On international flights (including U.S. portions of international trips), baggage coverage is limited to approximately $9.07 per pound, up to approximately $635 per checked bag. If you plan to check items more valuable than what's covered by the standard liability, see if your homeowner's policy covers your valuables, get baggage insurance as part of your comprehensive travel-insurance package, or buy Travel Guard's "BagTrak" product.

If your luggage is lost, immediately file a lost-luggage claim at the airport, detailing the luggage contents. Most airlines require that you report delayed, damaged, or lost baggage within 4 hours of arrival. The airlines are required to deliver luggage, once found, directly to your house or destination free of charge.

7 Health & Safety

Traveling to Jamaica should not adversely affect your health. Finding a good doctor in Jamaica is no real problem, and all of them speak English, of course.

Keep the following suggestions in mind:

- It's best to drink bottled water in Jamaica.

- If you experience diarrhea, moderate your eating habits and drink only bottled water until you recover. If symptoms persist, consult a doctor.
- The Jamaican sun can be brutal. Wear sunglasses and a hat, and use sunscreen liberally. Limit your time

Avoiding "Economy Class Syndrome"

Deep vein thrombosis, or as it's know in the world of flying, "economy-class syndrome," is a blood clot that develops in a deep vein. It's a potentially deadly condition that can be caused by sitting in cramped conditions—such as an airplane cabin—for too long. During a flight (especially a long-haul flight), get up, walk around, and stretch your legs every 60 to 90 minutes to keep your blood flowing. Other preventative measures include frequent flexing of the legs while sitting, drinking lots of water, and avoiding alcohol and sleeping pills. If you have a history of deep vein thrombosis, heart disease, or another condition that puts you at high risk, some experts recommend wearing compression stockings or taking anticoagulants when you fly; always ask your physician about the best course for you. Symptoms of deep vein thrombosis include leg pain or swelling, or even shortness of breath.

on the beach the first day. If you do overexpose yourself, stay out of the sun until you recover. If your exposure is followed by fever or chills, a headache, or a feeling of nausea or dizziness, see a doctor.

- Some of the biggest annoyances in Jamaica are the insects called "no-see-ums," which appear mainly in the early evening. You can't see these gnats, but you sure can "feel-um." Screens can't keep these critters out, so carry your favorite bug repellent.

You don't need to get any particular shots or vaccinations to travel in Jamaica, and most common medicines are available over the counter. If you need special medication, however, try to arrive in Jamaica with an adequate supply for the duration of your trip.

If you're traveling in the countryside, it's wise to take a small medical kit with you containing antacid, antiseptics, calamine lotion, Band-Aids, sunscreen, lip balm, water purification tablets, and insect repellent.

WHAT TO DO IF YOU GET SICK AWAY FROM HOME

We list **hospitals** and **emergency numbers** under "Fast Facts," p. 48.

If you suffer from a chronic illness, consult your doctor before your departure for Jamaica. For conditions like epilepsy, diabetes, or heart problems, wear a **Medic Alert Identification Tag** (© 800/825-3785; www.medicalert.org), which will immediately alert doctors to your condition and give them access to your records through Medic Alert's 24-hour hot line.

Pack **prescription medications** in your carry-on luggage, and carry prescription medications in their original containers. Also bring along copies of your prescriptions in case you lose your pills or run out. Carry the generic name of prescription medicines, in case a local pharmacist is unfamiliar with the brand name.

And don't forget sunglasses and an extra pair of contact lenses or prescription glasses.

Contact the **International Association for Medical Assistance to Travelers** (IAMAT) (© 716/754-4883 or, in Canada, 416/652-0137; www.iamat.org) for tips on travel and health concerns in the countries you're visiting, and for lists of local doctors. The United States **Centers for Disease Control and Prevention** (© 800/311-3435; www.cdc.gov) provides up-to-date information on health hazards by region or country and offers tips on food safety. The website **www.tripprep.com,** sponsored by a consortium of travel medicine practitioners, may also offer helpful advice on traveling

Healthy Travels to You

The following government websites offer up-to-date health-related travel advice.

- **Australia:** www.dfat.gov.au/travel/
- **Canada:** www.hc-sc.gc.ca/index_e.html
- **U.K.:** www.dh.gov.uk/PolicyAndGuidance/HealthAdviceForTravellers/fs/en
- **U.S.:** www.cdc.gov/travel/

abroad. You can find listings of reliable clinics overseas at the **International Society of Travel Medicine** (www.istm.org).

In Canada, contact **Health Canada** (© **613/957-2991;** www.hc-sc.gc.ca).

STAYING SAFE

Except for Haiti, Jamaica is the most potentially dangerous destination in the Caribbean. You can get into a lot of trouble in Jamaica or you can have a carefree vacation. Much depends on you, where you go, and what you do. Women traveling alone or even in pairs are especially vulnerable, as rapes are alarmingly common.

Walking alone at night, or even with a loved one, on a moonlit Jamaican beach is a romantic idea—but not smart. You could be mugged. And hitchhiking for both women and men is never a good idea

in Jamaica. There have been cases of "disappearances" in the remote hinterlands.

Petty crime also continues to be a major problem on the island, especially in the capital city of Kingston. Americans on many occasions have been robbed, the bandit turning violent if he faces resistance.

Bus travel in Jamaica is definitely not recommended. Buses are invariably overcrowded and the greatest venue for the pickpocket to practice his trade.

The good news? In major resort areas such as Montego Bay, the government is hiring more special foot police and bike patrols to enhance security. These megaresorts are virtually walled compounds with 24-hour guards. Smaller inns don't have such protection, however, so make sure that all your doors and windows are securely locked.

8 Specialized Travel Resources

TRAVELERS WITH DISABILITIES

Jamaican hotels rarely give much publicity to the facilities (if any) they offer persons with disabilities, so it's always wise to contact the hotel directly, in advance. Tourist offices probably won't be able to help you with such questions.

Get a free copy of *Air Transportation of Handicapped Persons* from the **U.S. Department of Transportation.** Write for Free Advisory Circular No. AC12032, Distribution Unit, U.S. Department of Transportation, Publications Division, 3341Q 75 Ave., Landover, MD 20785 (© **301/322-4961;** fax 301/386-5394;

http://isddc.dot.gov). Only written requests are accepted.

Many travel agencies offer customized tours and itineraries for travelers with disabilities. Among them are **Flying Wheels Travel** (© 507/451-5005; www.flyingwheelstravel.com); **Access-Able Travel Source** (© 303/232-2979; www.access-able.com); and **Accessible Journeys** (© 800/846-4537 or 610/521-0339; www.disabilitytravel.com). **Avis Rent a Car** has an "Avis Access" program that offers such services as a dedicated 24-hour toll-free number (© **888/879-4273**) for customers with special travel needs; special car features such as swivel seats, spinner knobs, and hand controls; and accessible bus service.

Organizations that offer assistance to disabled travelers include **MossRehab** (www.mossresourcenet.org); the **American Foundation for the Blind (AFB)** (© 800/232-5463; www.afb.org); and **SATH (Society for Accessible Travel & Hospitality)** (© 212/447-7284; www.sath.org). **AirAmbulanceCard.com** is now partnered with SATH and allows you to preselect top-notch hospitals in case of an emergency.

The community website **iCan** (www.icanonline.net/channels/travel) has destination guides and several regular columns on accessible travel. Also check out the quarterly magazine *Emerging Horizons* (www.emerginghorizons.com), and *Open World* magazine, published by SATH.

FOR BRITISH TRAVELERS Check out the **Royal Association for Disability and Rehabilitation (RADAR),** Unit 12, City Forum, 250 City Rd., London, EC1V 8AF (© **020/7250-3222;** fax 020/7250-0212; www.radar.org.uk).

GAY & LESBIAN TRAVELERS

Jamaica is the most homophobic island in the Caribbean, with harsh anti-gay laws, even though there's a large local gay population.

Many all-inclusive resorts, notably the famous Sandals of Jamaica, maintain strict no-gay policies. However, Hedonism II in Negril does allow gay travelers. So does the Grand Hotel Lido in Negril. Still, avoid open displays of affection—such as handholding on the streets—in Jamaica: You could be assaulted for trying it.

The **International Gay & Lesbian Travel Association (IGLTA)** (© **800/ 448-8550** or 954/776-2626; www.iglta.com) links travelers up with gay-friendly hoteliers, tour operators, and airline and cruise-line representatives. It offers monthly newsletters, marketing mailings, and a membership directory that's updated once a year. Membership is $200 yearly, plus a $100 administration fee for new members.

Above and Beyond Tours (© **800/ 397-2681;** www.abovebeyondtours.com) offers gay and lesbian tours worldwide and is the exclusive gay and lesbian tour operator for United Airlines. **Now, Voyager** (© **800/255-6951;** www.now voyager.com) is a San Francisco–based gay-owned and -operated travel service. **Olivia Cruises & Resorts** (© **800/631- 6277** or 510/655-0364; www.olivia.com) charters entire resorts and ships for exclusive lesbian vacations all over the world.

Gay.com Travel (© **800/929-2268** or 415/644-8044; www.gay.com/travel or www.outandabout.com) is an excellent online successor to the popular *Out & About* print magazine. It provides regularly updated information about gay-owned, gay-oriented, and gay-friendly lodging, dining, sightseeing, nightlife, and shopping establishments in every important destination worldwide.

The following travel guides are available at many bookstores, or you can order them from any online bookseller: *Spartacus International Gay Guide* (Bruno Gmünder Verlag; www.spartacusworld.com/gayguide/) and *Odysseus: The International Gay Travel Planner* (Odysseus Enterprises Ltd.); and the *Damron* guides (www.damron.com), with separate, annual books for gay men and lesbians.

SENIOR TRAVELERS

Except for a possible reduction on certain domestic airfares offered aboard **Air Jamaica Express,** the island itself is virtually devoid of discounts for senior citizens. Some car-rental companies may extend discounts to seniors, but arrange that before you land on the island. Once on the island, a senior is likely to pay the same prices that anybody else does.

Tying the Knot in Jamaica

During high season, some Jamaican resorts witness several weddings a day. Many of the larger resorts can arrange for an officiant, a photographer, and even the wedding cake and champagne. Some resorts will even throw in the wedding with the cost of your honeymoon at the hotel. Both the Jamaican Tourist Board and your hotel can assist with paperwork; participants must simply be in Jamaica for 24 hours before the ceremony. Bring birth certificates and affidavits saying you've never been married before. (If you've been divorced or widowed, bring copies of your divorce papers or a copy of the deceased spouse's death certificate.) The license and stamp duty costs J$5,000 ($80), and the ceremony can start at US$150 and go up from there, depending on how much legwork you do. Apply in person at the **Ministry of National Security and Justice,** 12 Ocean Blvd., Kingston, Jamaica (② **876/906-4908**).

The single best hotel for arranging wedding packages is **Half Moon** (② **800/ 626-0592**) in Montego Bay. **Sandals** properties in Montego Bay, Negril, and Ocho Rios (② **800/SANDALS;** www.halfmoonweddings.com) also have good packages.

Members of **AARP** (formerly known as the American Association of Retired Persons), 601 E St. NW, Washington, DC 20049 (② **888/687-2277;** www. aarp.org), get discounts on hotels, airfares, and car rentals. AARP offers members a wide range of benefits, including *AARP: The Magazine* and a monthly newsletter. Anyone over 50 can join.

Many reliable agencies and organizations target the 50-plus market. **Elderhostel** (② **877/426-8056;** www.elderhostel. org) arranges study programs for those aged 55 and over. **ElderTreks** (② **800/ 741-7956;** www.eldertreks.com) offers small-group tours to off-the-beaten-path or adventure-travel locations, restricted to travelers 50 and older. **INTRAV** (② **800/ 456-8100;** www.intrav.com) is a high-end tour operator that caters to the mature, discerning traveler (not specifically seniors), with trips around the world that include guided safaris, polar expeditions, private-jet adventures, and small-boat cruises down jungle rivers.

Recommended publications offering travel resources and discounts for seniors include: the quarterly magazine *Travel 50 & Beyond* (www.travel50andbeyond. com); *Travel Unlimited: Uncommon Adventures for the Mature Traveler* (Avalon); *101 Tips for Mature Travelers,* available from Grand Circle Travel (② **800/221-2610** or 617/350-7500; www.gct.com); and *Unbelievably Good Deals and Great Adventures That You Absolutely Can't Get Unless You're Over 50* (McGraw-Hill), by Joann Rattner Heilman.

FAMILY TRAVEL

Jamaica is one of the top family-vacation destinations in the Caribbean, and many of the island's resorts offer supervised children's activities, babysitters, family discounts, and special meals for kids.

To locate accommodations, restaurants, and attractions that are particularly kid-friendly, refer to the "Kids" icon throughout this guide.

Familyhostel (© **800/733-9753;** www.learn.unh.edu/familyhostel) takes the whole family, including kids ages 8 to 15, on moderately priced U.S. and international learning vacations. Lectures, field trips, and sightseeing are guided by a team of academics.

Recommended family travel websites include **Family Travel Forum** (www.familytravelforum.com); **Family Travel Network** (www.familytravelnetwork.com); **Traveling Internationally with Your Kids** (www.travelwithyourkids.com); and **Family Travel Files** (www.thefamilytravelfiles.com).

9 Planning Your Trip Online

SURFING FOR AIRFARE

The most popular online travel agencies are **Travelocity** (**www.travelocity.com,** or www.travelocity.co.uk); **Expedia** (**www.expedia.com,** www.expedia.co.uk, or www.expedia.ca); and **Orbitz** (**www.orbitz.com**).

Other helpful websites for booking airline tickets online include:

- www.biddingfortravel.com
- www.cheapflights.com
- www.hotwire.com
- www.kayak.com
- www.lastminutetravel.com
- www.opodo.co.uk
- www.priceline.com
- www.sidestep.com
- www.site59.com
- www.smartertravel.com

Also remember to check **airline websites,** especially those for low-fare carriers such as Southwest, JetBlue, AirTran, WestJet, and Ryanair, whose fares are often misreported or simply missing from travel agency websites. Even with major airlines, you can often shave a few bucks from a fare by booking directly through the airline and avoiding a travel agency's transaction fee. But you'll get these discounts only by **booking online:** Most airlines now offer online-only fares that even their phone agents know nothing about. For the websites of airlines that fly to and from your destination, go to "Flying to Jamaica," below.

For much more about airfares and savvy air-travel tips and advice, pick up a copy of *Frommer's Fly Safe, Fly Smart* (Wiley Publishing, Inc.).

SURFING FOR HOTELS

Shopping online for hotels is much easier in the U.S., Canada, and Caribbean than it is in the rest of the world. Also, many smaller hotels and B&Bs—especially outside the U.S.—don't show up on websites at all. Of the "big three" sites, **Expedia** may be the best choice, thanks to its long list of special deals.

In addition to **Travelocity, Expedia, Orbitz, Priceline,** and **Hotwire** (see above), the following websites will help you with booking hotel rooms online:

- www.hotels.com
- www.quickbook.com;
- www.travelaxe.net
- www.travelweb.com
- www.tripadvisor.com

It's a good idea to **get a confirmation number** and **make a printout** of any online booking transaction.

SURFING FOR RENTAL CARS

For booking rental cars online, the best deals are usually found at rental-car company websites, although all the major online travel agencies also offer rental-car reservations services. Priceline and Hotwire work well for rental cars, too; the only "mystery" is which major rental company you get, and for most travelers the difference between Hertz, Avis, and Budget is negligible.

Frommers.com: The Complete Travel Resource

For an excellent travel-planning resource, we highly recommend **Frommers. com** (www.frommers.com), voted Best Travel Site by *PC Magazine*. We're a little biased, of course, but we guarantee that you'll find the travel tips, reviews, monthly vacation giveaways, bookstore, and online-booking capabilities thoroughly indispensable. Among the special features are our popular **Destinations** section, where you'll get expert travel tips, hotel and dining recommendations, and advice on the sights to see for more than 3,500 destinations around the globe; the **Frommers.com Newsletter**, with the latest deals, travel trends, and money-saving secrets; our **Community** area featuring **Message Boards**, where Frommer's readers post queries and share advice (sometimes even our authors show up to answer questions); and our **Photo Center**, where you can post and share vacation tips. When your research is done, the **Online Reservations System** (www.frommers. com/book_a_trip) takes you to Frommer's preferred online partners for booking your vacation at affordable prices.

10 The 21st-Century Traveler

INTERNET ACCESS AWAY FROM HOME

Travelers have any number of ways to check their e-mail and access the Internet on the road. Of course, using your own laptop—or even a PDA (personal digital assistant) or electronic organizer with a modem—gives you the most flexibility. But even if you don't have a computer, you can still access your e-mail and even your office computer from cybercafes.

WITHOUT YOUR OWN COMPUTER

It's hard nowadays to find a city that *doesn't* have a few cybercafes. Although there's no definitive directory for cybercafes—these are independent businesses, after all—two places to start looking are at **www.cybercaptive.com** and **www.cybercafe.com**.

Hotel lobbies and tourist information offices around the world give you basic Web access for a per-minute fee that's usually higher than cybercafe prices.

Aside from cybercafes, most **public libraries** have Internet access. Avoid **hotel business centers** unless you're willing to pay exorbitant rates.

Most major airports now have **Internet kiosks** scattered throughout their gates. These give you basic Web access for a per-minute fee that's usually higher than cybercafe prices.

WITH YOUR OWN COMPUTER

More and more hotels, cafes, and retailers are signing on as Wi-Fi (wireless fidelity) "hotspots." Mac owners have their own networking technology: Apple AirPort. **Boingo** (www.boingo.com) and **Wayport** (www.wayport.com) have set up networks in airports and first-class hotel lobbies. IPass providers (see below) also give you access to a few hundred wireless hotel lobby setups. To locate other hotspots that provide **free wireless networks** in cities around the world, go to **www.personaltelco.net/index.cgi/ WirelessCommunities**.

For dial-up access, most business-class hotels throughout the world offer dataports for laptop modems, and a few thousand hotels now offer free high-speed Internet access. In addition, major Internet Service Providers (ISPs) have **local access numbers** around the world, allowing you to go online by placing a local call. The **iPass** network also has dial-up numbers around the world. You'll have to sign up with an iPass provider, who will then tell you how to set up your computer for your destination(s). For a list of iPass providers, go to www.ipass.com and click on "Individuals Buy Now." One

solid provider is **i2roam** (☎ **866/811-6209** or 920/235-0475; www.i2roam.com).

Wherever you go, bring a **connection kit** of the right power and phone adapters, a spare phone cord, and a spare Ethernet network cable—or find out whether your hotel supplies them to guests.

USING A CELLPHONE IN JAMAICA

The three letters that define much of the world's **wireless capabilities** are GSM (Global System for Mobiles), a big,

Flying with Film & Video

Never pack film—developed or undeveloped—in checked bags, as the new, more powerful scanners in U.S. airports can fog film. The film you carry with you can be damaged by scanners as well. **X-ray damage** is cumulative; the faster the film, and the more times you put it through a scanner, the more likely the damage. Film under 800 ASA is usually safe for up to five scans. If you're taking your film through additional scans, U.S. regulations permit you to demand hand inspections. In international airports, you're at the mercy of airport officials. On international flights, store your film in transparent baggies, so you can remove it easily before you go through scanners. Keep in mind that airports are not the only places where your camera may be scanned: Highly trafficked attractions are X-raying visitors' bags with increasing frequency.

Most photo supply stores sell **protective pouches** designed to block damaging X-rays. The pouches fit both film and loaded cameras. They should protect your film in checked baggage, but they also may raise alarms and result in a hand-inspection.

You'll have little to worry about if you are traveling with **digital cameras.** Unlike film, which is sensitive to light, the digital camera and storage cards are not affected by airport X-rays, according to Nikon. Still, if you plan to travel extensively, you may want to play it safe and hand-carry your digital equipment or ask that it be inspected by hand.

Scanners of carry-on items will not damage **videotape** in video cameras, but the magnetic fields emitted by the walk-through security gateways and handheld inspection wands will. Always place your loaded camcorder on the screening conveyor belt or have it hand-inspected. Be sure your batteries are charged, as you may be required to turn the device on to ensure that it's what it appears to be.

Online Traveler's Toolbox

Veteran travelers usually carry some essential items to make their trips easier. Following is a selection of handy online tools to bookmark and use.

- **Airplane Food** (www.airlinemeals.net)
- **Airplane Seating** (www.seatguru.com and www.airlinequality.com)
- **Foreign Languages for Travelers** (www.travlang.com)
- **Maps** (www.mapquest.com)
- **Subway Navigator** (www.subwaynavigator.com)
- **Time and Date** (www.timeanddate.com)
- **Travel Warnings** (http://travel.state.gov, www.fco.gov.uk/travel, www.voyage.gc.ca, or www.dfat.gov.au/consular/advice)
- **Universal Currency Converter** (www.xe.com/ucc)
- **Visa ATM Locator** (www.visa.com), **MasterCard ATM Locator** (www.mastercard.com)
- **Weather** (www.intellicast.com and www.weather.com)

seamless network that makes for easy cross-border cellphone use throughout Europe and dozens of other countries worldwide. In the U.S., T-Mobile, AT&T Wireless, and Cingular use this quasi-universal system; in Canada, Microcell and some Rogers customers are GSM; and all Europeans and most Australians use GSM.

If your cellphone is on a GSM system, and you have a world-capable phone such as many (but not all) Sony Ericsson, Motorola, or Samsung models, you can make and receive calls across civilized areas on much of the globe, from Andorra to Uganda, and certainly Jamaica. Just call your wireless operator and ask for "international roaming" to be activated on your account. Unfortunately, per-minute charges can be high.

World-phone owners can bring down their per-minute charges with a bit of trickery. Call up your cellular operator and say you'll be going abroad for several months and want to "unlock" your phone to use it with a local provider. Usually, they'll oblige. Then, in Jamaica, pick up a cheap, prepaid phone chip at a mobile-phone store and slip it into your phone.

(Show your phone to the salesperson, as not all phones work on all networks.) You'll get a local phone number—and much, much lower calling rates.

Otherwise, **renting** a phone is a good idea. While you can rent a phone from any number of overseas sites, including kiosks at airports and at car-rental agencies, we suggest renting the phone before you leave home. That way you can give loved ones your new number, make sure the phone works, and take the phone wherever you go—especially helpful when you rent overseas, where phone-rental agencies bill in local currency and may not let you take the phone to another country.

Two good wireless rental companies are **InTouch USA** (© **800/872-7626;** www.intouchglobal.com) and **Roadpost** (© **888/290-1606** or 905/272-5665; www.roadpost.com). Give them your itinerary and they'll tell you what wireless products you need. InTouch will also, for free, advise you on whether your existing phone will work in Jamaica; simply call © **703/222-7161** between 9am and 4pm EST, or go to http://intouchglobal.com/travel.htm.

11 Flying to Jamaica

THE MAJOR AIRLINES

There are two **international airports** on Jamaica: Donald Sangster in Montego Bay (© **876/952-3124**) and Norman Manley in Kingston (© **876/924-8452;** www.manley-airport.com.jm). The most popular flights are from New York and Miami. Remember to reconfirm all flights no later than 72 hours before departure. Flying time from Miami is 1¼ hours; from Los Angeles, 5½ hours; from Atlanta, 2½ hours; from Dallas, 3 hours; from Chicago and New York, 3½ hours; and from Toronto, 4 hours.

Some of the most convenient service to Jamaica is provided by **American Airlines** (© **800/433-7300** in the U.S.; www.aa.com) through hubs in New York and Miami. Throughout the year, one daily nonstop flight departs from New York's Kennedy Airport for Montego Bay. From Miami, at least two daily flights depart for Kingston and two daily flights depart for Montego Bay.

AmericaWest/US Airways (© **800/ 428-4322;** www.usairways.com) offers one flight daily from Charlotte, Ft. Lauderdale, Philadelphia, and Washington, D.C. **Northwest Airlines** (© **800/ 225-2525;** www.nwa.com) flies directly to Montego Bay daily from Minneapolis.

Air Jamaica (© **800/523-5585** in the U.S.; www.airjamaica.com) operates one or more flights daily to Montego Bay and Kingston from such cities as Miami, Fort Lauderdale, Orlando, Atlanta, Baltimore/Washington, D.C., Philadelphia, Chicago, Newark, Boston, Houston, Los Angeles, New York's JFK, and Toronto. The airline has connecting service within Jamaica through its reservations network to **Air Jamaica Express,** whose planes usually hold between 10 and 17 passengers. Air Jamaica Express flies from the island's international airports at Montego Bay and Kingston, and also to smaller airports around the island, including Boscobel (near Ocho Rios) and Tinson Pen (near Kingston).

Air Canada (© **888/247-2262;** www. aircanada.ca) flies from Toronto to Jamaica daily. The connection to Kingston is nonstop, but the flight to Montego Bay involves a change of planes in Miami. **British Airways** (© **0870/ 850-9850** in Britain; www.british airways.com) has four nonstop flights weekly to Montego Bay and Kingston from London's Gatwick Airport.

FLYING FOR LESS: TIPS FOR GETTING THE BEST AIRFARE

- Passengers who can book their ticket either **long in advance or at the last minute,** or who **fly midweek** or at **less-trafficked hours** may pay a fraction of the full fare. If your schedule is flexible, say so, and ask if you can secure a cheaper fare by changing your flight plans.
- Search **the Internet** for cheap fares (see "Planning Your Trip Online").
- Keep an eye on local newspapers for **promotional specials** or **fare wars,** when airlines lower prices on their most popular routes. You rarely see

---

Tips **Leave Your Cigarette Lighter at Home**

You cannot travel with a cigarette lighter on your person, in your carry-on, or even in your checked luggage. You may carry on up to four packs of matches. If you don't want to lose that sentimental lighter you've had for years, leave it at home and buy a disposable one when you get to your destination.

Tips   Getting Through the Airport

- Arrive at the airport 1 hour before a domestic flight and 2 hours before an international flight; if you show up late, tell an airline employee and he or she will probably whisk you to the front of the line.
- Beat the ticket-counter lines by using airport electronic kiosks or even online check-in from your home computer, from where you can print out boarding passes in advance. Curbside check-in is also a good way to avoid lines.
- Bring a current, government-issued photo ID such as a driver's license or passport. Children under 18 do not need government-issued photo IDs for flights within the U.S., but they do for international flights to most countries.
- Speed up security by removing your jacket and shoes before you're screened. In addition, remove metal objects such as big belt buckles. If you've got metallic body parts, a note from your doctor can prevent a long chat with the security screeners.
- Use a TSA-approved lock for your checked luggage. Look for Travel Sentry certified locks at luggage or travel shops and Brookstone stores (or online at www.brookstone.com).

fare wars offered for peak travel times, but if you can travel in the off-months, you may snag a bargain.

- Join **frequent-flier clubs.** Frequent-flier membership doesn't cost a cent, but it does entitle you to better seats, faster response to phone inquiries, and prompter service if your luggage is stolen or your flight is canceled or delayed, or if you want to change your seat. And you don't have to fly to earn points; **frequent-flier credit cards** can earn you thousands of miles for doing your everyday shopping. With more than 70 mileage awards programs on the market, consumers never had more options. Investigate the program details of your favorite airlines before you sink points into any one. Consider which airlines have hubs in the airport nearest you, and, of those carriers, which have the most advantageous alliances, given your most common routes. To play the

frequent-flier game to your best advantage, consult Randy Petersen's **Inside Flyer** (www.insideflyer.com). Petersen and friends review all the programs in detail and post regular updates on changes in policies and trends.

Internet users today can tap into the same travel-planning databases that were once accessible only to travel agents—and do it at the same speed. Sites such as **Frommers.com**, **Travelocity.com**, **Expedia.com**, and **Orbitz.com** enable consumers to comparison-shop for airfares, access special bargains, book flights, and reserve hotel rooms and rental cars. But don't fire your travel agent just yet: A seasoned, reliable travel agent remains an invaluable resource, particularly for complex itineraries.

Some websites, such as Expedia.com, send you **e-mail notification** when a cheap fare becomes available.

12 Packages for the Independent Traveler

Unlike many places, Jamaica is not a big market for escorted tours where you're hauled around on a bus and looked after constantly by a guide. You can, of course, take locally guided tours once you land.

Package tours are not the same thing as escorted tours. With a package tour to Jamaica, you travel independently but pay a group rate. Packages usually include airfare, a choice of hotels, and car rentals, and packagers often offer several options at different prices. In many cases, a package that includes airfare, hotel, and transportation to and from the airport will cost you less than just the hotel alone would have cost. That's because Jamaican packages are sold in bulk to tour operators—who then resell them to the public at a cost that sharply undercuts regular rates.

The best place to find a package tour is the travel section of your local Sunday newspaper. Also check the ads in the back of national travel magazines like *Arthur Frommer's Budget Travel, Travel & Leisure, National Geographic Traveler,* and *Condé Nast Traveler.*

Liberty Travel (✆ 888/271-1584 to be connected with the agent closest to you; www.libertytravel.com) is one of the biggest packagers in the Northeast, and usually has a full-page ad in Sunday papers. Check out its **Last Minute Travel Bargains** site, offered in conjunction with Continental Airlines (www.lastminute. com), with deeply discounted vacation packages and reduced airfares. **Northwest Airlines** (www.nwa.com) offers a similar service: Posted on Northwest's website every Wednesday, its **Cyber Saver Bargain Alerts** offer special hotel rates, package deals, and discounted airline fares.

Among the airlines themselves, your package options include those from **American Airlines Vacations** (✆ 800/321-2121; www.aavacations.com), **Delta Vacations** (✆ 800/221-6666; www.delta vacations.com), and **United Vacations** (✆ 888/854-3899; www.unitedvacations. com). Contact the airline that services your hometown most frequently. In addition, **Air Jamaica Vacations** (✆ 800/ LOVEBIRDS; www.airjamaicavacations. com) is affiliated with the national airline, and these folks know the country well.

The biggest hotel chains and resorts in Jamaica (such as **Sandals**) also offer package deals. If you know where you want to stay, call that resort about air-and-land packages.

FOR BRITISH TRAVELERS

ITC Classics, Concorde House, Forest Street, Chester CH1 1QR (✆ 01244/355-550; www.itcclassics.co.uk), offers all-inclusive packages (airfare and hotel) to Jamaica and customizes tours for independent travel. It publishes two catalogs.

Other Jamaican specialists operating out of the U.K. include big **Kuoni Travel,** Kuoni House, Dorking, Surrey RH5 4AZ (✆ 01306/742-222; www. kuoni.co.uk), and **Caribtours,** Kiln House, 210 New Kings Rd., London SW6 4NZ (✆ 020/7751-0660; www. caribtours.co.uk)—a small, very knowledgeable specialist.

Tips Don't Stow It—Ship It

Though pricey, it's sometimes worthwhile to travel luggage-free. Specialists in door-to-door luggage delivery include Virtual Bellhop (www.virtual bellhop.com), SkyCap International (wwww.skycapinternational.com), Luggage Express (www.usxpluggageexpress.com), and Sports Express (www. sportsexpress.com).

Tips Ask Before You Go

Before you invest in a package deal or an escorted tour:

- Always ask about the **cancellation policy.** Can you get your money back? Is there a deposit required?
- Ask about the **accommodations choices and prices** for each. Then look up the hotels' reviews in a Frommer's guide and check their rates online for your specific dates of travel. Also find out what types of rooms are offered.
- Request a complete **schedule** (escorted tours only).
- Ask about the **size** and demographics of the group (escorted tours only).
- Discuss what is included in the **price** (transportation, meals, tips, airport transfers, etc.) (escorted tours only).
- Finally, look for **hidden expenses.** Ask whether airport departure fees and taxes, for example, are included in the total cost—they rarely are.

13 Special-Interest Trips

For the traveler who likes to spice up a holiday with some more vigorous activity, Jamaica offers a number of quality options to entice you away from the beach.

BIKING

Some of the best bike tours in Jamaica are offered in Negril at **Rusty's X-cellent Adventures** (© 876/957-0155; http://rusty.nyws.com). See "Hitting the Beach & Other Outdoor Pursuits" in chapter 5.

Note that bike repair shops are almost nonexistent. Take along a repair kit if you plan to do some solo cycling.

GOLF

Jamaica has the best golf courses in the West Indies, with Montego Bay sporting the best championship links.

The Cinnamon Hill course at **Rose Hall Resort & Country Club** (© 876/953-2650; www.rosehallresort.com) is ranked among the top-five golf courses in the world by some; it's an unusual and challenging seaside and mountain course.

Golf at Half Moon (© 876/953-2211; www.halfmoongolf.com) at the Half Moon Resort features a championship course designed by Robert Trent Jones, Jr. **Ironshore Golf & Country Club** (© 876/953-2800) is another good course in Montego Bay. See "Beaches, Golf & Other Outdoor Pursuits" in chapter 4.

On the North Shore are **SuperClubs' Runaway Golf Club** (© 876/973-7319; www.superclubs.com) at Runaway Bay and **Sandals Golf & Country Club** (© 876/975-0119; www.sandals.com) at Ocho Rios. See "Sports & Outdoor Pursuits" in section 1, "Ocho Rios," in chapter 7.

In Mandeville, the **Manchester Country Club**, Brumalia Road (© 876/962-2403), is Jamaica's oldest golf course, recently expanded from 9 to 18 holes. Beautiful vistas unfold 660m (2,200 ft.) above sea level. See "Exploring the Area" in section 2, "Mandeville," in chapter 6.

HIKING

Because of possible dangers involved, it's often best to go on an organized tour, the best of which are offered by **Sun Venture Tours,** 30 Balmoral Ave., Kingston, Jamaica W.I. (© 876/960-6685; www.sunventuretours.com).

Besides the high Blue Mountains, where Sun Venture goes, another great place for hiking is from Port Antonio. You can hike various trails through the **Rio Grande Valley;** highlights include the 7-hour White River Falls jaunt along the banks of the White River and an easier walk to the Scatter Waterfalls, floating on a bamboo raft across the Rio Grande. The 11km (7-mile) Guava River Trail goes along the Guava River into the heart of the Blue Mountains. See "Beaches & Outdoor Pursuits" in chapter 8.

The **Maroon Country,** near Montego Bay, is also a place of challenging hikes—though it's best to hire a guide here.

HORSEBACK RIDING

The best riding is on the North Shore. Jamaica's most complete equestrian center is **Chukka Caribbean Adventures** (*© 876/972-2506;* www.chukka caribbean.com), at Richmond Landovery, less than 6km (4 miles) east of Runaway Bay. See "Sports & Outdoor Pursuits" in section 2, "Runaway Bay," in chapter 7.

Another good program is offered at **Rocky Point Riding Stables** (*© 876/953-2286*), Half Moon Club, Rose Hall, Montego Bay, housed in the most beautiful barn and stables in Jamaica. See "Beaches, Golf & Other Outdoor Pursuits" in chapter 4.

SCUBA DIVING

Diving is sometimes offered as part of all-inclusive packages by the island's major hotels. There are also well-maintained facilities independent of the hotels.

Near Montego Bay, **Seaworld Resorts** (*© 876/953-2180*), at the Cariblue Hotel on Rose Hall Main Road, offers scuba-diving excursions to offshore coral reefs that are among the most spectacular in the Caribbean. There are also PADI-certified dive guides, one dive boat, and all necessary equipment for either inexperienced or certified divers. See "Beaches, Golf & Other Outdoor Pursuits," in chapter 4.

Negril is a hotbed of diving. **Negril Scuba Centre** (*© 800/818-2963* or 876/957-9641; www.negrilscuba.com), in the Mariner's Negril Beach Club, Norman Manley Boulevard, is the area's most modern, best-equipped scuba facility. See "Hitting the Beach & Other Outdoor Pursuits," in chapter 5.

SNORKELING

The offshore reefs bordering the coast at Negril are excellent for snorkeling, many shallow enough to lure the beginner. The shoreline east of Ocho Rios to Galina Point is fringed by a coral reef of rainbow-hued marine life. Most resorts provide snorkeling equipment, but the activity isn't very well organized.

What the Meal Plans Mean

- **AP (American Plan):** This plan includes three meals a day (sometimes called "full board" or "full pension").
- **CP (Continental Plan):** A continental breakfast (that is, bread, jam, and coffee) is included in the room rate.
- **EP (European Plan):** This rate is always cheapest, as it offers only the room—no meals.
- **MAP (Modified American Plan):** Sometimes called "half-board" or "half-pension," this rate includes breakfast plus dinner or lunch.

TENNIS

All-Jamaica Hardcourt Championships are played in August at the **Manchester Country Club,** Brumalia Road, P.O. Box 17, Mandeville (© **876/962-2403**). The courts are open for general play during the rest of the year.

Sandals Grande Ocho Rios Beach & Villa Resort, Main Street, Ocho Rios (© **876/974-5691;** www.sandals.com), focuses more on tennis than does any other resort in the area. It offers three clay-surface and three hard-surface courts, all lit for nighttime play. Nonresidents must call and make advance arrangements with the manager.

In Montego Bay you'll find excellent tennis facilities at **Rose Hall Resort & Country Club,** at Rose Hall (© **876/953-2650;** www.rosehallresort.com); at the **Half Moon Resort** (© **876/953-2211;** www.halfmoon.com); and at **Tryall Club Jamaica,** St. James (© **876/956-5660;** www.tryallclub.com).

14 For the Cruise-Ship Traveler

Most cruise ships heading for Jamaica travel at night, arriving the next morning at the day's port of call, perhaps Montego Bay or Ocho Rios. In port, passengers can go ashore for sightseeing, shopping, and a local meal. Prices vary widely; consult a travel agent for the latest.

Agencies and tour companies offering cruise packages to Jamaica include: **Ambassador Tours,** 120 Montgomery St., Suite 400, San Francisco, CA 94104 (© **800/989-9000** or 415/357-9876; www.ambassadortours.com); **Cruises, Inc.,** 1415 NW 62nd St., Suite 205, Fort Lauderdale, FL 33309 (© **866/325-6893** or 800/854-0500; www.cruises inc.com); **Cruises of Distinction,** 2750 S. Woodward Ave., Bloomfield Hills, MI 48304 (© **800/634-3445**); **Cruise Masters,** Century Plaza Towers, 2029 Century Park E., Suite 950, Los Angeles, CA 90067 (© **800/242-9000** or 310/556-2925); **Kelly Cruises,** 1315 W. 22nd St., Suite 105, Oak Brook, IL 60521 (© **800/837-7447** or 630/990-1111); and **Hartford Holidays Travel,** 129 Hillside Ave., Williston Park, NY 11596 (© **800/828-4813** or 516/746-6670).

Also stay tuned to last-minute price wars brewing among such megacarriers as Carnival, Royal Caribbean, and Holland America (see below).

THE CRUISE LINES

Here's a brief rundown of some of the cruise lines serving Jamaica and the Caribbean. For detailed information, pick up a copy of one of our companion guides in this series, *Frommer's Caribbean Cruises & Ports of Call, Frommer's Caribbean Ports of Call,* or *The Unofficial Guide to Cruises.*

- **Carnival Cruise Lines** (© **888/CARNIVAL;** www.carnival.com): Offering affordable vacations on some of the biggest and most brightly decorated ships afloat, Carnival is the boldest, brashest, most successful mass-market cruise line in the world. Its vessels stop at Ocho Rios and Montego Bay. The cruises offer good value and feature nonstop activities. Food and party-colored drinks are plentiful, and the overall atmosphere is comparable to a floating theme park. Lots of single passengers opt for this line, as do families attracted by the line's well-run children's program.
- **Celebrity Cruises** (© **877/202-4345** or 305/539-6000; www.celebrity.com): Celebrity maintains eight stylish, medium to large ships that stop at Ocho Rios and Montego Bay. It's classy but not stuffy, several notches above mass-market lines. Accommodations are roomy and well equipped,

cuisine is refined, and service is impeccable.

- **Costa Cruise Lines** (© 800/462-6782 or 954/266-5600; www.costa cruises.com): Costa, the U.S.-based branch of a cruise line that has thrived in Italy for about a century, maintains hefty to megasize vessels. Two of Costa's vessels offer similar jaunts through the western Caribbean on alternate weeks, departing from Fort Lauderdale and calling at Ocho Rios. There's an Italian flavor and lots of Italian design on board here, and an atmosphere of relaxed indulgence.
- **Holland America Line** (© 877/SAIL-HAL; www.hollandamerica.com): Holland America is the most high-toned of the mass-market cruise lines. The ships offer solid value, with very few jolts or surprises, and attract a solid, well-grounded clientele of primarily older travelers (late-night revelers and serious partygoers might want to book cruises on other lines, such as Carnival). Cruises stop at deep-water mainstream ports such as Ocho Rios or Montego Bay, and last an average of 7 days, but in some cases 10 days, visiting such ports as Key West, Grand Cayman, St. Maarten, St. Lucia, Curaçao, Barbados, and St. Thomas.
- **Royal Caribbean International (RCI)** (© 800/562-7625; www.royal caribbean.com): RCI leads the industry in the development of megaships. Though accommodations are more than adequate, they are not upscale and tend to be a bit more cramped than the industry norm. Using either Miami, Fort Lauderdale, or Galveston as their home port, Royal Caribbean ships call regularly at Ocho Rios and Montego Bay. Most of the company's cruises last 7 days.

15 Getting Around

BY RENTAL CAR

Jamaica is big enough—and public transportation is unreliable enough—that a car is a necessity if you plan to do much independent sightseeing. Unfortunately, prices of car rentals in Jamaica have skyrocketed; it's now one of the most expensive rental scenes in the Caribbean. And fraud is a very real concern; stick with our choices below.

Most rental cars in Jamaica are picked up at the airport, not delivered to your hotel. Some hotels have car-rental desks, but in all cases we've found those desks' prices higher than if arrangements were made in advance. Most car-rental firms in Jamaica grant unlimited mileage; if the firm you're calling doesn't, switch to one that does.

You can usually book a rental car as part of a package tour, but if you're going on your own, here are some tips:

WHERE TO RENT Try **Budget** (© 800/472-3325, 876/952-3838 at the Montego Bay Airport, or 876/924-8762 in Kingston; www.budget.com); with Budget, a daily collision-damage waiver is mandatory and costs $15. **Hertz** (© 800/654-3131; www.hertz.com) operates branches at the airports in Montego Bay (© 876/979-0438) and Kingston (© 876/924-8028).

If you'd like to shop for a better deal with one of the local companies in Montego Bay, try **Jamaica Car Rental,** 23 Gloucester Ave. (© 876/952-5586; www.jamaicacarrentals.com), with a branch at the Sangster International Airport at Montego Bay (© 876/952-9496). You can also try **United Car Rentals,** 49 Gloucester Ave. (© 876/952-3077), which rents Mazdas, Toyotas, Hondas, and Suzuki jeeps, costing from $49 per day for a standard, $64 for automatic.

In Kingston try **Island Car Rentals,** 17 Antigua Ave. (© **876/929-5875;** www.islandcarrentals.com). It rents Hondas, Nissans, Toyotas, Suzukis, and others, with rates beginning at $49 daily in winter and $39 in the off season.

Expedia.com (www.expedia.com) and **Travelocity** (www.travelocity.com) can help you compare prices for rentals—and locate bargains—in Jamaica.

DRIVING IN JAMAICA   *Drive on the left side of the road.* You should exercise more than usual caution, and be especially cautious at night: Male drivers here are too reckless for comfort. Speed limits in towns are 50kmph (31 mph), and 80kmph (50 mph) outside towns. Gas is measured by the imperial gallon (a British unit of measurement that's about 25% more than a U.S. gal.); most stations don't accept credit cards. Your valid driver's license from home is acceptable for short-term visits to Jamaica.

ROAD MAPS   A coastal route designated by an A plus a number encircles Jamaica. It's well marked and easy to follow. More complicated are secondary roads, urban streets, and feeder roads, whose markings sometimes are infuriatingly unclear. Recognizing this problem, the Jamaica Tourist Board has issued one of the best maps of the island, the *Discover Jamaica* road map. It contains a detailed overview of the entire island, as well as blowups of Kingston, Montego Bay, Negril, Mandeville, Spanish Town, Port Antonio, and Ocho Rios; there's also a very useful street index to Kingston. Get it from any Jamaica Tourist Board office or car-rental agency.

AUTO BREAKDOWNS   In case of a breakdown, telephone your car-rental agency for assistance.

BY TAXI & BUS

Most cabs in Jamaica are older vehicles. Taxis in Kingston don't have meters, so agree on a price before you get in the car.

In Kingston and the rest of the island, special taxis and buses for visitors are operated by JUTA (Jamaica Union of Travellers Association) and have the union's emblem on the side of the vehicle. Look for a red Public Passenger Vehicle (PPV) plate.

Taxis can be flagged down on the street or summoned by phone. Rates are per car—not per passenger—and 25% is added to the metered rate between midnight and 5am.

Technically, JUTA cabs are supposed to have meters, but most of them are not in working order. Therefore, again, *agree on the price of the trip before booking.* Cab fares should be posted inside the taxi; if you don't see them, you have the right to request a copy from the driver. A 10% to 12% tip is usually added.

Avoid pirate or unlicensed taxis. Not only are they not metered—they are illegal and rarely carry insurance.

BY MOPED & MOTORCYCLE

The front desk of your hotel can usually arrange the rental of a moped or motorcycle. Expect a daily rate of about $45 for a moped or $70 for a Honda 550. Depending on the vehicle rented, a deposit of $100 to $300 is generally required.

BY PLANE

Most travelers enter the country via Montego Bay (although American Airlines and Air Jamaica also fly to Kingston). If you want to fly elsewhere on the island, you'll need to use the island's domestic air service, which is provided by **Air Jamaica Express.** Reservations are handled by **Air Jamaica** (© **800/523-5585** or 888/FLY-AIRJ in Jamaica; www.airjamaica.com). You can also reserve from home through a travel agent or American Airlines.

Air Jamaica Express offers scheduled flights daily between the resort areas. There are seven flights a day from Kingston to Montego Bay, two flights a day between Kingston and Ocho Rios, and two flights between Montego Bay and Ocho Rios—each about $70 per leg. Car-rental facilities are not available at Jamaica's smaller airports.

International Air Link (℃ **888/AIR-LINK** or 876/940-6660; www.intlairlink. com) also provides shuttle service between Montego Bay and Negril for $66 one-way.

16 Tips on Accommodations

Because of the island's size and diversity, Jamaica offers the widest array of accommodations in the Caribbean.

One increasingly popular option is the **all-inclusive resort.** Well-publicized, solidly financed, and boasting a wealth of facilities, these tend to be large resorts where all your drinking, dining, and sporting diversions are offered within the hotel compound as part of one all-inclusive price. Although they tend to limit your exposure to local life, they are convenient. (See "The All-Inclusive: Safe Haven, or Not for You?" box below.)

Another option is the **small hotel.** Jamaica offers many of these, a few of which are the finest in the Caribbean. There, on any given day, you'll be given an option of dining either within the hotel or at any of the independent restaurants that flourish nearby.

Other options include renting a **self-catering villa** or **apartment,** where you can save money by making your own meals in your own kitchen. Also noteworthy are Jamaica's simple but decent **guesthouses,** where low costs combine with maximum exposure to local life. Unfortunately, these sometimes lie far from beaches and offer few diversions or activities.

BOOKING A HOTEL ROOM

Reservation services usually work as consolidators, buying or reserving rooms in bulk, then dealing them out to customers at a profit. They do offer special deals that range from 10% to 50% off; but remember, these discounts apply to the inflated rack rates that guests rarely

end up paying. You're better off dealing directly with a hotel.

Here are a few of the best reservations services for Jamaican travel: **Hotels.com** (℃ **800/715-7666;** www.hotels.com) and **Quikbook** (℃ **800/789-9887,** includes fax-on-demand service; www. quikbook.com).

Online, try booking with **Frommers. com** and save up to 50%. **Microsoft Expedia** (www.expedia.com) features a "Travel Agent" that directs you to affordable lodgings.

LANDING THE BEST ROOM

Somebody has to get the best room in the house, and it might as well be you. In Jamaica the first question for most visitors is, "How far is my room from the beach?" Find this out before you go. Find out also what's included in the price—beach chairs, towels? It could make a big difference in your final bill.

Corner rooms are usually more spacious, more tranquil, and closer to the elevator. They often have more windows and light than standard rooms, and don't always cost more.

If you like to retire early, book a room away from the entertainment and the kitchen. Also ask if your windows can open, and if there are ceiling fans and/or air-conditioning.

Finally, when reserving ask if the hotel is under renovation. This is more likely to occur off season.

GUESTHOUSES

An entirely different type of accommodation is the guesthouse, where most Jamaicans themselves stay when they

The All-Inclusive: Safe Haven, or Not for You?

Of all the resorts of Jamaica, the all-inclusive has virtually taken over Ocho Rios, although Montego Bay and Negril have their fair share. The concept was pioneered by Jamaica's Butch Stewart with his Sandals properties (© **888/SANDALS**) and has since swept the Caribbean, including such islands as St. Lucia. Sandals caters only to couples (male/female), although most other resorts welcome all known couplings.

All-inclusives are not for the independent traveler. At the all-inclusive, you get all your meals and most activities paid for as part of a package. Some dine-around plans help you break the monotony of eating at the same resort every night. With their 24-hour security force, these all-inclusives give you more protection than the smaller, independent inns without such expensive patrolling.

If you're an adventure traveler, you may not want such womblike security. You may prefer to stay at a small inn or little hotel where you're free to roam throughout the day, returning to your bed after a night of rum and reggae on the town.

Like a mother hen, the all-inclusive will pamper you during your entire stay, even pick you up at the airport and haul you back there for your return flight. At the little independent inn or small hotel, you're more or less on your own. The choice is yours.

If you don't want to stick to the all-inclusives, one of the best travel agencies specializing in hotel deals is **Changes in L'Attitudes** (© **800/330-8272;** www.changes.com). For villas in Montego Bay, Ocho Rios, and Port Antonio, contact **Elegant Resorts International** (P.O. Box 80, Montego Bay, Jamaica; © **800/237-3237**).

travel. Prices average anywhere from $50 to $100 for a double per night, although this can vary widely.

The term "guesthouse" can mean anything, however. Some resemble simple motels built around swimming pools; others are made up of small individual cottages with kitchenettes, constructed around a main building containing a bar and restaurant serving local food. Some are surprisingly comfortable, often with private baths and a swimming pool. (You may or may not have air-conditioning; rooms are often cooled by ceiling fans or breezes through open windows—a security concern.)

Guesthouses can't be topped for value, however. Though bereft of frills, the guesthouses we've recommended are clean and safe for families or single travelers.

CONDOS, COTTAGES & VILLAS

If you're going as a family or group of friends, a housekeeping holiday can be one of the least-expensive ways to vacation in Jamaica. Self-catering accommodations are now available in many locations.

The more upscale **villas** have a staff, or at least a maid who comes in a few days a week, and they also provide the essentials for home life, including bed linens and cooking paraphernalia. **Condos** usually come with a reception desk and are often comparable to life in a suite in a big resort hotel. Nearly all condo complexes provide swimming pools (some have more than one pool).

Some **private apartments** in Jamaica are rented, either with or without maid service. This is more of a no-frills option than are the villas and condos. The apartments may not be in buildings with swimming pools, and they may not maintain a front desk to help you. Jamaican **cottages** often contain no more than a simple bedroom, small kitchen, and bath. During the winter, you'll need to reserve at least 5 or 6 months in advance.

Villas of Distinction, P.O. Box 55, Armonk, NY 10504 (© **800/289-0900;** www.villasofdistinction.com), offers private villas with one to six bedrooms and a pool. Domestic help is often included. Descriptions, rates, and photos of the villas are available online.

At Home Abroad, 405 E. 56th St., Suite 6H, New York, NY 10022-2466 (© **212/421-9165;** fax 212/533-0095; www.athomeabroadinc.com), has a roster of private upscale homes for rent in Jamaica, most with maid service.

VHR, Worldwide, 235 Kensington Ave., Norwood, NJ 07648 (© **800/633-3284** or 201/767-9393; fax 201/767-5510; www.vhrww.com), offers the most comprehensive portfolio of luxury villas, condominiums, resort suites, and apartments for rent in the Caribbean, including Jamaica. The company can also arrange for airfare and car rental.

Hideaways Aficionado, 767 Islington St., Portsmouth, NH 03801 (© **800/843-4433** in the U.S., or 603/430-4433; fax 603/430-4444; www.hideaways. com), publishes *Hideaways Guide,* a pictorial directory of home rentals worldwide, including Jamaica. It includes full descriptions so you know what you're renting. For most rentals, you'll deal directly with the owners. Other services include yacht charters, cruises, airline ticketing, car rentals, and hotel reservations. Annual membership is $185; membership information, listings, and photos are available online.

17 Tips on Dining Out

The bad news is that dining in Jamaica is generally more expensive than in either the United States or Canada. Restaurant prices are more in tune with Europe, as virtually everything must be imported except the fish and Caribbean lobster. Service charges are automatically added to most restaurant tabs, usually 10% to 15%. Even so, if service has been good, it's customary to tip extra.

To save money, many visitors prefer the Modified American Plan (MAP), which includes room, breakfast, and one main meal per day, almost always dinner. You can then have lunch somewhere else, or if your hotel has a beach, order a light a la carte lunch at the hotel, the cost of which is added to your bill. On some MAP plans, you can arrange in advance to exchange lunches for dinners, so you can go out a few times. This is true for affiliated resorts such as Sandals, which has more than one hotel in the same resort, as it does in Montego Bay and Ocho Rios.

The American Plan (AP), on the other hand, includes all three meals each day. Drinks, including wine, are usually extra. On this plan, it's cheaper and you don't need to rent a car or taxi at night, but you'll miss out on different dining experiences around your resort.

Before booking a hotel, it's wise to have a clear understanding of what is included in the various meal plans offered.

If you plan to eat out, here are some tips:

- In summer, only the most elegant establishments require men to wear jackets. Most top-rated places today ask only that a man wear a shirt with a collar.
- Check to see if reservations are required. In the winter you may find all the tables gone at some of the more famous places. Savvy guests often ask the concierge of a hotel to make reservations. At all places, wear a cover-up if you're lunching; don't enter a restaurant attired in a bikini.
- To save money, stick to regional food whenever possible. For a main dish, that usually means Caribbean lobster or fish (see "Jamaican Food & Drink," p. 265).
- Getting to a restaurant at night is difficult if you drive a rented car. The roads are badly marked, driving is on the left, and road conditions are poor. It's better to go by taxi. Some popular upscale restaurants will send a mini-van to your hotel.

18 Tips on Shopping

Crafts are a popular take-home item from Jamaica. **Woodcarvings** run the gamut from the horrible to the delightful; **baskets** are woven from palm fronds or the straw of an island plant known as the *jipijapa*. The island's inventory of woodcarvings and weavings is supplemented by establishments selling **leather goods** (sandals and shoes are often a good buy); locally made **jewelry** fashioned from gold, silver, onyx, and bone; and **clothing** (especially casual wear and sportswear) whose light textures nicely complement the heat of the tropics. Also noteworthy are the many **handbags** woven from straw or palm fronds, which are sometimes rendered more ornate through colorful embroidery applied by any of the island's "straw ladies."

Also noteworthy is the handful of **art galleries** that stock the paintings of local artists. Some art critics say the island's most valuable export, after aluminum, is its art. These paintings range from the banal and uninspired to evocative portrayals of universal themes.

Warning A Word on Marijuana

You will almost certainly be approached by someone selling *ganja* (marijuana)—in fact, that's why many travelers come here. However, drugs, including marijuana, are illegal, and imprisonment is the penalty for possession. You don't want to experience the Jamaican penal system firsthand. Don't smoke pot openly in public. Of course, hundreds of visitors do and get away with it, but you may be the one who gets caught, and the person selling to you might even be a police informant. Above all, don't try to bring marijuana back into the United States. There are drug-sniffing dogs stationed at the Jamaican airports, and they will check your luggage. U.S. Customs agents, well aware of the drug situation on Jamaica, have arrested many tourists who have tried to bring some home.

The Java of Kings

One of the world's most sought-after coffees, Blue Mountain Coffee is the drink of connoisseurs, favored from Tokyo to New York. The coffee is known for its good acidity, refined taste, particular sweetness, exquisite flavor, and an intense aroma.

The Blue Mountains north of Kingston reach a peak of 2,220m (7,400 ft.), making the coffee bean here one of the highest-elevation-grown coffees in the world. Introduced to Jamaica in 1728, the coffee is handpicked, and every stage of its production from hulling to sorting and grading is carefully supervised.

In Jamaica a ground 57-gram (2-oz.) gift pack usually retails for about $8, but it's probably far more expensive in your hometown if it's available at all. (Blue Mountain coffee beans in Japan, for example, sell for more than $60 per lb.)

The coffee is sold in most upscale gift shops in Jamaica, and makes an aromatic souvenir of your visit. We prefer to buy our supply while trekking through the Blue Mountains themselves. To locate where to buy the brew on-site (or nearly so), see "Exploring the Blue Mountains," in chapter 9.

Premium coffee is one of Jamaica's major exports, and you can buy it here much cheaper than at home.

Bargaining is welcome with handicrafts, especially in informal markets, but not in more formal stores. Expect a discount of around 15% to 20% off the original price.

19 Recommended Books

BOOKS
GENERAL

Catch a Fire: The Life of Bob Marley, by Timothy White (Guernsey Press, 1983), chronicles the reggae musician's life and career, from poverty to international fame.

Jamaican Folk Tales and Oral Histories, by Laura Tanna (Institute of Jamaica Publications, 1984), is a collection culled from the best Jamaican storytelling and told with humor and style.

The Cimaroons, by Robert Leeson (William Collins, 1978), is the story of an enslaved people who fought stubbornly for their freedom. Their story does not appear in many history books, yet is true and exciting.

X/Self, by Edward Kamau Brathwaite (Oxford University Press, 1987), one of the finest of the Caribbean poets, traces his African/Caribbean ancestry in an extraordinarily rich, imaginative sequence of poems.

HISTORY

The Gleaner Geography & History of Jamaica (Gleaner Company) is a regularly revised textbook through which Jamaican schoolchildren learn about their country. The latest edition is available in major bookstores around Jamaica.

TRAVEL

Tour Jamaica, by Margaret Morris (Gleaner Company, 1988), describes an island of infinite variety with interesting and warmhearted people. Covering six regions, the book provides data on places of interest, local personalities, and historic and topical anecdotes. Featured are 19 recommended tours.

The Adventure Guide to Jamaica, by Steve Cohen (Hunter Publishing, 1988), leads you on a tour of unforgettable parts of the island few visitors know how to reach.

CUISINE

The Jamaican Chef, by Byron Murray and Patrick Lewin (Life Long Publishers, 1990), provides recipes for an array of island dishes.

Traditional Jamaican Cookery, by Norma Benghiat (Penguin, 1985), includes local recipes never before written down, having been passed down by word of mouth.

FAST FACTS: Jamaica

Business Hours Banks are open Monday through Friday from 9am to 5pm. Store hours vary, but as a rule most business establishments open at 8:30am and close at 4:30 or 5pm Monday through Friday. Some shops open Saturday until noon.

Currency Exchange There are Bank of Jamaica exchange bureaus at both international airports (near Montego Bay and Kingston), at cruise ship piers, and in most hotels.

Doctors Many major resorts have doctors on call. If you need any particular medicine or treatment, bring evidence such as a letter from your home doctor.

Electricity Most places use the standard electrical voltage of 110, as in the U.S. However, some establishments still operate on 220 volts, 50 cycles. If your hotel is on a different current than your U.S.-made appliance, ask for a transformer and adapter.

Embassies, Consulates & High Commissions Calling embassies or consulates in Jamaica is a challenge. Phones will ring and ring before being picked up, if they are answered at all. Extreme patience is needed to reach a live voice on the other end. The embassy of the **United States** is located at the Jamaica Mutual Life Building, 2 Oxford Rd., Kingston 5 (✆ **876/929-4850**). The High Commission of **Canada** is situated at 3 West Kings House Rd., Kingston 10 (✆ **876/926-1500**). The High Commission of the **United Kingdom** is found at 28 Trafalgar Rd., Kingston 10 (✆ **876/510-0700**).

Emergencies For police and air rescue, dial ✆ **119**; to report a fire or call an ambulance, dial ✆ **110**.

Hospitals See "Fast Facts," in each regional chapter for the most convenient medical services to each destination.

Mail Instead of going to a post office, you can, in most cases, give mail to the hotel reception. Most hotels also sell stamps. Allow about a week for an airmail postcard or letter to reach North America. Increases in postal charges may be implemented at any time, so ask about the current rate before depositing mail. For mail to any business listed in this book, remember to include "Jamaica, W.I."

in the address. Call © **876/922-9431** in Kingston with questions. For important items, consider a courier service such as DHL (© **876/922-7333**) or Federal Express (© **876/952-0411**).

Newspapers & Magazines Jamaica supports three daily newspapers *(Daily Gleaner, The Jamaica Record,* and *Daily Star),* several weekly periodicals, and a handful of other publications. U.S. newsmagazines, such as *Time* and *Newsweek,* as well as occasional copies of the *Miami Herald,* are available at most newsstands.

Nudity Nude sunbathing and swimming are allowed at a number of hotels, clubs, and beaches (especially in Negril), but only where signs state that swimsuits are optional. Elsewhere, law enforcement officials won't even allow topless sunbathing.

Passports Allow plenty of time before your trip to apply for a passport; processing normally takes 3 weeks but can take longer during busy periods (especially spring). And keep in mind that if you need a passport in a hurry, you'll pay a higher processing fee.

For Residents of Australia: You can pick up an application from your local post office or any branch of Passports Australia, but you must schedule an interview at the passport office to present your application materials. Call the **Australian Passport Information Service** at © **131-232,** or visit the government website at www.passports.gov.au.

For Residents of Canada: Passport applications are available at travel agencies throughout Canada or from the central **Passport Office,** Department of Foreign Affairs and International Trade, Ottawa, ON K1A 0G3 (© **800/567-6868;** www.ppt.gc.ca).

For Residents of Ireland: You can apply for a 10-year passport at the **Passport Office,** Setanta Centre, Molesworth Street, Dublin 2 (© **01/671-1633;** www.irlgov.ie/iveagh). Those under age 18 and over 65 must apply for a €12 3-year passport. You can also apply at 1A South Mall, Cork (© **021/272-525**) or at most main post offices.

For Residents of New Zealand: You can pick up a passport application at any New Zealand Passports Office or download it from their website. Contact the **Passports Office** at © **0800/225-050** in New Zealand or 04/474-8100, or log on to www.passports.govt.nz.

For Residents of the United Kingdom: To pick up an application for a standard 10-year passport (5-yr. passport for children under 16), visit your nearest passport office, major post office, or travel agency or contact the **United Kingdom Passport Service** at © **0870/521-0410** or search its website at www.ukpa.gov.uk.

For Residents of the United States: Whether you're applying in person or by mail, you can download passport applications from the U.S. State Department website at **http://travel.state.gov**. To find your regional passport office, either check the U.S. State Department website or call the **National Passport Information Center** toll-free number (© **877/487-2778**) for automated information.

Pharmacies Prescriptions are only accepted by local pharmacies if they were issued by a Jamaican doctor. Luckily, hotels have doctors on call. If you need any particular medicine or treatment, bring evidence, such as a letter from your own physician. For the most convenient local pharmacies, refer to "Fast Facts" in each regional chapter.

Police Dial © **119.**

Radio & TV Jamaica is served by two major radio broadcasters. Radio Jamaica (RJR) is the more popular of the two, partly because of its musical mix of reggae, rock 'n' roll, and talk-show material. RJR's two island-wide services are known as Supreme Sound and FAME FM. The second broadcaster is Jamaica Broadcasting Corporation (JBC), which also operates the island's only television station (JBC-TV, established in 1963). Many of the better hotels offer CNN and other satellite channels.

Taxes The government imposes between 10% to 15% room tax, depending on your category of hotel. You'll be charged a US$37 departure tax at the airport, payable in either Jamaican or U.S. dollars. There's also a 20% government tax on rental cars and a 20% tax on all overseas phone calls.

Telephone, Telex & Fax Even the island's smallest hotels maintain their own fax machines. For telexes, contact the local branch of **Cleveland Walace Jamaica,** the country's telecommunications operators. In Kingston its address is 47 Halfway Tree Rd. (© **876/926-9700**).

Time During the winter, Jamaica is on Eastern Standard Time, the same as New York and Toronto. When the United States is on daylight saving time, however, it's 6am in Miami and 5am in Kingston; Jamaica does not switch to DST.

Tipping Tipping is customary in Jamaica. Typically 10% or 15% is expected in hotels and restaurants on occasions when you would normally tip. Most places add a service charge to the bill, but a little extra (3%–5%) is often expected for good service. Tipping is not "officially" allowed at all-inclusive resorts.

Useful Telephone Numbers Ambulance, © **110;** fire, © **110;** police, © **119;** time, © **117;** toll operator and telephone assistance on local and intraisland calls, © **112;** overseas calls operator, © **113;** Post and Telephone Department, © **876/922-9430.** You reach **MCI** at © **800/888-8000;** **AT&T** at © **800/CALLATT;** and **Sprint** at © **800/877-8000.**

Water It's usually safe to drink tap water island-wide; however, it's prudent to drink bottled water, if available. We do.

3

Suggested Itineraries

Vacations are getting shorter, and a lean-and-mean schedule is called for if you want to experience the best of Jamaica in a ridiculously small amount of time. If you're a time-stressed traveler, as most of us are, you may find these itineraries helpful. Think of them as "Jamaica in a nutshell."

Jamaica is arguably the most beautiful island in the Caribbean for scenery. Seeing its attractions is a joy. Getting to some of them is hell.

While touring Jamaica by car, you must drive on the left-hand side of the road. Breakdown assistance is quite limited in urban areas and virtually unavailable in rural sections.

Drivers and passengers in the front seat are required to wear seat belts (and will you ever need them!).

Drivers, if possible, should make every effort to avoid areas of high crime and civil strife. Most of these sudden explosions of violence take place in and around greater Kingston. Road blocks are sometimes employed by residents as protests to draw attention to particular issues. Extreme caution by drivers is urged. Keep the windows up and the doors locked when driving.

Most roads are paved, but suffer from ill repair, inadequate signage, and poor traffic-control markings. City roads are often subject to poorly marked construction zones, pedestrians, bicyclists, and, occasionally, livestock. Street corners are frequented by peddlers, window washers, and beggars walking among stopped cars. Small roads are often narrow and are frequently traveled at high speeds. Drivers should be aware of roundabouts, which are often poorly marked and require traffic to move in a clockwise direction. Motorists entering a roundabout must yield to those already in it. Failure to turn into the correct flow of traffic can result in a head-on collision.

The A1, A2, and A3 highways are the primary links among the most important towns and tourist destinations on the island. These roads are not comparable to American highways, and road conditions may be hazardous because of poor repair, inadequate signage, and poor traffic-control markings. The B highways and other rural roads are often very narrow and frequented by large trucks, buses, pedestrians, bicyclists, and open-range livestock. Highways are traveled at high speeds, but they are not limited-access and are subject to the hazards outlined above.

1 Exploring the North Coast in a Week: Montego Bay to Port Antonio

You can use the following itinerary to make the most out of a week in Jamaica, but feel free to drop a place or two to save a day to relax on the beach. One week provides just enough time, although barely, to introduce yourself to some of the best of the grand resorts on the island, especially Montego Bay and Port Antonio.

Jamaica's North Coast in One Week

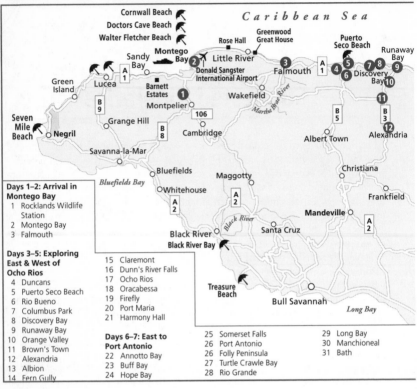

Cornwall Beach
Doctors Cave Beach
Walter Fletcher Beach

Caribbean Sea

Rose Hall
Greenwood
Great House

Puerto
Seco Beach

Runaway
Bay

Sandy
Bay

Montego
Bay

Little River

Falmouth

Discovery
Bay

Green
Island

Lucea

Donald Sangster
International Airport

Barnett
Estates

Wakefield

Montpelier

106

Grange Hill

Cambridge

Martha Brae River

Albert Town

Alexandria

Seven
Mile
Beach

Negril

Savanna-la-Mar

Bluefields

Bluefields Bay

Maggotty

Christiana

Frankfield

Whitehouse

Black River

Santa Cruz

Mandeville

Black River Bay

Treasure
Beach

Bull Savannah

Long Bay

Days 1–2: Arrival in Montego Bay
1 Rocklands Wildlife Station
2 Montego Bay
3 Falmouth

Days 3–5: Exploring East & West of Ocho Rios
4 Duncans
5 Puerto Seco Beach
6 Rio Bueno
7 Columbus Park
8 Discovery Bay
9 Runaway Bay
10 Orange Valley
11 Brown's Town
12 Alexandria
13 Albion
14 Fern Gully

15 Claremont
16 Dunn's River Falls
17 Ocho Rios
18 Oracabessa
19 Firefly
20 Port Maria
21 Harmony Hall

Days 6–7: East to Port Antonio
22 Annotto Bay
23 Buff Bay
24 Hope Bay

25 Somerset Falls
26 Port Antonio
26 Folly Peninsula
27 Turtle Crawle Bay
28 Rio Grande

29 Long Bay
30 Manchioneal
31 Bath

Days ❶ & ❷ Arrival in Montego Bay 𝒜𝒜𝒜

Fly to Jamaica and use Montego Bay as your gateway. It is Jamaica's premier resort with good airline connections from North America. You can pick up your rental car (advance arrangements are best) at the airport. Arm yourself with a good map and drive to your hotel. We don't suggest you launch the driving tour on your first day in Jamaica. The drive in from the airport will give you a good preview of driving conditions on the island. Perhaps after getting to your hotel of choice, you can relax and recuperate around the pool, sipping a rum punch. And then during your first evening you can enjoy some live reggae music and a bountiful buffet of Jamaican specialties

before turning in early after an exhausting day of departure and arrival hassles.

On the morning of Day 2, begin your road adventure of the island setting out for **Rose Hall Great House** (p. 95), formal locale of the "White Witch," which lies 15km (9¼ miles) east of the center of Montego Bay. Take the A1 highway east until you see the signposted turnoff near the community of Little River. After a 2-hour visit, get back on the A1 and continue east until you see the turnoff from A1 leading to **Greenwood Great House** (p. 94), former residence of the literary Barrett family. After a visit, you still have time to drive to **Falmouth** for lunch. The port town of Falmouth lies 37km (23 miles) east of Montego Bay. Before setting out to explore the town, stop first

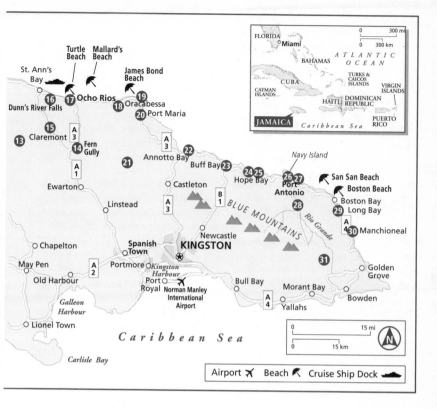

at the **Glistening Waters Restaurant and Marina** (p. 103) for a seafood lunch on the veranda overlooking the lagoon. After lunch, continue to Falmouth and take our walking tour of this historic seaport (see "Falmouth: Decaying Georgian Charm," in chapter 4).

After a day spent exploring the eastern coastline of Montego Bay, drive back to the center of the resort for the night. If you return by 4:30pm, you will still have time to see a unique sight in Jamaica: the **Rocklands Wildlife Station,** about 2km (1¼ miles) outside Anchovy. If you can make it here before closing at 5:30pm, Rocklands in the late afternoon attracts the most varied birdlife in Jamaica, winging in for the nighttime feeding (see "Interior St. James Parish," in chapter 4).

Anchovy lies on the western side of Montego Bay. Take the A1 until you reach Reading. At that point, cut south on Route B8 toward Anchovy. Return to Montego Bay for the night and perhaps an evening of feasting and listening to live reggae.

Days ❸, ❹ & ❺ Exploring East & West of Ocho Rios ★★

To keep from checking in and out of hotels frequently, you can use the North Coast of Ocho Rios as a base for all of the following excursions.

After checking out of your hotel, head east along A1 in the direction of **Falmouth** (see above). Beyond Falmouth, the A1 dips inland away from the sea until it reaches the little hamlet of **Duncans,** about 11km (7 miles) east of Falmouth and huddled under the hills of the Cockpit Country (see "The Cockpit Country," in chapter 4).

You'll find little here to detain you, except for a few local food joints and bars touting rum drinks. No one remembers when the clock tower last worked. Calypso fans know that the great singer, Harry Belafonte, once lived here in relative poverty. If you want to get out and stretch your legs, seek out the **Kettering Baptist Church** if it's open. Constructed in 1893, it honors William Knibb, a Baptist missionary. He is fabled in Jamaican history as an abolitionist. In 1840 he founded an emancipation village where runaway slaves enjoyed freedom.

Continue east beyond Duncans along the A1 to the little town of **Rio Bueno,** 51km (32 miles) east of Montego Bay. Rio Bueno is a fishing community that was the setting for the 1964 movie *A High Wind in Jamaica* (a classic you may find on the late show).

Rio Bueno was the place where Columbus first set foot in Jamaica on May 4, 1494 (or so it is believed). Offshore were anchored his caravels, the *Cardera, Nina,* and *San Juan.*

If you'd like a break, take time out to look at the 18th-century ruins of **Fort Dundas** behind the local school. It was named for Henry Dundas, the British secretary of war in the late 1700s. You can also walk over to **St. Mark's Anglican Church,** constructed on the water by the British in 1833. It has known greater days.

After Rio Bueno, the A1 runs along the sea until it reaches **Columbus Park,** which is a good place to stop for a picnic. You can secure the makings for a noonday respite at Montego Bay or at little joints in Rio Bueno. If you didn't prepare and bring along a picnic, you'll find a snack bar and a little tavern serving hot food. There's also a craft shop if you want a souvenir. Check out the museum here

before continuing on your way (see "Runaway Bay," in chapter 7).

Immediately to the east, reached along the A1, **Discovery Bay** comes into view. Opening onto a wide flask-shaped bay, Discovery Bay lies 8km (5 miles) east of Rio Bueno and 8km (5 miles) west of our next stopover at Runaway Bay. Locals make the claim that it was here that Columbus first landed in 1494, although some historians believe that Rio Bueno, as mentioned above, has a better claim.

You needn't spend a lot of time at Discovery Bay. The town is dominated by the Kaiser Jamaica Bauxite Company, and you can see large freighters loaded with the bauxite at the pier on the west side of the bay. Most of these freighters are headed for Russia. This so-called "red gold" is also shipped to refineries in the United States.

If you'd like an hour or so on the beach, take your trunks and head for **Puerto Seco Beach,** the best in the area. Its name, meaning "dry harbor," is said to have come from the reluctance of Columbus to land on a bay with no fresh water. There are full facilities and a snack bar here.

Continue east to **Runaway Bay,** which makes a more tranquil alternative choice for a hotel if you'd like to lodge here to explore the rest of the coast. Ocho Rios is larger and more bustling, however, with more activities going on.

Runaway Bay is for the escapist vacationers who want to flee the cruise-ship passengers arriving constantly at Ocho Rios. There's not a lot here. It's virtually a one-street village stretching for 3km (2 miles) along the A1. The name Runaway comes from the legend that the Spaniards fled from Jamaica to this point in 1655. Another legend suggests that the name comes from African slaves making a getaway from Cuba by canoe.

At this point in the tour you can dip south along the B3, following the signs past the little hamlet of Orange Valley to

Brown's Town, a large, bustling market town lying 11km (7 miles) south of Runaway Bay. For some motorists, this will be their first look at the "real Jamaica." Hopefully you'll arrive on one of the market days, Wednesday, Friday, and Saturday. Stroll through the tin-roofed, cast-iron Victorian market and be prepared for some powerful hawkers peddling their wares.

The views from this town are panoramic, a real taste of Jamaica's best scenery. Little food joints and tacky bars line the main street, and loud blasts of reggae music pierce the air.

Bob Marley fans will want to continue along the B3 south to **Alexandria,** a little hamlet of no importance, but a point from where you head east following the signs to Nine Mile and the **Bob Marley Centre & Mausoleum** (p. 189).

After paying your respects to the king of reggae, you can continue east from Nine Mile passing through the hamlet of Albion as you make your way to the town of Claremont, following the road signs. Once at Claremont you can hook up with the A1 north, leading to **St. Ann's Bay.** At this point you're back on the coast road, which is the A3 at this point. Follow it east into Ocho Rios if you have opted to make this resort your base for an exploration of the North Coast.

On the morning of Day 4 in Ocho Rios, you can set out to explore its immediate attractions, including **Dunn's River Falls** (p. 177) and the **Coyaba Gardens and Museum and Mahoe Falls** (p. 176), which are located 2km (1¼ miles) south of the town center. You can also fit in **Prospect Plantation** (p. 179), 5km (3 miles) east of Ocho Rios, returning to Ocho Rios in time to wander through the **Island Village** and the **Island Village Shopping Centre** (p. 178). Overnight once again in Ocho Rios.

On the morning of Day 5, set out to drive to the attractions east of Ocho Rios. But start the day by taking in one of the most scenic drives in Jamaica, heading south along the A3 to **Fern Gully,** a lush gorge. For driving directions, see p. 175. After this detour and a stopover here and there, return to Ocho Rios for the continuation of the tour.

Drive east 26km (16 miles) on the A3 in the direction of **Oracabessa.** A one-street town centered around a fruit and vegetable market, Oracabessa is best viewed on a Friday or Saturday. Gone are the notorious rum bars and gambling houses that flourished here at the turn of the 20th century when this was a major port for sending bananas to the United States. Ian Fleming wrote many of his James Bond stories at the property he purchased at **Goldeneye,** now a hotel (p. 164). Today you can visit the **James Bond Beach Club** Tuesday to Sunday from 9am to 6pm, just off Main Street along Old Wharf Road.

The A3 continues southwest until you reach **Port Maria,** which is 34km (21 miles) east of Ocho Rios and is one of the North Coast's most colorful towns opening onto a crescent-shaped bay. Most visitors come here to see **Firefly** (p. 177), just west of Port Maria. This was the Jamaican retreat of the playwright and actor, Nöel Coward. The world came to his doorstep, including celebrants of the Golden Age of Hollywood and even the Queen Mother of England.

While at Port Maria, you can also take a tour of the **Brimmer Hall Estate** (p. 176), which resides in the hills 3km (1¾ miles) from Port Maria. You can also swim in the pool of this 1817 estate.

On the way back to Ocho Rios for the night, we suggest a stopover at **Harmony Hall** (p. 178) on the A3, 6 km (3¼ miles) east of Ocho Rios. Once the main house for a sugar plantation, the hall today is one of the best shopping possibilities in the area, selling quality items, unlike the junk hawked on the streets. Return to Ocho Rios for the night.

Days ❻ & ❼ East to Port Antonio ✹✹✹

For a final look at Jamaica, we head east once again for the island's northwest sector, taking in our favorite destination on the island, historic Port Antonio, which is far removed from the hustle and bustle of either Montego Bay or Ocho Rios.

Leave Ocho Rios on the morning of Day 6, heading east along the A3, bypassing Oracabessa and Port Maria this time. Here, lush hills roll down to a coastline of white sandy beaches and the fabulous Blue Lagoon aquamarine pool. The A3 becomes the A4 at **Annotto Bay,** a battered old town, a one-street wonder, that is named after the red annatto dye once produced here. It's best to arrive at the main square on the market days of Friday and Saturday. Once it was a great banana shipping port in the 19th century, today seedy shanties line the waterfront. The place is like a time capsule of long ago, but it has its memories.

Sixteen kilometers (10 miles) to the east along the A4, **Buff Bay** comes into view. Farmers from the Blue Mountains come to market to sell their wares, often luscious fresh fruits and vegetables. The oldest building in town is the **St. George Anglican Church,** dating mostly from 1814, although some of the church has stood here since the late 17th century.

The other sights of interest, still to the east of Port Antonio, include **Hope Bay,** a 20-minute drive east of Buff Bay. Hope Bay is a fishing town filled with jerk stands, which is good to know if you're here at lunchtime.

A final stopover might be made at **Somerset Falls** to the immediate east of Hope Bay. Waters of the Daniels River pour down a deep gorge into a rainforest studded with waterfalls. This is one of the great beauty spots along the North Coast.

Continue east into Port Antonio where you can book a hotel for a 2-night stay.

On Day 7, go rafting on the **Rio Grande** (see "Beaches & Outdoor Pursuits," in chapter 8) before setting out on a drive. Rafting is experienced by nearly every visitor to Port Antonio. After that, head east along the A4, stopping first to look at the ruins of the **Folly Great House** on Folly Peninsula at East Harbour. Later, pass by the lavishly ornate **Trident Castle** at Turtle Crawle Bay (see "Exploring the Area," in chapter 8).

The A4 continues down the coastline in eastern Jamaica to the town of **Manchioneal,** 11km (6¾ miles) from Long Bay. The small fishing village is one of the most typical in Jamaica, and little jerk shacks line the shoreline if you're hungry.

After Manchioneal, continue south along the A4 until you see the turnoff to **Bath,** an evocative old spa town that seems to exist in a time capsule. If you're here for lunch, visit the **Bath Fountain Hotel and Spa.**

At this point because of the bad roads, you'd be advised to return northwest to Port Antonio for the night.

2 Circling 'Round the South Coast in a Week: Negril to Kingston

The tour outlined above is the pathway for mainstream tourism to the island, embracing the resorts that most visitors want to see. Except for **Negril,** which attracts thousands of visitors, the itinerary discussed here is more of a journey into unknown Jamaica, embracing the inland city of **Mandeville** and going to rarely visited **Spanish Town** and even **Kingston** itself, which the average visitor to Jamaica never sees.

Again, except for Negril, the South Coast doesn't offer the luxury of such resorts as Montego Bay and Ocho Rios. But you'll get a truer picture of what Jamaica is really like off the beaten path.

Day ❶ Arrival in Montego Bay 👁👁👁

You may have already seen this resort if you completed the 1-week tour outlined above. If you've seen the highlights of Montego Bay, you can spend Day 1 of the 2-week tour by doing something different. Montego Bay is famous for its beaches (see "Beaches, Golf & Other Outdoor Pursuits," in chapter 4). You can spend your day getting some R&R, which is what much of Jamaica is about. Or you can set out to do something more active, such as the **Hilton High Day Tour** of the historic plantation area or going on an evening cruise aboard the *Calico,* a gaff-rigged wooden ketch (see "Seeing the Sights," in chapter 4). Overnight in Montego Bay and try to get an early start for the tour west of Montego Bay the following morning.

Days ❷ & ❸ Southwest to Negril 👁👁👁

Make the popular and rather hedonistic resort of Negril your base for the next 2 days as you take in the sights of the far western section of Jamaica.

The drive west from Montego Bay takes you along the coast-hugging A1 to the community of **Reading** after a distance of 8km (5 miles). Its days as a major shipping port for sugar in colonial times are just a memory now. As you continue, you'll pass such exclusive and pricey resorts as Tryall and Round Hill, where the likes of Meryl Streep, Paul McCartney, and Demi Moore prefer to spend their holidays.

The first sizable town you'll come to is **Hopewell,** lying 8km (5 miles) west of Reading. This community is called the "dormitory" for the hotel workers of Montego Bay who journey east every morning to make their living at the resorts. There's little of interest here unless you arrive on a Saturday morning, when vendors from the hills descend on the local marketplace to hawk their wares, often fresh fruits and vegetables.

Immediately to the west of Hopewell, you arrive along the A1 at **Sandy Bay,** a hamlet founded as a free village for emancipated slaves, with a still-standing Baptist Church from 1848.

To the immediate west of Sandy Bay, **Miskito Cove** is a long, narrow inlet that is a favorite place for yachties to anchor, their luxuriant lifestyle in sharp contrast to the poverty of the region. Jerk shanties and beer joints pepper the area, which is rimmed with mangroves. The rock pillar offshore is said to resemble Queen Victoria in profile.

In this area, if time remains, you can visit the working farm of **Mayfield Falls & Mineral Springs** (see "Exploring the Area," in chapter 5).

After a visit, it's on to the largest town you will encounter en route to Negril. **Lucea,** pronounced "Lucy," 40km (25 miles) west of Montego Bay, was a bustling port town during the plantation era. Its crescent-shaped natural harbor, former stamping ground of Henry Morgan, is a shadow of itself today. Although the capital of the province of Hanover, Lucea today is a decaying Georgian town, its houses rotting in the sun. Its major attraction, the **Cleveland Stanhope Market,** is best seen on a Saturday. Pause at the large clock tower and restored town hall on **Alexander Bustamante Square,** officially dedicated by Queen Elizabeth in 1966.

After leaving Lucea, continue west for 6.5km (4 miles) to **Lance's Bay,** with its small, tempting sandy beaches. Our favorite for a dip is Guil Bay Beach. This peaceful cove is bordered by white sands.

As you head down the coast to **Green Island,** you will be immediately north of Negril and the famous swampland, **The Great Morass.** You may want to take your luncheon stopover at **Hurricane Park,** with many shady spots and a little nameless tavern that offers freshly cooked seafood. If you'd like to go for a dip, do so

Jamaica's South Coast in One Week

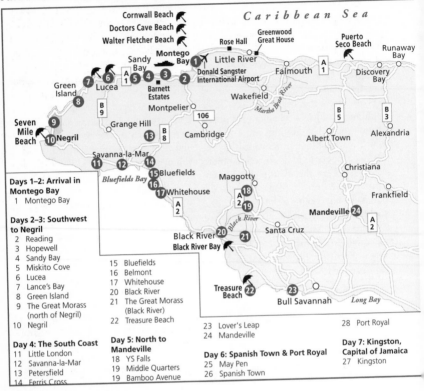

Days 1–2: Arrival in Montego Bay
1 Montego Bay

Days 2–3: Southwest to Negril
2 Reading
3 Hopewell
4 Sandy Bay
5 Miskito Cove
6 Lucea
7 Lance's Bay
8 Green Island
9 The Great Morass (north of Negril)
10 Negril

Day 4: The South Coast
11 Little London
12 Savanna-la-Mar
13 Petersfield
14 Ferris Cross

15 Bluefields
16 Belmont
17 Whitehouse
20 Black River
21 The Great Morass (Black River)
22 Treasure Beach

Day 5: North to Mandeville
18 YS Falls
19 Middle Quarters
19 Bamboo Avenue

23 Lover's Leap
24 Mandeville

Day 6: Spanish Town & Port Royal
25 May Pen
26 Spanish Town

28 Port Royal

Day 7: Kingston, Capital of Jamaica
27 Kingston

---

at **Half Moon Beach,** before pressing on to Negril where you can check into a hotel for 2 nights.

On Day 3, spend the morning enjoying **Seven Mile Beach** and perhaps have lunch in the area. In the afternoon, set out to explore the recreation area, the 122-hectare (300-acre) sight, **Royal Palm Reserve** (see "Exploring the Area," in chapter 5), which has been carved out of the massive local wetlands, the Great Morass, north of the center of Negril.

Here you can glimpse some of the best wildlife in Jamaica, perhaps even seeing the Jamaican woodpecker. Wooden boardwalks allow you to walk 2km (1¼ miles) into the wetlands for a closer encounter with the wildlife.

For a final excursion for the afternoon, you can visit the **Sir Alexander Bustamante Museum** at Blenheim, lying 6km (3¾ miles) inland from Green Island. It was the home of Bustamante, a national hero who is a sort of George Washington to Jamaicans. See "Exploring the Area" in chapter 5 for more information. Return to Negril for the night.

Day ❹ The South Coast 🎐🎐

On the morning of Day 4, leave Negril heading east along the A2. At this point, the main highway cuts inland away from the sea.

After leaving the resort, you'll pass through the low-lying **Negril Hills,** a bucolic Jamaica far removed from the bustling beach scene you've left behind.

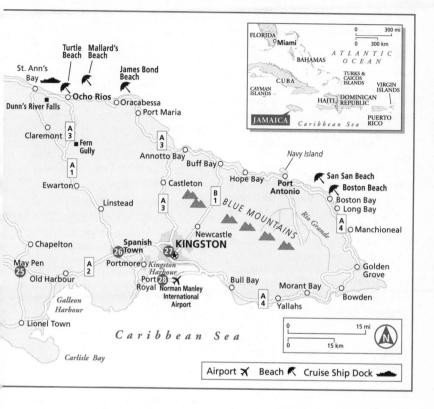

Most of the Rastas and other denizens who live in the ramshackle shacks here eke out a living by fishing. Bob Marley used to come here for R&R, and a sign points the way to **Bob Marley's Spring,** where the reggae king used to go skinny-dipping.

The first sizable town along the A2 is **Little London,** a study in dreariness. Pass it by, following the signs to the major port city of **Savanna-la-Mar,** which means "plain by the sea," although natives call it simply "Sav." It is the largest town in western Jamaica and the capital of the province of Westmoreland. Even so, it's dull and commercial. Instead of an intriguing old Jamaican city of the 18th and 19th centuries, you get hideously painted (if at all) concrete structures. The

reason for this is that a hurricane comes along several times a century and flattens the town. It has no developed attractions for visitors.

If you want to stop over, we suggest skipping Savanna altogether, and going 8km (5 miles) northeast of the city to the beautiful **Roaring River Park** (℃ 876/995-2094), open daily from 9am to 5pm and lying near the hamlet of Petersfield. The crystal clear mineral pool here and nearby caves make for a good break in your day on grounds that used to be a former sugarcane plantation. Water lilies and water hyacinths are profuse.

A local may point you to **Blue Hole Garden,** open daily 8am to 6pm. The blue hole is said to be bottomless, as its depth has never been probed. This sink-hole is enveloped by ginger torch and heliconia.

This whole area is one of the beauty spots of the South Coast, with small waterfalls and flowers everywhere, especially the white trumpet vine. There are some little stands selling food and drink.

Return to the coast and pick up the A2 as it continues east, this time hugging the coastline.

Just before you reach the town of Ferris Cross, you'll see **Paradise Park** (see "The South Coast," in chapter 6), a 405-hectare (1,000-acre) working cattle ranch that was used as a setting for some of the scenes in the hit film of yesterday, *Papillon.* Lying only 1.5km (1 mile) west of Ferris Cross, the park offers a chance for swimming in the Sweet River, hikes across lush terrain, and horseback riding. The grounds are open daily from 9am to 6pm.

Continuing east along the A2, you reach the twin towns of **Belmont** and **Bluefields,** with their fishing beaches. The approach to these towns is 19km (12 miles) southeast of Savanna-la-Mar. For more information on Bluefields and Belmont, see "The South Coast," in chapter 6.

After a visit the road continues southeast to the sea-bordering community of **Whitehouse,** 8km (5 miles) along the coast from Bluefields, still following the A2. Here you can pause to visit reggae star **Peter Tosh's Mausoleum.** Whitehouse is also the setting for the best hotel along the South Coast, **Sandals Whitehouse European Village & Spa** (p. 142). But this resort is for longer stays. As a motorist touring Jamaica, you'll look for inns or little hotels where you can check in one evening and check out the next morning.

Down the coast visitors arrive at **Black River,** where you will find two simple guest houses. Instead of checking in here, we suggest you press on for the night to Treasure Beach (see below).

Black River is the base from which to explore not only Black River, the second longest in Jamaica, but also the Great Morass. The Great Morass north of Black River evokes the Florida Everglades. See "The South Coast" in chapter 6 for touring information.

After your sightseeing, leave the A2 and continue southeast to **Treasure Beach** for the night. The small little town has the most diversified accommodations along the entire South Coast, our favorite nest being **Jake's** (p. 148).

Day ❺ North to Mandeville

Because of bad cross-country roads in Jamaica, Day 5 involves some backtracking, but it can be one of the most rewarding trips on this tour. If you arrived late in the afternoon, you can spend part of the morning exploring the sights around **Treasure Beach** itself. You can also follow the signs 11km (6¾ miles) southeast to **Lover's Leap.** One of the great panoramas along the South Coast unfolds here.

Return in the direction of Treasure Beach and backtrack to Black River. Here you can reconnect with the A2, which leaves the coast and moves inland, heading east to our final stopover for the day, Mandeville.

Two sights that you probably missed during your first stopover in Black River can be taken in a morning visit. **YS Falls** is among the most spectacular in the West Indies, lying 6km (3¾ miles) north of the A2 and signposted after you leave the village of Middle Quarters. After that hamlet, continue 13km (8 miles) north to reach the site.

Middle Quarters also marks the beginning of **Bamboo Avenue,** the Caribbean's most beautiful drive, lying between Middle Quarters and Lacovia. This 4km (2½-mile) highway is flanked by beautiful bamboo trees.

The A2 leads you east right into **Mandeville,** Jamaica's fifth-largest town (see

With More Time to Spare, Go Jamaican

With either of the above 1-week itineraries, you will have covered the major sights of Jamaica. But if your holiday schedule finds you with 2 weeks in Jamaica, spend your second week perfecting the fine points of being laid back and discovering in greater depth the multiple charms of the island. Here are some possibilities, any of which can profitably be repeated in case youre not sure you understood the details the first time. (A rigid assignment of specific activities to specific days would be completely un-Jamaican, so we've left the actual scheduling of these recommendations to you.)

- While sampling whichever of the island's rum drinks best appeals to your palate, you might experiment with having your hair braided into dreadlocks and learning the nuances of Jamaican patois, the island's unofficial language.
- Do some research into the Rastafarian religion, using what you learn to better appreciate the lyrics of reggae music.
- While sunning on an island beach, ponder the technical issues of the eventual construction of your own backyard jerk pit. Ask lots of questions about preferred cooking times and spices used during the jerk process.
- If you're interested in government, study the ideologies and practices of the island's political parties.
- Go shopping! Multiple opportunities for this art form present themselves throughout the course of any day, and by all means, don't limit yourself to whatever (and whoever) happens to approach you on the beach. Consider fine-tuning your respect (through visits to local art galleries) for the island's increasingly visible body of paintings, learning about the many woodcarvings produced by Jamaican artists, and watching for the cautious but subtle fashion statements that continue to emerge from the ateliers of the island's dressmakers.
- Read a book, meet people, go swimming, and, if only for the last week of your stay, BE JAMAICAN! (The locals will love it.)

"Mandeville," in chapter 6). Hotels and restaurants are limited but adequate for an overnight stopover. You can take a walking tour of the town in the afternoon and sample a real Jamaican local town—not a resort—as night falls.

Day ⑥ Spanish Town ⚐ & Port Royal ⚐

Leave Mandeville in the morning and get on the A2 once again. It dips southeast before heading east to the large town of **May Pen,** the capital of Clarendon Parish, just 58km (36 miles) west of Kingston. On the banks of the Minho River, May Pen lies midway between Mandeville and Spanish Town, which is the major destination for this day. On Friday and Saturday, a market is held south of the main square. Otherwise there is little of interest here.

We suggest bypassing May Pen, heading cross-country until you reach **Spanish Town** (see "Side Trips to Spanish Town & Port Royal," in chapter 9). You can spend 3 hours wandering this town and taking in its attractions, including the **Jamaica People's Museum of Craft & Technology.** Also check out the English cathedral with the Spanish name, **San Jago de la Vega,** dating from 1666.

Perhaps after a late lunch in Spanish Town, head for your final destination of the day, **Port Royal,** the once-notorious city signposted on an unnamed secondary road beginning southeast in Spanish Town.

Port Royal (see "Side Trips to Spanish Town & Port Royal," in chapter 9) is a shade of its former self, but once was called "the wickedest city on earth." You can walk around it and explore **Fort Charles** in an hour or two. We suggest you anchor in here for the night at **Morgan's Harbour Hotel & Marina** (p. 242), where you can also dine, your table opening onto a panoramic sweep of Kingston Bay and the Blue Mountains.

Day ❼ Kingston ☀, Capital of Jamaica

Your final look at Jamaica, its capital of Kingston, is also the most difficult. It is noisy and congested and possibly dangerous, yet filled with some intriguing sights. If you don't want the hassle of checking into another hotel for the night, you can stay at Morgan's Harbour (see above) for a second night, just venturing into Kingston for sightseeing for the day, returning to Port Royal at night.

Sights in Kingston that can easily fill up a day of sightseeing include the **National Gallery, Devon House,** the **Hope Botanical Gardens & Zoo,** and even the **Bob Marley Museum** (see "Seeing the Sights," in chapter 9). Try also to time it so that you can wander an hour or so through the **Kingston Crafts Market** (see "Shopping," in chapter 9).

Kingston is the major transportation hub of Jamaica, and flights are possible for other destinations in the Caribbean or for your return home.

3 Jamaica for Families

Jamaica offers many attractions for kids to enjoy. However, it is not the safest place to be, so you'll want to keep a hawk eye on your brood at every moment. Road travel is filled with some hazards, and casual walking can also be a bit hazardous because of reckless traffic. But, with proper precautions in place, you should have an enjoyable—and safe—experience discovering the island *en famille.*

In a capsule version, you can take in the highlights—just skimming the surface, of course—of Jamaica in just 1 week, with stopovers at the most popular resorts, including **Montego Bay, Negril, Ocho Rios,** and **Port Antonio.**

Day ❶ The Fun Begins at Montego Bay ☀☀☀

After your arrival in Montego Bay, check into a hotel for the night and try to arrange a returning booking for Day 4.

There's one attraction in Montego Bay for the entire family: the multi-million-dollar **Aquasol Theme Park** (p. 89), with its array of watersports activities, including a giant water slide. After you've checked out the attractions of this water-world, you can order lunch at an outdoor restaurant and get in some beach time on the sands of **Walter Fletcher Beach,** which is part of the theme park. All this fun is right in the heart of Montego Bay.

As the day wanes, we suggest a drive to the **Rocklands Wildlife Station** (p. 90). At this feeding station, you can caution your kids to remain quiet as they view the most flamboyant birds in Jamaica—including the doctor bird—come in for their daily pre-twilight feeding. Return to Montego Bay for the night and perhaps book a cruise on the *Calico,* a gaff-rigged wooden ketch sailing from the Montego Bay waterfront (see "Seeing the Sights," in chapter 4). Overnight in Montego Bay.

Day ❷ Southwest to Negril ✦✦✦

Ever since the hippie invasion of the late 1960s, the resort of Negril has been associated with more adult pleasures. But in the past decade or so, it has broadened its appeal and now embraces families. Plan an overnight stopover here on your whirlwind tour of Jamaica. Heading east along the A2, stop at **Mayfield Falls & Mineral Springs** (see "Exploring the Area," in chapter 5), which lies 6km (3¾ miles) east of the town of Lucea on Bamboo Bay. At this working farm, the entire family can swim in an underwater cave and stand in awe at all the waterfalls.

After continuing east, perhaps stopping for a picnic lunch at **Hurricane Park,** drive into Negril for the night. If you arrive in the afternoon, you can still get in some beach time along the fabled **Seven Mile Beach.** Avoid the nude section if you have small children unless your family is nudist-oriented.

Day ❸ The South Coast ✦✦

Leave Negril on the morning of Day 3, continuing east along the A2 and passing through the low-lying **Negril Hills,** going all the way to the major port city of **Savanna-la-Mar,** which has known greater glory. En route to Treasure Beach (see below), the best place to break up your day is at **Paradise Park,** a 405-hectare (1,000-acre) working cattle ranch, lying 1.5km (1 mile) west of the little town of Ferris Cross. The family can swim in the Sweet River here, take hikes, and even go horseback riding.

After a visit and perhaps a picnic lunch, continue on the A2 through the twin towns of **Belmont** and **Bluefields** until you reach **Whitehouse,** 8km (5 miles) along the coast from Bluefields. Here you can take a "safari," exploring **Black River,** the second-longest river in Jamaica, and a vast marshland called the **Great Morass** (see "The South Coast," in chapter 6).

As the afternoon fades, continue southeast along the A2 for the night until you reach **Treasure Beach.** This little resort makes the best stopover along the coast because it has the most diversified accommodations.

Day ❹ Return to Montego Bay ✦✦✦

On the morning of Day 4, drive west along the A2, following the same route you took to get here. Your goal for your final days in Jamaica is the North Coast. However, because of poor road conditions, reaching Ocho Rios by an inland route is a journey into hell. Therefore, it's necessary to do all this backtracking along the A2 to the final two destinations discussed here.

When you reach Montego Bay, check into a hotel (perhaps the same one where you booked before) and plan a day of R&R with your entire family. Most kids at this point want more hours on the beach. However, if your family wants to continue sightseeing, make it the old town of **Falmouth** (see "Falmouth: Decaying Georgian Charm," in chapter 4). After a good night's sleep, you'll be ready to set out the following morning to enjoy the major highlights of Jamaica's North Coast, which is far more touristy than the South Coast you've just visited.

Days ❺ & ❻ Exploring East & West of Ocho Rios ✦✦

Follow the A1 east to Ocho Rios. You'll spend a good part of the day on bad roads on the way to Ocho Rios from Montego Bay. This is the most family-friendly resort in Jamaica, and you'll want to spend at least 2 nights here, preferably at a resort such as **Beaches Boscobel Resort & Golf Club** or **FDR (Franklyn D. Resort),** which targets the family trade.

On your first day, after driving along Jamaica's notorious bad roads, your family may want to dispense with driving for the rest of the day and head for the beach.

Mallard's Beach in the center of Ocho Rios is the most convenient.

On the morning of Day 6 you can set out to do some touring. The major attraction at Ocho Rios, the 546m (600-feet) **Dunn's River Falls,** is not suitable for small children. More appropriate family-friendly fun includes such active attractions as **rafting on the White River** or **playing with dolphins** (p. 174).

If you'd like to go for a short but scenic drive, the lush gorge **Fern Gully** is one of the beauty spots of the North Coast. If time remains in the day, a final attraction of interest to families is **Coyaba Gardens and Museum and Mahoe Falls** (p. 176).

Day ❼ East to Port Antonio ✿✿✿

The family fun continues as you set out on the morning of Day 7 to visit historic **Port Antonio** in the east.

Along the way, stop off at **Harmony Hall** (p. 178), 6km (3¾ miles) east of Ocho Rios. This art gallery, crafts store, and restaurant is more of interest to adults than children (but you deserve some sightseeing too). The hall makes the best stopover after some potentially hazardous driving out of Ocho Rios. At least the whole family can enjoy some cold drinks before continuing with the tour.

Alternatively you can take in the 90-minute jitney tour of **Prospect Plantation** (p. 179), a working plantation—featuring pimentos, allspice, and limes—spread over 405 hectares (1,000 acres).

After arriving in Port Antonio, check into a hotel for the night. You can either head for the beach if you're tired of touring or take the entire family **rafting on the Rio Grande,** a tradition started by film actor Errol Flynn, who once lived in the area.

For your final night in Jamaica, we suggest you take the entire family for dinner at **Norma's at the Marina** (p. 201). Not only is this the finest restaurant in the area but it will also give you a chance to see Port Antonio's newest attraction, its marina.

After a night's rest, head out the following morning for your return home.

4

Montego Bay & the Northwest Coast

Despite a large influx of visitors, **Montego Bay** retains its own identity. A thriving business-and-commercial center, it functions as the main market town for most of western Jamaica, supporting both cruise-ship tourism and a growing industrial center. Mo Bay, as it's known, is even served by its own airport, **Donald Sangster International.**

This is the most cosmopolitan of Jamaican resorts, not as hedonistic as Negril but also not as crowded as Ocho Rios. As such, Montego remains the grande dame of island resorts. The draw of Mo Bay is its deluxe hotels, such as the Ritz-Carlton, Half Moon, Round Hill, and Tryall.

As in much of Jamaica, your choice of resort here often matters more than your choice of area. If you're determined to honeymoon with your sweetie, go for one of the Sandals properties; if you want to hang with the jet-set, take a villa at Round Hill.

If you're seeking authentic or traditional Jamaica, however, this area is probably not for you.

1 Orientation

ARRIVING BY PLANE   Most arrivals in Jamaica are at **Donald Sangster International Airport** (✆ 876/952-3124), 3km (1¾ miles) east of the center of Montego Bay. Those booked into resorts at Negril or Ocho Rios and its satellite, Runaway Bay, also use the Mo Bay airport as a point of entry into Jamaica.

In winter, the busy season for tourism in Jamaica, lines move smoothly. Things move more slowly during the summer months, despite dwindling numbers of tourists—partly because many Jamaicans from Canada and the United States arrive during those months to visit family. They often bring suitcases packed with gifts and supplies; inspection of these items can cause endless delays. (Jamaica's Customs and Immigration officers are zealous.)

After clearing Immigration, there is a **currency exchange office.** You can change money here into Jamaican dollars. Nearly all places on the island will accept the Yankee dollar—in fact, some vendors will specifically request it—but if you plan to go to local dives, they'll usually accept American dollars, but at a rate that's not as good as what you'd have gotten at a bona-fide bank. Our advice? Pick up a little Jamaican cash here at the airport, where you'll get a far better exchange rate than at your hotel.

In recent years, the numbers of **ATMs** has greatly increased within Jamaica. They're now readily available within most of the shopping malls and tourist zones frequented by cruise ship passengers and foreign visitors. Although it's true that you can find

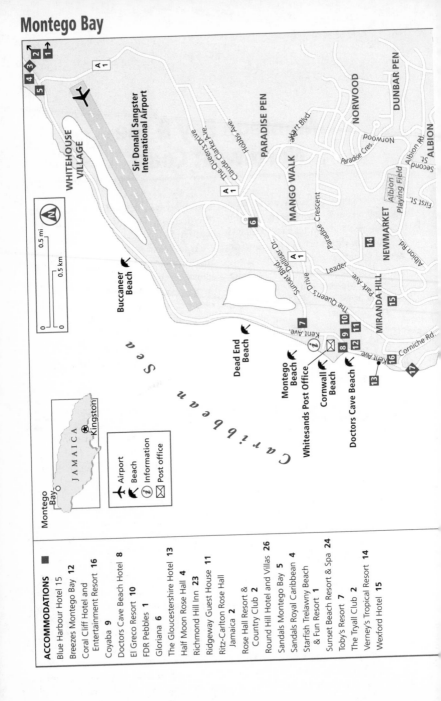

Montego Bay

ACCOMMODATIONS

Blue Harbour Hotel **15**
Breezes Montego Bay **12**
Coral Cliff Hotel and
  Entertainment Resort **16**
Coyaba **9**
Doctors Cave Beach Hotel **8**
El Greco Resort **10**
FDR Pebbles **1**
Gloriana **6**
The Gloucestershire Hotel **13**
Half Moon Rose Hall **4**
Richmond Hill Inn **23**
Ridgeway Guest House **11**
Ritz-Carlton Rose Hall
  Jamaica **2**
Rose Hall Resort &
  Country Club **2**
Round Hill Hotel and Villas **26**
Sandals Montego Bay **5**
Sandals Royal Caribbean **4**
Starfish Trelawny Beach
  & Fun Resort **1**
Sunset Beach Resort & Spa **24**
Toby's Resort **7**
The Tryall Club **2**
Verney's Tropical Resort **14**
Wexford Hotel **15**

Montego
Bay

JAMAICA
Kingston

✈ Airport
🏖 Beach
ⓘ Information
⊠ Post office

WHITEHOUSE
VILLAGE

Sir Donald Sangster
International Airport

Buccaneer
Beach

Dead End
Beach

Montego
Beach

Whitesands Post Office

Cornwall
Beach

Doctors Cave Beach

Caribbean Sea

PARADISE PEN

MANGO WALK

NORWOOD

DUNBAR PEN

ALBION

Norwood

Paradise Cres.

Paradise Crescent

NEWMARKET

Albion
Playing Field

First St.

Second St.

Albion Rd.

Albion St.

MIRANDA HILL

Leader

Park Ave.

Corniche Rd.

Kent Ave.

Sunset Blvd.

The Queen's Drive

Delisser Dr.

Kent Ave.

The Queen's Drive

Claude Clarke Ave.

Hobbs Ave.

Fairy Blvd.

0.5 mi
0.5 km

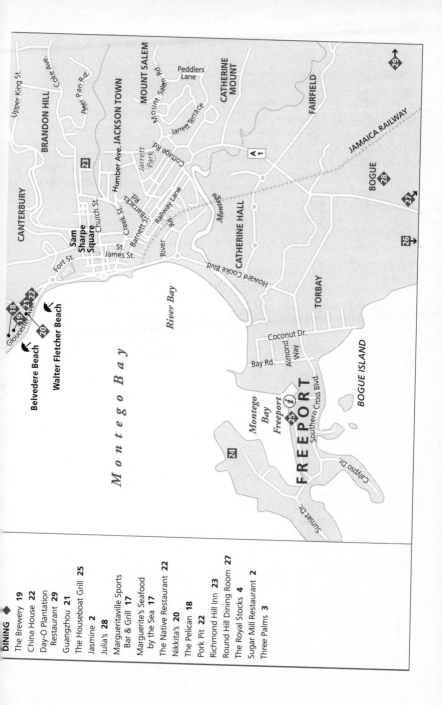

DINING ◆

The Brewery **19**
China House **22**
Day-O Plantation
  Restaurant **29**
Guangzhou **21**
The Houseboat Grill **25**
Jasmine **2**
Julia's **28**
Margueritaville Sports
  Bar & Grill **17**
Marguerite's Seafood
  by the Sea **17**
The Native Restaurant **22**
Nikkita's **20**
The Pelican **18**
Pork Pit **22**
Richmond Hill Inn **23**
Round Hill Dining Room **27**
The Royal Stocks **4**
Sugar Mill Restaurant **2**
Three Palms **3**

ATMs at the airport, some Frommer's readers have noted that some of these machines have occasionally run out of cash.

Warning: Once you retrieve your luggage at the airport, hang on to it, though luggage theft at the airports is less common than in years past, the police having made successful efforts at cleaning things up.

GETTING FROM THE AIRPORT INTO THE CITY   Some of the major resorts, such as the Sandals properties, keep vans waiting at the airport to carry guests right to the hotel for free. Other properties do not, however, especially the less expensive ones. If you're staying at one of these, you must take a taxi (unless you're picking up a rental car at the airport); there is no public bus service from the airport into Montego Bay.

Use only special taxis or vans operated by **JUTA,** the **Jamaica Union of Travellers Association** (© **876/957-4620**), or taxis operated by its government-sanctioned counterpart, JCAL Tours (Jamaica Co-operative Automobile & Limousine Tours; © **876/952-7574**). Do *not* get into a "pirate taxi," even if the driver promises to cut the going rate in half; cheating tourists is disturbingly common. JUTA tariffs are controlled, and you'll recognize its vehicles by the union emblems and red license plates. A list of official tariffs is posted at the airport—but it's still important to agree on the price before setting out, to avoid potential disagreements later.

VISITOR INFORMATION   The main office of the **Jamaica Tourist Board** is on Gloucester Avenue (© **876/952-4425**), opposite the entrance to Cornwall Beach. It is open Monday to Friday 8:30am to 4:30pm and on Saturday from 9am to 1pm. A small branch office of the tourist board is in the arrivals hall of Donald Sangster Airport, just at the point where new arrivals line up for approval of their passports, before they retrieve their luggage. According to a spokesperson from that office, most of the staff's function here involves reserving hotel rooms for visitors arriving in Jamaica without reservations. When visiting, ask for a free map of Montego Bay.

GETTING AROUND   Taxis are generally the way to get around, as there is no practical bus service in Montego Bay and no minivan shuttles except those maintained by hotels—and they're usually reserved strictly for the use of registered guests. There is, however, a loose cohesion of quasi-official minivans (referred to as "route taxis") that follow vaguely predetermined routes, usually along major highways leading in and out of town. The best and most reliable of these communal vehicles bear red-colored license plates whose numbers contain the letters "PP" (an abbreviation for "public passengers") somewhere within their sequences, and the words "route taxis" will be written on the outside of their doors. There are no individual signs indicating anything approaching a clearly designated bus stop, but locals know the points where they should stand along traffic arteries heading in and out of town. Rides cost between $1 and $2, depending on the distance you want to travel, and fares are usually collected before you get in. If you opt for this awkward and inconvenient mode of transport, pre-determine the fare before you board.

You can walk to most places within the center of Montego Bay itself, especially along Gloucester Avenue. In other cases, summon a licensed taxi. These have red license plates. A few of them have meters, but more often, government-sanctioned fares between most commonly requested destinations and points of departure are prominently posted inside each vehicle. If you want to hail a taxi to go somewhere outside of town, most of the cabs can be found along Gloucester Avenue.

For the truly adventurous, getting around by bike or motorcycle is another possibility, but frankly, the country's narrow, deeply potholed roads, the many blind curves, and the general hysteria associated with road traffic make transport by bicycle hazardous. Two-wheeled bike transit isn't particularly popular even among Jamaicans, and it's much less so for foreign visitors. If you still want to risk life and limb on a two-wheeled conveyance (and we hope that you won't), your hotel might either lend you a bike or rent you one. Whereas the law requires the use of a helmet for motorcycle riders, no such mandate is necessary for pedal bikes.

FAST FACTS: Montego Bay

Banks For money exchanges and/or other banking needs, the two best choices are **Scotiabank** (© 876/952-4440) and **National Commercial Bank** (© 876/952-3640), both on Sam Sharpe Square in the center of Mo Bay. Each maintains a 24-hour ATM and opens Monday to Thursday 8:30am to 4:30pm, Friday 8:30am to 4pm. Both are part of the Cirrus system, so participating cards work in their machines. Ironically, most of the ATMs we ran across in Jamaica dispense U.S. dollars only, but if there's any confusion, the currency dispensed by each machine is clearly indicated on the outside.

Bookstores If you'd like to do some light reading on the beach, you can go to **Sangster's Bookshop,** 2 St. James St. (© 876/952-0319), the largest book outlet in Montego Bay. It's open Monday to Saturday 8:30am to 6pm. Another retailer is **Henderson's Book Store,** 27 St. James St. (© 876/952-2551), open Monday to Saturday 8:30am to 6pm.

Business Hours Stores' policies vary, but in general they open Monday to Saturday 8:30am to 4:30 or 5pm. With the notable exception of some shops that cater specifically to the cruise ship trade, Sunday gets sleepy in Montego Bay, except at the hotels.

Doctors & Dentists All major hotels have a doctor or dentist on call. For emergency treatment, go to the hospital (see "Hospital," below). If you will need medicine or any particular treatment while in Montego Bay, bring a letter from your home physician before arriving on the island.

Drugstores One of the best pharmacies in Montego Bay is **Clinicare Pharmacy,** 14A Market St. (© 876/952-8510), open Monday to Saturday from 9am to 8pm and Sunday 10am to 6pm. Note that local pharmacies will only accept a prescription if it has been issued by or "endorsed by," (i.e., countersigned by) a Jamaican doctor. If whatever ails you might be handled with an over-the-counter medication, ask the pharmacist to recommend something.

Emergencies Dial © **110** to report a fire or call an ambulance. Dial © **119** for the police.

Hospital The biggest hospital in Montego Bay is **Cornwall Regional Hospital** at Mount Salem (© 876/952-5100). An alternative clinic, Montego Bay Hope (© 876/953-3649), is associated with the Half Moon resort. There's also the Doctor's Hospital in the suburb of Freeport (© 876/979-8983 or 876/953-6008).

Patients in emergency situations who can afford it are sometimes flown to Miami, where medical facilities are better.

Internet Access Your best bet if your hotel isn't equipped is **Irie Tech,** 17 Harbour St. (© **876/971-6057;** irietech2@cwjamaica.com). It's open Monday to Saturday 9am to 7pm.

Laundry & Dry Cleaning If your hotel doesn't offer guest laundry facilities, you can drop off laundry at **Fabricare Centre,** 4 Corner Lane (© **876/952-6897**), which also features 1-hour dry cleaning. Hours are Monday to Saturday 7:30am to 5pm. Offering much the same service, including 1-hour dry cleaning, is **Quality Laundry & Dry Cleaners,** 11 Perry St. (© **876/952-6105**), open Monday to Saturday 8am to 5:30pm.

Mail Include "Jamaica, W.I." in all island addresses. At press time for this edition, the island had no zip codes, despite efforts that had been made throughout 2005 to inaugurate them within the Jamaican postal system.

Maps Go to the tourist office (see above) for a good map of Montego Bay.

Photo Supplies Film can be purchased at **Salmon's,** 32 St. James St. (© **876/952-4527**), open Monday to Thursday 9am to 7pm, Friday and Saturday 9am to 8pm; and **Ventura,** 22 Market St. (© **876/952-2937**), open Monday to Friday 9am to 5pm and Saturday 9am to 6pm. Each of these stores also processes photos.

Post Office Many visitors buy Jamaican stamps as collector's items, as they are often flamboyant. The chief post office in Montego Bay is in the center of town at 122 Barnett St. (© **876/952-7389**). It is open Monday to Friday 8am to 5pm.

Safety Montego Bay is far safer as a destination than Kingston. All the major resorts, especially the all-inclusives, have private security guards patrolling the grounds; on-site you'll probably run into few problems. As is the case anywhere in the world, security is less tight when you leave the premises of your hotel. One annoying inconvenience involves the occasional hustler—peddling souvenirs, flesh, drugs, or whatever—who might pester you. Most of them are harmless; a few, though, are muggers or pickpockets, so be careful around them. As for wandering around Montego Bay's narrow, dark streets at night—suffice to say that it's a bad idea. Take comfort in the fact that in recent years, the situation in heavily touristed areas is much better than it was in the mid-1990s, thanks to increased police supervision.

Telephone Hotels sometimes add outrageous surcharges to long-distance calls. For that reason, some frugal travelers purchase a **Cable & Wireless Phone Card**—available at most hotel desks and within many gift shops—for J$200 (US$3.20), allowing you to talk to places in the U.S. and Canada for about 11 minutes. For more information, call © **888/225-5295.**

Travel Agencies There is no local representative for American Express in Montego Bay. However, with an American Express card you can get a personal check cashed at **Great Vacations,** 2 Market St. (© **876/971-6750**), open Monday to Friday 8:30am to 5pm, Saturday 9am to 1pm. This office can also make travel arrangements for you. Another leading travel agent is **Trafalgar Travel,** 14B Market St. (© **876/979-1556**), which is open Monday to Friday 8:30am to 5pm, Saturday 10am to 1pm.

2 Where to Stay

The Montego Bay region boasts a superb selection of hotels, ranging from very expensive world-class resorts to notable bargains. There's also a broad scale and diverse selection of all-inclusive resorts, which are all reviewed together for easy comparison at the end of this section. Most of the big full-service resorts are frequently included in package tours. Booking a package will make the rates much more reasonable. See "Packages for the Independent Traveler" and "Tips on Accommodations" in chapter 2.

Each type of property attracts a different crowd. The deluxe properties such as Round Hill, Tryall, and Half Moon are for veterans of Caribbean travel. Many guests at these resorts are repeat visitors, and in some cases have visited them 20 or more times; if you're not a member of this club, however, you might feel a bit out of place.

The all-inclusive resorts tend to attract young, starry-eyed couples and honeymooners on their first trips to Jamaica. These places tend to be a little noisy, decadent, and no-holds-barred as a result.

Finally, the smaller resort properties listed here as moderately or inexpensively priced tend to attract middle-age couples (as opposed to the young crowd at Sandals-type places). Guests at these smaller properties tend to be more experienced travelers, often Europeans, and are independent-minded enough to view the hotel mostly as a place to bunk down at night.

MAKING RESERVATIONS

If you arrive without a reservation (not recommended in Jamaica), begin your search for a room as early in the day as possible. If you arrive late at night without a reservation, you may have to take what you can get—often in a price range much higher than you'd like to pay.

Montego Bay has become a year-round destination, and summers aren't as tranquil as they once were. Nonetheless, hotels still have lower occupancy from mid-April to mid-December. Off-season discounts, which can be substantial, are granted at resorts during slow times.

VERY EXPENSIVE

Half Moon ✸✸✸   Opening onto 162 hectares (400 acres) that includes 3.2km (2 miles) of coastline, much of it edged with white-sand beach, this is one of the Caribbean's grandest and most appealing hotels. It's bigger than Round Hill (which can sometimes be just a bit snobbish) and consequently has far more activities, amenities, restaurants, and a better beach. And we consider it much more inviting than its newer, and much less dramatic or appealing, competitor, the Ritz-Carlton. It also has topnotch landscaping and an astounding number (51) of swimming pools, some of which are linked to individual villas, others associated with clusters of villas. About 13km (8 miles) east of Montego Bay's city center and 10km (6¼ miles) from the international airport, this is a classic, and 1 of the 25 best hotels in the world according to *Condé Nast Traveler*. It's a grand and appealing place, a true luxury hideaway with undeniable taste and style.

Accommodations include conventional small hotel rooms, grand suites, and a collection of superbly accessorized private villas (most villas have private pools and a full-time staff). Each unit is comfortably furnished with mahogany furniture, some of it made within on-site workshops that are considered a triumphant example of this mega-resort's tendency toward at least some degree of self-sufficiency. Furnishings throughout carry an English colonial/Caribbean motif, with a private balcony or patio, plus a state-of-the-art bathroom with a shower/tub combo. Queen Anne–inspired furniture is set off by vibrant Jamaican paintings, and many units contain mahogany four-poster beds. Note, however, that there are a few older, smaller rooms here, and that some accommodations are quite a ways away from the beach (golf carts are the favored form of transportation on this sprawling resort)—make sure to request the specific type of room you want when making your reservation.

The Sugar Mill Restaurant, our favorite in Montego Bay, is beside a working water wheel from a bygone sugar estate (see "Where to Dine," later in this chapter). The Seagrape Terrace offers delightful meals alfresco. Il Giardino, set within a convincing replica of a Renaissance palazzo, serves savory Italian cuisine. Planned for 2007 is a pan-Asian/Indian restaurant, to be known as The Akbar Restaurant. The resort also has a steakhouse, designed like an English pub (The Royal Stocks, which is recommended separately later in this chapter); a contemporary Jamaican restaurant; and both miniature and full-scale golf courses. Half Moon, thanks to its own on-site hospital, school, furniture-making facilities and upholstery shops, security force, and lavishly accessorized physical plant, is the most completely self-contained resort facility in Jamaica—there's a good chance you'll never leave the grounds.

Half Moon Post Office, Rose Hall, St. James, Montego Bay. ℃ **800/626-0592** in the U.S., or 876/953-2211. Fax 876/953-2731. www.halfmoon.com. 402 units. Winter $410–$645 double, from $695 suite; off season $240–$350 double, from $350 suite. Children under 12 stay free in parent's room. MAP (breakfast and dinner) $85 per person extra. Ask about golf and spa packages. AE, DC, DISC, MC, V. **Amenities:** 7 restaurants; 7 bars; 4 pools; 18-hole golf course; 13 tennis courts (9 lit); fitness club; spa; Jacuzzi; 2 saunas; bike rental; children's activities; car rental; room service (7am–11:30pm); babysitting; laundry service; medical center; croquet; squash; deep-sea fishing; dive shop; horseback riding. In room: A/C, TV, dataport, kitchenette (in some), minibar, hair dryer, iron, safe.

Ritz-Carlton Rose Hall Jamaica ★★ Kids   The newest of the grand dame resorts of Mo Bay (that includes Half Moon and Round Hill), this blockbuster complex is big, bustling, upscale, and impressive, sprawling as it does across an adequately wide stretch of white-sand beach. (Clients seeking a better beach are shuttled to the nearby Rose Hall Beach Club, site of many motorized and non-motorized watersports.) One of its major draws is the White Witch Golf Course, a 15-minute shuttle ride away. Its public areas try, at least, to duplicate the ambience of a traditional Jamaican great house that's been updated and modernized into a big-time and oversized icon to "the good life." Come here if you're looking for a somewhat sanitized stopover in a hotel saturated with international comforts, including a full-service spa. Frankly, this is not our favorite of the ultra-upscale resorts of Montego Bay—it lacks the sense of fantasy (gazebos, lavish gardens, bougainvillea burgeoning over lattices, etc.) of Half Moon, and it utterly lacks the intimacy of Round Hill. This is not even the most impressive Ritz-Carlton in the chain. For such a big and supposedly topnotch venue, the pool isn't big enough. Accommodations, however, are appropriately luxurious, but with an upscale motif that could have been imported from virtually any luxury hotel in North America. Each features a deluxe bathroom with tub/shower combos.

Rose Hall, Montego Bay. ℃ **800/241-3333** in the U.S. or Canada, or 876/953-2800. Fax 876/518-0110. www.ritz carlton.com. 427 units. Winter $429–$800 double, from $800 suite; off season $300–$650 double, from $650 suite. Children under 12 stay free in parent's room. AE, DISC, MC, V. **Amenities:** 6 restaurants; 2 bars; pool; 18-hole golf course; 2 tennis courts; health club and spa; Jacuzzi; nonmotorized watersports; children's activities; business center; 24-hr. room service; babysitting; laundry service; dry cleaning; nonsmoking rooms; rooms for those w/limited mobility. In room: A/C, TV, dataport, minibar, beverage maker, hair dryer, iron, safe.

Round Hill Hotel and Villas ✦✦✦ Opened in 1953 on a small, private, white-sand beach, Round Hill is a legend, an icon, and the most prestigious address in Jamaica, even though it lacks the extensive facilities (and in some cases, the whimsical sense of romantic fantasy) of Half Moon. It originated as a small, clubby compound of private villas supervised by Lord Monson, on the grounds of a 45-hectare (110-acre) plantation devoted to the production of pineapples and allspice, attracting the aristocracy of Europe and some of the biggest media and entertainment moguls of the New World. By far the most spectacular accommodations here are those cloistered away on the surrounding hillsides, within white-sided villas. The look of these luxurious villas is kept upscale, elegant, cutting-edge, and theatrical thanks to frequent renovations, acres of mahogany and marble, and the skill of some of the best architects in North America and Europe. Less grand accommodations are within a rambling, two-story building (Pineapple House) set at the edge of the sea, overlooking a swimming pool that was enlarged early in 2006. The decor inside Pineapple House is all white, light-hearted, and airy, with four-poster bamboo beds.

Breakfast is brought to your room or served on the dining terrace. Informal luncheons are held in an intimate straw hut with an open terrace in a little sandy bay. Standard Jamaican and Continental dishes are served on a candlelit terrace or in the Georgian colonial room overlooking the sea. Ralph Lauren decorated the cocktail area.

Rte. A1 (P.O. Box 64), Montego Bay. © 800/972-2159 in the U.S., or 876/956-7050. Fax 876/956-7505. www.round hilljamaica.com. 74 units. Winter $570 double, from $1,250 villa; off season $350 double, from $780 villa. Extra person $90. MAP (breakfast and dinner) $90 per person extra. AE, DC, DISC, MC, V. **Amenities:** Restaurant; 3 bars; pool; 5 tennis courts (2 lit); health club and spa; limited room service; babysitting; laundry service; nonsmoking rooms; dive shop. *In room:* A/C, dataport, kitchen (in some), fridge, beverage maker, hair dryer, iron, safe.

The Tryall Club ✦✦✦ *Kids* This is a top choice for vacationers who are serious about golf and who want the privacy and isolation of a private cottage surrounded by verdant landscaping and good security. With more spacious grounds than almost any other Jamaican hotel, this stylish and upscale resort sits 19km (12 miles) west of town on the site of an 880-hectare (2,200-acre) former sugar plantation. It has neither the fine beach of Half Moon, nor the elegant house-party atmosphere of Round Hill, but nonetheless, it's one of Jamaica's grandest resorts. The property lies along a 2km (1¼-mile) beachfront and is presided over by a 165-year-old Georgian-style great house. Throughout, you'll find a deep respect for golf, with many important tournaments played on the rolling greens of the resort's topnotch golf course.

The accommodations in luxurious villas are decorated in cool pastels with English colonial touches. Each is artfully positioned amid lush foliage and designed for privacy, with a private pool and a self-contained kitchen. Each has ceiling fans and some have air-conditioning, along with big windows framing sea and mountain views. Bedrooms are upscale and exceedingly spacious, with luxurious beds, private patios or terraces, and tile floors. Bathrooms are roomy, with plenty of counter space and a shower/tub combination. The most formal of the resort's dining areas is in the great house, but it's not the equal of the options available at Half Moon and the Ritz-Carlton. There's also a casual beach cafe, more for convenience than good food.

Many clients here are CEOs, so the hotel has opened an Internet room. On other fronts, Tryall is winning recognition as one of the most eco-sensitive resorts in the Caribbean, winning acclaim as a "Green Globe Hotel."

St. James (P.O. Box 1206), Montego Bay. © 800/238-5290 in the U.S., or 876/956-5660. Fax 876/956-5673. www.tryallclub.com. 69 villas. Winter $3,080–$3,850 1-bedroom villa, $5,200–$6,600 2-bedroom villa. Off season

$1,925–$2,750 1-bedroom villa, $2,310–$2,750 2-bedroom villa. MAP (breakfast and dinner) $85 per person extra. AE, DC, DISC, MC, V. **Amenities:** 2 restaurants; 4 bars (1 swim-up); pool; championship 18-hole par-71 golf course; 9 Laykold tennis courts; fitness center; children's programs; Internet room; salon; massage; babysitting; laundry service; nonsmoking rooms; rooms for those w/limited mobility; deep-sea fishing; snorkeling; windsurfing; horseback riding. *In room:* A/C (in some), ceiling fan, TV, kitchen, fridge, beverage maker, hair dryer.

EXPENSIVE

Coyaba 🌀🌀   On a lovely strip of private beachfront, this small resort evokes a British colonial atmosphere. It was established in 1994 by American/Jamaican-Chinese entrepreneurs, the Robertson family, and built from scratch at a cost of $4 million. Set a 15-minute drive east of the center of Montego Bay, it's centered on an adaptation of an 18th-century great house.

Accommodations in the main building overlook the garden; those in the pair of three-story outbuildings lie closer to the beach and are somewhat more expensive. The decor is plantation-style, with traditional prints, expensive chintz fabrics, French doors leading onto private patios or verandas, and mahogany furniture. Hand-carved bedsteads, often four-posters, are fitted with luxury coverings. The roomy bathrooms have combination shower/tubs. Its bedrooms are modern and well maintained, and some units have been upgraded to junior suites with small refrigerators and such special amenities as irons and ironing boards. The hotel's main and most formal restaurant, the Vineyard, serves first-rate Jamaican and Continental dinners.

Little River Post Office, Montego Bay. (C) **877/232-3224** or 876/953-9150. Fax 876/953-2244. www.coyabaresort jamaica.com. 50 units. Winter $300–$400 double; off season $200–$250 double. All meals $110 per person extra. Children age 11 and under get a 50% discount on meals. AE, MC, V. **Amenities:** 3 restaurants; 3 bars; pool; lighted tennis court w/free tennis clinic; health club and spa; Jacuzzi; watersports; car-rental desk; limited room service; massage; laundry service; nonsmoking rooms; rooms for those w/limited mobility; nanny service. *In room:* A/C, TV/VCR, coffeemaker, hair dryer, iron/board, safe.

Rose Hall Resort & Country Club 🌀 *Kids*   If you have to be directly on a great beach, this place isn't for you, but if you want to escape the more impersonal all-inclusives like the Sandals clones in favor of a more authentic Jamaican experience, then check in here. On a thin strip of white-sand beach, this 12-hectare (30-acre) resort stands along the north-coast highway 14km (9 miles) east of the airport. On a former sugar plantation, the hotel abuts the 200-year-old home of the legendary White Witch of Rose Hall (see the box on p. 95), now a historic site. The seven-story H-shaped structure features a large, attractive lobby on the ground floor; upstairs, all the guest rooms have sea views and come with a small private balcony. The tiled bathrooms with tubs and showers are well maintained.

Facing massive competition from the newly opened (and superior) Ritz-Carlton, Rose Hall has spent millions on renovations, improving and upgrading its accommodations with new designer furniture. Bathrooms have received a makeover with granite countertops, new plumbing fixtures, and Bath & Body Works amenities. The hotel's six restaurants are good but not sublime.

Rose Hall (P.O. Box 999), Montego Bay. (C) **800/468-0389** in the U.S., or 876/953-2650. Fax 876/518-0203. www.rosehallresort.com. 488 units. Winter $245–$360 double; off season $195–$295 double. Breakfast and dinner $65 per person extra. AE, DC, DISC, MC, V. **Amenities:** 6 restaurants; 4 bars (2 swim-up); 3 pools; 3 whirlpools; 18-hole golf course; 6 lit all-weather Laykold tennis courts; fitness center; sailboats; children's programs; limited room service; massage; babysitting; laundry service; dry cleaning; nonsmoking rooms; rooms for those w/limited mobility. *In room:* A/C, TV, dataport, hair dryer, beverage maker, iron, safe.

MODERATE

Coral Cliff Hotel and Entertainment Resort ☆ (Value)

For good value, the Coral Cliff may be your best bet in Montego Bay, as it's only a 2-minute walk from Doctors Cave Beach, and about 2km (1¼ mile) west from the center of town. The hotel grew from a colonial-style building that was once the private home of Harry M. Doubleday (of the famous publishing family). The public areas of this place are now as busy and popular as virtually any other hotel in Montego Bay, thanks to the presence of about 100 small-stakes slot machines, open to the public, including non-residents. Many of the light, airy, and spacious bedrooms open onto sea-view balconies. The rooms, as befits a former private house, come in a wide variety of shapes and sizes, most of them containing old colonial furniture, wicker, and rattan. Most units have twin beds. The bathrooms are small in the older bedrooms, but more spacious in the newer wing out back. Each is tidily maintained and has a combination shower/tub. Decent Jamaican and international dishes are served at Ma Lou's restaurant.

165 Gloucester Ave. (P.O. Box 253), Montego Bay. ℂ 876/952-4130. Fax 876/952-6532. www.coralcliffjamaica.com. 12 units. Winter $110–$180 double, $120–$190 triple, from $180 suite; off season $80–$90 double, $92–$105 triple, from $140 suite. AE, MC, V. **Amenities:** 2 restaurants; bar; pool; health club; spa; babysitting; laundry service; library; small-scale gaming lounge (slot machines only). *In room:* A/C, TV, dataport, safe.

Doctors Cave Beach Hotel ☆ (Value)

This three-story hotel offers great value and lies in the bustle of the town's commercial zone, a minute's walk across the seafronting boulevard from Doctors Cave Beach, the busiest and most crowded, but with the best sands, in the Montego Bay area. It has its own gardens on 1.6 hectares (4 acres) of tropical gardens. The well-maintained rooms are simply but comfortably furnished, and suites have kitchenettes. Rooms are rated standard or superior; the latter are more spacious and have balconies with a view. All units have tile floors, queen-size or twin beds (suites have king-size beds), and small but efficiently organized tiled bathrooms with combination shower/tubs. The food is more authentic than at other resorts.

Gloucester Ave. (P.O. Box 94), Montego Bay. ℂ 876/952-4355. Fax 876/952-5204. www.doctorscave.com. 85 units. Winter $110–$130 double, $145 suite for 2; off season $105–$125 double, $130 suite for 2. Extra person $25. MAP (breakfast and dinner) $29 per person extra. AE, DC, MC, V. **Amenities:** Restaurant; bar; pool; health club; Jacuzzi; limited room service; rooms for those w/limited mobility. *In room:* A/C, TV, refrigerator (only in suites), beverage maker, safe.

Richmond Hill Inn ☆ (Finds)

If you're an avid beach lover, you should know in advance that the nearest beach is a 5-minute drive away from this hotel. But for immediate access to one of the loveliest and most panoramic terraces and bar areas in Montego Bay, it's hard to beat. It was built in 1806 as the homestead of the Dewar family (the scions of scotch). Only a short but very thick wall of the original villa remains, but what you'll find is a sweepingly panoramic hilltop aerie ringed with urn-shaped concrete balustrades, a pool terrace suitable for sundowner cocktails, and comfortable, slightly fussy bedrooms done up in lace-trimmed curtains, homey bric-a-brac, and pastel colors. Each accommodation comes with a midsize bathroom with tub/shower combination. Maid service is included in the rates. Frankly, we're surprised that the bar here isn't more consistently crowded, mobbed even, as an after-work drinking destination, as the view and setting are indeed idyllic.

Union St. (P.O. Box 362), Montego Bay. ℂ 876/952-3859. Fax 876/952-6106. www.richmond-hill-inn.com. 20 units. Winter $70–$180 double, off season $58–$150 double; suites for 2, year-round $250–$300. MC, V. **Amenities:** Restaurant; bar; pool; limited room service; babysitting; maid service. *In room:* A/C, TV, fridge, coffeemaker, iron, safe.

INEXPENSIVE

Blue Harbour Hotel On a hillside overlooking the harbor, midway between the airport and town off the A1, this small four-story hotel offers basic service in a friendly atmosphere. Rooms here are simple, while the suites offer kitchenettes to help you save even more money. For dinner, the hotel offers the option of a dine-around plan that includes 10 of Montego Bay's restaurants. (Transportation to and from the restaurants is provided.) Facilities include a swimming pool, air-conditioned lounge, and coffee shop serving breakfast and light lunch. Tennis courts are nearby; arrangements can also be made for golf, deep-sea fishing, scuba diving, and island tours. The hotel operates a shuttle once a day to Doctors Cave Beach, leaving at 10am.

6 Sewell Ave. (P.O. Box 212), Montego Bay. ℂ 876/952-5445. Fax 876/952-8930. http://fly.to/jamaica. 25 units. Winter $68–$98 double, $70–$86 triple; off-season $54 double, $70 triple. Each additional person $15. Children 11 and under stay free in parent's room. Rates include continental breakfast. AE, MC, V. **Amenities:** Coffee shop; lounge; pool; nearby sports such as golf and tennis; tour desk; limited room service; nonsmoking rooms; rooms for those w/limited mobility. *In room:* A/C, TV, kitchenette (in some), safe.

El Greco Resort This three-story, cream-and-pale-green hotel sits at the top of a rocky bluff, across the seafronting boulevard from the sea, high above the surf, sand, and well-oiled bodies of Doctors Cave Beach. A private elevator links the hotel's cliff-top site to a point near the beachfront. Surrounded by a landscaped garden into which are nestled both a swimming pool and a pair of tennis courts (lit for night play), the resort is well maintained and well priced. It's smack in the middle of Montego Bay's densest concentration of honky-tonk commercialism—yet the location enables guests to rise above the congestion a bit. This hotel catches the trade winds, and most (but not all) of the rooms offer a sweeping view over the sea. Apartments contain full kitchenettes and have pure white ceramic floor tiles. The bedrooms are air-conditioned, though not the living rooms, which have ceiling fans instead; 32 larger two-bedroom units occupy the building's uppermost floor. Each unit comes with a midsize private bathroom with a shower. There's both a bar and a restaurant on the premises, although many of the guests opt to cook.

11 Queens Dr. (P.O. Box 1624), Montego Bay. ℂ 888/354-7326 in the U.S., 800/597-7326 in Canada, or 876/940-6116. Fax 876/940-6115. www.elgrecojamaica.com. 96 apts. Year-round $125–$134 1-bedroom apt; $184–$194 2-bedroom apt. Rates include breakfast. AE, MC, V. **Amenities:** Restaurant; bar; pool; tennis court; limited room service; rooms for those w/limited mobility. *In room:* A/C, cable TV, dataport, kitchen, fridge, iron, safe.

Gloriana *Value* This hotel seems to go out of its way to welcome visitors, offering them everything from live entertainment to tours across Jamaica. There's even a whirlpool-style swimming pool. Lying a 10-minute walk to Doctors Cave Beach, the property offers midsize bedrooms that front a garden, a mountain, the airport, or the pool. Rooms are comfortably furnished, often in bold Jamaican colors. Bathrooms are compact and adequate with showers. The hotel also maintains 24-hour security.

1–2 Sunset Blvd., Montego Bay. ℂ 876/979-0669. Fax 876/979-0698. www.hotelgloriana.com. 75 units. Winter $75 double; off season $45–$60 double. AE, MC, V. **Amenities:** Restaurant; bar; pool; spa; 24-hr. room service. *In room:* A/C, TV, small fridge (in some units).

The Gloustershire Hotel *Value* Lying along "Hip Strip," this well-run hotel fronts Doctors Cave Beach and is set in the midst of Jamaican restaurants, bars, dance clubs, and watersports kiosks. In spite of the increased size of this hotel, it still offers a touch of Jamaican hospitality not found in the larger resorts. Guests enjoy the bubbling Jacuzzi out back and meet fellow guests around the pool. Rooms are midsize and

Honeymooning at Half Moon

Although the couples-only Sandals properties offer honeymoon packages, our advice is to skip those and opt for either a wedding or a honeymoon (perhaps both) at **Half Moon** (p. 71). We consider its romance packages the best in the Caribbean.

The resort offers three different wedding packages and one honeymoon package. Couples planning to celebrate both even get a special bonus if they book at least 25 rooms for attending family and friends: Half Moon gives the bride and groom a complimentary ceremony and 7 nights' free accommodations, a savings of up to $8,500.

You can also order services a la carte. The Standard Wedding Plan includes a marriage officer, a bottle of champagne, a bouquet of flowers for the bride and a boutonniere for the groom, a wedding cake, a professional video, a roll of 36 pictures and negatives, and—if needed—a best man and maid of honor to act as witnesses, all at a total cost of around $900. The Royal Wedding Plan includes all of the above, plus a $50 gift voucher redeemable at selected shops in the Half Moon Shopping Village, a bottle of Half Moon rum, two Half Moon watches, and the services of a calypso band for 15 minutes. That package costs $1,300.

For more information, call ⓒ **876/953-2211** (ⓒ 800/626-0592 in the U.S.), or log on to **www.halfmoonweddings.com**.

attractively and comfortably furnished, the more expensive opening onto the sea. Other hotels open onto a garden in back. On the patio of an English-style pub, guests enjoy lunches of Jamaican specialties such as jerk pork or British fish and chips. More elaborate food is served in the exotic Waterfall Restaurant, with both international and authentic Jamaican dishes.

Gloucester Ave., Montego Bay. ⓒ 877/574-8497 in the U.S. or 876/952-4420. Fax 876/952-8088. 88 units. Winter $115–$130 double, $135 junior suite; off season $110–$125 double, $130 junior suite. MC, V. **Amenities:** Restaurant; pub; pool; Jacuzzi. *In room:* A/C, TV.

Ridgeway Guest House *(Finds)*   This warm B&B, far removed from the impersonal megaresorts (and their megaprices), is a great find. The helpful owners offer free pickup from the airport and transport to Doctors Cave Beach, a 15-minute walk or 5 minutes by car. They are constantly improving their property—a two-story white-painted building set among flowers and fruit trees from which guests may help themselves, perhaps having an orange-and-grapefruit salad. The large rooms are decorated in a tropical motif with two or three queen-size beds. The marble bathrooms have modern fixtures, including a combo tub and shower, and TV is available in a public area. Some rooms feature air-conditioning, TVs, and phones; others are equipped with ceiling fans only, and lack televisions or phones. The hotel next door opens its restaurant to Ridgeway guests.

34 Queens Dr. (P.O. Box 1237), Montego Bay. ⓒ 876/952-2709. Fax 876/952-9282. www.ridgewayguesthouse.com. 4 units. Winter $55–$70 double, $65–$80 triple; off season $45–$60 double, $55–$70 triple. Children 11 and under stay free in parent's room. MC, V. **Amenities:** Nearby restaurant; TV lounge; car-rental desk; laundry service; rooftop garden. *In room:* A/C (in some), TV, fridge, hair dryer, no phone (in some units).

Toby's Resort   This resort is a 5-minute walk from Doctors Cave Beach. Despite the traffic and crowds around it, the almond, mango, and grapefruit trees that surround the two-story main building, cottages, and swimming pools create a sense of rural isolation. You'll also find a restaurant serving Jamaican cuisine, a flower shop, a minigym, a bandstand for occasional concerts, and a bar. Bedrooms all have either a terrace or a balcony, and each unit's small, tiled bathroom has a shower. This hotel is also a showcase for Jamaican and foreign art.

1 Kent Ave. (P.O. Box 467), Montego Bay. (C) 876/952-4370. Fax 876/952-6591. www.tobyresorts.com. 65 units. Winter $100 double, $135 triple; off season $90 double, $115 triple. MAP $25 a day. AE, DISC, MC, V. **Amenities:** Restaurant; 2 bars; 2 pools; small gym; game room; limited room service. *In room:* A/C, TV, iron/board, no phone.

Verney's Tropical Resort   In a verdant setting that's a 10-minute walk from the urban congestion of Montego Bay, this hotel—formerly known as the Verney House Hotel—offers a feeling of remote calm. You can still get to where the action is by making a short trek downhill, or kick back on the sand by heading to one of several beaches (such as Cornwall Beach) that lie about 5 minutes away by foot. The inn also provides free van transportation to and from the beach. Each unit sports white walls and simple furnishings, creating the sense that you're in a private home. The restaurant and bar both overlook the swimming pool.

3 Leader Ave. (P.O. Box 18), Montego Bay. (C) 876/952-2875. Fax 876/979-2944. www.verneyhousehotel.com. 25 units. Winter $63 double, $77 triple, $85 quad; off season $55 double, $65 triple, $77 quad. AE, MC, V. **Amenities:** Restaurant; bar; pool; babysitting. *In room:* A/C, TV, iron, safe.

Wexford Hotel *Kids*   Especially good for families on a budget, this hotel lies within a 5-minute walk of Doctors Cave Beach. This hotel has a small pool and a patio (where calypso is enjoyed in season). The apartments have living/dining areas and kitchenettes, so you can cook for yourself. All rooms have patios shaded by gables and Swiss chalet–style roofs, and each has a tiled, shower-only bathroom. The restaurant serves some zesty Jamaican dishes in a setting that evokes a 1950s Howard Johnson's.

39 Gloucester Ave. (P.O. Box 108), Montego Bay. (C) **888/790-5264** or 876/952-2854. Fax 876/952-3637. www.thewexfordhotel.com. 60 units. Winter $115–$120 double, $130 apt; off season $105–$110 double, $120 apt. Up to 2 children under 12 stay free in parent's room. MAP (breakfast and dinner) $34 per person extra. AE, DISC, MC, V. **Amenities:** Restaurant; bar; pool; limited room service; laundry service; babysitting; rooms for those w/limited mobility. *In room:* A/C, TV, kitchenettes (in some), safe.

ALL-INCLUSIVE RESORTS

All-inclusive resorts charge one price for a lengthy stay (usually a week), folding accommodations and dining into one package. Once you've paid up, you can forget about watching the dinner bill or getting dinged for every little tour, hike, or boat ride you take on the property.

Note that when you book into one of the following all-inclusives, you either take your meals on-site or buy a dine-around plan that enables you to patronize the eateries at other, similar resorts. Either way, though, you're likely to find most of the food rather mediocre. In no case will it compare to the fare served at sophisticated restaurants in such major U.S. cities such as New York or Boston.

Of course, those big-city restaurants don't open onto a beach—and the weather here's much better in wintertime. So there are advantages to these Mo Bay resorts, but just remember: Creative cuisine is not one of them.

Breezes Montego Bay *¢¢*   A five-story complex, this SuperClub—called "a sandbox for your inner child"—is the only major hotel directly on the sands of Montego

Bay's most popular public beach, Doctors Cave. It's adult and indulgent, but without the raucous partying of Hedonism II in Negril (a member of the same chain). Bedrooms are tastefully furnished and breezy, overlooking either the beach or the garden that separates the hotel from the traffic of Montego Bay's main commercial boulevard, Gloucester Avenue. Rooms range from intimate cabins to lavish suites. The cabin rooms, 31 in all, are similar to a ship's cabin, with a queen-size bed. Slightly larger are the deluxe rooms, with twins or a king-size bed. The best are the deluxe oceanfront rooms, with king-size beds, and the oceanfront suites. All units have bathrooms with shower/tub combinations.

Informal but good meals are served at Jimmy's Buffet, a terrace overlooking the pool and the beach. More formal meals, with a more refined cuisine, are dished out at the candlelit Pastafari, an Italian restaurant.

Gloucester Ave., Montego Bay. ℂ 877/467-8737 in the U.S., or 876/940-1150. Fax 876/940-1160. www.superclubs.com. 124 units. Winter $254–$400 double; off season $211–$373 double. Rates include all meals, drinks, airport transfers, and most activities. AE, DC, DISC, MC, V. No children under 14 accepted. **Amenities:** 2 restaurants; 4 bars; pool; 2 tennis courts; golf; fitness center; rooftop Jacuzzi; disco; billiards; table tennis; dive shop; kayaks; sailing; snorkeling; windsurfing. *In room:* A/C, TV, beverage maker, hair dryer, iron, safe.

FDR Pebbles ✿ *Kids*   No, it's not named after the U.S. president. This resort, which pioneered at Runaway Bay, has invaded Montego Bay and almost overnight become the most family-friendly place in the area. It's even better than its parent outside Ocho Rios. FDR lies a 35-minute drive east of the airport, opening onto the waterfront and a beach. The resort is an all-inclusive property of cedar-wood accommodations designed with real Jamaican flair, offering spacious living and bedroom areas, shower/tub combination bathrooms, plus generous balconies opening onto a view. It's most suited for families with two children, although a larger family can be very comfortable in adjoining units. Everything is geared towards family fun, with an array of activities including fishing and swimming in a nearby river and hiking along nature trails. Each family is assigned a "vacation nanny" who helps with housekeeping and babysitting.

First-rate ingredients are fashioned into a rather standard repertoire of both Jamaican and American dishes. Portions are exceedingly generous.

Main St., Trelawny (P.O. Box 1933). ℂ 888/FDR-KIDS in the U.S. or 876/617-2500. Fax 876/617-2512. www.fdr holidays.com. 96 units. Winter $220–$310 per person double; off season $160–$280 per person double. Children under 6 stay free in parent's room. Rates are all-inclusive. AE, DISC, MC, V. **Amenities:** 2 restaurants; 3 bars; pool; tennis court; Jacuzzi; kids' club; teen center; Internet cafe; babysitting; nonsmoking rooms; rooms for those w/limited mobility; dance club; hiking; volleyball; kayaks; scuba diving; snorkeling; Sunfish sailboats; biking. *In room:* A/C, TV.

Sandals Montego Bay ✿   It isn't the most glamorous, or the most upscale of the Sandals resorts, but the chain's management makes it their flagship, the one that they cite as an example of the Sandals philosophy and management style at its purest. Favored by honeymooners, it lies next to Whitehouse Village on the largest private beach in Mo Bay, even better than the one at Sandals Royal Caribbean. Located on a 7.6-hectare (19-acre) site, this all-inclusive also has a big party atmosphere (whereas Sandals Royal Caribbean is more refined and subdued). Everything is included in this resort's all-inclusive price: snacks, nightly entertainment (including the notorious toga parties), and unlimited drinks night or day at one of four bars. Lots of entertainment and sports facilities are available on the property, and many guests never leave its walls. There's one drawback: The resort lies literally at the edge of the airport, and planes fly overhead all day. Thankfully, the airplanes now landing at Montego Bay are less noisy than those of a dozen years ago that would rattle the rum glasses.

As noted above, many of Sandals' corporate policies were originally hammered out and then refined within this resort. Originally built in the mid-1960s, and acquired by Sandals in 1981, its walls are now semi-antique in comparison to newer hotels nearby. But thanks to massive enlargements over the years, and an aggressive upgrade early in the millennium, you might not even notice. Accommodations are either in villas spread along 510m (1,700 ft.) of the white-sand beach or in the main house, where most bedrooms face the sea and include private balconies. All units contain plantation-inspired mahogany four-poster beds meticulously crafted in Indonesia. Try to avoid booking 1 of the 10 rooms positioned immediately above the dining area; these don't have balconies and may be noisy. The best units are the grand luxe ocean- or beachfront units, with private balconies or patios. Each unit here is equipped with a first-rate bathroom with a tub/shower combo. Rates are the most complicated in Jamaica, with nearly a dozen different price structures in effect at various times of the year (sometimes only for a week!). Always check carefully the various plans and possible discounts before booking here. The cuisine is in the typical Sandals chain-style format—plenty of it, but nothing too imaginative. The best option is Tokyo Joe's, serving six-course Asian dinners. The Oleander Room, with its "white-glove service," features Jamaican and Caribbean cuisine.

Kent Ave. (P.O. Box 100), Montego Bay. ℂ **800/SANDALS** in the U.S. and Canada, or 876/952-5510. Fax 876/952-0816. www.sandals.com. 251 units. Year-round $590–$1,550 daily per couple. Rates include all meals, drinks, and activities. AE, DC, DISC, MC, V. **Amenities:** 5 restaurants; 4 bars; 4 pools; 4 tennis courts; spa facilities and health club; 4 Jacuzzis; 2 saunas; watersports; salon; massage; laundry service; nonsmoking rooms; rooms for those w/limited mobility; dive shop; Internet cafe. *In room:* A/C, cable TV w/pay-per-view movies, dataport, coffeemaker, hair dryer, iron, safe.

Sandals Royal Caribbean ✹✹   This middle-bracket branch of the all-inclusive Sandals chain (they define it as one of their "classic," but not one of their "signature," properties) pays more frequent and deeper homage to the aesthetics and manners of the British colonial empire than any other member of the chain. Tranquil and just a bit more sedate than some of its counterparts within the same chain, it lies astride an appealing private beach. References to things English abound: Buildings bear British-inspired names that include, among others, Caernarvon, Kensington, and Arundel, and afternoon teas are widely publicized and popular, beginning at 4pm. There are modern touches as well, including a private, clothing-optional island reached by boat.

The spacious rooms range from standard to superior to deluxe. Best are the grand luxe beachfront rooms, with private patios or balconies. Each unit has a small but well-equipped private bathroom with a shower/tub combination. The cuisine is more varied here than at the other Mo Bay Sandals, with, for example, Royal Thai, a Thai/Indonesian restaurant on an offshore island. The Regency and The Pavilion serve a rather good Jamaican-inspired cuisine, among other options.

Mahoe Bay (P.O. Box 167), Montego Bay. ℂ **800/SANDALS** in the U.S. and Canada, or 876/953-2232. Fax 876/953-2788. www.sandals.com. 181 units. Winter per person $305–$390, from $420 suite; off season per person $285–$350, from $400 suite. Rates include all meals, drinks, and activities. 2-night minimum stay required. AE, DISC, MC, V. No one under 18 allowed. **Amenities:** 4 restaurants; 7 bars (2 swim-up); 4 pools; 4 whirlpools; 3 lit tennis courts; fitness center; sauna; 24-hr. room service; massage; coin-operated laundry; dry cleaning; nonsmoking rooms; rooms for those w/limited mobility; canoes; kayaks; sailing; scuba diving; snorkeling; water-skiing; windsurfing. *In room:* A/C, TV, beverage maker, hair dryer, iron, safe.

Sunset Beach Resort & Spa 🄺🄸🄳🅂   This all-inclusive hotel is a member of a small-scale chain that's owned and operated by a Jamaica-based family. It opened in 1998 and aims for a marketing niche that's just a touch less upscale (and less expensive) than

(Fun Fact Moving to the Beat at Jamaica's Music Festivals

For about 4 days during the third week in July, during what might otherwise have been a slow tourist season, Montego Bay comes alive with the pulsating sounds of reggae, thanks to a well-known music festival that seems to captivate the imaginations of virtually everyone in town. The event is known as **Reggae Sumfest** (not to be confused with "Reggae Sunfest," an event that has been discontinued), and it occurs amid the soundstages and jerk food stalls at Catharine Hall, a government-funded arts and entertainment development beside the Roseway Bypass in Montego Bay's industrial suburb of Freeport. Throughout most of the year, this site is usually littered, vacant, and dusty, but during reggae festivals, it's virtually overrun with grooving, jiving, gossiping, and flirting music lovers from throughout Jamaica.

The mid-winter counterpart of this festival is Air Jamaica's **Jazz and Blues Festival,** which is conducted over a 2-day weekend in late January on the grounds of the Cinnamon Hill golf course at Rose Hall Resort & Country Club. Both events share the same promoters, who have managed to snag the musical talents of artists who have recently included Ziggy Marley, Cocoa Tea, the Melody Makers, Bares Hammond, the Mystic Revealers, and Morgan Heritage—some of the biggest names in reggae, both from Jamaica and abroad. Many local hotels are fully booked for the festival, so advance reservations are necessary. Tickets to either event range in price from $12 to $45 each, depending on the event. Musical venues tend to begin at between 7 and 7:30pm, and many participants opt to bring blankets and folding chairs for placement on the lawns that surround the bandstands from which emanate highly addictive streams of jiving music.

Any branch of Jamaican Tourist Board can provide information about packages and group rates for the festivals and fill you in on other musical and cultural events held throughout the year in Jamaica.

that occupied by the Beaches and Sandals groups. The complex consists of three separate beaches; two canary-yellow, 10-story towers containing a total of 300 units; and a 120-room annex, the Beach Inn, whose low-rise design allows guests closer and more immediate access to the sand. Accommodations are outfitted in a subdued motif that includes vague references to tropical design, but tends to be more soothing (and blander) than the decor of many of its competitors. Rooms are fairly spacious, with comfortable beds, plus medium-size bathrooms with tubs and showers.

Meals, featuring a varied cuisine, are served at each of the property's four restaurants which focus, respectively, on Italian, Pacific Rim, Jamaican/Caribbean, and International. There's also nightly entertainment.

Montego Freeport Peninsula, P.O. Box 1168, Montego Bay. ⓒ **800/234-1707** or 876/979-8800. Fax 876/953-6744. www.sunsetbeachresort.com. 430 units. Winter $280–$340 double, $400–$500 suite for 2; off season $260–$320 double; $380–$480 suite for 2. AE, MC, V. **Amenities:** 4 restaurants; 6 bars; 3 pools (2 w/swim-up bars); minigolf; 4 lit tennis courts; fitness center/health club; spa; Jacuzzi (suitable for up to 25 people at a time); children's programs ("Club Mongoose" for pre-teens and "Pirates' Cove" for teens); game rooms; coin-operated laundry; rooms for those w/limited mobility; disco; nighttime entertainment, small-stakes casino (slot machines only); shuffleboard courts; giant chess and checkerboards; beachfront volleyball; watersports that include snorkeling, paddle boats, kayaking; Internet cafe. *In room:* A/C, cable TV, minibar (in some units), hair dryer, safe.

Starfish Trelawny Beach & Fun Resort ⚐ (Kids)   Following a $5-million much-needed renovation of a property that has managed to survive throughout many past incarnations, under many previous administrations, this all-inclusive is one of the best value vacations on the island. At this hotel, families and family values reign supreme, thanks to low, all-inclusive prices for basic life support and some well-conceived and well-executed children's programs. Whereas each of the most basic food and amenities are included as part of the all-inclusive price, there's a higher percentage of upscale diversions that are not included in the price than at virtually any other all-inclusive hotel in the region, thereby allowing families to pick and choose those activities they don't want to pay for. The result is low prices for generic vacations, with extra fees imposed for additional gewgaws and frills, such as scuba diving. Designed with three interconnected wings, much like the shape of an airplane propeller, it opens onto a stretch of powder-white, soft, sandy beach. The location is 37km (23 miles) east of the Mo Bay airport. The most spacious rooms are the garden cottages, which each house two adults and two children. For those who must have an ocean view, the resort rents some "superior" rooms, suitable for two adults and one child, with a balcony overlooking the beach. The least expensive units have a mountain or garden view, with a balcony, each housing three adults and one child. The wide range of sports and amenities make this an alluring choice. The food is fairly standard, but there's a Japanese restaurant with teppanyaki tables and a pasta-and-pizza restaurant. Four-course gourmet dinners are served in the Casablanca Restaurant.

North Coast Hwy, Falmouth. © **800/659-5436** or 876/954-2451. Fax 876/954-2450. www.superclubs.com. 350 units. Winter $108–$152 per person double; off season $88–$140 per person double. Rates are all-inclusive. AE, DC, MC, V. **Amenities:** 5 restaurants; 6 bars; 4 pools; minigolf; 4 lit tennis courts; fitness center; sauna; children's center; massage; babysitting; laundry service; disco; Internet cafe; badminton; basketball; ice skating; rock climbing; trapeze; dive shop; sailing; snorkeling; windsurfing. *In room:* A/C, TV, minibar, hair dryer, iron, safe.

3 Where to Dine

The Montego Bay area offers some of the finest—and most expensive—dining in Jamaica. But if you're watching your wallet and don't have a delicate stomach, some intriguing food is sold right on the street. For example, on Kent Avenue you might try spicy jerk pork. Seasoned spareribs are also grilled over charcoal fires and sold with extra-hot sauce. Naturally, either dish goes down better with a Red Stripe beer. Cooked shrimp are sold on the streets of Mo Bay; they don't look it, but they're very hotly spiced, so be forewarned. If you're cooking your own meals, you might want to buy a fresh lobster or the catch of the day from a Montego Bay fisherman on the harbor.

EXPENSIVE

Day-O Plantation Restaurant ⚐⚐ (Finds) INTERNATIONAL/JAMAICAN
Here's your chance to wander back to Jamaica's plantation heyday. This place was originally built in the 1920s as the home of the overseer of one of the region's largest sugar producers, the Barnett Plantation. The restaurant occupies a long, indoor/outdoor dining room that's divided into two halves by a dance floor and a small stage. Here, owner Paul Hurlock performs as a one-man band, singing and entertaining the crowd while his wife, Jennifer, and their three children manage the dining room and kitchen.

Every dish is permeated with Jamaican spices. Try the chicken plantation-style, with red-wine sauce and herbs; filet of red snapper in Day-O style, with olives, white wine, tomatoes, and peppers; or, even better, one of the best versions of jerked snapper in Jamaica. We also like the grilled rock lobster with garlic butter.

Day-O Plantation, Lot 1, Fairfield. © **876/952-1825.** Reservations suggested. Main courses $14–$32. AE, MC, V. Tues–Sun noon–11pm. 8-min. drive west of town off Rte. A1 toward Negril. Private van transportation provided; ask when you reserve.

Jasmine ☆☆ INTERNATIONAL   Small, boutique-y, and intimate, this is the most upscale and most fussed-over restaurant within the also-recommended Ritz-Carlton Rose Hall resort. As such, non-residents (some of them hotel insiders themselves from competing hotels) have used a meal here as an excuse to check out the premises of Montego Bay's newest five-star hotel. To reach the dining room, depending on which access doors are open at the time, you might have to pass through the rambling length of a less upscale restaurant, Horizons, next door. Jasmine's occupies a jewel-like circular room that, if you squint your eyes and if the illumination is by candlelight, you might almost imagine was transplanted directly from a château in France. Twelve intricately laid tables accent tones of blue-gray and white, and flickering candles set the mood. Additional seating is available on an outdoor veranda. What impresses here is the sense of intimacy, romance, and stylish internationalism. Delectable menu items include Asian spring rolls, a napoleon of blue crabmeat, Jamaican pumpkin and carrot soup, Singapore-style lobster chili, spice-encrusted loin of lamb, Asian-style grilled filet mignon, and five-spice marinated pork loin.

In the Ritz-Carlton Rose Hall resort, Rose Hall, Montego Bay. © **876/953-2800.** Reservations recommended. Main courses $38–$45. AE, DC, MC, V. Daily 6:30–9:30pm.

Julia's ☆ CONTINENTAL   Julia's food, although competently prepared and using fresh ingredients whenever possible, can hardly compete with the view. The winding jungle road you take to get here is part of the before-dinner entertainment. After a jolting ride to a setting high above the city and its bay, you pass through a walled-in park that was the site of a private home built in 1840 for the Duke of Sutherland. The long, low-slung modern house boasts sweeping, open-sided views over the rolling hills and faraway coastline. Wills Green, the man running the place, draws on the styles of both the Caribbean and central Europe to prepare filet of fresh fish with lime juice and butter, lobster, shrimp, and many different kinds of pasta. Also look for such dishes as the mixed grilled seafood, cheesecake of the day, and their delicious raspberry tart.

Julia's Estate, Bogue Hill. © **876/952-1772.** Reservations required. Main courses $20–$41. AE, DISC, MC, V. Daily 5:30–11pm. Private van transportation provided; ask when you reserve.

Finds Mo Bay Street Meat

The densest concentration of street food in Montego Bay is available at the junction of Gloucester Avenue and Kent Road. (The .8km/½-mile strip of beach-fronting boulevard stretching along both sides of that junction is also known as Bottom Rd. or, less formally, as the "Hip Strip," the edges of which are lined with bars, food stands, and shops catering to the beach trade.) At any of these stands, you might try authentic jerk pork or seasoned spareribs, grilled over charcoal fires and sold with extra-hot sauce; order a Red Stripe beer to go with it. Peppered and cooked shrimp are also sold on the streets of downtown Mo Bay, especially along Saint James Street; they don't look it, but they're very spicy, so be warned. And if you have an efficiency unit with a kitchenette, you can buy fresh lobster or the catch of the day and make your own dinner.

Nikkita's &&& MODERN JAMAICAN   This is the newest, and in terms of cuisine, the most ambitious, restaurant in Montego Bay. It occupies a prominent ochre-colored building along Montego Bay's "Hip Strip," in the heart of town. Inside, the decor might remind you of a stylish restaurant you might have found in Florida, with dark wood trim and a floral, slightly Florentine twist. There are two distinctly different venues within this place: a posh-looking and deliberately upscale bar and a restaurant. Menu items are carefully researched, more "fussed over" than within any other restaurant in the neighborhood, and artful. Examples include a country veal and pork pâté; a terrine of grilled vegetables; a "gateau" of smoked marlin and ackee, served with bammy bread; or a whole baked lobster that's removed from its shell, diced, and mixed with diced scallops, crabmeat, and shrimp, and then put back into its shell.

Gloucester Avenue. ✆ 876/979-6373. Reservations recommended for dinner. Main courses $29–$60. AE, DC, DISC, MC, V. Daily 6–10pm. Bar remains open till 3am.

Richmond Hill Inn & INTERNATIONAL/CONTINENTAL   This plantation-style house dates from 1806, when it was built in a spectacularly panoramic position by owners of the Dewars whiskey distillery. Today, it functions as an unpretentious hotel (see "Where to Stay," earlier in this chapter) with a restaurant and bar that every Jamaican in Montego Bay seems to like. Even if you opt not to dine here, drop in for its dozens of comfortable, open-air seats, and an atmosphere that might have been lifted, intact, from the nostalgia-permeated 1960s. Food is well-prepared and flavorful, with few ambitions about presenting cutting-edge novelties. Lunches focus on salads, light platters, and sandwiches; dinners include a sautéed shrimp, an excellent house salad, stuffed breast of chicken, filet of red snapper, and a choice of dessert cakes. Many of the dishes are of a relatively standard international style, but others, especially the lobster, are worth the trek up the hill.

Top of Union St. ✆ 876/952-3859. Reservations recommended. Lunch salads and platters $4–$25; dinner main courses $17–$43. DISC, MC, V. Daily 7am–10pm. Take a taxi (a 4-min. ride uphill, east of the town's main square).

Round Hill Dining Room & INTERNATIONAL   One of the top dining rooms in Montego Bay, within an also-recommended resort that's one of the most legendary in Jamaica, this place has attracted a smattering of celebrities with its sophisticated surroundings. To reach the dining room, you'll have to pass through the resort's open-air reception area and proceed along a winding path through a garden. Part of the fun here involves a pre-dinner drink within a bar that evokes the mahogany walls and clubby accessories of an upscale country club. (Ralph Lauren designed the bar's decor, taking care to retain the framed photographs of many of the celebrity visitors of the past 50 years.) Dinner is served on either an outdoor terrace perched above the surf or (during inclement weather) under an open-sided breezeway. The menu changes nightly, offering an array of well-prepared dishes, from Mediterranean to Jamaican, from American to Italian pastas. For example, shrimp and pasta Caribe is sautéed with chopped herbs, cream, and wine; and Rasta pasta is tossed with vegetables and basil. Caribbean veal is stuffed with spicy crabmeat and seared, and the catch of the day is served jerked, broiled, Cajun-blackened, or steamed with butter, herbs, and ginger. Other, more classic dishes, include rack of lamb, pan-seared scallops, or medallions of lobster sautéed with cream and served over fettuccine. Afternoon tea and sandwiches are served daily, without charge, at 4pm. Three nights a week (Monday, Wednesday, and Friday), the evening meal is conducted as a series of upscale buffets, some of them presented, replete with elaborate table settings and even more elaborate food presentations, from tables and chairs set directly on the sands of the beach.

In the Round Hill Hotel and Villas, along Rte. A1, 13km (8 miles) west of the center of Montego Bay. © 876/956-7050. Reservations required. Main courses $23–$42; fixed-price dinners during designated, buffet-style "theme nights" $42–$65. AE, DC, MC, V. Daily 12:30–2:30pm and 7:30–9:30pm.

Sugar Mill Restaurant ✿✿ INTERNATIONAL/CARIBBEAN   Widely publicized, and undeniably romantic, this is the signature restaurant of the Rose Hall Half Moon Resort—one of the most upscale and desirable in Montego Bay. It occupies a verdant, landlocked site immediately adjacent to the ruin of what used to be a water wheel for a now-defunct sugar plantation, about a 3-minute shuttlebus transfer from the lobby of the resort that contains it. The lovely, nostalgia-soaked setting and the elaborate and exquisite cuisine make this place a perennial favorite. Guests dine by candlelight either indoors or on an open terrace with a view of a pond, the water wheel, and plenty of greenery. Lunch can be a relatively simple affair, a daily a la carte offering, preceded by Mama's pumpkin soup and followed with homemade rum-and-raisin ice cream. For dinner, try one of the chef's zesty versions of jerk pork, fish, or chicken. He also prepares the day's catch with considerable flair. Smoked North Coast marlin is a specialty. On any given day, you can ask the waiter what's cooking in the curry pot. Chances are it will be a Jamaican specialty such as goat, full of flavor and served with island chutney.

At the Half Moon Rose Hall, along Rte. A1. © 876/953-2314. Reservations required. Main courses $30–$48. AE, DC, DISC, MC, V. Daily 7–9:30pm. A minivan can be sent to most hotels to pick you up.

Three Palms ✿ JAMAICAN/INTERNATIONAL   This restaurant sits across from one of the largest hotels in Montego Bay. With its cedar-shingled design and trio of steeply pointed roofs, it has the air of a country club. Not everything is ambrosial on the menu, but the cooks turn out a predictable array of good pasta and seafood dishes. Many of the flavors are Mediterranean, especially the lobster tails and other seafood dishes. Two intriguing chef's specialties are "grouper round down" (grouper served with shrimp, squid, and mussels) and pan-seared snapper with beans, rice, and fresh vegetables.

Across from the Wyndham Rose Hall Resort, Rose Hall. © 876/953-2650. Reservations recommended. Main courses $20–$25. AE, MC, V. Thurs–Tues 6–9:30pm.

MODERATE

The Houseboat Grill INTERNATIONAL   The setting for this unusual and very laid-back restaurant is a houseboat built around 1960 that floats at permanent anchor from a pier beside Freeport Road. You can enjoy a pre-dinner drink and watch the sunset from a chair on the main deck before descending into the boat's innards for a meal that's composed of culinary ideas from virtually everywhere. Specialties include New Zealand mussels in a Thai-style red curry; pan-seared pork medallions with apple-pecan stuffing and a brandy-flavored cream sauce; and filet of red snapper with Thai-style tamarind sauce and garlic-flavored green beans. Although the kitchen closes around 10pm, the bar opens every day at 4pm and remains open until whenever the owners feel like shutting it down.

Freeport Rd. © 876/979-8845. Reservations recommended. Main courses $16–$20. MC, V. Tues–Sun 6–9:30pm. Closed 2 weeks in Aug.

Fun Fact If Only Columbus Had Prevailed

When Christopher Columbus and his men sailed into what is now Montego Bay, the explorer named it *El Golfo de Buen Tiempo* or "The Gulf of Good Weather." The name didn't stick. The Spanish conquistadores preferred *Bahía de Manteca.* Literally translated, that means "Lard Bay." The Spanish fleets used to anchor in the bay and send men ashore to hunt down wild hogs. From the fatty flesh of these animals, they made "hog butter" to cook with on the long journey back to Europe. Eventually Manteca evolved into Montego.

Marguerite's Seafood by the Sea and Margueritaville Sports Bar & Grill INTERNATIONAL/SEAFOOD   This two-in-one restaurant across from the Coral Cliff Hotel and Gaming Lounge specializes in seafood served on a breeze-swept terrace overlooking the sea. There's also an air-conditioned lounge with an adjoining "Secret Garden." The chef specializes in exhibition cookery at a flambé grill. The menu is mainly devoted to seafood and fresh fish, but there are also numerous innovative pastas and rather standard meat dishes. The changing dessert options are homemade, and a reasonable selection of wines is served. The sports bar and grill features a 34m (110-ft.) water slide, live music, satellite TV, watersports, a sun deck, and a straightforward menu of seafood, sandwiches, pasta, pizza, salads, and snacks—nothing fussy. Naturally, the bartenders specialize in margaritas. Immediately adjacent to Marguerite's, and under the same management, is The Blue Note Bar, a consistently popular after-dark venue that seems to get more crowded, more permissive, and more hip as the evening progresses.

Gloucester Ave. ℂ **876/952-4777.** Reservations recommended for Marguerite's Seafood by the Sea. Main courses $14–$42; snacks and platters from $10. AE, MC, V. Restaurant daily 6–10:30pm; sports bar daily 10:30am–5am.

The Royal Stocks ℱ INTERNATIONAL   It defines itself as a reasonably priced steakhouse and English pub that's owned by, but not on the premises of, one of the most posh and best-accessorized resorts in Montego Bay—Half Moon. Consequently, even if you're staying at that hotel, you'll still have to take one of the hotel's shuttle buses to reach it. Frankly, despite that minor inconvenience, we consider its offbeat location a virtue, since you'll get to mingle with a staff of hip and smart locals, and a clientele of diners that derive mostly from four or five upscale resorts within the immediate neighborhood. The decor successfully combines the best of woodsy Olde England with the Jamaican tropics, although in the competition, Olde England usually prevails. (There's a dart board, a timbered ceiling, and some medieval iconography.) One of the best things about this place is its staff. Start your meal with a platter of Jamaican smoked marlin, move on to dishes that include steak and kidney pie, Milanese-style Parmesan chicken, bangers and mash, Penzance-style fish and chips, fisherman's pie, and "Canterbury" chicken–and-ham cobbler. There's even four different variations of burger, including one that's known as "the Best British."

In the Half Moon Shopping Center, Half Moon, Rose Hall. ℂ **876/953-9770.** Reservations recommended. Burgers, sandwiches, and salads $6–$17; platters $14–$16. AE, DC, MC, V. Daily 9am–10pm.

INEXPENSIVE

The Brewery AMERICAN/JAMAICAN   This is more a bar than a full-scale restaurant, but lunch and dinner are served. Basic hamburgers, salads, and sandwiches are available, and there's also a daytime special buffet featured on Monday, Wednesday, and

Friday, costing J$300 (US$4.80). You can enjoy drinks and a meal on the outside patio overlooking the ocean. The best time to come for drinks is during happy hour, from 4 to 6pm daily. On Friday and Saturday nights, they have disco nights, and the bar has karaoke on Thursday.

In Miranda Ridge Plaza, Gloucester Ave. ✆ 876/940-2433. Reservations not accepted. Main courses J$480–J$650 (US$7.70–US$10). AE, MC, V. Daily 11am–2am.

China House *Value* CHINESE   Forget the tacky commercial surroundings, which evoke a fast-food outlet in the States. The cooks here dish up an array of lip-smackingly good dishes, platter after platter of fresh, tasty Chinese food. In the densest concentration of stores and souvenir shops on Montego Bay's tourist strip, this high-ceilinged restaurant lies across Gloucester Avenue from the sea. The well-prepared food is served in copious portions. Lobster in black-bean sauce is a specialty, and the cooks also prepare several Cantonese dishes exceedingly well.

32 Gloucester Ave. ✆ 876/952-5240. Reservations not accepted. Main courses J$400–J$900 (US$6.40–US$14). AE, MC, V. Daily 10am–10pm.

Guangzhou CHINESE   This is about your only choice for Chinese food along the "Hip Strip." If you live in such places as New York or San Francisco, don't get too excited about dining here. Nonetheless, what you're served isn't bad. The food is very familiar: a selection of lobster, shrimp, chicken, and pork from lo mein to Singapore noodles. The same menu is served at both lunch and dinner. We've found lunch here a bit gloomy, but dinner is better. The chefs, incidentally, are actually from China.

Gloucester Ave. ✆ 876/952-6200. Reservations not accepted. Main courses J$280–J$725 (US$4.50–US$12). MC, V. Mon–Sat noon–9:45pm; Sun 5–9:45pm.

The Native Restaurant ✻ JAMAICAN/INTERNATIONAL   Open to the breezes, and set along the edge of the busy avenue leading along the coastline into the center of Montego Bay, this is a casual but convivial restaurant that's favored by many of the year-round residents of Montego Bay. The dining room occupies a covered, open-sided veranda that's open to the breezes on three sides. The congenial owner, Boris Reid, serves some of the finest Jamaican dishes in the area, many of which seem to taste better when they're preceded with "An Old Native Special," which is described as "a rum punch with a kick." Appetizers include ackee and salt fish and jerk reggae chicken, or smoked marlin, which you can follow with steamed fish or jerk chicken. A more exotic specialty is Boonoonoonoos; billed as "A Taste of Jamaica," it's a big platter with a little bit of everything—meats, fish, and vegetables. Desserts are among the resort's best.

29 Gloucester Ave. ✆ 876/979-2769. Reservations recommended. Main courses $12–$32. AE, DC, DISC, MC, V. Daily 7:30am–10:30pm.

The Pelican JAMAICAN   A Montego Bay landmark, near the St. James Parish Library, the family-friendly Pelican has been serving good food at reasonable prices for more than a quarter century. Most of the dishes are at the lower end of the price scale, unless you order shellfish. Many diners come here at lunch for one of the well-stuffed sandwiches, juicy burgers, or barbecued chicken. You can also choose from a wide array of Jamaican dishes, including stewed peas and rice, curried goat, Caribbean fish, fried chicken, and curried lobster. A "meatless menu" is also featured, and includes such dishes as a vegetable plate. The soda fountain serves old-fashioned sundaes with real whipped cream.

Gloucester Ave. ✆ 876/952-3171. Reservations recommended. Main courses $14–$24. AE, MC, V. Daily 7am–11pm.

(Moments A True Taste of Jamaica

Wherever you go in Jamaica, you'll see ramshackle stands selling **jerk pork**. There is no more authentic local experience than to stop at one of these stands and order a lunch of jerk pork, preferably washed down with a Red Stripe beer. Jerk is a way of barbecuing spicy meats on slats of pimento wood, over a wood fire set in the ground. You can never be quite sure what goes into the seasoning, but the taste is definitely of peppers, pimento (allspice), and ginger. You can also order jerk chicken, sausage, fish, and even lobster. The cook will haul out a machete and chop the meat into bite-size pieces for you, then throw them into a paper bag.

Pork Pit ☆ JAMAICAN   This joint is the best place to go for Jamaican jerk pork and jerk chicken, and the location is right in the heart of Montego Bay, immediately across the boulevard from the Aquasol Theme Park. Many beachgoers desert their towels at noontime and head over here for a big, reasonably priced lunch. Picnic tables encircle the building, and everything is open-air and informal. A half-pound of jerk meat, served with a baked yam or baked potato and a bottle of Red Stripe, is usually enough for a meal. The menu also includes steamed roast fish.

27 Gloucester Ave. ✆ 876/952-3663. Reservations not accepted. 1 lb. of jerk pork $10. MC, V. Daily 11am–11pm.

4 Beaches, Golf & Other Outdoor Pursuits

BEACHES

Cornwall Beach (✆ **876/952-3463**) is a long stretch of white sand with dressing rooms, a bar, and a cafeteria. The grainy sand and good swimming have made it a longtime favorite. Unlike some of Jamaica's remote, hard-to-get-to beaches, this one is near all the major hotels, especially the moderately priced ones. Unfortunately, it can be crowded in winter (mostly with tourists, not locals). This is a good beach for kids, with gentle waters and a gently sloping ocean bottom. The beach is open daily from 9am to 5pm. Admission is $3.25 for adults, $1.65 for children.

   Doctors Cave Beach, on Gloucester Avenue (✆ **876/952-2566** for the beach club), is arguably the loveliest stretch of sand bordering Montego Bay. Its gentle surf, golden sands, and fresh turquoise water make it an inviting place to swim, and there's always a beach-party atmosphere. Placid and popular with families, it's the best all-around beach in Montego Bay. Sometimes schools of tropical fish weave in and out of the waters, but usually the crowds of frolicking people scare them away. Since it's almost always packed, especially in winter, you have to get there early to stake out a beach-blanket-size spot. Admission is $5 for adults, $2.50 for children age 12 and under. Open daily 8:30am to sunset. The beach club here has well-kept changing rooms, showers, restrooms, a food court, a bar, a cybercafe, and a sundries shop. Beach chairs and umbrellas can be rented daily.

   Frankly, you may want to skip all these public beaches entirely and head instead for the **Rose Hall Beach Club** (✆ **876/680-0969** for the beach club), on the main road 18km (11 miles) east of Montego Bay. The club offers .8km (½ mile) of secluded white-sand beach with crystal-clear water, plus a restaurant, a bar, a covered pavilion, an open-air dance area, showers, restrooms, hammocks, changing rooms, beach volleyball courts, beach games, and a full watersports program. Admission is $6 for adults, $3 for children. Hours are daily from 9am to 5pm.

SPORTS & OUTDOOR PURSUITS

DEEP-SEA FISHING   **Seaworld Resorts,** whose main office is at the Cariblue Hotel, Rose Hall Main Road (© **876/953-2180;** www.diveseaworld.com), operates flying-bridge cruisers, with deck lines and outriggers, for fishing expeditions. A half-day fishing trip costs $400 for up to four participants.

DIVING, SNORKELING & OTHER WATERSPORTS   Some of the best dive sites in the area include **Rose Hall Reef,** a shallow reef teeming with marine life and underwater visibility of 7 to 14m (20 to 40 ft.). A large pillar of coral rising to the surface is called "Fairy Castle" by local divers. Nurse sharks often swim at this reef, and you can invariably see grunts, soldier fish, and red snapper. Named after the James Jones novel, *Go to the Widowmaker,* the ominously named **Widowmakers Cave** starts at 12m (40 ft.) with its entrance cave stretching for 24m (80 ft.). As you swim into its cavernous depth, you're greeted with barracuda, reef fish, and other denizens of the deep, along with such natural wonders as gorgonians, black coral, and sponges. At the aptly named **Chub Reef,** the site is teeming with Bermuda Chubs and other rainbow-hued marine life in 8m (24 ft.) of water. The coral caverns here are particularly stunning. Finally, **The Point,** whose wall drops to 60m (200 ft.), is for very experienced divers only. Expect strong currents and exotic black coral, deep-water gorgonians, sponges, and other marine life. **Seaworld Resorts** (see above) also operates scuba-diving excursions, plus sailing, windsurfing, and more. Its dives plunge to offshore coral reefs—among the most spectacular in the Caribbean—with three certified dive guides, one dive boat, and all the equipment for both inexperienced and already-certified divers. One-tank dives cost $45; night dives are $65.

Kids A Waterworld for Families

For years, the Walter Fletcher Beach was a sunny, well-maintained beach, without too many improvements, positioned a short walk from the heart of Montego Bay. In 2004, a team of entrepreneurs added a compound of entertainment options, fenced everything in, and renamed it the **AquaSol Theme Park** (© **876/979-9447** or 876/940-1344). Now, its sands bustle with scantily clad sunbathers and swimmers throughout the day. Then, beginning at around 8pm every Friday to Sunday, the site experiences a change of clientele when mobs of both Jamaicans and foreign visitors hang out for hours in the moonlight, jamming and gossiping till the wee hours. Foreign visitors pay a $5 entrance fee, which allows access to a watersports kiosk, a pier where glass-bottomed boats are moored, a strip of sand, a beauty salon, a bar and grill-style restaurant, a gym/health club with a private local membership, and a disco/bar with views of the sea, a collection of caged macaws, and surges of reggae and soca. Admission is $5 for adults, $3 for children under 12. Regardless of which of the facilities you opt to patronize, the entire compound is open Monday to Thursday 9am to 7pm, and 9am to at least midnight, and sometimes, later, depending on business, on Friday to Sunday.

North Coast Marine Sports (© 876/953-2211), located at the Half Moon resort, offers everything from scuba diving to Sunfish, snorkel gear, kayaks, and more. They can arrange for deep-sea fishing trips and snorkel cruises, too.

Doctors Cave Beach is part of the **Montego Bay Marine Park,** which was established to protect the wide variety of marine life among the coral reefs right offshore from the popular beaches. You can rent snorkel gear from the beach club at Doctors Cave, or from the beach clubs at any of the local beaches.

You might also like to head across the channel to check out **Coyaba Reef, Seaworld Reef,** and **Royal Reef,** which are full of barjacks, blue and brown chromis, yellow-headed wrasses, and spotlight parrotfish. You must have a guide here, as the currents are strong and the wind picks up in the afternoon. If you're not staying at a resort offering snorkeling expeditions, then Seaworld is your best bet. For about $30 per hour, a guide swims with you and points out various fish.

GOLF   The **White Witch of Rose Hall Golf Course,** part of the Ritz-Carlton Rose Hall (© 876/518-0174), is one of the most spectacular courses in the Caribbean, situated on 80 hectares (200 acres) of lush greenery in Jamaica's old plantation country. The course is named after Annie Palmer, the notorious "White Witch" and mistress of Rose Hall nearby. Ten minutes from the deluxe resort by wheels, the course was created by Robert von Hagge, who designed the course to wind up and down the mountains, with panoramic vistas of the sea visible from 16 of the 18 holes. Greens fees are $139 for hotel guests, $159 for nonguests.

The Cinnamon Hill course at **Rose Hall Resort & Country Club** ☻☻ (© 876/953-2650) has a noted course with an unusual and challenging seaside-and-mountain layout, built on the shores of the Caribbean. Its 8th hole skirts the water, and then doglegs onto a promontory and a green thrusting 182m (600 ft.) into the sea. The back 9 are the most scenic and interesting, rising up steep slopes and falling into deep ravines on Mount Zion. The 10th fairway abuts the family burial grounds of the Barretts of Wimpole Street. The 90m-high (300-ft.) 13th tee offers a rare panoramic view of the sea and the roof of the hotel, and the 15th green is next to a 12m (40-ft.) waterfall, once featured in a James Bond movie. Amenities include a fully stocked pro shop, a clubhouse, and a professional staff. Guests pay $131 for 18 holes, or $75 for 9 holes; nonguests pay $154 for 18 holes and $89 for 9 holes. Cart rental and the use of a caddy are included in the greens fees.

The excellent course at the **Tryall Club Jamaica** ☻☻☻ (© 876/956-5660), 19km (12 miles) from Montego Bay, is so regal that it's often the site of major tournaments. For 18 holes, guests of Tryall are charged $85 in winter, $40 the rest of the year. In winter the course is usually closed to nonguests; the rest of the year, they pay a steep $125.

Moments Meeting Some Feathered Friends

At the **Rocklands Wildlife Station,** about 2km (1¼ mile) outside Anchovy on the road from Montego Bay, St. James (© 876/952-2009), you can have a Jamaican doctor bird perch on your finger to drink syrup, feed small doves and finches millet from your hand, and watch dozens of other birds flying in for their evening meal. Don't take children age 5 and under to this sanctuary, as they tend to bother the birds. Admission is $10; open daily from 9am to 5:30pm.

Moments **Swimming with the Dolphins**

Montego Bay's **Half Moon** (p. 71) features daily sessions of swimming with the dolphins at its **Dolphin Lagoon** in a natural cove in the vicinity of Sunrise Beach. For $155 per person, you get into the water with some of Flipper's cousins for a bottlenose kiss and a dorsal-fin ride. A trimmed-down close encounter with the dolphins—called "Beach Encounter"—costs $89 per person. Before joining the program, a trainer gives a briefing about the "politically correct" ways to mingle with these friendly sea animals. For more information or to make reservations in advance, call ℰ **800/626-0592.**

Golf at Half Moon (ℰ **876/953-2211;** www.halfmoongolf.com) at the Half Moon resort features a championship course designed by Robert Trent Jones, Sr. with manicured and diversely shaped greens. Half Moon hotel guests pay $125 for 18 holes including caddy and cart; nonguests pay $130. Carts cost $35 for 18 holes, and caddies (which are mandatory) are hired for $20.

The **Ironshore Golf & Country Club,** Ironshore, St. James, Montego Bay (ℰ **876/953-3681**), is another well-known par-72 course. Privately owned, it's open to all golfers. Greens fees for 18 holes are $50, plus $35 for a cart and $15 for a caddy.

HORSEBACK RIDING   A good program is offered at the **Rocky Point Riding Stables** at the Half Moon Club, Rose Hall, Montego Bay (ℰ **876/953-2286**). Housed in the most beautiful barn and stables in Jamaica, it offers around 30 horses and a helpful staff. A 90-minute beach or mountain ride costs $60.

RAFTING   **Mountain Valley Rafting,** P.O. Box 23, Montego Bay (ℰ **876/ 956-4920**), offers somewhat tame and touristy excursions on the Great River, which depart from the Lethe Plantation, about 16km (10 miles) south of Montego Bay. Skip that, and head over to Falmouth, 45km (28 miles) to the east, where rafting on the **Martha Brae** is an adventure. To reach the starting point from Falmouth, drive approximately 5km (3 miles) inland to **Martha Brae's Rafters Village** (ℰ **876/ 952-0889**). The rafts are similar to those on the Rio Grande, near Port Antonio; you sit on a raised dais on bamboo logs. The cost is $45, with two riders allowed on a raft, plus a small child if accompanied by an adult (but use caution). The trips last 1¼ hours and operate daily from 9am to 4pm. It's not necessary to wear swimsuits. Along the way, you can stop and order cool drinks or beer along the banks of the river. There's a bar, a restaurant, and two souvenir shops in the village.

TENNIS   **Half Moon** ☆☆☆, outside Montego Bay (ℰ **876/953-2211**), has the finest courts in the area. Its 13 state-of-the-art courts, 7 of which are lit for night games, attract tennis players from around the world. Lessons cost $25 to $35 per half-hour, $50 to $65 per hour. Residents play free, day or night. The pro shop, which accepts reservations for court times, is open daily from 7am to 9pm. If you want to play after those hours, switch on the lights yourself. If you're not a hotel guest, you must purchase a day pass ($40 per person) at the front desk; it allows access to the resort's courts, gym, sauna, Jacuzzi, pools, and beach facilities.

Tryall Club Jamaica, St. James (ℰ **876/956-5660**), offers nine hard-surface courts, three lit for night play. Day games are free for guests; non-guests pay $30 per hour. There's a $20 per hour charge to light the courts after dark. At least four on-site pros provide lessons for $25 to $35 per half-hour, or $45 to $60 per hour.

Rose Hall Resort & Country Club, Rose Hall (© **876/953-2650**), outside Montego Bay, is an outstanding tennis resort, though not the equal of Half Moon or Tryall. Wyndham offers six hard-surface courts, each lit for night play. The resident pro charges $40 per hour for lessons, $35 for 45 minutes, or $30 for 30 minutes.

5 Seeing the Sights

WALKING TOUR   A STROLL THROUGH MONTEGO BAY

Start: Fort Montego.
Finish: St. James Parish Church.
Time: 1½ hours.
Best Times: 10am–4pm.
Worst Times: 8–10am and 4–6pm because of very heavy traffic.

Most of the Montego Bay area's first-rate sights, such as the great houses, lie outside the city.

But the downtown area does at least merit a morning of your time for a look around. Everyone at some point seems to stroll **Gloucester Avenue,** home to hotels, restaurants, shops, street vendors, taxi drivers, and hair braiders. From there, it's possible to make a brief tour of the town.

If you don't mind fending off hustlers, you can stroll through the center of Montego Bay. Allow about 1½ hours to see the major landmarks.

We like to begin our walk north of Walter Fletcher Beach at:

❶ Fort Montego

Above Gloucester Avenue and up Miranda Hill on Queen's Drive, the fort is long gone. Originally it had 17 cannons, of which only a trio remain. The fort never saw much action, and what it did see was of the comic variety—a Jamaican slapstick film.

Immediately south of the fort and reached by going southeast along Gloucester Avenue is a roundabout at the beginning of Howard Cooke Drive. This is the site of the:

❷ Old Fort Craft Park

See "Shopping," below for more details. You'll be awash in T-shirts, woodcarvings, shell jewelry, baskets to fit cobras of any size, and vendors peddling fruits and vegetables.

Afterward, you can walk 1 block to the east along Union Street until you reach the landmark:

❸ Georgian House

This 18th-century residence—really two buildings—was built by a rich tradesman who wanted one house for his wife and the other for his mistress.

Return to Fort Street, going only 1 block to the south to reach:

❹ Sam Sharpe Square

Sam Sharpe was the local hero who spearheaded the Christmas Rebellion of 1831 that eventually led to the freeing of Jamaica's slaves. The cobblestone square bearing his name is still a rallying point for protests and political speeches.

At the northwest corner of the square is a bronze statue commemorating Sharpe, who was hanged in this very square.

Walking Tour: A Stroll through Montego Bay

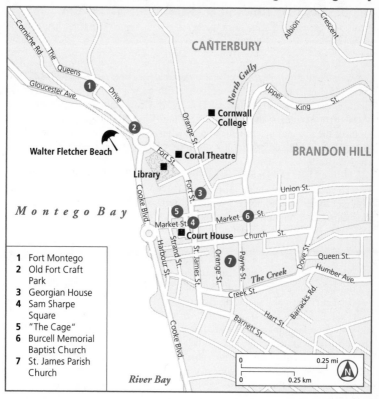

CANTERBURY

Corniche Rd.
The Queens
Gloucester Ave.
Drive

1

2

Walter Fletcher Beach

Albion
Crescent

North Gully
Orange St.
Upper
King St.

■ Cornwall College

■ Coral Theatre

BRANDON HILL

Library

Fort St.

Cooke Blvd.

3

Union St.

Montego Bay

5
Market St. **4**
Market St. **6**

Strand St.
Harbour St.
St. James St.
Cooke Blvd.

Orange St.

■ Court House
Church St.

Payne St.

7
The Creek
Creek St.

Barnett St.

Dove St.
Queen St.
Humber Ave.

Barracks Rd.
Hart St.

River Bay

1 Fort Montego
2 Old Fort Craft Park
3 Georgian House
4 Sam Sharpe Square
5 "The Cage"
6 Burcell Memorial Baptist Church
7 St. James Parish Church

0   0.25 mi
0   0.25 km

In the northwest corner you can also see another grim monument called:

⑤ "The Cage"

This foreboding brick structure dates from 1806. Its name is apt: It was used as a lockup for both escaped slaves and drunks arrested on the street, most often British sailors on shore leave.

Leaving Sam Sharpe Square, head east along Market Street for 2 blocks until you come to:

⑥ Burcell Memorial Baptist Church

Dating from 1824, this church is named for its founder, the preacher Thomas Burcell; Sam Sharpe himself once served as a deacon here. The present church is a reconstruction, as slave owners burned the original church to protest Burcell's support of the emancipation movement. Sharpe's remains lie in the church's vault.

Continue to walk east along Market Street for another block until you approach the intersection with East Street. Take East Street south to Church Street. Once here, head west again in the direction of Sam Sharpe Square. On your left you'll come to:

⑦ St. James Parish Church

Shaped like a Greek cross, this is one of the best examples of mid-18th-century architecture on the island. The present church is a reconstruction; the original church was destroyed in the devastating earthquake that rocked Mo Bay in 1957.

THE BEST ATTRACTIONS IN & AROUND MONTEGO BAY

If you can tear yourself away from the beach to take some excursions, here's the pick of the litter.

TOURS & CRUISES

Croydon Plantation, P.O. Box 1348, Catadupa, St. James (© **876/979-8267**), is a 38km (24-mile) ride from Montego Bay. It can be visited on a half-day tour from Montego Bay (or Negril) on Tuesday and Friday. Cruise-ship passengers can visit on Wednesday. Included in the $55 price are round-trip transportation from your hotel, a tour of the plantation, a taste of tropical fruits in season, and a barbecued-chicken lunch. Most hotel desks can arrange this tour, which is rather touristy and not worth a half-day for most visitors.

A **Hilton High Day Tour,** booked through Beach View Plaza (© **876/952-3343;** www.jamaicahiltontour.com), includes round-trip transportation on a scenic drive through historic plantation areas. Your day starts with continental breakfast at an old plantation house. You can roam the 40 hectares (100 acres) of the plantation and visit the German village of Seaford Town or St. Leonards village nearby. Calypso music is played throughout the day, and a Jamaican lunch is served at 1pm. The cost is $64 to $75 per person for the plantation tour, breakfast, lunch, and transportation. Tour days are Tuesday, Wednesday, Friday, and Sunday.

Day and evening cruises are offered aboard the *Calico,* a 17m (55-ft.) gaff-rigged wooden ketch that sails from Margaritaville on the Montego Bay waterfront. An additional vessel, *Calico B,* also carries another 40 passengers. You can be transported to and from your hotel for either cruise. The daily voyage departs at 10am and returns at 1pm offering sailing, sunning, and snorkeling (with equipment). The cruise costs $40. On the *Calico's* evening voyage, which goes for $25 and is offered daily from 5 to 7pm, cocktails and wine are served as you sail through the sunset. For information and reservations, call **Calico Pirate Cruises** (© **876/940-4465**) a few days in advance.

THE GREAT HOUSES

Occupied by plantation owners, each great house of Jamaica was built on high ground so that it overlooked the plantation itself and was in sight of the next house in the distance. It was the custom for the owners to offer hospitality to travelers crossing the island by road. While these homes are intriguing and beautiful, it's important to remember that they represent the sad legacy of slavery—they were built by slaves, and the lavish lifestyle of the original owners was supported by the profits of slave labor. The two great houses below can be toured in the same day.

Greenwood Great House ✦ Some people find the 15-room Greenwood even more interesting than Rose Hall (see below) because it's undergone less restoration and has more literary associations. Erected between 1780 and 1800, the Georgian-style building was the residence of Richard Barrett (cousin of poet Elizabeth Barrett Browning). Elizabeth Barrett Browning herself never visited Jamaica, but her family was one of the largest landholders here. An absentee planter who lived in England, her father once owned 33,600 hectares (84,000 acres) and some 3,000 slaves. On display is the original library of the Barrett family, with rare books dating from 1697, along with oil paintings of the family, Wedgwood china, rare musical instruments, and a collection of antique furniture.

On Rte. A1, 23km (14 miles) east of Montego Bay. © **876/953-1077.** Admission $12 adults, $6 children under age 12. Daily 9am–6pm.

The White Witch of Rose Hall

Annie Mae Paterson, a beautiful 18-year-old spitfire measuring only 4' 11" tall, arrived at the **Rose Hall Great House** near Montego Bay on March 28, 1820, to take up residence with her new husband, the Honorable John Rose Palmer. The house was said to affect her badly from the moment she entered it. Born in 1802 in England of half-English, half-Irish stock, she had moved to Haiti with her merchant parents when she was 10. When they died soon after from yellow fever, she was adopted by her Haitian nanny, who was rumored to be a voodoo priestess who educated her young charge in the arts of the occult. When the nanny died, the young white woman came to Jamaica, husband-hunting.

Several months after the marriage, when her husband discovered her affair with a young slave, he is said to have beaten her with a riding whip. John Palmer died that night. Before long, rumors were swirling that his young wife had poisoned his coffee.

With her husband buried, Annie Palmer began a reign of terror at Rose Hall. Fearing her slave lover might blackmail her, she watched from the back of a black horse while he was securely tied, gagged, and flogged to death. Legend says that she then began to drift into liaison after liaison with one slave after another. But she was fickle: When her lovers bored her, she had them killed.

Partly because of her training in the occult arts during a childhood spent in Haiti, her servants called her the "*Obeah* (voodoo) woman," the daughter of the devil, and "the White Witch of Rose Hall."

Although some scholars claim that they can produce no evidence of this legendary figure's cruelty or even of her debauchery, her story has been the subject of countless paperback Gothic novels.

When Ms. Palmer was found strangled in her bed in 1831, evidence surfaced that the murderer was Takoo, a freed slave seeking vengeance for a curse that Annie—in a fit of jealous rage—had placed on his beloved granddaughter, which had caused that granddaughter "to wither and die." Her household servants, as well as the overseer of her plantation, Ashman, who recorded most of the grisly events in his diary, just wanted her buried as soon as possible in the deepest hole they could dig. Fearing her return from the dead, the household servants hastily burned most of her possessions, fearing that they were permeated with remnants of her spirit. Evidence of the building being haunted grew stronger as a succession of tragedies befell most of the subsequent owners.

Rose Hall Great House ✹   The legendary Rose Hall is the most famous great house on Jamaica, and the legends associated with it are so riveting and spellbinding that we urge you to visit, even at the expense of a day at the beach. The subject of at least a dozen Gothic novels, it was immortalized in the H. G. deLisser book, *White Witch of Rose Hall*. The house was begun in 1750 by George Ash, an English planter, and completed in 1780 by John Palmer, a wealthy British planter. At its peak, this was

---

Tips **Getting Past the Security Guard**

Jamaica, especially the area about Montego Bay, is filled with great houses left over from the plantation era fueled by a slave economy. With few exceptions, these great houses—often decaying—are closed to the public. Over the years, we've found that exchanging some money with the local groundskeeper or security guard will gain us entry into the private grounds and gardens. Of course, you shouldn't actually go inside a great house and invade people's living quarters, but it's a great way to see a *Gone with the Wind* side of Jamaica rarely viewed by the casual visitor.

---

a 2,640-hectare (6,600-acre) plantation, with more than 2,000 slaves. At the time, it was considerably larger than what you'll see today, thanks to two additional wings, connected to the main house at the time by open breezeways, which were never rebuilt. Many of the macabre legends associated with the place derived from Annie Palmer, wife of the builder's grandnephew, John Rose Palmer, who became the focal point of fiction and fact (see "The White Witch of Rose Hall" box, below). Annie was said to have murdered several of her husbands while they slept and eventually suffered the same fate herself. Having collapsed into ruins after an abandonment that lasted for more than 130 years, the house was richly restored between 1966 and 1971 by members of the Delaware-based Rollins family, owners of the nearby Ritz-Carlton. Listen carefully to the guide, who will probably be dressed in a plaid-patterned frock that emulates equivalent costumes that were standard fare for generations. Her tale of sexual intrigue, insanity, sado-masochism, and murder ranks as one of the hottest celebrity exposés in Jamaica. The dark and brooding Annie's Pub is on the building's ground floor. There, a rum-laced "witches brew" goes for $2.50. Two of the antiques within the Great House, incidentally, were donated by the late Johnny Cash, friends of the Rollins family, present owners of the building.

Rose Hall Hwy., 15km (9¼ miles) east of Montego Bay. ℂ 876/953-2323. Admission $15 adults, $10 children. Daily 9am–6pm. Last tour at 5:15pm.

6 Shopping

Be prepared to be pursued by aggressive vendors. Selling a craft item may mean the difference between having a meal or going hungry, and that situation often leads to a feverish attempt to peddle goods to potential customers, all of whom are viewed as rich. *Warning:* Occasionally this harassment turns ugly or even violent, so watch your back if you decide to turn it on an angry vendor.

The main shopping areas are at **Montego Freeport,** within easy walking distance of the pier; **City Centre,** where most of the duty-free shops are, aside from those at the large hotels; and the **Holiday Village Shopping Centre,** located across from the Holiday Inn, on Rose Hall Road, heading from Montego Bay toward Ocho Rios.

If you have time for only one shopping complex, make it **Old Fort Craft Park,** as its handicrafts are more varied. It's grazing country for both souvenirs and more serious purchases. This shopping complex with 180 vendors (all licensed by the Jamaica Tourist Board), fronts Howard Cooke Boulevard (up from Gloucester Ave. in the heart of Montego Bay, on the site of Fort Montego). You'll see wall hangings, hand-woven

> ### *Tips* When "Duty-Free" Isn't
>
> Some so-called "duty-free" prices are actually lower than stateside prices, but then the government hits you with a 10% "general consumption tax" on all items purchased. Even so, you can still find good duty-free items here, including Swiss watches, Irish crystal, Italian handbags, Indian silks, and liquors and liqueurs. Appleton's rums are an excellent value. Tía María (coffee-flavored) and Rumona (rum-flavored) are the best liqueurs. Khus Khus is the local perfume. Jamaican arts and crafts are available throughout the resorts and at the Crafts Market (see below).

straw items, and wood sculpture. You can even get your hair braided. Be aware that vendors can be very aggressive. If you want something, be prepared to bargain.

What's the best souvenir shop in Montego Bay that isn't part of any larger crafts market? It stands alone on the Hip Strip, surrounded by less appealing shops on at least one side. It's **Tropical Treasures,** Shop #1, 55 Gloucester Ave. (© 876/971-8531). Open daily from 9am to 7pm, under the ownership of the genuinely charming Sam Chhugani, it offers handmade gift items, a wide range of Jamaican rums, cigars, jerk spices, and coffees, CDs by Jamaican musicians, rum cakes, some very intriguing beachwear, and some of the most attractive women's dresses we've seen—the kind that make most women look fluid, graceful, nubile, and sexy. Many were crafted in India, come in "one size fits all" motifs, seem appropriate for cocktail parties within moonlit gazebos, are undeniably sexy, and rarely exceed $50 in price.

At the **Crafts Market,** near Harbour Street in downtown Montego Bay, you can find a good selection of handmade souvenirs of Jamaica, including straw hats and bags, wooden platters, straw baskets, musical instruments, beads, carved objects, and toys. That jipijapa straw hat is important if you're out in the island sun.

One of the most intriguing places for shopping is an upscale minimall, **Half Moon Plaza,** on the coastal road about 13km (8 miles) east of the commercial center of Montego Bay. It caters to the guests of the Half Moon resort, and the carefully selected merchandise is upscale and expensive. On the premises are a bank, about 25 relatively upscale boutiques, and a private and well-respected prep school named in honor of the longtime manager of Half Moon, Heinz Simonowitz.

Klass Kraft Leather Sandals, 44 Fort St. (© 876/952-5782), offers sandals, caps, and leather accessories made on location by a team of Jamaican craftspeople.

Golden Nugget, 8 St. James Shopping Centre, Gloucester Avenue (© 876/952-7707), is a duty-free shop with an impressive collection of watches and

---

Grooving on Marley's Reggae Beat

The Bob Marley Experience at the Half Moon Shopping Village, North Coast Highway (© 876/953-3946), provides a keen insight into the reggae star's life. On-site you can visit a shop stuffed with Marley memorabilia, everything from CDs to T-shirts, from postcards to incense. Marley's exclusive clothing line, the "Tuff Gong Collection" of denim wear, is also sold here—and there's a free 15-minute documentary on Marley's life and music showing continuously in a wide-screen theater seating about 70.

> **(Tips) Avoiding the Mo Bay Hustle**
>
> With some 2 million tourists arriving each year, often with fat wallets, the Mo Bay hustle developed. Although the government has improved the situation considerably, time was in the 1990s that you couldn't walk more than a few steps before a hustler approached or cornered you.
>
> Rivaled by Ocho Rios, the Mo Bay hustler is still an annoying presence and works hard to keep you from walking around the resort and enjoying it on your own terms.
>
> Sometimes even a simple "no" is not enough to free yourself from the bondage of your uninvited guest. If a hustler will not leave, you can threaten to call a resort patrol, a group of police officers hired by the government to prevent harassment of visitors. The patrol (both men and women) wear dark-blue quasi-military uniforms with black berets and are easy to spot.
>
> Some vendors try to peddle themselves as guides. Some try to sell junky souvenirs such as carvings. Many are peddling drugs, especially ganja (marijuana).
>
> Be careful of pickpockets when shopping the markets, and don't let a carver etch your name on a piece of wood. He will later claim you ordered him to do so. Resist having jewelry put on your body; similarly, if someone places a straw hat on your head, you'll be billed whether you want it or not.

a fine assortment of jewelry, plus cameras and a wide assortment of French perfumes.

Copasetic, Half Moon Shopping Village (© **876/953-3838**), is a good outlet for Jamaican crafts, including pottery, jewelry, and straw products.

The best selection of native art is found at the **Gallery of West Indian Art,** 11 Fairfield Rd. (© **876/952-4547**), with a wide selection of paintings not only from Haiti and Jamaica, but Cuba as well, along with Jamaican hand-carved wooden animals—even some painted hand-turned pottery.

Mezzaluna, Half Moon Shopping Village, Half Moon Plaza (© **876/953-9683**), is an upscale women's boutique selling lingerie, La Perla perfumes, and various garments, along with chic accessories such as belts.

7 Montego Bay After Dark

Nightlife is not guaranteed at Montego Bay's top hotels. In winter the restaurants and bars of the Ritz-Carlton or Half Moon have the most diverse amusements. After dark it's sleepy at Round Hill and Tryall.

The following clubs attract mainly a crowd of 20- to 40-somethings.

A highly visible and popular nightspot in Mo Bay is a two-in-one restaurant, **Marguerite's Seafood by the Sea** and **Margueritaville Sports Bar & Grill,** Gloucester Avenue (© **876/952-4777**), across from the Coral Cliff Hotel. It specializes in moderately priced seafood and margaritas served on a breezy terrace overlooking the sea. The sports bar and grill features a 33m (110-ft.) Hydroslide, live music, satellite TV, a sun deck, a CD jukebox, and a straightforward menu of seafood, sandwiches, pasta, pizza, salads, and snacks—nothing fussy.

What's our favorite down-home evening hangout in Montego Bay? It's **Scotchies,** Coral Gardens Main Highway (the A1), in Ironshore (© **876/953-8041**). Set behind a dusty-looking cement-block barrier, about 5km (3 miles) east of Montego Bay's town center, it's the place where after-office Jamaicans meet and greet one another in a setting that's well-lubricated with rum, jerk food, and music. A lot of friendships and romances have been sparked at this place. The thing that surprises us the most about it is its setting, behind a masonry wall that's coated with the dust of a nearby construction project. Kenny Rogers and jazz singer Alicia Keys have both been spotted here, along with a healthy mixture of local residents and hip tourists. A half-pound portion of jerk pork, chicken, or sausage costs J$350 (US$5.60); a half-pound portion of jerk fish goes for J$300 (US$4.80). Red Stripes cost J$80 (US$1.30), and a portion of roasted breadfruit, yams, or sweet potatoes, J$100 (US$1.60) each. MasterCard and Visa are both accepted. Technically, the place opens every day around 2pm, shuffling along on a low-key level until 6pm, when it gets crowded. It's packed by around 8:30pm, when there's some kind of live music performed. The joint usually closes by 2am.

The newest and most deliberately upscale bar in Montego Bay is **Nikkita's,** on Gloucester Avenue (© **876/979-6373**). Much of its creative forces are lavished on the restaurant which is attached to this bar, but since the bar does a healthy and sometimes bustling business in its own right, many people come here just for a cocktail or two amid a dark-paneled decor that might have been lifted intact from a stylish watering hole in San Francisco or London. Rum punches cost $4.50 each; a shot of Jack Daniels costs $8. It's open daily from 6pm until 3am.

Where should you go if you're looking to hang out someplace that's a bit earthier and rowdier than Nikkita's? Consider a restaurant and nightspot with the most whimsical name of any in Jamaica, the **Jamaica Bobsled Café,** 69 Gloucester Ave. (© **876/940-7009**). Prefaced with the bright colors of the Jamaican flag, and an oversized digital clock that counts down the minutes to the next Winter Olympic Games, this is a tongue-in-cheek reminder of one of the most effective public relations and press campaigns in the history of Jamaica: the Jamaican bobsled team. Prominently displayed is the actual bobsled that was used by the Jamaican team in the 1992 Winter Olympic Games in Calgary. Burgers, platters, and salads at this place cost from $5 to $9 each. It's open Monday to Thursday from 10am to 2am; Friday to Sunday from 7am to 2am.

Cricket Club, at Wyndham Rose Hall (© **876/953-2650**), is more than just a sports bar; it's where people go to meet and mingle with an international crowd. Televised sports, karaoke singalongs, tournament darts, and backgammon are all part of the fun. It's open daily from 8pm to 2am; there's no cover.

Moments Rum & Reggae—& an Escape

When you want to escape, head for **Time 'n' Place,** just east of Falmouth (© **876/954-4371**). From Montego Bay, you'll spot the sign by the side of the road before you reach Falmouth: "If you got the time, then we got the place." On an almost deserted 3km (1¾-mile) beach sits this funky beach bar built of driftwood. Sit back in this relaxed, friendly place and listen to the reggae from the local stations. You can order the island's best daiquiris, made from fresh local fruit, or stick around for peppery jerk chicken or lobster. Time 'n' Place isn't completely undiscovered—somehow, fashion editors of *Vogue* have swooped down on the place, using it as a backdrop for beach fashion shots.

Moments **Hunting the Green Flash**

In Jamaica, people gather for what's known as a "sundowner" to watch the day's last flickering rays.

The place we head for our sundowner is **Richmond Hill Inn** (p. 75). This 1806 plantation-style house was once owned by the Dewars, of Scotch whisky fame. Perhaps out of memory of the long-ago occupants, a Scotch will do. But those fruit punches seem to win out instead. In a building constructed of limestone and molasses, you can wander among antiques and take your drink out onto the terrace for a grand sweep of the resort and the bay.

Count yourself lucky if you see a sudden "green flash" the moment the sun sets. This rare refraction of sunlight, which sometimes occurs in the West Indies on cloudless evenings, is said to guarantee true love to couples who witness it.

We've enjoyed the atmosphere at **Sun Daze,** 39 Gloucester Ave. (© **876/952-9391**), which has an authentic Jamaican laid-back feel—complete with a constant flow of calypso and reggae music from as early as 10am daily (for the diehards) until 2am. This restaurant/club draws an equal mixture of locals and visitors, nearly all under 40

If you want to stick to the more familiar, try **Witches Nightclub,** Holiday Inn Sun-Spree Resort (© **876/953-2485**). Nonguests of the hotel can pick up a pass at the front desk for $95, which allows them all-inclusive privileges at the nightclub. The pass includes a buffet and all the drinks and dancing you can handle. The house/disco/jazz music is as imaginative as what you'll find at a club in the United States. It's open daily from 6pm to 2am.

The Brewery, Gloucester Avenue (© **876/940-2433**), is one of the city's most popular nightlife hangouts. It's a cross between an English pub and a Jamaican jerk-pork pit. There's a woodsy-looking bar where everyone is into Red Stripe and reggae, lots of neo-medieval memorabilia, and a covered veranda in back overlooking busy Gloucester Avenue.

When it comes to gambling parlors, Mo Bay is no San Juan, much less Las Vegas. If you must, there's the **Coral Cliff Gaming Lounge** on Gloucester Avenue (© **876/952-4130**), open 24 hours so that locals can play for small stakes at its slot machines—nearly 100 in all. Don't expect large jackpots. On site is a big-screen TV and bar, drawing a Bud-swilling sports crowd.

8 Falmouth: Decaying Georgian Charm

WALKING TOUR   **STROLLING THROUGH FALMOUTH**

Start: Water Square.

Finish: St. Peter's Anglican Church.

Time: 45 minutes.

Best Times: 10am–4pm.

Worst Times: 8–10am and 4–6pm—more traffic then.

Walking Tour: Strolling through Falmouth

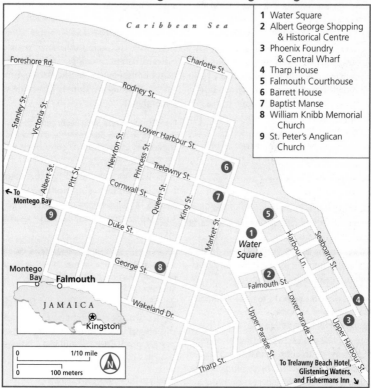

1 Water Square
2 Albert George Shopping & Historical Centre
3 Phoenix Foundry & Central Wharf
4 Tharp House
5 Falmouth Courthouse
6 Barrett House
7 Baptist Manse
8 William Knibb Memorial Church
9 St. Peter's Anglican Church

Caribbean Sea

Foreshore Rd.
Charlotte St.
Rodney St.
Stanley St.
Victoria St.
Lower Harbour St.
Newton St.
Princess St.
Trelawny St.
Albert St.
Pitt St.
Cornwall St.
Queen St.
King St.
← To Montego Bay
Duke St.
Market St.
Water Square
Harbour Ln.
Seaboard St.
Montego Bay
Falmouth
George St.
Falmouth St.
Upper Parade St.
Lower Parade St.
Upper Harbour St.
JAMAICA
Kingston
Wakeland Dr.

0 — 1/10 mile
0 — 100 meters

Tharp St.
To Trelawny Beach Hotel, Glistening Waters, and Fishermans Inn ↘

The port town of **Falmouth** lies on the north coast of Jamaica, 37km (23 miles) east of Montego Bay. It makes for an interesting morning or afternoon tour. Laid out in 1790, Falmouth is the best-preserved Georgian town on the island, although it is ramshackle. Talks of restoration are just hot air at this point, and it's hard to imagine that such a sleepy town was once the busiest port in Jamaica (most of its port business shifted east to the larger harbor at Kingston long ago). Don't be surprised to share the streets today with wandering donkeys and goats.

Leave your car at Water Square; you can explore the town on foot in about an hour.

The best place to begin your walk is:
❶ Water Square
The town's center, this is a large, spacious plaza at the east end of Falmouth. It was named for a large old circular stone-built reservoir erected in 1798 to store water from the Martha Brae River.

Facing Water Square is:
❷ Albert George Shopping & Historical Centre
This is still a market, rather claptrap but thriving, with little handicrafts stores. It was constructed in 1895.

From here, walk 1 block east toward the water to see:

❸ Phoenix Foundry & Central Wharf

At the corner of Lower Harbour and Thorpe streets, the foundry dates from 1810. In its heyday it manufactured iron bedsteads for the British army. In back is a sad reminder of Falmouth's past, the Central Wharf, where slaves were brought ashore to be auctioned off to plantation owners.

To the immediate west of the foundry stands:

❹ Tharp House

Near the junction of Thorpe and Seaboard streets, this was the in-town residence of John Tharp, notorious as the largest slave owner on the island. Today it's still disliked by locals, but for a different reason: It shelters the Falmouth tax office.

After viewing the property, continue northwest along Seaboard Street to:

❺ Falmouth Courthouse

This is the grandest building in town, a Georgian courthouse constructed in the Palladian style with Doric columns. The courthouse is guarded by cannons on each side. Originally the courthouse dated from 1815, but a fire swept through it in 1926. The present building is a reconstruction.

From the courthouse, head northwest along Seaboard Street until you come to Market

Street, cutting right at this point and heading in the direction of the sea. You'll come to:

❻ Barrett House

This was the Falmouth townhouse of Edward Barrett, a rich planter, and one of many houses owned by the Barrett family (of which Elizabeth Barrett Browning was a member).

From Barrett House, walk south again as if returning to Water Square. At the intersection of Market and Cornwall streets, you come to the:

❼ Baptist Manse

This was once the abode of the island's most passionate abolitionist, William Knibb, a Baptist preacher who angered sugar planters with his fiery speeches attacking slavery.

After seeing the manse, continue down Market Street until you come to Duke Street, at which point you head west. After 1 block, turn left on King Street to see:

❽ William Knibb Memorial Church

At the corner of George and Duke streets, this chapel was rebuilt following its burning by the British during the Christmas Rebellion of 1831.

Return to Duke Street and continue 4 blocks west to:

❾ St. Peter's Anglican Church

Built in 1795 and enlarged in 1842, this is the oldest extant building in Falmouth and the second oldest church on the island. Visit its interior to see its stained-glass windows.

WHERE TO STAY

Fisherman's Inn Dive Resort (Rose's by the Sea)   Set on the coastal road just outside the commercial center of Falmouth, immediately adjacent to the also-recommended Glistening Waters, this is a well-designed roadside inn that might remind you of a pub-hotel in Britain. Much attention is devoted to the woodsy-looking restaurant, where main courses at lunch cost from $5 to $20 and dinners range from $13 to $40; menu items include filet mignon, stir-fried beef with soy and oriental herbs, and chicken breast stuffed with cheese and chopped callaloo. Despite its appeal as a restaurant, there's an interesting hotel configuration here as well: It includes a swimming pool set in a concrete wharf jutting into the waters of the phosphorescent bay, a gazebo-style pool bar, and a walkway and wooden pier accessing the bedrooms—which are built on pilings above the sea. Each of these has a private veranda or patio, white tile floors, white-painted furniture, and a sense of low-key coziness that only a

---

Moments **Market Day**

On Wednesday morning from 8am to noon, Falmouth hosts the biggest flea market in the country, with hundreds of booths linking the marketplace and overflowing into the streets. Take time out to buy a loaf of bammy (cassava bread) and pick up the makings of a picnic.

---

small, intimately organized hotel can convey. All the units come with small private bathrooms with shower.

Rock Falmouth, Trelawny. © 876/954-4078. 10 units. Year-round $120–$125 double. AE, MC, V. **Amenities:** Restaurant; bar; pool; 24-hr. room service; babysitting; nonsmoking rooms; rooms for those w/limited mobility. *In room:* A/C, TV, iron, safe.

WHERE TO DINE

Glistening Waters Restaurant and Marina *Finds* SEAFOOD   Residents of Montego Bay often make the 45km (28-mile) drive out here along the A1 just to sample the ambience of old Jamaica. This well-recommended restaurant and sports bar, with a veranda overlooking the lagoon, is housed in what was originally a private clubhouse for the aristocrats of nearby Trelawny. (The furniture here may remind you of a stage set for *Night of the Iguana*.) Menu items usually include local fish dishes, such as snapper or kingfish. Other specialties include three different lobster dishes, three different preparations of shrimp, three different conch viands, fried rice, and pork chops. The food is just what your mama would make—if she came from Jamaica. And the waters of the lagoon contain a rare form of phosphorescent microbe which, when the waters are agitated, glows in the dark. Ask about evening booze cruises, which cost $15 per person, including one drink, where you can observe this phenomenon. Departures are nightly at about 7pm.

Rock Falmouth, Trelawny (between Falmouth and the Trelawny Beach Hotel). © **888/991-9901** toll-free in Jamaica, or 876/954-3229. Main courses $9–$34. AE, MC, V. Daily 10am–9:30pm.

9 Interior St. James Parish

Most visitors, including many who have visited Montego Bay multiple times, never leave the coastline. Yet you can take an interesting self-guided driving tour deep into the lush interior of St. James Parish. This tour touches only on destinations nearer to Montego Bay.

At the village of **Reading,** west of Montego Bay, take Route B8 (it's signposted) into the tropical interior. The elevation rises as you drive along the aptly named **Long Hill,** which runs parallel to the Great River Valley. From below you can see tropical palms and ferns.

Six kilometers (3¾ miles) south of Reading, you come to the village of:

LETHE   This is a base for rafting the Great River. Before driving from Montego Bay, arrange rafting trips in advance. **Mountain Valley Rafting,** Lethe Hanover (© **876/956-4920**), offers excursions on the Great River that depart from the Lethe Estate, 16km (10 miles) south of Montego Bay. Rafts cost $40 for up to two people. Trips last 45 minutes and operate daily from 8am to 5pm. The rafts are composed of bamboo trunks with a raised dais to sit on. In some cases, a small child can accompany two adults on the same raft, although due caution should be exercised if you choose to do this. Ask about pickup by taxi at the end of the rafting run. For $55 per person, a half-day experience includes transportation to and from your hotel, an hour's rafting, lunch, a garden tour of the Lethe property, and a taste of Jamaican liqueur.

The Northwest Coast

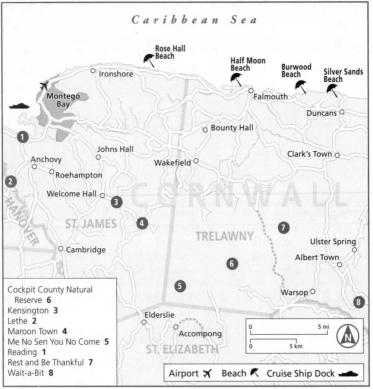

Cockpit County Natural
  Reserve **6**
Kensington **3**
Lethe **2**
Maroon Town **4**
Me No Sen You No Come **5**
Reading **1**
Rest and Be Thankful **7**
Wait-a-Bit **8**

Airport ✈   Beach ⚓   Cruise Ship Dock ⛴

Also at Lethe you'll find one of the most graceful **stone bridges** ☆ in Jamaica, spanning the Great River and dating from 1828. Who built this bridge of heavy stones? Slave labor, of course. The decaying ruins of a former sugar mill standing forlornly on the riverbank will make you reach for your camera. It's one of the most evocative sights in St. James of a long-gone plantation era.

Nearby lies another attraction:

ROCKLANDS WILDLIFE STATION   For more information, including times to visit, refer to the box, "Meeting Some Feathered Friends," earlier in this chapter. To reach this site, you must turn off the B8 some 183m (600 ft.) south of the signposted turnoff to Lethe. A steep dirt road leads up to Rocklands, which is one of the most favored spots in all the West Indies for birders, who have been flocking here since a feeding station opened in 1958. The area abounds in bird life, including the hummingbird, orange quit, ground dove, and saffron finch. You also might see the national bird of Jamaica, the streamer-tailed doctor bird.

10 The Maroon Country

A strange, eerie part of Jamaica lies in the hills southeast of Montego Bay. Few visitors from abroad venture here. The landscape begins 2km (1¼ miles) south of Montego Bay along Fairfield Road (which is not in the best of shape).

BACK-ROADING SOUTHEAST OF MONTEGO BAY

If you follow bumpy Fairfield Road, you will eventually reach Maroon Town, lying on the periphery of the rugged and bleak **Cockpit Country** (see below).

The first hamlet of historical interest is:

KENSINGTON A tiny town some 21km (13 miles) south of Mo Bay, Kensington doesn't offer much to see today. But history buffs will be interested to know that in this remote outpost the famous slave uprising of 1831 was launched, bringing on the Christmas Rebellion that eventually led to the emancipation of slaves in the British colonies. A ridge-top plantation was set afire, and the rebellion broke out of control before the slaves were eventually subdued.

The only sign of this rebellion today is a plaque along the road, placed here by the Jamaican National Heritage Trust to commemorate the moment.

Continue 5km (3 miles) southeast to:

MAROON TOWN This town was settled by the remnants of the Trelawny Town Maroons. A Jamaican colonel, John Guthrie, signed a peace treaty here with the Maroons in 1745, though it only lasted until 1795.

11 The Cockpit Country

The foreboding landscape of the Cockpit Country is one of the most desolate and eerie territories in all the West Indies. For those who'd like to combine some adventure into that holiday by the beach, a tour through this rugged terrain is recommended— if you're in good shape, that is.

The forest-clad limestone hills of the Cockpit Country are shaped like witches' hats. This is wild "karst" terrain, of the type also found in Puerto Rico. The land is filled with weathered limestone covering 1,295 sq. km (500 sq. miles). Much of the Cockpit Country remains uninhabited and, even today, still hasn't been explored in depth.

Conical hillocks were dissolved by an elaborate drainage system of caves and sinkholes. No other region of the Caribbean has such intriguingly named settlements: Wait-a-Bit, Rest and Be Thankful, and Me No Sen You No Come.

Jamaica at present classifies the Cockpit Country as a **National Reserve,** although there is a movement afoot to have it declared a national park. Because the Maroons function almost independently of the Jamaican government, they are fiercely opposed to national park status, fearing it would intrude upon their independence.

Warning: Trails here are overgrown, so guides are imperative. No foreigner should attempt this exploration without skilled guidance. Sinkholes appear suddenly and without warning, and hikers who fall into them can be seriously injured or killed. The land is also a mosquito breeding factory. These pests are hungry for blood—*yours*—so be prepared. You should also take plenty of water and adequate provisions.

The company we recommend most for guided tours is **Cockpit Country Adventure Tours** ✆ (© **876/610-0818;** www.stea.net). Guides are experienced and were trained by the U.S. Peace Corps. The easiest tour is called "Burnt Hill Nature Walk," costing $55 per person. The second tour, "Rock Spring Cave and River Adventure," is a medium adventure including some visits to caves. The cost here is $65 per person. The most difficult jaunt is the "Quashie River Sink Cave Exploration," costing $70 per person, and going into the difficult territory of the Quashie River, as well as exploring the 4km (2½-mile) Quashie Cave, known for its "cathedral room" and its underground waterfall.

In all cases, it is necessary to hire two guides for each trip, even if only one person goes along. So it's recommended that you go with other people.

Negril

On the arid western tip of Jamaica, **Negril** has had a reputation for bacchanalia, hedonism, marijuana, and nude sunbathing since hippies discovered its sunny shores during the 1960s. The resort became more mainstream during the early 1990s as big-money capitalists built megaresorts, many of them managed by SuperClubs, Sandals, Couples, or the relative newcomers, the Spain-based Riu chain. But despite the creeping sense of corporate encroachment on a domain once dominated by laid-back hippies, some resorts still reserve stretches of beach for nude bathers, and illegal ganja is still (more or less discreetly) peddled.

Clothed or unclothed, visitors are drawn to the white sands of Seven Mile Beach and some of the best snorkeling and scuba diving in Jamaica. Opening onto a tranquil lagoon protected by a coral reef, the beach here is set against a backdrop of sea grapes and coconut palms. Resorts, in synch with local building codes that forbid the construction of buildings that rise above the canopy of trees, are invariably low-rise designs that blend more or less gracefully into the flat, sandy landscape.

There are really two Negrils. The relatively earthy and funky West End is the site of modest cottages, boutique-style hotels and guesthouses, and local restaurants loaded with Jamaican spirit. The more formal and more upmarket Negril is on the East End, set on either side of the highway leading into town from the east (from Montego Bay). The best and most substantial resorts line this panoramic beachfront. The town center itself offers bucketfuls of Jamaican zest and color, but little of formalized interest.

WHICH ONE'S FOR YOU: NEGRIL OR MO BAY?

Throughout the 1940s and 1950s, when Montego Bay was a magnet for some of the richest and best-known celebrities in the world, Negril was little more than a fishing village. Throughout the 1960s and '70s, it became well known as a destination for hippies who appreciated the cheap and readily available ganja and the laid-back lifestyle. But beginning in the early 1980s, Negril has redefined itself as a serious tourist competitor to Montego Bay. But despite the fact that Negril is catching up in the tourism game, the two resorts remain markedly different in their flavor and in what they have to offer: And despite some new first-class hotels that have opened, Negril is not in the same league as Montego Bay when it comes to famous, posh, or legendary hotels.

For the serious golfer, Mo Bay is also the better choice, with several of the finest courses in the Caribbean. And for those who view sightseeing as part of their holiday, Montego Bay offers the most diversified attractions in Jamaica. In marked contrast, Negril, other than its beaches, is not blessed with great sights.

What, then, does Negril offer? There is no more laid-back place in the Caribbean for sunning by day and "sinning" after dark. For those who want to hang out—*literally*—Negril has the only officially sanctioned nude beach in all Jamaica. Negril is a sensual, fun-loving Eden where you can find shelter in everything from a Rastafarian hut to an overcrowded Jacuzzi where fellow guests may be naked. And if you hate fancy French restaurants, but enjoy hallucinogenic brownies and 11km-long (6¾-mile) beaches, then Negril is the place for you.

Ironically, despite a well-deserved reputation for libertine behavior among otherwise conservative adults, for some reason, Negril has become increasingly popular in recent years as a destination for families with young children.

One caution: Though the temptation to take a moonlit walk on an isolated stretch of Negril's legendary beach is powerful, resist strolling along its most isolated sections. It's possible you could be mugged at night, or worse.

1 Orientation

ARRIVING BY PLANE

If you're coming from abroad, leaving such cities as Miami or New York, try to fly into the **Donald Sangster International Airport** in Montego Bay. See "Orientation" in chapter 4 for more details.

From the airport at Montego Bay, it is an 81km (50-mile) drive southwest to Negril, a trip that usually takes 2 hours but could take more or less, depending on traffic conditions. The road winds scenically past ruins of sugar estates and great houses.

It is unwise to fly into Kingston if your destination is Negril. Kingston is 242km (150 miles) to the east and at least a 4-hour drive, maybe more.

GETTING FROM THE AIRPORT TO NEGRIL

If you've booked into one of the all-inclusives such as Sandals, a hotel van will carry you from the airport at Mo Bay into Negril. Arrangements for your arrival and pickup are made in advance, at the time of booking, and most of the large all-inclusive resorts clearly signpost their respective rendezvous points within the Montego Bay airport.

If you don't have a transfer to your hotel arranged, we do not recommend the public bus between Montego Bay and Negril, even though it's a cheap, one-way ride priced at about $4 per passenger. The crowded minibus is uncomfortable, there isn't room for much luggage, and vendors of souvenirs have been known to prey upon the tourists.

It's better to take a private minivan. We've found the most reliable to be **Tourwise** (© 876/952-4943), charging $21 one-way. This van will drop you right at your final destination in Negril. If you don't see a Tourwise minivan waiting at the Mo Bay airport, call © 876/974-2323.

Another option is to go from Sangster Airport to Negril by taxi, though this is a pricey choice. The one-way fare ranges from $60 to $80; always negotiate it *before* getting into the car with your things.

Still another option is renting a car. For information on car rentals, see "Getting Around" in chapter 2. From the airport in Montego Bay, you drive west along the A1 for about 90 minutes to reach Negril.

En route, the only town of any size you'll pass through is **Lucea,** built around a harbor at a point 40km (25 miles) east of Negril. If you're driving, it hardly merits a stopover, although in British colonial days it was more important than Mo Bay.

Locals call it "Lucy." If you visit at all, the best time to stop is on Saturday morning when the market around the harbor is both active and colorful, from about 7am to noon. Otherwise, we'd suggest you drive on, heading straight for the more glamorous retreats of Negril.

Finally, if you're really in a hurry, Negril has a small airport for short-hop domestic flights. **International Air Link** (© **888/AIR-LINK** or 876/940-6660; www.intl airlink.com) flies the Kingston-to-Negril run as a direct charter. The airfare for these scheduled charter flights—three passengers or more—can range from as low as $60 to as high as $95 per person, depending on the flight.

These shuttle flights land at the **Negril Aerodrome** at Bloody Bay, 11km (6¾ miles) north of Negril's central hotel belt. There's no scheduled bus service from the airstrip to Negril Village, but taxis are plentiful: Though the fare is to be negotiated with a driver, count on spending at least $8 for the short ride.

VISITOR INFORMATION

Regrettably and to the surprise of many visitors, the **Jamaica Tourist Board** has shut down its offices in Negril. Seekers of information are referred to the office in Montego Bay, which is hardly a practical solution for most visitors. See "Orientation" in chapter 4 for contact information.

ORIENTING YOURSELF IN NEGRIL

Of all the resorts of Jamaica, Negril offers the simplest geography. Many visitors view Negril as one long street.

The South Negril River divides the resort in two, with Long Bay and its beaches lying north of the river and West End lying to the south of it.

Set inland from the beach about 91 to 137m (300–450 ft.), **Norman Manley Boulevard** begins near the Norman Manley Sea Park, close to the point where the South Negril River empties into Long Bay. This two-lane highway, flanked by hotels and restaurants, continues north to Long Bay Beach Park and eventually the airport.

Negril Village (the heart of Negril) consists mainly of two unimpressive shopping plazas, a bank or two, some tacky stores, and some housing developments in a distant section known as "Red Ground." (Most of Negril's local population lives here.)

The two main squares, **Negril Plaza** and **Coral Seas Plaza,** lie south of the traffic circle fronting **Negril Square.** At the parking lot here, you can hail a taxi to take you where you want to go. This sector marks the beginning of **Sheffield Road,** the main highway leading out of town to the city of Savanna-la-Mar. Here you'll find the most convenient gas station in Negril, along with a health clinic and the police station.

South of the South Negril River is a rock-studded limestone plateau. When American hippies arrived back in the 1960s, they settled here, calling the place **"the Rock."** Hotels here are intimate, attracting an independent backpacker clientele.

Eventually, West End Road leads to the **West End** and becomes Lighthouse Road as it winds its way to **Negril Lighthouse** ⊛, some 5km (3 miles) south of Sunshine Village at Negril Village. The lighthouse stands 30m (100 ft.) above the sea at the westernmost tip of Jamaica. The West End is the only sector that evokes the Negril of old, though it becomes increasingly congested and developed with each passing year. As you travel beyond the lighthouse, you'll find a few places to escape the madding beach crowds.

GETTING AROUND NEGRIL

Negril is very spread out, stretching for miles. Some visitors walk where they want to go, but it's a long hike if you're heading to the northern edge of Long Bay or to the West End—some of these places may be 11 to 16km (6¾–10 miles) from your hotel. Also, walking along the roads of Negril after dark isn't recommended because of potential muggers and because of the dangers from fast-moving cars on the narrow roads of the town's West End.

So you'll need transit. The upscale resorts, including the all-inclusives, operate shuttles from the northern tip of Long Bay into Negril Village. Because the West End's hotels aren't on the beach, the more prosperous ones also operate shuttles to the beach; small inns don't.

Otherwise, you can do as the locals do and take the minibus that runs all day long up and down Norman Manley Boulevard and even into the West End. Most rides cost $2; the bus runs until early evening, sometimes later.

In lieu of the uncomfortable minivan, you might hail a taxi. Cabbies operate all over Negril, the licensed ones displaying a red medallion. In theory, fees are regulated by the government, but in years of going to Negril, we've never encountered a meter that wasn't broken.

So negotiate your fare before getting into the cab. Most trips should cost from $4 to $5, depending on where you're going. If a cabbie demands $20, look for another taxi. Taxis are most plentiful at Coral Seas Plaza and the Negril Crafts Market. Your hotel will often call a cab for you; if they won't, phone the JUTA (© **876/957-9197**) cab association for one.

You can also get around Negril by bike. Bicycles are available at most resort properties.

Instead of peddling up and down Seven Mile Beach or across the rocky cliffs of the West End, many visitors prefer to rent a motor scooter. The best supplier of those is the aptly named **Dependable Bike Rental,** at Vernon's Car Rental, Plaza de Negril (© **876/957-4354** or 876/957-3585). This outfitter doesn't rent bicycles, only motor scooters costing from $25 to $30 per day plus a $250 deposit taken on your credit card. Jeeps can be rented here, as well: A Suzuki convertible jeep begins at $50 a day.

Unlike in the U.S., helmets are not mandatory in Jamaica, but you should wear one for your own safety: Roads are potholed and often dangerous, with patches of sand and gravel making it easy to skid out of control. Helmets are included in the rental fee.

If you'd like to escape the traffic and the crowds along Norman Manley Boulevard, the best place to go biking, in our view, is into the **Negril Hills,** which lie beyond the Negril Lighthouse along West End Road (see above). A bike tour here can be in relative isolation as you pass along the most often deserted beaches of greater Negril and even past some landing strips where private planes depart with illegal cargoes of marijuana for the mainland United States.

FAST FACTS: Negril

Airport For information about domestic short-hop flights, call the Negril Aerodrome at © **876/957-5016.**

Banks The best, most central bank is **Scotiabank,** Plaza de Negril (© **876/957-4236**), open Monday, Thursday, and Friday 8:15am to 4pm, and Tuesday and Wednesday 8:15am to 3pm. Its ATMs are open 24 hours.

Emergencies For emergencies, dial © **119**. The Negril Police Headquarters (© **876/957-4268**) lie some 183m (600 ft.) east of the Shell gas station on Sheffield Road. For an ambulance or to report a fire, dial © **110**.

Internet Access The best place to go, outside your hotel, is the **Coral Seas Beach Hotel,** Norman Manley Boulevard (© **876/957-3997**), open daily 9am to 5pm. Nonguests are permitted to use the facilities.

Library The small **Negril Library,** West End Road (© **876/957-4917**), is open Monday to Thursday 10am to 6pm, Friday 10am to 5pm, Saturday 10am to 3pm.

Mail Include "Jamaica, W.I." in all island addresses. At press time for this edition, the island had no zip codes, despite efforts that had been made throughout 2005 to inaugurate them within the Jamaican postal system.

Medical Services For a non-life-threatening emergency, there are several choices. The **Negril Beach Medical Centre,** Norman Manley Boulevard (© **876/957-4888**), is open daily from 9am to 5pm. And the **Negril Health Centre** sits on Sheffield Road (© **876/957-4926**) between the police station and the Shell gas station. Each charges about J$100 (US$1.60) to see a doctor.

Post Office & Mail The **Negril Post Office** (© **876/957-9654**) is located on West End Road next to the Craft Market. It is open Monday to Friday 8am to 5pm. Expect long lines. Instead of the overcrowded post office, we use the **Airpak Express** (© **876/957-5051**) at the Negril Aerodrome, 11km (6¾ miles) outside town. UPS packages arrive here, and letters can be mailed internationally.

Pharmacy The best outlet is the **Negril Pharmacy,** shop no. 14 in the Coral Seas Plaza (© **876/957-4076**), open Monday to Saturday 9am to 7pm, Sunday 10am to 4pm.

Safety The all-inclusives and the first-class resorts have 24-hour security guards. The lower-rent properties rarely do, and theft—including night burglary—is distressingly commonplace in these places. Try to secure your room at night, and don't leave windows open no matter how tempting cooling trade winds are.

Tourists are rarely robbed at gunpoint, but muggings and pickpocketing are occasionally reported. Guard your valuables, and take all the usual precautions while traveling in Negril. Be extremely careful, especially at night, about opening your door to strangers—even those who claim to be members of the hotel staff.

Also be careful of the drivers who race around Negril in battered cars. Some Jamaican males think they are "king of the road," and it is a fool who doesn't get out of their way. Regrettably, the same sense of machismo also afflicts some of the town's cabbies. You may need to warn your driver that you prefer to take a few minutes longer on your ride.

Telephone Resort hotels often add ridiculous surcharges to overseas calls. To beat this game, head for **Negril Calling Service,** shop no. 19, Plaza de Negril (© **876/957-3212**), open 9am to 7:30pm daily.

Travel Agents If you need to make travel arrangements once you've landed here, the most reliable agency is **Caribic Vacations,** Norman Manley Boulevard (© **876/957-3309**).

2 Where to Stay

The choice and variety of lodgings in Negril are a bit bewildering, from funky and rustic to first-class and opulent; no place in the West Indies offers more bizarre accommodations than Negril. You can stay in a deluxe four-poster bed that was recently warmed before you by a departing Jimmy Buffett; a guesthouse where Bob Marley and a girlfriend used to hang out; or the B&B of an eccentric lady from England who will serve you a proper "cuppa" on her Wedgwood tea set. It's all up to you.

Most visitors want a hotel or resort along **Seven Mile Beach** opening onto Long Bay. Here are all the famous (or infamous) all-inclusive resorts that have secured the best beachfront property, leaving the lesser resorts to fight for their own places in the sun. Many had to build across the main street as a result—something to consider.

For the escapist, the **West End's** inns and small B&B-type places are the places to go, although these properties open onto rocky cliffs instead of a beach. Nevertheless, they are much preferred by independent types and are certainly more adventurous. (Note that some of these cliff-side resorts will not allow families with children under 8 to check in, for fear they might fall from the cliffs; most of the paths don't have protective rails.) West End cottages and huts are far cheaper than the resorts on Long Bay. Regrettably, they are also easy for night burglars to penetrate. (See "Safety" in "Fast Facts: Negril," above.)

If you're seeking really rock-bottom bargains in simple rustic huts that are almost camplike, try to book one of the dozen units offered by **Da Gino's,** an Italian restaurant (p. 128). Other dining spots that rent cheap rooms include **LTU Pub** (p. 129) and **Kuyaba on the Beach** (p. 128).

Note: Negril's all-inclusive resorts, most of which would fall into our "Very Expensive" or "Expensive" categories, are treated separately beginning on p. 118.

EXPENSIVE

Sea Splash Resort ✦   Partly because of its small size, this beachfront resort, originally built in 1990, has a friendly, personable feeling and none of the snobbishness exhibited by the staff of The Caves (p. 119). Much more intimate than the megaresorts nearby, and evoking a small-scale condominium complex in Florida, it lies on a small but carefully landscaped sliver of beachfront land planted with tropical vegetation that includes lavish displays of arbor-hugging blue-flowered vines known as thumburgia. Suites are spacious, comfortable, and stylishly decorated. All are the same size and contain the same amenities—a kitchenette, a balcony or patio, large closets, and either a king-size bed or twin beds—although the suites on the upper floor have higher ceilings and feel more spacious than the others. Living areas contain sofa beds, ideal for small families. The bathrooms come with showers but not bathtubs. The in-house restaurant, Norma's, is recommended separately (p. 125). Incidentally, Hugh Wint, the cosmopolitan and charming Jamaica-born manager of this place, used to work at the much more upscale Round Hill, and is locally famous for having once been forced to tell Princess Diana that Round Hill was fully booked and that she'd have to change the dates of her arrival there.

Norman Manley Blvd. (P.O. Box 3123), Negril. ℭ **888/790-5264** or 876/957-4041. Fax 876/957-4049. www. seasplash.com. 20 units. Winter $145 double; $181–$243 suite for 2; off season $97 double, $120–$165 suite for 2. Extra person $25. AE, DC, DISC, MC, V. **Amenities:** Restaurant; bar; pool; Jacuzzi; limited room service; babysitting; laundry service; rooms for those w/limited mobility. *In room:* A/C, TV, kitchenette (in suites only), coffeemaker, hair dryer, safe.

MODERATE

Charela Inn ⚜   Simplicity, a sense of calm, a well-managed restaurant, and good value for the money are the hallmarks of this seafront inn whose sprawling, low-slung design is reminiscent of a Spanish hacienda. This place sits on the main beach strip on 1 hectare (3 acres) of landscaped grounds. The building's inner courtyard, with a tropical garden and a round, not-particularly large freshwater pool, opens onto one of the widest (75m/250 ft.) sandy beaches in Negril. Try for 1 of the 20 or so rooms with a view of the sea. Accommodations are generally spacious, often with hints of Jamaican character in their wicker or Jamaica-made mahogany furnishings and ceiling fans. A few of the rooms have mahogany planks covering the ceilings. Each has a private patio or balcony. Most of the efficiently outfitted bathrooms have shower/tub combinations, but some have showers only.

Le Vendôme (p. 125), facing the sea and the garden, offers a sophisticated combination of upscale French and low-down Jamaican cuisine. Several times a week during high season, the hotel offers some kind of live entertainment.

Norman Manley Blvd. (P.O. Box 33), Negril. ✆ 876/957-4648. Fax 876/957-4414. www.charela.com. 49 units. Winter $166–$221 double; off season $114–$155 double. MAP (breakfast and dinner) $40 per person extra. 5-night minimum stay required in winter. AE, MC, V. **Amenities:** Restaurant; bar; pool; 24-hour room service; laundry service; nonsmoking rooms; rooms for those w/limited mobility. *In room:* A/C, TV, dataport, beverage maker (in some units), hair dryer, safe.

Crystal Waters *Kids*   This is an excellent choice for families with young children. Unlike other resorts, the housekeeper assigned to you here is like a personal maid who takes over all the cooking and babysitting. The place is a long-established old-timer and much respected locally for simple accommodations at reasonable prices. The accommodations are tropically decorated, furnished with a mixture of hardwoods and wicker, plus a small bathroom with shower. The villas include ceiling fans (plus air-conditioning) and full kitchens. There's also a freshwater pool.

Norman Manley Blvd. (P.O. Box 3018), Negril Beach, Negril. ✆ **876/957-4284.** Fax 876/957-4889. www.crystal waters.net. 10 villas. Winter $150–$165 1-bedroom villa; $260–$300 2-bedroom villa, $430 3-bedroom villa; off season $115–$130 1-bedroom villa, $180–$220 2-bedroom villa, $305 3-bedroom villa. Maximum of 2 people per bedroom. MC, V. Closed in Sept. **Amenities:** 2 pools; Jacuzzi; watersports; children's pool and playground equipment; activities desk; 24-hr. room service; in-room massage; babysitting; laundry service. *In room:* A/C, TV, dataport, kitchen, fridge, coffeemaker, hair dryer, iron, safe, cellphone, microwave.

Idle Awhile Resort ⚜ *Finds*   One of Negril's newest resorts is also among its most intimate and personal. Right on a choice spot on Seven Mile Beach, the inn offers deluxe bedrooms with king-size beds and large verandas, and eight junior suites, each with a kitchenette and enclosed patio. There are also larger suites available with more living area and a more spacious veranda. Catering to families, singles, or couples, the resort offers guest privileges at the large sports complex at the nearby Couples Swept Away (p. 120). Bedrooms are nestled in tropical gardens. On a luxury-living note, if you book a one-bedroom suite, you can hire a cook for another $15 per day, plus groceries. The chef will go grocery shopping for you and prepare you regional Jamaican dishes.

Norman Manley Blvd., Negril. ✆ **877/243-5352** or 876/957-3303. Fax 876/957-9567. www.idleawhile.com. 13 units. Winter $170–$180 double, $220 junior suite, $290 1-bedroom suite; off season $115–$130 double, $170 junior suite, $180–$200 1-bedroom suite. AE, MC, V. **Amenities:** Restaurant; bar; limited room service; babysitting; laundry service/dry cleaning. *In room:* A/C, TV, dataport, kitchenette (in some rooms), minibar, safe.

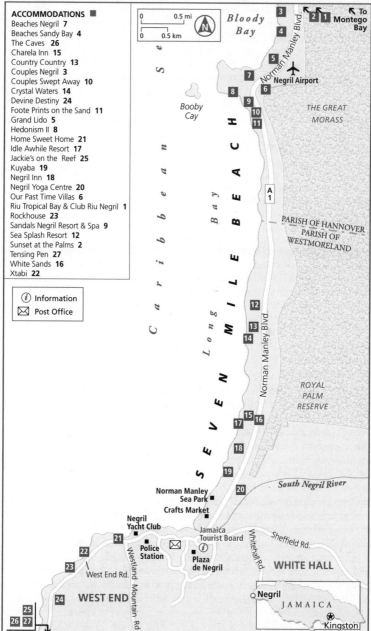

ACCOMMODATIONS ■
Beaches Negril **7**
Beaches Sandy Bay **4**
The Caves **26**
Charela Inn **15**
Country Country **13**
Couples Negril **3**
Couples Swept Away **10**
Crystal Waters **14**
Devine Destiny **24**
Foote Prints on the Sand **11**
Grand Lido **5**
Hedonism II **8**
Home Sweet Home **21**
Idle Awhile Resort **17**
Jackie's on the Reef **25**
Kuyaba **19**
Negril Inn **18**
Negril Yoga Centre **20**
Our Past Time Villas **6**
Riu Tropical Bay & Club Riu Negril **1**
Rockhouse **23**
Sandals Negril Resort & Spa **9**
Sea Splash Resort **12**
Sunset at the Palms **2**
Tensing Pen **27**
White Sands **16**
Xtabi **22**

(i) Information
⊠ Post Office

Bloody Bay
To Montego Bay
Negril Airport
Booby Cay
THE GREAT MORASS
Norman Manley Blvd.
A 1
PARISH OF HANNOVER
PARISH OF WESTMORELAND
Caribbean Sea
Long Bay
SEVEN MILE BEACH
Norman Manley Blvd.
ROYAL PALM RESERVE
South Negril River
Norman Manley Sea Park
Crafts Market
Negril Yacht Club
Jamaica Tourist Board
Police Station
Plaza de Negril
Whitehall Rd.
Sheffield Rd.
WHITE HALL
Westland Mountain Rd.
West End Rd.
WEST END
Negril
JAMAICA
Kingston

Jackie's on the Reef *(Finds)* The setting is a soaring concrete building that looks as though it was never quite completed; the result evokes a postmodern cathedral, thanks to long corridors that spill into sunlit communal areas. In Jackie Lewis's own words, "This is a healing joint," welcoming a revolving series of practitioners imported for temporary sojourns from Manhattan. Treatments might include facials, body massages, reflexology, and more. Most bedrooms are generous in size with mosquito netting draped over beds in old plantation style; however, there are no TVs, phones, air-conditioning, or even fans, and furnishings are rather simple, with usually just twin beds and small tables in the rooms. Each comes with a shower-only bathroom. The hotel lies 11km (6¾ miles) from the nearest beach, but there's a small seawater pool and a ladder down to the reef for swimming.

West End Rd., Negril. (C) 876/957-4997 or 718/469-2785 (New York state). www.jackiesonthereef.com. 3 units, 1 cottage. Winter $150 per person; summer $125 per person. Rates include breakfast, dinner, and yoga class. No credit cards. Drive 4km (2½ miles) past the oldest lighthouse in Negril; just keep heading out the West End until you come to the sign. Children not accepted. **Amenities:** Dining room; small seawater pool; spa; snorkeling; outdoor massage; laundry service; yoga; meditation. *In room:* No phone.

Tensing Pen *(★★)* One of the most unusual and intimate inns in Negril defines itself as "a boutique collection of cottages," catering to sophisticated international (often European) clients with simple tastes from a position near the town's western edge. With strong links to Negril's past as a New Age refuge for counter-culture American and British expatriates during the '60s and '70s, it is now considerably more elegant than what it was during its earliest hippy-centered origins. During the hurricanes of 2005, the inn suffered major damage to parts of its cliff-bordering premises, but immediately activated major architectural changes to its cottages that have changed the look and feel of the place forever. Sea-fronting cottages, which had previously been raised high above the ground, South Seas style, on massive timbers, are now supported by massive masonry piers that are bigger than any equivalent foundations in Negril, adding a space-age, high-tech look that's oddly incongruous within a venue that's otherwise small-scale, low-tech, eco-friendly, and charming. The entire compound is positioned at the top of a vertiginous cliff, a 10-minute stroll from Negril's landmark lighthouse, about 6km (3¾ miles) south of the center of town. Hidden away from the world, the place is a little gem. On ¾ of a hectare (2 acres) of grounds, you're surrounded by tropical planting. Laze in the hammocks or sunbathe on the terraces hewn out of rock. Accommodations usually contain a four-poster bed—crafted either from bamboo or from Jamaican mahogany—draped in mosquito netting, plantation house–style. Handmade tiles, tropical woods, bamboo rockers, ceiling fans, and louvered windows set the tone. No room contains a TV—a deliberate omission that's favored by a clientele who appreciate an escape from media in general. Bathrooms with shower/tub combinations are a bit cramped.

The resort contains the scariest-looking bridge in Negril. Fashioned from timber and planking, and without a handrail, it stretches over the water between two rocky headlands, allowing, if you dare, deepwater plunges into the watery depths—at your own risk, of course. The nearest beach is a 10- to 15-minute drive or a 30-minute walk away, but many of the clients of this place swim locally, off the rocks.

One of the most appealing aspects of the place involves its restaurant. Open only to residents and their invited guests, it occupies a long, low, communal building whose design (and the way its beams have been lashed together with a combination of hempen twine and nails) was imported directly from central Africa. English-born

Richard Murray is the elegant, eco-sensitive host whose stories about the early days of Negril could fill a small, gossipy book.

Everyone who checks in here, we've been told, asks about the origin of the hotel's name. Tensing Norgay was the Sherpa tribesman who guided Sir Edmund Hilary in his historic ascent of Mount Everest. The Murray family's pet dog was a Lhasa Apso named Tensing in honor of that guide. Since the dog came to view the entire hotel compound as his exclusive fiefdom, the hotel's name was changed to Tensing Pen, with Pen referring to a fenced-in area for restraining animals.

Lighthouse Rd. (P.O. Box 3013), Negril. © 876/957-0387. Fax 876/957-0161. www.tensingpen.com. 15 units. Winter $175–$554 double; off season $103–$396 double. Rates include breakfast. AE, MC, V. **Amenities:** Restaurant; bar; babysitting; laundry service; rooms for those w/limited mobility. *In room:* A/C (in some), ceiling fan, fridge, no phone.

INEXPENSIVE

Country Country ✫   The owners of this intimate hotel were determined to outclass their competitors, so they turned to celebrity decorator Ann Hodges, the creative force behind the gorgeous decor in many of the much more expensive Island Outpost properties. A narrow meandering path stretches from the coastal boulevard to the white-sand beach, where watersports await. Along the way is a collection of neo-Creole, clapboard-sided buildings that drip with elaborate gingerbread and cove moldings, each inspired by an idealized vision of vernacular Jamaican colonial architecture. The buildings are a rainbow of peacock hues highlighting the separate architectural features of each building. Inside, concrete floors keep the spacious interiors cool. Each unit has a vaguely Victorian feel, with comfortable furnishings, plus a shower-only bathroom. There's a beachfront bar and grill offering good-tasting, moderately priced dishes. Insiders have compared this hotel to what you might expect deep within Jamaica's untrammeled south coast.

Norman Manley Blvd. (P.O. Box 39), Negril. © 888/790-5264 or 876/957-4273. Fax 876/957-4342. www.country negril.com. 17 units. Winter $160–$180 double; off season $120–$140 double. Rates include breakfast. AE, MC, V. **Amenities:** Restaurant; bar; limited room service; laundry service; nonsmoking rooms. *In room:* A/C, TV, fridge, beverage maker, hair dryer, safe.

Devine Destiny ✫ *Finds*   This is one of the best—and best-designed—resorts in the West End, utterly devoid of the funky-hippie motif that characterizes most of its competitors. Set in an isolated neighborhood 366m (1,200 ft.) from the sea and cliffs, it's a relatively large complex plunked down in the middle of a counterculture neighborhood that until quite recently shunned resorts.

The architecture might remind you of an upscale hacienda in Argentina, with sprawling wings, terra cotta, tile work, mahogany furniture, and such decorative touches as a stone column in the lobby where water drips from a fountain. More than any of its competitors, this place gives the feeling of a coherently planned resort. There's a shuttle bus to Seven Mile Beach, which beats the 2-hour walk, and an on-site restaurant serves simple fare. Many clients here come on European group tours.

Summerset Rd., West End (P.O. Box 117), Negril. © 876/957-9184. Fax 876/957-3846. www.devinedestiny.com. 43 units. Winter $69–$119 double, $169 suite; off season $49–$74 double, $119 suite. Children 11 and under stay free in parent's room. AE, MC, V. **Amenities:** Restaurant; bar; pool; Jacuzzi; pool table; shuttle bus to beach; laundry service. *In room:* A/C, TV (in some units), kitchenette, safe (available to rent).

Foote Prints on the Sands   Dane and Audrey Foote started this enterprise in the mid-1980s; it has since expanded and occupies some of the choicest beachfront along Seven Mile's sandy stretch. The rooms, four of which contain kitchenettes, are tropically outfitted with hardwood furnishings, air-conditioning, and private bathrooms with shower and tub. From the outside, they look like a futuristic and angular cluster of two-story buildings, each painted in vivid tones of beige and bright gold. The hotel restaurant serves three meals daily, specializing in Jamaican and American food. Barbecues and music liven up the place on Friday nights.

Norman Manley Blvd. (P.O. Box 100), Negril. ℂ **888/790-5264** or 876/957-4300. Fax 876/957-4301. www. footprintshotel.com. 30 units. Winter $135–$145 double, $165 double w/kitchenette; off season $85–$95 double, $115 double w/kitchenette. Extra person $30 in winter, $20 off season. AE, DISC, MC, V. **Amenities:** Restaurant; bar; limited room service; babysitting; laundry service. *In room:* A/C, TV, kitchenette (some units), coffeemaker, hair dryer, iron/board.

Home Sweet Home *(Finds)*   This is a cozy, down-home place that almost re-creates Negril's hippie heyday. You might find your groove here just as writer Terry McMillan did; she visited while doing research for her novel, *How Stella Got Her Groove Back.* "Home" is a concrete building with a garden with lots of greenery and flowering plants. When you see the bedrooms, you'll realize many visitors have slept here before you. All accommodations have ceiling fans, a radio and a cassette player, plus a balcony or veranda, but no TV or phone (only suites have a phone). Every unit is equipped with a small bathroom with shower. There's a sun deck on the cliffs, and you can swim, dive, or snorkel. A simple restaurant serves three inexpensive Jamaican meals a day.

West End Rd. (P.O. Box 3002), Negril. ℂ/fax **800/925-7418** in the U.S., or 876/957-4478. www.homesweethomeresort. com. 14 units. Winter $110–$250 double, $200 penthouse; off season $74–$180 double, $150 penthouse. Extra person $15. Children 11 and under stay free in parent's room. AE, MC, V. **Amenities:** Restaurant; bar; pool; Jacuzzi; bike rentals; 24-hr. room service; massage in room or on the cliff; babysitting; laundry service; rooms for those w/limited mobility. *In room:* A/C, kitchenette, coffeemaker, safe, no phone.

Kuyaba *(Value)*   This is one of the more appealing hotels along Negril's beach, with an artfully designed collection of bedrooms and a distinguished clientele. It occupies a long and narrow strip of sandy soil stretched between the coastal road and the beach. Accommodations are within buff-colored, Iberian-inspired, two-story buildings that contain terra-cotta floors, mahogany four-poster beds, tub/shower bathrooms, lots of mahogany louvers and trim, and rates that—considering the quality of the rooms— are a relative bargain. The suites are an especially good value. Part of the appeal of this place derives from the in-house, beachfront restaurant, Kuyaba on the Beach (p. 128). Permeated with a Polynesian whimsy, it has the most elaborately engineered setting of any restaurant on Negril's beach.

Norman Manley Blvd. (P.O. Box 2635), Negril. ℂ **876/957-4318.** Fax 876/957-9765. www.kuyaba.com. 18 units. Winter $70–$97 double, $106 suite; off season $56–$77 double, $85 suite. Extra person $12 per night. AE, MC, V. **Amenities:** Restaurant; bar. *In room:* A/C, TV (in some units), kitchenette (in some units), safe, no phone.

Negril Yoga Centre *(Finds)*   Set on 1.4 flat and verdant hectares (3½ acres) of thriving vegetation across the road from the beach, this place offers a collection of artfully mismatched accommodations that have evolved over time. It began as the original yoga school in Negril.

Three of the units lie within La Casa Blanca, a cement-sided building whose angularity evokes a work by Le Corbusier. The remaining units all lie within funky-looking wood-and-concrete cottages, each with a ceiling fan but no air-conditioning. Overall, the aura is artfully spartan and carefully synchronized with nature, permeated with a Zen-like calm. The social center is an open-aired pavilion where the owner teaches Hatha yoga for $10 per class. Meals cost from $6 to $15 and are served at 3 and 7pm, depending on which seating is available.

Norman Manley Blvd. (P.O. Box 48), Negril. ℂ/fax **876/957-4397.** www.negrilyoga.com. 12 units. Winter $35–$65 double; off season $30–$50 double. MC, V. **Amenities:** Dining room; massage; nonsmoking rooms; rooms for those w/limited mobility; yoga. *In room:* Kitchenette, fridge, no phone.

Our Past Time Villas *Value*   Picture this as a good value B&B on attractively land-scaped grounds. In a town full of all-inclusive resorts, this is an oasis of independence for the self-sufficient type of visitor who likes renting a unit with a kitchenette and preparing some meals in-house, although there's also a good alfresco restaurant on-site serving tasty Jamaican specialties. The location is choice as well, at the beginning of Seven Mile Beach. Accommodations here are fairly simple but tastefully decorated in a vaguely Caribbean motif, and each comes with a private balcony or a patio. The better units open onto views of the sea. Each rental contains a small bathroom with shower, and accommodations fall into three categories: a regular double room, a studio and kitchenette, and a two-bedroom apartment with kitchenette.

Norman Manley Blvd. (P.O. Box 45), Negril. ℂ **876/957-5503.** Fax 876/957-5422. www.ourpasttimenegril.com. 17 units. Winter $100–$120 double, $110–$130 studio, $210–$240 2-bedroom apt.; off season $50–$90 double, $70–$120 studio, $130–$200 2-bedroom apt. Additional person $20. AE, MC, V. **Amenities:** Restaurant; bar; limited room service; babysitting; laundry service. *In room:* A/C (in most units), TV, kitchenette (in some units), safe.

Rockhouse *★★*   Artful, funky, and permeated with a sense of whimsy and fun, this boutique inn stands in stark contrast to hedonistic all-inclusive resorts like Sandals, and it offers very affordable rates. Scattered along a cliff-edged stretch of coastline that took massive amounts of labor to tame, it's a cross between a South Seas island retreat and an African village, with a distinct sense of international hip and low-key media glamour. A team of enterprising young Australians restored and expanded this place, which was one of Negril's first hotels (the Rolling Stones hung out here in the 1970s). Accommodations are simple stone-and-timber cottages, scattered along a winding series of pathways atop the cliffs. Each has a ceiling fan, a queen-size four-poster bed draped in mosquito netting, an open-air shower, and a romantic emphasis on flicker-ing candles and moonlit views of the sea. Four cottages have sleeping lofts with extra queen-size beds. Less than half a kilometer (¼ mile) from the beach, Rockhouse has a ladder that extends down to a rock-edged cove where you can swim and snorkel. The in-house Rockhouse Restaurant (p. 126) is one of the most appealing parts of this hip and in its own, understated way, elegant hotel.

West End Rd. (P.O. Box 3024), Negril. ℂ **876/957-4373.** Fax 876/957-0557. www.rockhousehotel.com. 34 units. Winter $150 studio, $275 villa; off season $125 studio, $225 villa. No children under 12 allowed. AE, MC, V. **Amenities:** Restaurant; 2 bars; pool; nonsmoking rooms; rooms for those w/limited mobility; snorkeling. *In room:* A/C, minibar, safe.

White Sands *★ Kids*   This low-key property is informal and family-run, offering good value. Most of its bedrooms open onto the beach, although some less desirable units are across the street. Accommodations range widely from a basic double to a four-bedroom, four-bathroom villa with a pool. The smallest units on the property, with either double beds or twins, attract the frugal traveler. Deluxe rooms have vaulted ceilings and overlook the beach. Families prefer the one-bedroom apartments, with a bedroom, living room, dining room, and kitchen. Most units come with full bathroom with shower only. The four-bedroom villa, across the road from the beach,

is ideal for families or groups. Families also appreciate that children 11 and under stay free.

Norman Manley Blvd. (P.O. Box 60), Negril. © 876/957-4291. Fax 876/957-4674. www.whitesandsjamaica.com. 40 units, 1 villa. Winter $67–$72 double, $134 1-bedroom apt, $443 villa; off season $54–$75 double, $94 1-bedroom apt, $288 villa. AE, DISC, MC, V. **Amenities:** Beach bar and grill; pool; game room; rooms for those w/limited mobility. *In room:* A/C, kitchen, fridge, coffeemaker, iron, no phone.

Xtabi The land that's owned by this resort is bisected by West End Road in a way that places the simpler, less-expensive units on the landward side, and the larger, more-glamorous units (in this case, cottages) on a cliff above the sea. Units on the landward side have air-conditioning and efficient, unpretentious layouts and furnishings. Those near the sea don't have air-conditioning but are larger and benefit from more-direct access to sea breezes. All the units contain a neatly kept private bathroom with shower, and a few of them have bathtubs. If you stay here, don't expect direct access to a sandy beach. A combination of ladders and spiral staircases descend, somewhat precariously, down to a set of sandy-bottomed, rock-sided inlets where the surf roils around during heavy seas. Safer and easier is a dip in the hotel's pool. The resort's social center is an octagonal bar area with a large ocean-fronting patio. Drinks are served continuously between 8am and 11pm; lunches are simple affairs of conch, sandwiches, or salad; dinners are more elaborate, with grilled pork chops and filet mignon, lobster thermidor, and conch steaks. The resident manager is Scotland-born Alan Young, who, when prompted, can tell some of the funniest off-color jokes in Negril. The name "Xtabi," incidentally, translates from the Arawak as "meeting place of the gods."

Lighthouse Rd., Negril. © 876/957-4336. Fax 876/957-0827. www.xtabi-negril.com. 24 units. Winter $65–$110 double, $210 seafront cottage for 2; off season $55–$87 double, $120 seafront cottage for 2. Extra person $27 winter, $17 off season. AE, MC, V. **Amenities:** Restaurant; bar; pool; babysitting; laundry service. *In room:* A/C (in some units), kitchenette, iron, safe, no phone.

ALL-INCLUSIVE RESORTS

All-inclusive resorts fold the cost of lodging, meals, and often extras such as drinks or sports into one price. The advantage of staying at one of these places is that you can more or less chart the cost of your vacation in advance, providing you don't spend a lot of extra money on entertainment, shopping, excursions, or transportation. Another element all-inclusives offer that most other properties, especially smaller ones, don't is security: Most of these resorts can afford to hire guards to protect the grounds 24 hours a day.

However, because you're paying for food in advance, you'll feel obligated to dine on-site every night—and the food tends to be unremarkable at best. If you view food as an integral part of your holiday, it might be better to check into a property where you are not a part of a meal plan.

Beaches Negril ♠ *Kids* Enjoying a high occupancy rate, this colorful, low-rise resort was established in 1997 as the family-oriented wing of the Sandals chain—an all-inclusive outfit that remains stoically opposed to allowing children into most of its other resorts. Designed like a cluster of clapboard-sided cabanas, arranged in patterns that create a series of small, intimate outdoor spaces, it occupies a highly desirable 8-hectare (20-acre) lot studded with palms and sea grapes adjacent to a sandy beach. At Beaches Negril you can either spend time with your kids or relax on the beach in the knowledge that they're entertained and supervised elsewhere, thanks to a roster of child and teen activities in segregated areas (where adults can enter only at their children's invitation, believe it or not). Among the devices used to entertain parents and children alike are costumed but living and breathing versions of characters from Sesame Street, including Elmo and Zoe. There's a replica of an ancient Roman aqueduct on site, and an impressively vertiginous waterslide, where participants shoot down a stream of water within a plastic tube that rises to the height of a four-story building. Accommodations are clustered in three individual villages, each of which is subdivided into a cluster of cement and wood buildings accented with cedar shingles. All units come equipped with midsize private bathrooms with tub or shower.

The resort's five restaurants include the unpretentious Blazing Paradise Beach Grill and the formal Seville Room, where the standard Jamaican and international cuisine and the decor evoke Andalusia. There's live entertainment nightly, usually music from a local reggae band. Overall, this place is bolder, more exuberant, and splashier than the "other" Beaches, which is recommended next.

Norman Manley Blvd., Negril. © 800/BEACHES or 876/957-9270. Fax 876/957-9269. www.beaches.com. 215 units. Winter $2,000–$2,760 double, $2,940–$6,391 suite for 2; off season $1,770–$2,490 double, $2,520–$5,880 suite for 2. Rates are all-inclusive for 3 nights. AE, MC, V. **Amenities:** 5 restaurants; 7 bars; 3 pools; 2 tennis courts; exercise room; limited spa facilities, 3 whirlpools; sauna; watersports; tour desk; massage; babysitting; laundry service; dry cleaning. *In room:* A/C, cable TV, coffeemaker, hair dryer, iron, safe.

Beaches Sandy Bay ✿ *Kids*

In massive renovations early in the millennium, more than $3.5 million worth, this ocean-bordering resort reopened its doors late in 2003 to show a design that evokes Georgian-inspired colonial Jamaica. Spread across 2.4 hectares (6 acres) of lush landscaping, it fronts 305m (1,000 ft.) of white-sand beach that's just a bit less wide than the one in front of its counterpart at Beaches Negril, recommended immediately above. Unlike many Negril resorts, which cater to couples or adults only, this sprawling property caters to singles, couples, and, especially, families with children. The resort is positioned less than a mile from the also-recommended Beaches Negril (see above), so as such, clients of either of the two resorts often, without charge, use the facilities of the other. Loaded with facilities to divert and amuse children, the resort is laid-back, casual, and less animated and rah-rah than its larger and more "Americanized" Beaches counterpart down the road. This one tends to attract higher percentages of Canadian and European clients who appreciate the relative calm and the decreased emphasis on nightlife options. Since meals are included, it comes as good news that the hotel employs many talented chefs to maintain restaurants that feature both Italian and Caribbean fare—there's also a beachfront grill.

Norman Manley Blvd., Negril. © 800/BEACHES or 876/957-5100. Fax 876/957-5229. www.beaches.com. 128 units. Winter $550–$610 double, $670–$970 suite; off season $480–$540 double, $610–$910 suite. 2-night minimum stay. Rates all-inclusive. **Amenities:** 3 restaurants; 3 bars; 2 pools; 2 lit tennis courts; fitness center; watersports; kids activities; salon; laundry service/dry cleaning; entertainment; rooms for those w/limited mobility. *In room:* A/C, TV, kitchenette (in some units), beverage maker, hair dryer, safe.

The Caves ✿

Although the nearest beach is a 12-minute ride away, Negril's most atmospheric and elegant small inn still attracts international celebrities. In spite of its fame, however, there are drawbacks. There's a sense of snobbishness at this member of Chris Blackwell's Outpost hotels, generally the finest in the Caribbean, and the prices are very high compared to the competition. The hotel is on ¾ of a hectare (2 acres) of land that's perched above a honeycombed network of cliffs, 10m (32 ft.) above the surf on a point near Negril's lighthouse, close to Jamaica's westernmost tip. The setting, though lavishly publicized, is difficult to negotiate with its stairwells and catwalks.

Accommodations, well suited for groups of friends traveling together, are in breezy units within five cement and wood-sided cottages, each with a thatched roof and sturdy furniture. Matisse could have designed them. None has air-conditioning, and the windows are without screens. A TV and VCR can be brought in if you request them. Many of the units contain alfresco showers.

Sumptuous meals are prepared only for guests and are included, along with domestic Jamaican drinks from the bar, as part of the all-inclusive price.

P.O. Box 3113, Lighthouse Station, Negril. ℗ **800/OUTPOST** in the U.S. and Canada, or 876/957-0270. Fax 876/957-4930. www.islandoutpost.com/thecaves. 10 units. Winter $665–$695 double; off season $515–$535. Rates include all meals and self-service bar. AE, MC, V. No one under 16 allowed. **Amenities:** 2 restaurants; bar; saltwater pool; spa; Jacuzzi; sauna; bikes; airport transfers; laundry service; nonsmoking rooms; snorkeling. *In room:* A/C (in some), ceiling fan, TV, dataport, minibar, beverage maker, hair dryer, safe.

Couples Negril ✸ Loving couples are welcomed at this romantic resort, lying on 300m (1,000 ft.) of white-sand beach fronting Bloody Bay, 8km (5 miles) from the center of Negril. The formula worked in Ocho Rios (p. 163), so it was repeated here. A rival of the Sandals properties, this love nest is the site of many weddings and honeymoons. On 7 hectares (18 acres) facing crescent-shaped Negril Harbour, this resort caters to those who want back-to-back scheduled activities, including volleyball, croquet, basketball, "mixology" classes, horseshoe-tossing tournaments, reggae dance classes, bocce, and more. Each of the good-size units contains a king-size bed and a CD player (bring your own tunes), plus a balcony or patio with a view of the bay or of the lush gardens. Furnishings, though standard, are comfortable, and everything is well-maintained at regular intervals, including the shower/tub combination bathrooms. The best doubles are the beachfront suites, which have Jacuzzis and hammocks. No building in the complex is higher than the tallest palm tree within the surrounding gardens. On the west side of the property, nude sunbathing is permitted within a compound that's virtually self-sufficient—at least during daylight hours and in terms of food and beverage, sports activities, and Jacuzzis—from the rest of the hotel.

The food is good, and you have a choice of three restaurants, including Otaheite (which was named after a species of Jamaican apple), serving a Caribbean fusion cuisine. Mediterranean and Continental menus are also served. A resident band plays nightly and there's special entertainment planned throughout the week, including Caribbean dinner buffets with music. Six separate minivan excursions (including outings devoted to golf, shopping, and a catamaran cruise) are included as part of this hotel's all-inclusive rates. In 2005, the resort added a pair of additional Jacuzzis.

Bloody Bay (P.O. Box 35), Negril. ℗ **800/COUPLES** in the U.S., or 876/957-5960. Fax 876/957-5858. www.couples. com. 234 units. Rates are per couple: winter $559–$783 double, $746–$944 suite for 2; off season $535–$636 double, $681–$814 suite for 2. Rates include all meals, drinks, and activities. AE, MC, V. No one under 18 allowed. **Amenities:** 3 restaurants; 7 bars; 2 pools; golf; 4 tennis courts (2 of them lit for night play); fitness room w/aerobics classes; 4 Jacuzzis; watersports; game room; tour desk; limited room service; laundry service; basketball court; dive shop; glass-bottom-boat trips; Sunfish sailing. *In room:* A/C, TV, minibar (in some), coffeemaker, hair dryer, iron, safe.

Couples Swept Away ✸✸ This is one of the best beachside hotels in Negril—it's certainly the one most conscious of both sports and relaxation, and the one that, thanks to its popularity, is the fastest growing. All-inclusive, it caters to singles and couples eager for an ambience that incorporates the possibility of many different diversions, including scuba and golf at no extra charge, but with absolutely no organized schedule and no pressure to participate if you just want to relax. As a staff member told us (privately, of course), "We get the health-and-fitness nuts, and Hedonism

and, to a slightly lesser degree, Sandals, get the sex-crazed." The resort occupies 30 flat and sandy acres, which straddle both sides of the highway leading in from Montego Bay. Whereas most of the resort's accommodations and most of its food and beverage facilities occupy the beach-fronting 8-hectare (20-acre) side of the compound, most of the sports and fitness facilities, including its very large swimming pool, are on the compound's 4-hectare (10-acre) "landward" side.

The accommodations are contained within 38 two-story villas clustered together and accented with flowering shrubs and vines, a few steps from the 11km (6¾-mile) beachfront. Depending on your tastes, they come with or without a TV or minibar and, as such, are priced accordingly. Each room is airy and spacious, with a ceiling fan, a king-size bed, and (unless the vegetation obscures it) sea views. Wooden shutters let sunlight and breezes in. Units contain showers only.

The cuisine here is more health conscious and of better quality than that served at Sandals and Hedonism II, with specialty restaurants that focus on, among others, Thai, Caribbean/Jamaican, and international cuisine. The resort's social center is its international restaurant, Feathers, which lies in an open-sided covered pavilion directly astride the beach. There's also an informal beachfront restaurant and bar, plus a veggie bar serving fresh fruit, juices, pita sandwiches, salads, and vegetarian dishes. At press time for this edition, a brand-new "Great House"—conceived as a reception and administrative center—was under construction. *Note:* Non-residents of this resort can (and often do) use the sports facilities on its landward side for $20 a day, and local fitness enthusiasts visit the gym facilities as part of long-term memberships.

Norman Manley Blvd. (P.O. Box 3077), Negril. ℭ 800/COUPLES in the U.S. and Canada, or 876/957-4061. Fax 876/957-4060. www.couples.com. 212 units. Winter $590–$833 double suite; off season $538–$693 double suite. Rates are all-inclusive. Ask about spa packages. AE, MC, V. No children under 18. **Amenities:** 6 restaurants; 8 bars; 3 pools; 10 tennis courts; health club and spa; 3 Jacuzzis; sauna; bikes; tour desk; airport transfers; room service (continental breakfast only); laundry service; racquetball; squash; glass-bottom-boat trips; sailing; scuba diving; sea kayaking; snorkeling; water-skiing; windsurfing. *In room:* A/C, TV (in about half of the units), coffeemaker; hair dryer, iron, safe.

Grand Lido *(Overrated)*

Billing itself as a "super-inclusive" resort, the Grand Lido sits on a landscaped 8.9-hectare (22-acre) stretch of beachfront that's immediately adjacent to the more raucous Hedonism II. Although it is touted as the most upscale of Jamaica's SuperClubs resorts, it sometimes falls a bit below expectations. The "contemporary Jamaican-style" lobby might seem a bit impersonal, and some readers have claimed that the place lacks good service. But SuperClubs has done a lot to overcome that, and things, we think, are getting better, especially since the management of SuperClubs is heavily invested in the site as the chain's flagship. And it has also won many awards from organizations that include Condé Nast and AAA.

Rooms are sun-flooded and comfortable, each with a vaguely Hispanic/Mediterranean theme. Each is relatively spacious, containing either a patio or a balcony that (except for a few) overlooks the beach. Most units are split-level, with CD players, king or twin beds, and large bathrooms with tubs and showers. The elegant hardwood furniture in the rooms was handmade in Jamaica. In addition to a cavernous main dining room, there are five additional "specialty" restaurants serving, among others, Japanese food (in Munasan), casual Italian food (in the Cafe Lido); Jamaican/Caribbean food (in the Reggae Café), and upscale Italian food (in Piacere). Guests can also sample a late-night disco, piano bar, pool tables, and nine bars. Note that the smaller of the resort's two beaches is reserved for nudists; if you're particular about who you'd like to see going around nude, or if you dislike views of nude bathers

altogether, ask for a "swimwear-side" unit. Children are not allowed on the grounds of this resort: only couples and singles over 16 years old.

Bloody Bay (P.O. Box 88), Negril. (Ⓒ) **877/GO-SUPER** in the U.S., or 876/957-5010. Fax 876/518-5148. www.grandlido. com. 210 units. Winter $1,780–$2,900 suite for 2; off season $1,634–$2,570 suite for 2. Rates are all-inclusive for 4 days/3 nights. AE, MC, V. Children 16 and under not accepted. **Amenities:** 6 restaurants; 9 bars; 2 pools; 4 tennis courts; gym; health club; spa facility w/many options for massage outdoors; 4 Jacuzzis; sauna; pool tables; business center; salon; 24-hr. room service; laundry service; nonsmoking rooms; rooms for those w/limited mobility; disco. *In room:* A/C, TV, minibar hair dryer, safe.

Hedonism II ⟅&⟆ Devoted to the pursuit of sophomoric pleasure—and with less class than Couples Negril—Hedonism II packs the works into a one-package deal, including all the drinks and partying anyone could want. The complex lies at the northeast end of Negril Beach, close to the town's only airport—a small-scale affair that mostly accepts flights from within Jamaica. Of all the members of the SuperClubs chain, this is the most raucous. It's a meat market, deliberately inviting its mainly single guests to go wild for a week. One manager boasted that the resort holds the record for the most people in a Jacuzzi at once.

The rooms are stacked in dull two-story clusters dotted around a sloping 9-hectare (22-acre) site about 3km (1¾ miles) east of the town center. When it was built, local architects cited it as a good example of an eco-sensitive resort whose highest point didn't surpass the height of the surrounding treetops. This is not a couples-only resort—singles are both accepted and encouraged, and in some cases have included a startling (sometimes alarming) collection of horny single males from venues as diverse as rah-rah college fraternities or sports teams. The hotel will find you a roommate if you'd like to book on the double-occupancy rate. Staff members here might include some of the most jaded souls in Jamaica. For the record, they're nominally forbidden from participating in any of the on-site shenanigans, but behind closed doors, one will never know. Also for the record, most of the raucousness here is sheathed within mostly heterosexual venues, with same-sex couplings, when they occur at all, being relegated to venues that are much less blatant. How do the locals cope with all this? In the words of a local cab driver who has spent years maneuvering guests around Jamaica, "Hedonism begins in the space between your ears, then spills outward from there." We strongly advise you that no one should check into Hedonism who's unprepared for the venue and ambience. More than any other hotel in Jamaica, if you're uptight or tense about letting go, or if you prefer to let go in demure and discreet environments, this is not the place for you.

Accommodations don't have balconies but are spacious. Each has a king-size or twin beds fitted with upscale linen and with mirrors hanging over the beds. Each bathroom has a shower/tub combination.

On one section of this resort's beach, clothing is optional. It's called the "Nude" section; the other is known as "the Prude." The resort also maintains a secluded beach on nearby Booby Cay, where guests are occasionally taken for picnics.

There's nightly entertainment, along with a live band, a high-energy disco, and a piano bar with karaoke facilities. International cuisine, a bit bland, is served as part of an ongoing series of daily buffets. In addition, there are three different specialty restaurants, one of which is focused exclusively on Japanese cuisine. There's also a clothing-optional bar, a prude bar, a grill, facilities for rock-climbing (climb at your own risk!), a lovely swim-up bar (on the "prude" side of the beach); and one of the best gyms of

---

> **Fun Fact** **The Naked Truth**
>
> Nude bathing is allowed at a number of hotels, clubs, and beaches (especially in Negril), but only where there are SWIMSUITS OPTIONAL signs. Elsewhere, the law will not even allow topless sunbathing.

---

any in Negril. The spa facilities (treatments within which cost extra), as of 2005, are for the most part new and lavish.

Negril Beach Rd. (P.O. Box 25), Negril. ⓒ 800/859-7873 in the U.S., or 876/957-5070. Fax 876/957-5214. www. superclubs.com. 280 units. Winter $449–$589 double; off season $380–$511 double. Rates include all meals, drinks, and activities. AE, DC, DISC, MC, V. Children not accepted. **Amenities:** 4 restaurants; 6 bars; 2 grills; 2 pools; 6 tennis courts; exercise rooms; sauna; free airport transfers; massage; nonsmoking rooms; 1 room for those w/limited mobility; dance club; Internet cafe; basketball court; volleyball court; aerobics; 2 badminton courts; 2 indoor squash courts; dive shop; glass-bottom-boat rides; sailing; scuba diving; snorkeling; water-skiing; windsurfing. *In room:* A/C, coffeemaker, hair dryer, safe.

Negril Inn ★

About 5km (3 miles) east of the town center in the heart of the 11km (6¾-mile) beach stretch, this is one of the smallest and most reasonably priced all-inclusive resorts in Negril. Because of its size, it's very low-key. The resort, not confined to couples only, offers very simple but comfortably furnished guest rooms with private balconies, in a series of two-story structures in a garden setting. Each unit has a small tiled bathroom with a shower/tub combination.

Included in the package are all meals, all alcoholic drinks (except champagne), and nightly entertainment. The restaurant is rather good.

Norman Manley Blvd. (P.O. Box 59), Negril. ⓒ 876/957-4209. Fax 876/957-4365. www.negrilinn.com. 46 units. Year-round $180 double, $225 triple. Rates are all-inclusive. AE, MC, V. **Amenities:** Restaurant; bar; pool; 2 tennis courts; fitness center; Jacuzzi; room service (breakfast only). *In room:* A/C, hair dryer, iron, no phone.

Riu Tropical Bay & Club Riu Negril ★ Kids

Two of the newest blockbuster hotels of Negril occupy immediately adjacent plots of beachfront, beside the highway leading in from Montego Bay, east of Negril's town center. The smaller, older, and nominally more upscale of the two is Riu Tropical Bay, which opened in 2001 as the first Riu resort in Jamaica. Efforts were made by the Spain-based chain that owns both properties to render the mammoth size of this place a bit less obvious, to imbue it with some boutique-y features, and to place a bit less emphasis on children's activities than at its neighbor/sibling. As such, clients at Riu Tropical Bay get a bit more emphasis on romance and laid-back-ness than at the even bigger hotel (Club Riu) next door. Club Riu, built in 2003, has a larger physical plant (pedestrian traffic is encouraged, without charge, between the two resorts), greater numbers of children, and a more obvious mass-market tone than within its sibling. Both resorts occupy sprawling, low-rise premises whose labyrinthine buildings are each painted in Riu's trademark colors, a fiesta-like tone of orchid-inspired violet. Both focus exclusively on cost-conscious all-inclusive programs, and both offer nonstop rounds of communal activities, including dance classes. If you don't mind the occasional sense of anonymity, Riu poses serious competition for the other cost-conscious all-inclusive hotels of Negril.

Norman Manley Blvd. (Bloody Bay Beach), Negril. ⓒ 876/957-5900. Fax 876/957-5727. www.riu.com. 420 units for Club Riu. 416 units for Riu Tropical Bay. Winter $488–$598 double, $740 suite. Off-season $368–$478 double, $622 suite. Rates are all-inclusive. AE, DC, MC, V. **Amenities** (shared by both resorts): 8 restaurants; 12 bars; 6 pools; golf; 4 lit tennis courts; 2 fitness centers; spa; watersports; 2 centers for kids activities; game room; car-rental kiosk; 2 gift

shops; 2 salons; 24-hr. room service; laundry service/dry cleaning; evening entertainment; discos; Internet cafe; aqua-aerobics classes; small-scale casino (slot machines only); rooms for those w/limited mobility. *In room:* A/C, ceiling fan, TV, minibar, beverage maker, hair dryer, safe.

Sandals Negril Beach Resort & Spa 🏵

On 5 hectares (13 acres) of prime beach-front land a short drive east of the center of Negril, Sandals Negril is an all-inclusive, couples-only resort that attracts a basically young, convivial, and unsophisticated audience. Imbued with a beachy, fretwork-trimmed design that evokes a Victorian-Colonial theme, it's a bit more active and freewheeling than the more formal and somewhat more restrained Sandals properties in Ocho Rios and Montego Bay. The casual but comfortably furnished rooms have a tropical motif and mahogany, planta-tion-inspired furniture, including four-poster beds. Completely renovated early in the millennium, rooms are generally spacious, each with a marble bathroom with a shower/tub combination. Most units open directly onto the beach—in fact, of the 223 units, only 27 don't offer views of the sea. In fact, here, more than at many other Sandals, you'll be so close to the sea that you'll hear the sound of the waves through-out the night. Unfortunately, so close to the sea, hurricanes, when they come, tend to do a lot of damage, so if, during the lifetime of this edition, you hear of tropical storms hitting Jamaica, ask about the condition of this hotel before you book.

Rates include all meals; snacks; unlimited drinks, day and night, at the resort's four bars (including two swim-up pool bars); and nightly entertainment, including theme parties. The Bayside is the main dining room, but guests can also eat at one of the spe-cialty restaurants. The Sundowner offers white-glove service and Caribbean cuisine. Low-calorie health food is served beside the beach at the 4C's Grill. Kimonos features Japanese cuisine. Barefoot by the Sea, housed in a huge thatch-covered building beside the beach, focuses on seafood.

Norman Manley Blvd. (P.O. Box 112), Negril. ✆ **800/SANDALS** in the U.S. and Canada, or 876/957-5216. Fax 876/957-5338. www.sandals.com. 223 units. 2-night minimum stay. Winter $360–$435 double, $455–$750 suite; off-season $345–$415 double, $435–$750 suite. Rates are all-inclusive. AE, DISC, MC, V. Children under 16 not accepted. **Amenities:** 5 restaurants; 4 bars; 2 pools; 4 tennis courts; fitness center w/saunas; full-fledged spa w/aerobics classes; airport transfers; limited room service; massage; coin-operated laundry; nonsmoking rooms; canoeing; scuba diving; snorkeling; Sunfish sailing; windsurfing. *In room:* A/C, TV w/pay movies, minibar, beverage maker, hair dryer, iron/board, safe.

Sunset at the Palms (Value) (Kids)

This all-inclusive hotel appeals to travelers who want to get away from it all without spending a fortune; it's an especially good choice for families with kids. The feeling overall is like something you'd have expected in the South Pacific, thanks to its design as a compound of low-rise wooden buildings set within a forest, across the coastal road from a beach called Bloody Bay, an eastern exten-sion of Seven Mile Beach. The 4 hectares (9 acres) of gardens are planted with royal palms, bull thatch, and a rare variety of mango tree. Scattered throughout are Asian sculptures, rich, jungle-inspired landscaping, and an appealing sense of Jamaican per-missiveness. Photos of the layout have been featured within *Architectural Digest.*

The simple but stylish cabins are small timber cottages, none more than two stories high, rising on stilts. Each offers two spacious and comfortable bedrooms, plus a bal-cony, a shower-only bathroom, and dark-grained furniture, including four-poster beds and big armoires, evoking Indonesia and/or the South Pacific. Many units were upgraded and improved after the hotel's takeover by a Jamaica-based chain, the Sun-set Group, early in the millennium. Of the three hotels within the chain, this is by far

the smallest and the most consciously boutique-y in its allure. A high percentage of the clientele here derives from Britain, Germany, and Holland.

Norman Manley Blvd. (P.O. Box 118), Negril. ⓒ 800/234-1707 in the U.S., or 876/957-5350. Fax 876/957-5381. www.sunsetatthepalms.com. 85 units. Winter $375 double, $575 suite; off season $325 double, $525 suite. Rates are all-inclusive. Children under age 2 stay free in parent's room; children age 2–12 are $25 extra. AE, MC, V. **Amenities:** 2 restaurants; bar; pool; tennis court; fitness center; spa services; Jacuzzi; bike rental; car rental; limited room service; laundry service; scuba diving; snorkeling. *In room:* A/C, TV, beverage maker, hair dryer, iron (in executive suites).

3 Where to Dine

Negril has more raffish, fun dining spots than anywhere else in Jamaica; this town makes some of the dining spots in Mo Bay look duller than a British teahouse.

The best item on almost any menu is fresh fish (it's often fried, but you can usually get it grilled). Jerk chicken is another popular local dish. Pasta is found on almost every menu. Finally, you'll find more vegetarian options here than anywhere else in the country. Don't be surprised to even occasionally encounter ganja cakes on some menus in the West End. (Yes, they *are* hallucinogenic—and technically illegal to consume.)

EXPENSIVE

Le Vendôme ★ JAMAICAN/FRENCH   This place some 6km (3¾ miles) from the town center enjoys a good reputation. You don't have to be a guest of the Charela Inn, in which the restaurant lies, to sample the cuisine, which owners Daniel and Sylvia Grizzle describe as a "dash of Jamaican spices" with a "pinch of French flair." Within a covered breezeway that's open on two sides to a view of the gardens, you can order dishes that include foie gras from the Landes region of France (priced at from $48–$62 per plateful, depending on its size), snails prepared in the style of Burgundy, assorted seafood appetizers, or a Jamaican vegetarian plate. Main courses include pastas, including a delectable version with lobster; Caribbean-style pork chops; duck in orange sauce; shrimp in garlic sauce; grilled lobster; and locally caught red snapper in coconut sauce. And if you really want to go native, the menu even offers curried goat meat. For dessert, try a sugared crêpe stuffed with homemade ice cream and drizzled with coffee liqueur. Many of the wines and champagnes offered here are imported from France.

In the Charela Inn, Negril Beach. ⓒ 876/957-4648. Reservations recommended for Sat dinner. Continental breakfast $5; English breakfast $10; lunch platters $3.50–$21; dinner main courses $29–$42. AE, DC, DISC, MC, V. Daily noon–2:30pm and 6:30–10pm.

Norma's on the Beach at Sea Splash ★★ INTERNATIONAL/JAMAICAN
The very durable matriarch Norma Shirley is hailed as the finest chef in Jamaica. Although it's unlikely that she'll appear on the premises at the time of your arrival, the chefs use her recipes for their inspiration—a cookery characterized by such regional products as callaloo (a spinachlike vegetable), papaya, and corn-fed free-range chicken. To reach the place, you'll have to proceed down a long, jungle-landscaped pathway from the parking lot (near the sea-hugging boulevard), through the gardens of the Sea Splash resort, to a pair of lattice-ringed wooden decks and pavilions beside a stretch of Seven Mile Beach. Pick your preferred dining venue—there are at least two, one of which lies at the top of a flight of wooden stairs. The menu is seasonally adjusted, with offerings that may include jerk pork or jerk chicken, stuffed chicken breasts, coconut chicken, Old Harbour (i.e., spicy) shrimp, quesadillas, smoked

marlin, and penne pasta dotted with jerk chicken. Lunches are invariably simpler, with burgers, coconut shrimp, fish burgers, and tuna melts.

In the Sea Splash Resort, Norman Manley Blvd. ℭ **876/957-4041.** Reservations recommended. Breakfast $4.95–$8.95; lunch main courses $6.95–$22; dinner main courses $13–$24. AE, DC, MC, V. Daily 7:30am–10:30pm.

Rick's Café *Overrated* SEAFOOD/STEAKS   At sundown, everybody in Negril heads toward the lighthouse along the West End strip to Rick's Café, whether they want a meal or not. Of course, the name was inspired by the old watering hole of Bogie's *Casablanca*. There was once, in the dim consciousness of counter-culture Negril, a real Rick (Richard Hershman), who first opened this bar as a hippy hangout back in 1974, but he's long gone. And his original vision of Rick's was pilfered long ago by big-money, big-time tourism corporations who don't mind trading in on the ganja-based, free-love, Rasta-inspired legends of Negril's yesteryear.

Don't expect anything small scale: The original rickety version of Rick's was blasted to smithereens during the hurricanes of 1998 and 2005, and the newest mostly masonry incarnation has walls thick enough to survive a small atomic bomb. You might be dismayed by the tour buses and minivans that disgorge hundreds of foreign visitors into the overcrowded parking lot of this place throughout the day and early evening, every day and every evening throughout the year. Security guards keep the place sanitized, and there's a heavy-handed emphasis on this site as a venue for the bronzed, the steroid-buffed, the beautiful, and for anyone who wants to be. There are even a phalanx of bikini-clad (male) Jamaican bodybuilders who pose decoratively, for hours, atop rock walls that frame views of the sea, the cliffs, and the setting sun. Management claims that the sunset here is the most glorious in Negril, and after a few fresh-fruit daiquiris, you might agree with them. (Actually, the sunset is just as spectacular at any of the waterfront hangouts in Negril, if nothing is blocking the view, although the view from here is infinitely better accessorized.) Casual dress as you'd expect to see in a shopping mall in central Florida is the order of the day, and recorded reggae and rock comprise the background music. Steps lead down from the clifftops to a rock-ringed swimming area, far below, and often, catamarans float immediately offshore, having disgorged passengers hauled in from resorts nearby. If you're hungry, ask for a menu, which in addition to describing the food, waxes nostalgically about the original role of Rick's as a counter-cultural mecca for refugees from the corporate world. If you want dinner, you can order dishes that include shellfish linguine, jerk chicken pasta, tropical chicken salads, sautéed Caribbean shrimp, smoked pork loin with pineapple glaze, and chicken that's either jerked or barbecue, according to your tastes. The food is rather standard, and expensive for what you get, but that doesn't keep the tour bus crowds away from the sunset party. Everything's a bit too touristy and tacky, we'd say. Neither Bogie nor the original Rick would have tolerated this.

West End Rd. ℭ **876/957-0380.** Reservations accepted for parties of 6 or more. Alcoholic drinks $4–$8; main courses $14–$22. AE, MC, V. Daily noon–10:30pm for food, till 2am for drinks.

Rockhouse Restaurant ✦ INTERNATIONAL   This is a gorgeous setting for enjoying some of the best food, and some of the most sophisticated clifftop engineering, in Negril. Perched above the cliffs of the previously recommended Rockhouse hotel, it was developed by a team of Australian and Italian entrepreneurs who designed a bridgelike span, equivalent to a railway trestle, high above the surging tides of a rocky inlet on Negril's West End. You may get a touch of vertigo if you lean over the railing. This place attracts a hip international crowd. Enjoy a drink or two at the bar,

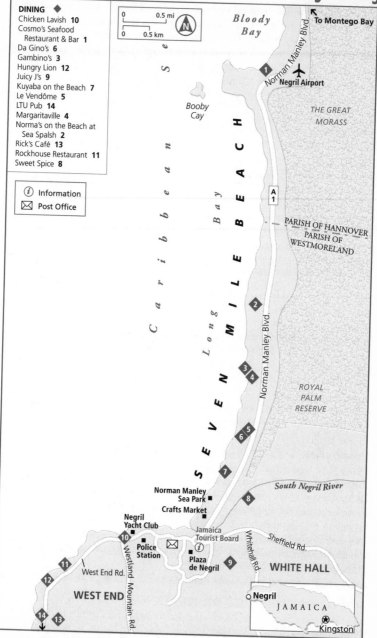

DINING ◆
Chicken Lavish **10**
Cosmo's Seafood
   Restaurant & Bar **1**
Da Gino's **6**
Gambino's **3**
Hungry Lion **12**
Juicy J's **9**
Kuyaba on the Beach **7**
Le Vendôme **5**
LTU Pub **14**
Margaritaville **4**
Norma's on the Beach at
   Sea Spalsh **2**
Rick's Café **13**
Rockhouse Restaurant **11**
Sweet Spice **8**

ⓘ Information
✉ Post Office

Bloody Bay
To Montego Bay
Negril Airport
Norman Manley Blvd.
THE GREAT MORASS
Caribbean Sea
Booby Cay
Long Bay
SEVEN MILE BEACH
A 1
Norman Manley Blvd.
PARISH OF HANNOVER
PARISH OF WESTMORELAND
ROYAL PALM RESERVE
South Negril River
Norman Manley Sea Park
Crafts Market
Negril Yacht Club
Police Station
Jamaica Tourist Board
Plaza de Negril
Westland Mountain Rd.
Whitehall Rd.
Sheffield Rd.
WHITE HALL
West End Rd.
WEST END
Negril
JAMAICA
Kingston

which is built with glossy tropical hardwoods and coral stone, with views sweeping out over the limestone coral cliffs, before your meal. Menu items, which are always supplemented with daily specials, may include a seasonal platter of smoked marlin, fried calamari and crab, blackened mahi-mahi with mango chutney, Jamaican-style jambalaya, lobster Thermidor, coconut or curried chicken, and an upscale version of Jamaican peppered pork with yams.

In the Rockhouse, West End Rd. ℭ 876/957-4373. Reservations required for dinner. Main courses $12–$30. AE, MC, V. Daily 7am–10:30pm.

MODERATE

Da Gino's ITALIAN Four octagonal, open-sided dining pavilions, separated from Negril's beachfront by a strip of trees, evolved as the escapist dream of Gino Travaini, the Italy-born owner. Pastas and bread are made fresh daily. The best chef's specialties feature linguine with lobster, filet of beef with peppercorns, various forms of scaloppine, and huge platters of grilled seafood.

On the premises are a dozen very simple huts, each octagonal, rustic, and camplike, that rent for between $60 and $120 each, double occupancy, depending on the season. Each has a TV, a very basic kitchenette, and a ceiling fan, but no air-conditioning.

In the Hotel Mariposa Hideaway, Norman Manley Blvd. ℭ 876/957-4918. Reservations recommended. Main courses $10–$28. MC, V. Daily 7am–10pm.

Gambino's ★ ITALIAN Adjacent to the more visible and better-known Margaritaville, with an outdoor deck that opens directly onto the sands of the beach, this restaurant mixes Jamaican and Italian food better than almost any other eatery in Negril. You may begin with a psychedelic house special drink (they include Beachcomber's rum punch, a Miami Vice, and a strawberry daiquiri), and then head for a chair at one of the wrought-iron tables for a meal. Menus here run to fresh salads, grilled fish, spaghetti Alfredo, veal or chicken parmigiana, and a very good version of fettuccine with lobster.

In the Beachcomber Club Hotel, Norman Manley Blvd. ℭ 876/957-4170. Reservations recommended for dinner. Lunch burgers, salads, and platters $5–$25; dinner main courses $9–$27. AE, MC, V. Daily 7:30–10:30am, noon–2:30pm, and 7:30–10pm.

Hungry Lion ★ (Finds) RASTAFARIAN/INTERNATIONAL Some of the best seafood and vegetarian dishes are found at this laid-back alfresco hangout on the cliffs. Instead of the usual Red Stripe beer, you can visit the juice bar and sample the tropical punches with or without rum. Menus change daily, depending on what's available in the local markets. About seven main courses are offered nightly, mostly seafood and vegetarian platters, featuring grilled kingfish steak and pan-fried snapper. Lobster is prepared in many different ways, and everything is accompanied by rice and peas along with steamed vegetables. The homemade desserts are luscious, especially the pineapple-carrot cake, our favorite.

West End Rd. ℭ 876/957-4486. Reservations not accepted. Main courses $10–$18. AE, MC, V. Daily 5:30–11pm.

Kuyaba on the Beach ★ (Value) INTERNATIONAL The setting is about as rustic, laid-back, and funky as you'll find—the perfect venue for slugging back two or three of the house special cocktails, which include "screaming bananas" and a party-colored, rum-based concoction known as a "kuyaba rainbow." Tables are set on a wooden deck, built on poles buried deep in the sands of the beach. The menu has been considerably

improved—better market-fresh ingredients and more flavor. Starters that are special-ties include jerk sausage served with shrimp wrapped in bacon, or a bowl of "real Jamaica"—a choice of red peas (actually beans), cream of pumpkin, or pepper pot. Pasta dishes are winning, especially conch-laced spaghetti with a garlic, wine, and tomato sauce, or angel-hair pasta studded with cream. Caribbean lobster is a standard feature. Some of our favorite dishes include crab and pumpkin cakes with a papaya mustard, or coconut curried conch with a mango-and-papaya chutney. For dessert, there's nothing finer than the Jamaican rum cake or the mango cheese cake. The name is Arawak for "feasting, drinking, and dancing," something that happens whenever a musician drops by to play some live reggae or soca.

In the Hotel Kuyaba, Norman Manley Blvd. © 876/957-4318. Reservations recommended for dinner. Main courses $10–$23; sandwiches and salads $6–$9. AE, MC, V. Daily 8am–11pm.

LTU Pub INTERNATIONAL   Built from concrete, with an outside that's painted red and white, the place doubles as a simple 10-room hotel. But it's best known for the restaurant, atop a cliff 11m (35 ft.) above the sea. Meals may consist of grilled fish, especially snapper filets; several different preparations of shrimp; grilled steaks; burg-ers; and salads, including an especially flavorful version made with lobster. You'll find this place around the corner from Rick's Café.

The 10 rooms at this hotel occupy five concrete "villas" set within the garden; all have air-conditioning and ceiling fans; none has TV or phone.

West End Rd. © 876/957-0382. Reservations recommended for dinner. Sandwiches and salads $4–$15; main courses $10–$22. AE, MC, V. Daily 8am–11pm.

INEXPENSIVE

Chicken Lavish ★ *Finds* JAMAICAN   Established in the early 1960s, this is the most durable and long-lived of the low-budget eateries in Negril. We particularly love its name. Just show up on the doorstep of this place along the West End beach strip and see what's cooking. Curried goat is a specialty, as are fresh fried fish and pork chops. The red snapper is caught in local waters. But the big draw is the restaurant's namesake, the chef's special Jamaican chicken. It's amazingly consistent, fried or served with curry or sweet-and-sour sauce. He'll tell you, and you may agree, that it's the best on the island. If you really want to go upscale, the lobster that's served here, when available, is either pan-fried or grilled and served with garlic butter. Ironically, this utterly unpretentious restaurant has achieved something like cult status among counterculture travelers who have eaten here for as long as most of them can remem-ber. Don't, by any means, expect glamour—everything is congenially battered and weather-beaten, but the food is "lavish" albeit completely down-home. Red Stripe, banana daiquiris, or paw-paw (papaya) juice, with or without rum, are the drinks of choice. You can dine on the roofed veranda, or ask for takeout.

West End Rd. © 876/957-4410. Reservations not accepted. Main courses $5–$20. MC, V. Daily 10am–11pm.

Cosmo's Seafood Restaurant & Bar ★ *Finds* SEAFOOD/JAMAICAN   One of the best places to go for local seafood enters on a Polynesian thatched *bohío* (beach hut) open to the sea and bordering the main beachfront. In this rustic setting, Cosmo Brown entertains locals and visitors. You can order his famous conch soup, or conch in a number of other ways, including steamed or curried. He's also known for his savory kettle of curried goat, or you may prefer freshly caught seafood or fish,

depending on what the catch turned up. Unless you order shellfish, most dishes are rather inexpensive.

Norman Manley Blvd. © **876/957-4784**. Reservations not accepted. Main courses $8–$18. AE, MC, V. Daily 9am–10pm.

Juicy J's JAMAICAN   The more you look at this place, the more you'll probably like it. It's weatherbeaten and a bit battered, but completely respectable—the kind of place where either a gaggle of hippies or members of a local church's choir might meet for a meal and some prayers. At breakfast, try ackee and salt fish or fish stewed in brown sauce and served with plantain—a fine, thoughtfully prepared example of what most Jamaicans consider standard morning fare. If that doesn't appeal to you, consider the "hungry man breakfast," a platter piled high with eggs cooked to your liking, steak, bacon, home fries, and toast. To acclimate yourself, head past the mismatched chairs and tables of the front rooms to the pinewood bar in back, meet the staff, and have a glass of fruit punch, coffee, beer, or rum. Then select from a list of good-tasting food that includes grilled, steamed, or (our favorite) *escoveitch* of fish; four different preparations of chicken, including a version with curry; lasagna; or lobster.

Negril Sq. (behind Scotia Bank). © **876/957-4213**. Reservations not accepted. Breakfast platters J$200–J$350 (US$3.20–US$5.60); lunch and dinner main courses J$350–J$1,200 (US$5.60–US$19). MC, V. Daily 7am–11pm.

Margaritaville AMERICAN/INTERNATIONAL   It's practically Disney-gone-Jamaican at this rowdy bar, restaurant, and entertainment complex. Thanks to the loaded buses that pull in for a field trip from some of Negril's all-inclusive hotels, it's a destination in its own right. People party here all day and night. There's an on-site art gallery where most of the works are by the very talented U.S.-born artist Geraldine Robins, and at the gift shops you might actually be tempted to buy something. Every evening beginning around 9pm there's live music or perhaps karaoke. Permanently moored a few feet offshore is a pair of Jamaica's largest trampolines, whale-size floaters that feature high-jumping contests by any participant whose cocktails haven't affected them yet. Rock climbing is also available. Drinks are deceptively potent. In this party atmosphere, you don't expect the food to be that good, but it might happily surprise, even though it consists of such fare as shrimp-and-tuna kebobs. You'll find Southern fried chicken, along with the standard club steaks and burgers.

Norman Manley Blvd. © **876/957-4467**. Reservations not accepted. Burgers and sandwiches $8.75–$9.75; main courses $12–$25. AE, MC, V. Daily 8am–11pm.

Sweet Spice ★ (Kids) JAMAICAN   This is everybody's favorite mom-and-pop eatery, a real local hangout. It's set beside the road leading south out of Negril, within a clapboard-sided house that seems to grow bigger each year, and which is painted an electric shade of blue. Food is simple, cheap, and bountiful, served amid a decor of plastic tablecloths, tile floors, and windows covered with louvers and screens (but without glass). The Whytes welcome guests warmly and serve portions that are large, satisfying, and home-style. Bring Grandma, Mom, Dad, the kids—many Jamaican families do. You get what's on the stove or in the kettle that night, perhaps the fresh catch of the day or a conch steak. The grilled chicken is done to perfection, and shrimp is steamed and served with garlic butter or cooked in coconut cream. A number of curry dishes tempt, including concoctions made with goat, lobster, and chicken. Meals come with freshly cooked, Jamaica-grown vegetables. The fruit juices served

here in lieu of alcoholic beverages are truly refreshing, and the menu is the same at lunch and dinner.

1 White Hall Rd. ⓒ **876/957-4621.** Reservations not accepted. Main courses J$300–J$1,120 (US$4.80–US$18). MC, V. Daily 9am–11pm.

4 Hitting the Beach & Other Outdoor Pursuits

BEACHES

HITTING THE BEACH

Beloved by the hippies of the 1960s, **Seven Mile Beach** 🎯🎯 is still as beautiful as ever, but it's no longer the idyllic retreat it once was. Resorts now line this beach, attracting an international crowd. Nudity, however, is just as prevalent: This beach promotes a laid-back lifestyle and carefree ambience more than any other in Jamaica or, perhaps, in the Caribbean. Clean aquamarine waters, coral reefs, and a backdrop of palm trees add to the appeal. When you tire of the beach, you'll find all sorts of resorts, clubs, beach bars, open-air restaurants, and the like. Vendors hawk everything from Red Stripe beer to ganja.

Except for the crowds and harassment, this is one of the prettiest beaches in Jamaica—though the harassment can be a big turnoff. One Frommer's reader found the constant hassle "high-octane—never ending. I was offered everything almost on an hourly basis from the hustler himself to drugs. A simple 'no' often wouldn't do."

In the spirit of the place, topless bathing is common along the entire stretch of the beach, although a small section near Cosmo's Restaurant officially condones total nudity. Many of the big resorts also have nude beaches. The hottest and most exotic is found at **Hedonism II,** although **Grand Lido** next door draws its fair share. When these hotels rent "rooms with a view," theirs is no idle promise: Nude beaches at each of these resorts are in separate and "private" areas of the resort property. Security guards keep Peeping Toms at bay; photography is not permitted. Most of the resorts also have a nude bar, a nude hot tub, and a nude swimming pool.

If you want to escape the hair-braiders, hustlers, aloe masseurs, nude bodies, reggae music, and the rest, escape to **Long Bay Beach Park** at the far northern end of Negril Beach. Out beyond the hotel belt, this stretch of beach is set against a backdrop of picnic tables and changing rooms. We've found it the least crowded of all Negril's beaches, even during the busy winter months. On our latest visit, we didn't even detect a whiff of ganja here.

If you have kids in tow, take them to **Anancy Fun Park** on Norman Manley Boulevard, close to the Poinciana Beach Resort. It offers an array of activities ranging from miniature golf to a merry-go-round, train ride, pedal boating, fishing, and other attractions. The park is open daily from sunup to sundown, charging no admission—you are charged, however, for rides or activities. The park is corny but recommended for children.

A favorite retreat for us—and we're letting you in on a secret—is the half-moon-shaped **Bloody Bay Beach** 🎯 lying beyond Long Bay Beach Park. Nude bathers do frequent the place, and because of its relative emptiness there is some danger of a possible mugging or theft, even during the day. That's the only downside; otherwise, it's wonderful. Use the center of the beach, near an open-air barbecue where the smell of jerk pork permeates the air.

BIKE TOURS

Rusty's X-cellent Adventures, Hilton Avenue, P.O. Box 104 (© **876/957-0155;** http://rusty.nyws.com), choreographs some of Jamaica's most hair-raising and best-conceived bike tours. The outfit was founded by Ohio-born Rusty Jones. Tours begin and end at his house, on a side road (Hilton Ave.) just west of Negril's lighthouse. He's the region's expert on the dozens of relatively dry—that is, not muddy—single-track goat and cow paths that provide aerobic exercise and drama for all levels of bike riders. Customized tours last between 2 and 4 hours, cost $35 per person, and never include more than four riders at a time. Tours are primarily geared to "hard-core mountain bikers," even though there are ample opportunities for newcomers to the sport, as well. There's a running commentary on cultural and horticultural diversions en route. Bikes, helmets, water canteens, and accessories are included in the price as part of the experience; advance reservations are essential.

You can also rent a bike (available at most Negril resorts) and explore at will, although you're not likely to find as dramatic scenery as you will on a guided tour.

BOATING

Boating is a major sport in Negril, but you don't see a lot of large craft, especially fishing vessels, prevalent on the North Coast. In Negril, visitors mainly take to the waters in canoes, runabouts, and dugouts. The major hotels rent Sailfish, Sunfish, and windsurfers.

The best outfitter is **Aqua Nova Water Sports** at the Negril Beach Club (© **876/957-4754**). Its program features an array of activities, including a morning snorkel-and-lunch cruise, an island picnic, a sunset snorkel cruise, and a clothing-optional cruise. It also offers the best array of watersports, including fishing trips, jet skiing, WaveRunners, water-skiing, parasailing, and glass-bottom reef trips.

Depending on what you want to do, prices are wide-ranging, with fishing trips being the most expensive. You can, for example, take the morning snorkel lunch cruise for $55, the sunset snorkel cruise for $65, or a glass-bottom reef trip for $25. Parasailing costs $35, and a 4-hour fishing trip costs about $400.

GOLF

Negril Hills Golf Club, Sheffield Road (© **876/957-4638**), is Negril's only golf course. Although it doesn't have the cachet of such Montego Bay courses as Tryall, it's your only choice in western Jamaica. The 91-hectare (225-acre) course lies in the foothills of Negril at Sheffield, 5km (3 miles) east of the resort. The course is known for its water hazards and undulating fairways. This is one place where if your ball goes into the water, you shouldn't try to retrieve it—unless you want to fight a crocodile for it. On-site are a restaurant (the food is mediocre) and pro shop. Greens fees for this 18-hole, par-72 course are $58, and club rental is $18. Carts and caddies, which are not obligatory, cost $35 and $14, respectively. Anyone can play, but advance reservations are recommended before 7am.

HORSEBACK RIDING

Check out **Country Western Horse Rental** (© **876/955-7910**), Bay Road, Little London. Here you can go for a 2-hour ride for $50. Rides follow the coastline before venturing into the Negril Hills. See **Rhodes Hall Plantation** (© **876/957-6334**) under "Exploring the Area," below, for yet another option.

SCUBA DIVING & SNORKELING

Negril offers some of the best and most challenging underwater life for scuba divers of any resort in Jamaica. There are no really deep walls prevalent along the North Coast, but the offshore reefs here teem with marine life. Many of them are shallow, making them ideal for neophytes who want to break into the sport. Even in front of Seven Mile Beach are undercuts and caverns, attracting the diver or snorkeler.

The most famous dive site is **"The Throne Room"** ⚓, with a depth ranging from 12 to 21m (40–70 ft.). The site enables divers to enter at one end and ascend into the open air at the other. The orange elephant ear sponges that flourish here are the largest we've ever seen in Jamaica.

The Sands Reef Club, named after a nearby hotel, has a depth range of 12 to 24m (40–80 ft.). This shallow reef drops off to a sandy shelf, and is noted for its purplish sea fans and its gorgonians and coral heads. There is much to see here, from black durgeons to tube sponges, from squirrelfish to goatfish.

With a depth of 12 to 21m (40–70 ft.), **"The Caves"** indeed consists of sea caverns—one large, the other small. There is a linking tunnel between the two. Black coral and sponges grow in profusion along with gorgonians. There is a sea kingdom of other residents, too, including sea cucumbers and stingrays.

Long a favorite with divers, **Kingfish Point** ⚓, with depths of around 27m (90 ft.), lures the most experienced divers because of its depths. The marine life here is the most varied of the dive sites, including both the elephant ear and the yellow tube sponge, the hogfish and the damselfish, along with both brain and star coral and marigold-colored crinoids. The huge boulders of star coral are among the most dramatic along the coast, along with deepwater sea fans and sea plumes.

Negril Scuba Centre, in the Negril Beach Club Hotel, Norman Manley Boulevard (© 800/818-2963 or 876/957-9641), is the most modern, best-equipped scuba facility in Negril. Beginner dive lessons are offered daily, as well as multiple-dive packages for certified divers; full scuba certifications and specialty courses are also available. A resort course, designed for first-time divers with basic swimming abilities, costs $75 and includes all instruction, equipment, a lecture on water and diving safety, and one open-water dive. A one-tank dive costs $35 per dive plus $5 for equipment rental (not necessary if divers bring their own gear). More economical ($55) is a two-tank dive, which must be completed in 1 day.

Watersports equipment is readily available at any of at the kiosks along Negril's beaches. Each of these outlets is operated by **Seatec Water Sports** (© 876/957-4401), charging roughly the same rates as Negril Scuba Centre (see above). Jet skis cost $40 to $50 for a 30-minute ride; snorkeling is $15 to $20 per person for a 60-minute excursion by boat to an offshore reef with equipment; 20-minute banana-boat rides are $10; parasailing is $30 for a 12-minute ride; and water-skiing is $30 for a 15-minute tow-around.

SPORTFISHING

Stanley's (© 876/957-0667) does deep-sea fishing trips in the waters off Negril. Catches turn up such game fish as wahoo, tuna, blue marlin, and sailfish. Bait, tackle, and beverages are included in the price. Six people can rent a fishing boat for $400 for a trip lasting 4 hours. An 8- to 9-hour trip, including lunch, will cost six fishermen about $750.

5 Exploring the Area

The chief attraction of Negril is **Seven Mile Beach** (see "Beaches," above). Many beach buffs visit Negril and don't care to see much else. There are actually a few sights, though Negril has none of the multifaceted or historical attractions found in a place like, say, Montego Bay.

ROYAL PALM RESERVE

The 122-hectare (300-acre) **Royal Palm Reserve** ✦ recreation site carved into the Great Morass is the easiest part of the massive local wetlands to explore. To reach it, take the road to Savanna-la-Mar at the southern end of Negril, turning left at the signpost and going along a dirt road to reach the beginning of the reserve. Here you'll find much wildlife, including sea hawks, ospreys, and the Jamaican woodpecker. The swamp is also home to egrets, butterflies, doctor birds, herons, and the endangered Jamaican black parakeet. Wooden boardwalks enable you to walk 2km (1¼ miles) or so into the wetlands for a close encounter with it all. Take along plenty of mosquito repellent.

The showpiece of the reserve is Cotton Tree Lake, home to numerous waterfowl, including wild ducks and the Jamaican pond turtle. A nature museum informs about the plant and animal life of the reserve. There is also a riverside bar and another lakeside restaurant and bar specializing in natural juices and Jamaican dishes.

The visitor center (© **876/957-3736**) is open daily from 9am to 5pm, and tours cost $10 for adults and $5 for children 12 and under.

IN THE ENVIRONS

Should you wish to escape and discover that Jamaica is not just a beach, you can take a day off and head for **Rhodes Hall Plantation,** especially if you like to ride horses. Both neophyte and champion riders are catered to here. A 2-hour ride takes you through banana and coconut groves and high into the hills. A crocodile watch is one of the highlights of the tours. You can also tour the 202-hectare (500-acre) plantation and go scuba diving or fishing.

Horseback riding is available Sunday through Friday from 7am to 5pm, averaging $60 per ride. For more information, call © **876/957-6333.** The location of the plantation is 5km (3 miles) north of Negril at Green Island.

GREEN ISLAND

You can explore the area north of Negril on your scooter or in a rented car. Follow the main highway, the A1, as it passes through the wetlands of The Great Morass. A good stop along the way is at the shady **Hurricane Park** (you'll see a sign) with a bar. You can order a rum punch here, a cold soft drink, or perhaps the grilled catch of the day.

Another recreational site is reached by traveling 914m (3,000 ft.) or so to the west of Hurricane Park. Here you'll come to **Half Moon Beach,** which takes its name from sands likened to "crushed diamonds." Expect to find a thatched dive serving some Jamaican dishes, most often seafood the local fishermen brought in.

Continue 3km (1¾ miles) west of Green Island Harbour to **Rhodes Mineral Springs and Beach,** with several thatched bars aggressively seeking to slake your thirst. The beach is small but inviting. It's the site of a spontaneous beach party most Sunday nights.

Ann Bonney & Her Dirty Dog

It was at Bloody Bay, off the coast of Negril, that one of the most notorious pirates of all time, Calico Jack Rackham, was finally captured in 1720. His is a name that will live in infamy, along with Blackbeard's. He was captured with his lover Ann (also Anne) Bonney, the most notorious female pirate of all time. (The bay isn't called "bloody," however, because of these pirates. Whalers used to disembowel their catch here, turning the waters red with blood.)

After tracking her husband, a penniless ne'er-do-well sailor named James Bonney, to a brothel in the Virgin Islands, Ann slit his throat. However, she soon fell for Captain Jack Rackham, who was known as "Calico Jack." Some say he came by his nickname because of the colorful shirts he wore; others claim it was because of his undershorts.

Until he met this lady pirate, Calico Jack hadn't done so well as a pirate, but she inspired him to greatness. In a short time, they became the scourge of the West Indies. No vessel sailing the Caribbean Sea was too large or too small for them to attack and rob. Ann is said to have fought alongside the men, and according to reports, was a much tougher customer than Calico Jack himself. With her cutlass and marlinspike, she was usually the first to board a captured vessel.

It was late in October, off the Negril coast, when Calico Jack and all the pirates were getting drunk on rum, that a British Navy sloop attacked. Calico Jack ran and hid, but Ann fought bravely, according to reports. She flailed away with a battle-ax and cutlass.

Calico Jack and the other captured pirates were sentenced to be hanged. Ann, however, pleaded with "milord" that she was pregnant. Since British law did not allow the killing of unborn children, she got off though her comrades were sentenced to death. Her final advice to Calico jack: "If you'd fought like a man, you wouldn't be hanged like the dirty dog you are." So much for a lover's parting words. Ann's father in Ireland purchased her release and she opened a gaming house in St. Thomas where she prospered until the end.

MAYFIELD FALLS & MINERAL SPRINGS ★★

Another intriguing excursion takes you to Miskito Cove, 6km (3¾ miles) east of Lucea on Bamboo Bay—an idyllic spot discovered by yachters who often anchor there. If you're there at noon, you're greeted with the smell of jerk chicken cooking in various shacks.

Rising south of the cove is a series of green hills called the Dolphin Head Mountains. Reach them via the A1 road to **Mayfield Falls & Mineral Springs** (ⓒ 876/971-6580), at Mayfield. This is a working farm near the village of Pennycooke, 16km (10 miles) south of Miskito Cove. Take in the waterscapes as you walk through a bamboo village. There are more than a dozen waterfalls, and you can swim into an underwater cave. The full-day tour is $65 including transfers.

The easiest way to enjoy the experience without the hassle is booking a half-day excursion through **Caribic Vacation** (ⓒ 876/957-3309 in Negril). You're transported to the site and fed lunch for a total cost of $48 per person; this daily tour lasts from 9am to 1pm.

BLENHEIM

Those with a sense of Jamaican history, especially Jamaican Americans, might want to journey to the tiny hamlet of Blenheim, 6km (3¾ miles) inland from Green Island. Administered by the Jamaican National Trust, this is the site of the free **Sir Alexander Bustamante Museum** ★ (℃ 876/922-1287). Bustamante was a national hero, the nation's first prime minister; he is kind of the George Washington of Jamaica. Born in modest surroundings (as this rustic three-room shack reveals), he eventually rose to the position of prime minister and helped break British colonial rule. Queen Elizabeth II later knighted him. The hilltop museum displays mostly photos and memorabilia.

6 Shopping

At long last, Negril has a shopping mall to equal the ones found in Mo Bay or Ocho Rios. It's the **Time Square Mall** (℃ 876/957-9263), lying on Norman Manley Boulevard across from the much-frequented nightclub Bourbon Each. More than five duty-free shops and souvenir stores await you, including a courtyard cafe.

This mall offers Negril's best selection of watches (from Chaumet to Patek Philippe), jewelry (including some from the collections of Chopard and Mikimoto), and gifts and accessories such as a wide assortment of pens and writing instruments. Crafts are sold here, along with perfumes, books, cigarettes, cigars, film, liquor, dresses, and Blue Mountain coffee. The first and only cigar store (Cigar World) in Negril is also here, with a walk-in humidor, selling genuine *Habanos* or Cuban cigars. Jamaican cigars are also sold.

If you're staying in a housekeeping or self-catering apartment, you can pick up groceries at the **Hi-Lo Grocery Store** in the Hi-Lo Shopping Centre on West End Road. Here's your chance to enjoy Blue Mountain coffee, Jamaican spices, and locally grown fruits and vegetables.

Just off Norman Manley Boulevard, as you head south into Negril Village, you come upon the **Negril Crafts Market.** A collection of shacks, this is the largest center for crafts in the area, though they're sold virtually everywhere, including along the beach. Woodcarvings, beds, jewelry, and other items fill the market. Haggling is expected; begin by offering half the price you're quoted.

The worst shopping is at the overpriced boutiques found at first-class hotels, especially the all-inclusives. But they come in handy when you're seeking postcards, souvenirs, suntan lotion, or swimwear in a pinch.

Other vendors can be found at **Fi Wi Plaza** on West End Road, between a traffic circle and "Sunshine Village." The most expensive (but not always best) crafts are sold at **Rutland Point Market** in the north of Negril.

7 Negril After Dark

Some of the best reggae bands in Jamaica, often from Kingston and often Bob Marley wannabes, show up in Negril. Alfred's and Risky Business are both major venues for reggae performances. All establishments listed below are located on Norman Manley Boulevard unless otherwise noted.

Alfred's (℃ 876/957-4735) is a Jamaican experience where travelers will still feel welcome. Though catering more to locals, there's much intermingling, no cover, and a mix of ages here. You can also order a bite to eat until 11pm. Particularly interesting is

the beach-party area, with a stage for live reggae and jazz acts. You can also boogie on the dance floor inside, shaking to hits you'll hear at clubs stateside. Alfred's puts on a show 3 nights a week (Sunday, Tuesday, and Friday) and there is a $5 cover charge.

Bourbon Beach (© 876/957-4405) is the most popular and versatile hangout on Negril Beach. The club features live reggae 3 nights a week. The rum and Red Stripe flow freely through the day and night—at least from 9am to 11pm (and often much later). The club also serves food, including jerk chicken or fresh fish and lobster.

Norma's on the Beach at Sea Splash (© 876/957-4041) is the bar that's associated with the most famous independent restaurant in Negril, linked as it is to the most famous restaurateur (Norma) in Jamaica, and recommended separately in "Where to Dine," earlier in this chapter. But even if you aren't particularly hungry, you might have a merry and rollicking time hanging out at the lattice-trimmed bar here, looking at the waves, the moon, and the other clients. The venue, at its best, can be convivial and even festive, with hints of Jamaican chic and occasionally, humor. The bar is open daily 7am to midnight.

The Jungle, in Mariner's Negril Beach Club (© 876/957-4005), is the most crowded, horny, exuberant, and famous disco and nightclub in Negril, with a penchant for attracting sports and music-industry celebrities. (Even trash-TV king Jerry Springer did a turn here.) Its slogan? "Unleash the Animal." The scene gets so mobbed during spring break that movie crews have actually flown in from the United States to film it. Most of the perspiration here is spilled on the ground level, where four bars and dance floors rock and roll with music that varies according to the night's individual theme. Head for the upper level for the much-needed "cool-downs" that, at least here, have developed into a laid-back art form all their own. Red Stripe and rum punches are the drinks of choice for a crowd that really seems to enjoy their estrogen and testosterone highs. Fortunately, security here at least appears to be tight, with a prominent sign in front that declares, "No prostitutes or gigolos, no drugs, no soliciting, no misconduct," and a forbidding-looking bar that locks the place up tighter than a jail during off-hours. The cover charge is $9 for men (referred to on signs at the entrance as "Tarzans") and $7 for women (referred to as "Janes"). The Jungle Arcade is a gaming room with around 100 slot machines. The club is open Wednesday to Saturday from 8:30pm until the last patron staggers back to his or her hotel.

Mary's Bay Boat Bar & Grill, West End Road (© 876/454-2284), the brainchild of a U.S. ex-pat, William H. Miller, lies just before Mi Yard Music Bar & the Love Boat, about a 10-minute walk west from the center of Negril. This popular bar opens onto a panoramic sweep of Negril's Seven Mile Beach. It offers a wide selection of drinks and serves an array of hot tasty Jamaican dishes. Live reggae music is presented on Tuesday night after 9pm. The bar is also a magnet during the day with showers and lockers, chaise longues, and an Internet cafe. Boat charter services—featuring fishing, snorkeling, and sunset cruises—also operate out of here.

The hotspot during spring break, **Margaritaville** (© 876/957-4467) is a popular venue at night. It attracts the Bud and Marlboro crowd to its four open-air bars with large-screen TVs playing both music and sports videos. Karaoke is a Sunday regular, and various events are staged here, including bikini and wet T-shirt competitions.

Cosmo's Seaford Restaurant & Bar (© 876/957-4784) is also popular after dark. Located on the beach, it offers recorded music, everything from old hits to soca. You can play pool, drink, and mingle.

Risky Business (© 876/957-3008) sits a few feet from the waves. It can be sleepy or manic, depending on what music is playing. In season you can order burgers and sandwiches, and the Red Stripe is cheap year-round. Basically, it's a young hangout whose traditional party nights are Monday, Thursday, and Saturday, beginning at 9pm. Friday night (crazy Fridays) features karaoke. There's no cover, even when the place is rocking.

For the hottest night in Negril, don a toga and head for **Hedonism II** (© 876/957-5200), the most notorious all-inclusive in Jamaica. It's known for wild and raunchy parties. Nonguests are allowed entrance if they purchase a $75 night pass. At first this might seem steep, but it's really not when you consider that for this fee you are allowed all the food and drink you can consume—plus the entertainment. Fellow guests in thong bikinis and bondage suits are just part of the scenery. On-site is the resort's hottest disco, where action begins at 11pm and often goes on until 3am.

MXIII, on West End Road (no phone), more than any other nightclub in Negril, can either blow you away with its high-energy pulsations or simply present a ripped-up bandstand without energy and lights, depending on whether or not there's a musical act scheduled. There's no permanent bar—only temporary vendors selling colorful drinks from coolers. Expect a spontaneous, difficult-to-pin-down schedule heavy on soca and reggae.

The South Coast & Mandeville

While Negril (see chapter 5) gets the crowds, the **South Coast** of Jamaica has only recently begun to attract visitors. The Arawak once lived in sylvan simplicity along these shores before their civilization was destroyed. Early Spanish settlers came here searching for gold; today's traveler comes looking for the untrammeled sands of its secluded beaches. Fishermen still sell their catch at colorful local markets, and the prices, as they say here, are "the way they used to be" in Jamaica.

Most visitors here come east from Negril through Savanna-la-Mar to the high-country, British-style town of **Mandeville,** then on to a boat tour up the Black River, home of freshwater crocodiles. (Those with more time hit Treasure Beach first before going on to Mandeville.)

The area attracts an adventure-oriented visitor who doesn't want to be picked up in a minivan and hauled to an all-inclusive hotel behind a guarded compound with canned entertainment. It's a sleepy place devoid of duty-free stores, musicians in yellow shirts singing "Yellow Bird," and toga parties. Instead of air-conditioning, you get mosquito nets and ceiling fans.

Yet the beaches here are the equal of those of Mo Bay or Ocho Rios. Restaurants, for the most part, are of the sort you'd have found along the roadside in Jamaica in the 1950s—and some of them are still charging 1950s prices. Local lifestyles, too, remain mostly unchanged by time.

This last frontier of Jamaica will no doubt be invaded by tourism within the next decade or so. But for now it appears, at least in its more remote parts, a sleepy dream from long ago.

1 The South Coast ⊀

Think of this as the undiscovered Jamaica, though the region is beginning to attract more visitors every year; they're drawn by Jamaica's sunniest climate.

Local adventures are plentiful on the South Coast. Among the most popular is a boat tour up the Black River, once a major logging conduit. Another favorite is the trip to the Y. S. Falls, where seven spectacular cascades tumble over rocks in the foothills of the Santa Cruz Mountains, just north of the town of Middle Quarters.

BLUEFIELDS & BELMONT

These twin fishing villages are approached via the A1 highway, 19km (12 miles) to the southeast of Savanna-la-Mar. Bluefields Beach (actually a series of small beaches) is one of the finest in the area, drawing visitors every weekend from as far away as Kingston.

EXPLORING THE AREA

To reach the South Coast, head east from Negril, following the signposts to Savanna-la-Mar along Sheffield Road; the highway isn't particularly good until it broadens into the

A2 at Savanna. After passing through the village of **Bluefields,** continue southeast to the small town of **Black River,** which opens onto Black River Bay.

From Black River you can take the A2 north and northeast to the city of **Mandeville.** Or you can continue along the coast to **Treasure Beach,** though the road narrows at this point. If you'd like to continue to the very end of the road, head east to attractions at quaintly named Lover's Leap, Alligator Pond, and Milk River Bath.

WHERE TO STAY

Shafston Great House (Value)
For the uncomplaining frugal traveler who does not require state-of-the-art maintenance, this historic house is the domain of the best-known fellow in town, Frank Lohmann. The place is very popular with young people from Germany. On the grounds is the most-photographed tree in the area, a mammoth silk cotton tree framed against a backdrop of pimento fields. The view from this hilltop is panoramic, as well. Bedrooms are large, comfortably furnished, and quite plain; only two have private (shower-only) bathrooms, however. Ten more old-fashioned rooms are located in the great house, the rest in a newer extension, most sharing bathrooms; campsites are also available for rent, at $35 per night. There's a rustic Jamaican restaurant here, too, serving regional specialties.

Bluefields. ℂ **876/869-9212.** www.shafston.com. 20 units (3 w/private bathroom). Year-round $100 double w/no bathroom; $168 double w/bathroom. Rates include meals. MC, V. **Amenities:** Restaurant; bar; pool; Jacuzzi; guided tours; laundry service; rooms for those w/limited mobility. *In room:* No phone.

The Villas at Bluefields Bay ★★★ (Finds)
These exclusive private waterfront villas—built by American architect Debbie Moncure with her husband Braxton—are an ideal retreat. Right on their own white-sand beach, with private pools, they are the ultimate in South Coast luxury. *Caribbean Travel & Life* even goes so far as to say they're Jamaica's best, though that's a bit of hyperbole. One local said that guests are "just married, just remarried, just ourselves, just ourselves and the kids, or just escaping the kids."

Set among lush foliage, these villas feel remote and secluded, yet lie only a 40-minute drive from Negril. Each villa is perfect for a honeymoon or romantic week; all are furnished with tub and shower combinations. Antique armoires and Irish linens provide additional grace notes. Two of the villas, Hermitage and San Michele, can even sleep up to eight guests. You dine on crystal and fine china, and each villa has its own staff, including a chef, a waiter, a gardener, laundry worker, maid, and night attendant. Guests of the various villas meet at The Treehouse—a beach pavilion—for drinks, waterfront lunches, to change bathing suits, or to mingle.

Bluefields Bay, Bluefields. ℂ **202/232-4010** (Alexandria, VA). Fax 703/549-6517. www.bluefieldsvillas.com. 5 villas. Winter $4,500–$7,000 double; off season $3,500–$4,900 double. Rates are weekly and all-inclusive. No credit cards. **Amenities:** Villa kitchen with chef; beach pavilion for lunch and drinks; private pool; tennis court; spa treatments; airport transfers; babysitting; laundry service; horseback riding nearby; deep-sea fishing. *In room:* A/C, bar.

BEACHES & OUTDOOR PURSUITS

Bluefields Bay stretches for 10km (6¼ miles) along the coast and is broken up by a number of little coves. Here you'll find a string of sandy beaches separated from one another by mangroves. Walk along and select your favorite spot on the sands.

Along the western fringe of the bay stands **Paradise Park** ★ (ℂ **876/955-2675**), a 404-hectare (1,000-acre) cattle-and-dairy farm that has been in the same family for more than a century. It is centered around an 18th-century property on a tropical

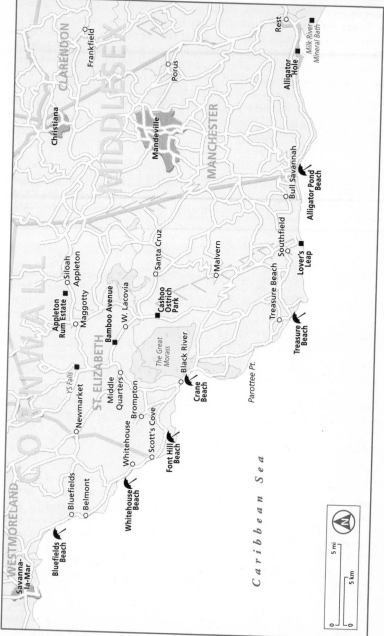

savanna with luxuriant growth. Horseback riding can be arranged, and afterward explore the grounds of the estate on trails cut through a tropical forest full of bird life. In May and June, you can pick mangoes right off the trees. The waters here are ideal for swimming, and you can picnic in the park: Picnic tables and open barbecue grills are provided. You can also swim in the Sweet River. The park lies 2km (1¼ miles) west of Ferris Cross, along the main A2 highway between Negril and Black River. Admission costs $5, riding tours cost $30; the whole experience takes about 4 hours.

At a section called **Bluefields Beach Park,** you'll find most of the local vendors, terrible toilets, and jerk stalls. Because the fish is likely to be fresher than the pork or chicken, this is a good place to order jerk fish, along with a Red Stripe beer. Locals make highly prized hammocks, which are sold along the road in this area.

WHITEHOUSE ⚑

From Bluefields, the A2 road winds south to Whitehouse for 8km (5 miles) along the coast. Local life is expected to change permanently with the opening of a Beaches resort in the future, the first to go up along this coast. If you come before the change eventually occurs, you'll still find a fishing village of small shops and vegetable stalls (busiest on Wed and Sat mornings).

EXPLORING THE AREA

Just off the A2 at Belmont, you can visit the **Peter Tosh Museum,** in a small green-and-gold building, open daily from 9am to 5pm. Technically, no admission is charged but you'll be asked for a donation. The Bob Marley Centre & Mausoleum (p. 189) at Nine Mile, reached from Ocho Rios, is more interesting, unless you liked reggae star Tosh's music better.

Bluefields was also the home of Philip Gosse (1810–88), an English naturalist who lived here for 18 months beginning in 1844 and wrote two books. His former abode is now privately owned and in poor condition, but you can walk by it, as it lies adjacent to the police station in Bluefields. In the gardens of the house grows a breadfruit tree said to have been planted as a seedling by Captain Bligh of *Mutiny on the Bounty* fame.

Snorkeling is good right off the shoreline. You can often get the owner of a local boat to take you over to nearby **Moor Reef** for $35 per hour. Some of the boats hold as many as six snorkelers.

WHERE TO STAY

Sandals Whitehouse European Village & Spa ⚑   Local sociologists hailed this massive new resort as the most significant development in the history of Jamaica's mostly undiscovered south shore. The resort opened in 2005, occupying a 3.2km (2-mile) stretch of beachfront, on an 18-hectare (45-acre) tract whose sheer size would have been unthinkable in more richly developed regions of, say, Jamaica's north shore. Ironically, despite its isolation from more populated parts of the country, it's only a 90-minute drive from the Montego Bay Airport, a shorter time than what would be required to drive from that airport to any of the Sandals properties in either Ocho Rios or Negril.

About 75% of the clientele is North American, the balance comprised mostly of Europeans. In preparation for its opening, Sandals interviewed 5,000 candidates for a mere 500 job openings within the new resort. The result is a team of hitherto inexperienced but innately charming locals, specifically trained by Sandals to be attentive and sensitive to the needs of the guests. Know in advance that because of its isolation, you'll probably venture only rarely from the confines of this place.

The layout consists of one very large public area, known locally as "the piazza," the animated site of six of the resort's seven restaurants. In addition to a dining venue that focuses exclusively on buffets, specialty restaurants on-site include eateries devoted to Italian, Asian fusion, Caribbean, grilled items, and steakhouse cuisine. There's also an open-to-view kitchen chugging out confections for an on-site coffee shop and pastry bar. Pools are appropriately theatrical, and lodgings lie within three distinctly individual clusters of buildings (Sandals refers to them as "villages") positioned to one side of the piazza. Their themes are devoted to a blue-painted French decor, a terra-cotta painted Dutch decor, and a red-and-ocher-colored Italian decor. Here, as at other Sandals, the motto is, "You bring the love, we'll provide the rest." A bit corny, but you get the point that the resort is for lovers. Especially conducive to romance is a spectacular piano bar whose angles are deliberately arranged to showcase sunsets.

Whitehouse Westmoreland (P.O. Box 5000), Jamaica. © **876/640-3000.** Fax 876/640-3001. www.sandals.com. 360 units. Winter $375–$480 per person double, from $510 per person suite; off season $360–$465 per person double, from $495 per person suite. AE, DC, MC, V. **Amenities:** 7 restaurants; 4 bars; 4 pools (plus 3 whirlpools); 2 tennis courts; fitness center; gym; spa treatments; scuba diving and other watersports; car rental; limited room service; dry cleaning; theater; night club.. *In room:* A/C, TV, hair dryer, safe.

WHERE TO DINE

Culloden Café ⊕ INTERNATIONAL   Set beside the coastal road stretching between Bluefields and Whitehouse, this restaurant is housed within an aristocratic-looking blue-painted villa that originally functioned as the childhood home of its owners and chef. The cozy and scarlet-colored interior opens to reveal a view of a formal garden and putting-green lawns that sweep down to the edge of the sea in vistas that evoke a tropical view of the English countryside. The charming owner is Ann Lyons, a former editor at a New York City publishing house. She directs a polite, well-rehearsed staff who prepare flavorful food that's considerably broader in scope—and more sophisticated—than anything else in the area. Menu items include locally caught fish that might be blackened, New Orleans–style; *escoveitch* of fish (a whole fish served in a peppery vinegar sauce); quesadillas stuffed with guacamole; or curried banana soup. Dessert may include Key lime cake, mango cheesecake, Blue Mountain coffee flan, or a frothy version of Pavlova—fruit and whipped cream in a meringue shell.

Culloden District, Whitehouse. © **876/963-5344.** Reservations recommended. Main courses J$400–J$800 (US$6.40–US$13). MC, V. Wed–Mon noon–9pm.

BEACHES & OUTDOOR PURSUITS

The best beach is reached by going along a small trail past the Alexander Seaview Shopping Square. It's sleepy here during the day, but comes alive when fishermen return in the early evening, bringing the day's catch.

BLACK RIVER

The A2 continues to the southeast until you come to the waterfront settlement at Black River, the main town of **St. Elizabeth Parish.** There are more attractions to be visited from here than anywhere else along the South Coast. Allow 2 days for exploring the entire region if you have the time, including, if you so care, a day trip to Mandeville (see "Mandeville," later in this chapter).

EXPLORING THE AREA

Reached along the A2 directly south of Whitehouse, going via South Sea Park, is **Scott's Cove,** a deep inlet that forms the frontier between the parishes of Westmoreland and

St. Elizabeth. Here you'll find several fish and bammy stalls with vendors hawking their wares. (Bammy, for the uninitiated, is fried pancake-shaped cassava bread.)

Immediately to the southeast stands the 1,274-hectare (3,150-acre) **Font Hill Wildlife Sanctuary** ⊛, strung along 3km (1¾ miles) of seafront. Birders from all over the world flock here to see herons, egrets, and much rarer species such as blue-winged teals. Listen for the sound of the whistling duck. This is also a habitat for the ground dove, the smallest bird of that species. Give wide berth to the dozens of crocodiles that still inhabit the district.

You can follow a dirt trail here down to **Font Hill Beach,** a small strip of white sands set against a backdrop of sea grapes. The swimming is good here, as the waters are clear, which invites snorkelers to the offshore reefs. This is one of the ideal places for a picnic with supplies you picked up at Scott's Cove.

VISITOR INFORMATION

The local office of the **Jamaica Tourist Board** is in the Hendricks Building, 2 High St., Black River (© **876/965-2074**), open Monday to Friday 9am to 5pm.

WHERE TO STAY

Invercauld Great House & Hotel   In 1889, when Black River's port was one of the most important in Jamaica, a Scottish merchant imported most of the materials for the construction of this white-sided manor house. Today the battered but much-enlarged house functions as a very basic hotel. Rooms are clean, stripped down, and simple, usually with mahogany furniture made by local craftspeople. The hotel has gradually added five small houses filled with suites; these come with either a king-size bed or twin beds, and the units each also have a fold-out couch, are air-conditioned, have cable TVs and phones, and either patios or verandas. Most rooms come with a tub and shower; the rest only have showers.

High St., Black River. © 876/965-2750. Fax 876/965-2751. www.invercauldgreathousejamaica.com. 52 units. Year-round $59–$97 double; $85–$155 suite. MC, V. On the harborfront, a few blocks west of Black River's commercial center. **Amenities:** Restaurant; bar; pool; tennis court; limited room service; babysitting; laundry service; rooms for those w/limited mobility. *In room:* A/C, TV, iron.

Waterloo Guest House   We wouldn't want to recommend anything more rickety, old-fashioned, and worn than this place—which drips character, at least, from its wooden verandas and gingerbread trim. Accommodations are found in the main house and also in a more modern, far less attractive motel-like unit out back. The main-house accommodations feature air-conditioning and private bathrooms with showers; those in the duller unit don't always have air-conditioning but do come with shower-only bathrooms. Furnishings are extremely modest, and the place is quite worn, even battered. Locals do flock here to the on-site restaurant and bar.

44 High St., Black River. © 876/965-2278. Fax 876/965-9207. 20 units. Year-round J$1,800–J$3,000 (US$29–US$48) double. MC, V. **Amenities:** Restaurant; bar; pool; car-rental desk; limited room service; laundry service; rooms for those w/limited mobility; Internet access. *In room:* A/C (in some units), TV (in some units), coffeemaker, iron, fridge.

WHERE TO DINE

Bridge House Inn JAMAICAN   This is a simple and very Jamaican restaurant. The cement-sided structure was built in the early 1980s; it's done with a beachfront motif and set within a grove of coconut palms and sea grapes. Patrons include mostly a cross-section of Jamaicans, including the occasional conference of librarians or nurses.

Menu items—everything is home style—include complete dinners (fish, chicken, curried goat, oxtail, stewed beef, or lobster) with soup and vegetables, served politely and efficiently by a staff of hardworking waiters. A separate bar area off to the side dispenses drinks.

14 Crane Rd., Black River. ✆ 876/965-2361. Reservations not necessary. Full meals $15–$30. MC, V. Daily 7am–10pm. On the eastern outskirts of Black River, on the opposite side of the town's only bridge from the commercial center.

EXPLORING THE TOWN

Come here for a glimpse of old Jamaica before it disappears completely. Because the town appears to be in decay during the day, we prefer it under the kind, rosy glow of sunset while walking along its waterfront. You might also walk along High Street (the main street), taking in old colonial buildings, some in the West Indian gingerbread style and others mere rip-offs of Georgian architecture.

At the east end of High Street sits the **Hendricks Building,** site of the tourist office (see above). This battered old structure dates from 1813. Also on "The High," you can see the old **courthouse** with its porticoes and the **town hall** with its pillared facade opening onto a mammoth banyan tree. Nearby you'll spot the **Parish Church of St. John the Evangelist,** dating from 1837.

BLACK RIVER ⭐ & THE GREAT MORASS ⭐⭐

The second longest river in Jamaica and a vast marshland called the Great Morass are the Jamaican equivalent of the Florida Everglades. This sprawling mass of animals, bird life, and lush vegetation is the most evocative section in Jamaica—a Tarzan-like jungle setting.

Five Jamaican rivers meet in the 32,374-hectare (80,000-acre) Morass, a soggy mass of crocodile-filled swamps, mangroves, and marshland with plenty of bird life, such as egrets, herons, ducks (both the whistling and ringed-neck species), and the blue-winged teal, among others.

The savanna is also filled with rare plant life such as butterfly ginger, bull thatch, saw grass, water hyacinths, pancake lilies, guaco bushes, potato slips, and wild cane, to name just a few. The red mangrove seen here is especially stunning: It sends its roots as deep as 12m (40 ft.) into the murky swamplands. You can also see royal palms and the remains of the logwood trees that once brought prosperity to Black River.

For a look at the Black River, its mangrove swamps, and crocodiles, the best tours are offered by **South Coast Safaris.** Tours are led by the town's most popular local character, extrovert Charles Swabey. The 1½-hour tour covers 19km (12 miles) upstream and back and costs $15 for adults, $7.50 for children; tours leave daily at 9 and 11am and 12:30, 2, and 3:30pm. Children under 3 go free but probably shouldn't be taken at all, unless they are held onto firmly. South Coast Safaris is at 1 Crane Rd., Black River (✆ **876/965-2513**).

EXPLORING THE AREA

Most visitors come here for a so-called "safari" adventure along the Black River and into the Great Morass. However, it's also possible to see many land-based sights, especially if you take the A2 north and east to Mandeville.

YS FALLS ⭐⭐⭐ (Kids)   Among the most spectacular falls in the West Indies, rivaled only by the tourist-trodden Dunn's River Falls at Ocho Rios (p. 177), these eight falls drop a panoramic 36m (120 ft.) in majestic tiers separated by beautiful pools ideal for

---

Finds Plenty Water Deh 'Bout

Jamaica's most bizarre bar, the **Pelican Bar** at Parottee Point (© **876/354-4218**), lies on a shoal off this point and stands in shallow water on stilts made from acacia trees. Surely there is no more ramshackle bar in the Caribbean than the little hut of Floyd (real name Denever Delroy Forbes). Under a half-thatched half-tarp roof, he serves yachties and boaters seeking a pit stop as they head up the Black River. This rickety structure looks as if it's going to fall into the sea at any minute, but is usually packed with patrons. Many drinkers enjoy their rum punches or their Red Stripe beer while standing in the shallow waters around the patchwork bar of wood and other materials called "tings." Amazingly, if you notify him in advance, Floyd will even cook your dinner—fresh fish, fried or steamed, or maybe freshly caught Caribbean lobster for that special treat. His stove? Two car wheel rims fired by wood. His house cocktail is Pelican Perfection, a concoction made with lime juice, sugar, white rum, and ginger beer.

---

swimming. The lush setting is framed by limestone cliffs and junglelike growth. A crew of engineers dug a basin out of the riverbank, thereby creating a large and beautiful freshwater swimming pool whose waters are constantly replenished by the swift-flowing waters. The falls lie on the privately owned YS Estate, 6km (3¾ miles) to the north of the A2 highway; the turnoff is signposted 2km (1¼ miles) east after you leave the village of Middle Quarters, about 13km (8 miles) north of Middle Quarters.

Kids love this estate, which includes a playground and tractor rides. It's open Tuesday to Sunday from 9:30am to 3:30pm, charging an admission of $12. There's a little thatched dining hut on-site serving chicken and burgers, if you didn't pack a lunch. For more information, call © **876/997-6360.**

In the hamlet of **Middle Quarters,** women stand along the roadside hawking peppery shellfish. Fiery hot, these crayfish (locally called "swimps") are caught in the river and then cooked at little open-air roadside grills.

BAMBOO AVENUE 🌟🌟🌟   Middle Quarters, along the A2 north from Black River, marks the beginning of Bamboo Avenue—the most beautiful drive in the West Indies. Lying between Middle Quarters and Lacovia, this 4km (2½-mile) stretch of bamboo trees is a grand scenic treat. Planted in the early 20th century to provide a respite from the hot sun for sugar cane workers, the bamboo trees stretch across the road, linking to form a canopy over the road, which narrows to a kind of tunnel that flutters in the trade winds. It's a dramatic sight, and along the road hawkers of coconuts and peanuts ply their trades. Stop anywhere along the way for a snack and a refreshing drink of coconut water.

CASHOO OSTRICH PARK *Kids*   Ostriches are not associated with Jamaica, but they thrive on this 40-hectare (100-acre) estate lying 6km (3¾ miles) south of East Lacovia (at the eastern end of Bamboo Ave.). Some of these birds weigh more than 159 kilograms (350 lb.); their eggs alone can weigh 2 kilograms (4½ lb.) or more. The owner has also installed a little petting zoo and playground with rabbits, ducks, and donkeys, among other tame animals. For adults, there's a bar along the riverside where you can rest in hammocks, enjoying a respite from touring. (Crocodiles inhabit the river, so don't be tempted to take a dip.) The park is open Tuesday to Sunday from

10am to 4:30pm, costing J$275 (US$4.40) for admission or J$175 (US$2.80) for ages 12 and under. For more information, call © **876/966-2222.**

SANTA CRUZ   The last town of any importance you'll pass after Bamboo Avenue en route to Mandeville is Santa Cruz, a thriving market town supported in part by a large factory. The best stopover is at **Hind's Restaurant & Bakery,** Santa Cruz Plaza (© **876/966-2234**), serving Jamaican cuisine daily from 7am to 6pm (until 7pm Fri–Sat, closed on Sun). Main courses cost J$145 to J$325 (US$2.30–US$5.20). Many locals come here for breakfast, the favorite dish being ackee and salt fish. Main meals include such hair-on-your-chest dishes as stewed oxtail, tripe and beans, and curried goat. The faint-of-heart can order baked goods such as a rum cake. No credit cards are accepted.

APPLETON RUM ESTATE   This estate is the oldest rum producer in the English-speaking West Indies. The estate has been producing award-winning rums since 1749. At the end of a tour, in which you're shown how cane is turned into rum, you're treated to complimentary samples of cane juice, called "high wine," and all the flavorful rums they can produce. The tour takes 45 minutes to 1 hour and is available Monday to Saturday from 9am to 4pm, costing $14 per person. Call © **876/963-9215.**

TREASURE BEACH   Departing from the main A2 at Black River, a secondary road dips to the southeast taking you to Treasure Beach. This section is very different from the rest of Jamaica, evoking at times the more arid parts of Arizona. Sheltered by the Santa Cruz Mountains to the north, it doesn't get the heavy rainfall that showers over the lusher parts of the island. You are more likely to encounter towering cacti instead of junglelike growth.

Since the opening of Jake's (see "Where to Stay," below), which *Vogue* dubbed the "chicest shack in the Caribbean," more and more international tourists are drawn to this remote part of Jamaica.

WHERE TO STAY

Blue Marlin Villas ✦✦   On a broad beach of gold-colored sand, these luxury villas sprawl across a bit over 1 hectare (2½ acers) of well-landscaped gardens with views. The compound borders the fishing community of Great Bay, which is the best swimming beach along the south coast. Blue Marlin is a four-bedroom villa with three bathrooms, and is elegantly furnished with a combination of comfortable contemporary pieces with a mixture of Jamaican antiques, including an extra large four-poster bed in some of the bedrooms. Extra services include a housekeeper and cook, a maid, and a full-time gardener. The other villa on site is the two-story Coquina, which has three attractively furnished bedrooms and three bathrooms. These villas are your most *luxe* choice for living along the South Coast, but rentals require a minimum 3-night stay. Additional nights are pro-rated at one-seventh of the weekly rate.

(P.O. Box 5), Treasure Beach, Jamaica. ©/fax **876/965-0459.** www.bluemarlinvillas.com. 7 units. $558–$945 double. Rates represent 3 nights lodgings. 15% off-season discounts. No credit cards. **Amenities:** Garden. *In room:* Ceiling fans, no phone.

Golden Sands Guest House *Value*   Popular with backpackers and others, this is the best bargain along the coast, although it's not for everyone. Four buildings that make up this compound lie at the edge of a long beach of good sands. A garden separates the property from the beach. The bedrooms are very spartan but well kept, each cooled by an overhead fan. All units contain twin beds and a small bathroom where

the water is never hot but kind of tepid. Management provides bed linens and towels. Guests cut down on meal costs by purchasing supplies at one of the local markets and cooking their own meals. The outdoor bar is a popular gathering place at night, attracting an international crowd of visitors that range from Germany to Manitoba. The most luxurious and private way to stay here is to rent the one-bedroom cottage. Sometimes guests wait until the fishing boats come in, to unload their rainbow-hued catch of the day. Then they purchase their dinner on the spot, with a guarantee that it's very fresh.

Calabash Bay. © 876/965-0167. 24 units. Year-round $45 double; $80 cottage. No credit cards. **Amenities:** Breakfast room. *In room:* A/C (in cottage only), ceiling fans, TV, kitchenette, no phone.

Jake's ★★ *(Finds* This is one of the most eccentric and off-beat hotels in Jamaica. Perched on a cliff side overlooking the ocean and set within a labyrinth of badly marked roads, adjacent to a rocky beach that benefits from the occasional dumping of truckloads of sand, Jake's is a special haven. It occupies a series of earth-colored Casbah-style buildings, each individually decorated and exploding with colors—everything from funky purple to Pompeian terra cotta. Each contains mosquito netting, flickering candles, and a CD player with a very hip collection. All units come with a well-maintained bathroom with tub-and-shower combination. Likewise, as a means of avoiding infestations of flying insects, lighting is kept deliberately dim. Our favorite accommodations here are the trio of Octopussy villas, each with a large amount of living space and a spacious bedroom with an open-air deck on the rooftop jutting out over the water. For an extra sense of romance, the villas offer alfresco showers.

There's also a raffish-looking bar attracting guests and well-meaning locals, an amoeba-shaped pool, and a barrage of fishers and drivers who'll familiarize you with local activities and tours. The hotel restaurant is recommended separately in "Where to Dine," below.

Jake's is owned by Chris Blackwell, the man who brought the world Bob Marley and U2. It is run by Jason Henzell, son of Perry Henzell, who produced *The Harder They Come*, the hippest Caribbean film of all time.

Calabash Bay, Treasure Beach. © 800/OUTPOST or 876/965-0635. Fax 876/965-0552. www.islandoutpost.com/jakes. 26 units. Year-round $115–$395 double; $250–$800 villa, plus 18.25% service and taxes. AE, MC, V. **Amenities:** 2 restaurants; bar; pool; game room/media room; bicycles; Internet room; limited room service; babysitting; laundry service; kayaks. *In room:* A/C (in some units), full kitchen (in some units), minibar, fridge (in some units), coffeemaker, hair dryer, safe, no phone.

Marblue Domicil ★ *(Finds* A stylish little guesthouse with only three bedrooms has opened along this yet-to-be-discovered coast. Each of the comfortably furnished, though rather simple, bedrooms opens onto the sea. These oceanfront rooms contain private balconies where guests sit out to watch the sunset at night. During the day, guests can be seen wandering Treasure Beach. The staff will inform you of all the activities available in the area in addition to swimming; these include snorkeling and taking excursions into the Santa Cruz Mountains. The furnishings are rather stylish and designed by the owners and handmade out of cedar wood. Beds are queen-size and covered in Egyptian cotton. Guests consistently praise the food served here, with a daily changing menu that includes such delights as shrimp and lobster with a garlic-laced aioli sauce.

Treasure Beach. ©/fax 876/965-3408. www.marblue.com. 8 units. Winter $159–$229 double; off season $139–$199 double. Rates include breakfast. MC, V. **Amenities:** Restaurant; bar; pool; massages; laundry service; nonsmoking rooms. *In room:* A/C (in 3 units), fridge, beverage maker, hair dryer, iron.

Sunset Resort & Villas On a masonry terrace above the seacoast, a short walk from the moored fishing boats of Calabash Bay, this hotel doesn't have the international cachet or the sense of fun of nearby Jake's. But for an older and more conservative clientele, it's a solid alternative. Built in stages beginning in the late 1970s, on a 2.2-hectare (5½-acre) site, Sunset Resort might remind you of an enlarged version of a 19th-century sea captain's house, thanks to a two-story central core and horseshoe-shaped pair of symmetrical wings that enclose a pool. The bedrooms, however, are larger than those at Jake's, though with none of their decorative flair. Each has non-controversial, low-slung furnishings, some made with New England–style knotty pine. Most rooms come with tub-and-shower combinations. There's a restaurant (The Red Lobster) and bar on-site.

Calabash Bay, Treasure Beach. ✆ 876/965-0143. For reservations, contact South Enterprises, 2875 S. Main St., Suite 203, Salt Lake City, UT 84115. ✆ 800/786-8452 or fax 800/487-2749. www.sunsetresort.com. 17 units. Year-round $124–$163 double; $200 1-bedroom suite for 2; $324 2- or 3-bedroom suite, w/kitchen, for 2–6 occupants. AE, MC, V. **Amenities:** Restaurant; lounge; pool; bike rentals; limited room service; babysitting; rooms for those w/limited mobility; outdoor barbecue; free snorkeling gear; fishing. In room: A/C, TV, minibar, coffeemaker, iron, safe, no phone.

Treasure Beach Hotel Set on a steep, lushly landscaped hillside above a sand beach with active surf, this white-sided hotel was built in the mid-1970s about 2km (1¼ miles) west of Pedro Cross. Although its staff is young and inexperienced, this is the largest hotel in the area, and is often the hotel of choice for Jamaican honeymooners. The origins of this property actually date from the 1930s when it was a retreat for asthmatics. Its centerpiece is a long and airy rattan-furnished bar whose windows look down the hillside to the beach and the hotel's 4.4 hectares (11 acres). Bedrooms lie within a series of outlying cottages. Each unit has a ceiling fan and a veranda or patio, plus a small bathroom with tub-and-shower combination.

Treasure Beach, P.O. Box 5, Black River, St. Elizabeth. ✆ 800/526-2422 or 876/965-0110. Fax 876/965-2544. www.treasurebeachjamaica.com. 36 units. Winter $105–$153 double; off season $80–$121 double. AE, MC, V. **Amenities:** Restaurant; bar; 2 pools; Jacuzzi; limited room service; babysitting; laundry service; rooms for those w/limited mobility. In room: A/C, TV, fridge (in some units), hair dryer, iron, safe (in some units).

WHERE TO DINE

Jack Sprat INTERNATIONAL This is the less formal and slightly less expensive of the two restaurants associated with the also-recommended Jake's Hotel, the most eccentric hotel along Jamaica's south coast. A raffish-looking decor is inspired by the colors of ripe lemons and limes. It opens onto broad lawns where blankets are sometimes spread for clients to read, sun bathe, or nap. The venue is about as laissez-faire and laid-back as anything you'll find in Jamaica. Menu items are simple, outdoors-y, with picnic-y fare, including burgers, steaks, fried fish, and a wide array of pizzas, each of which is suitable as a main course for two diners at a time. The most popular are the versions topped with shrimp or savory chunks of lobster, with herbs.

On the grounds of Jake's Hotel. ✆ 876/965-3583. Reservations not necessary. Pizzas J$400–J$900 (US$6.40–US$14); main courses J$350–J$980 (US$5.60–US$16). AE, DC, MC, V. Daily 10am–10pm.

Jake's ★★ JAMAICAN/INTERNATIONAL Even if the sheer eccentricity of Jake's prevents you from an overnight here, you should absolutely dine here. Part of its allure stems from its raffish charm and unpredictability—you never know who might show up to divert and entertain you during a meal. (Likely candidates include everyone from Kingston's most prominent doctors to loquacious local philosophers who will predict your future through a rum-induced haze.) Jake's offers two distinctly

> ⟨Finds⟩ **Reggae, Jerk Barbecue & Callaloo Fritters**
>
> At Treasure Beach there are ramshackle thatched-roof huts where you can order a Red Stripe beer and escape from the fierce sun under a cooling palm tree. Our favorite is **Winsome s on the Beach** at Frenchman's Bay (no phone), where you can order freshly made fish chowder, callaloo fritters, and chicken adobe, the house specialty, which is cooked in a coconut milk and ginger-laced tomato sauce. Grilled kingfish in *escoveitch* (pickled carrots, onions, and specialties) is another specialty. Along Treasure Beach Road you'll come upon **Diners Delite** (no phone), serving such classic Jamaican dishes as okra and salt fish, chicken stew, and braised oxtail.

different dining experiences: a romantic and secluded covered veranda out back, and a much more sociable front porch where tables are hand-painted in psychedelic patterns inspired by the 1960s. Menu items are announced on a chalkboard and may include pumpkin, red bean, or pepper-pot soups; fish tea (a clear broth checkered with herbs); and conch, callaloo, or cod fritters. More substantial fare includes plantain chips or carrot strips served with smoked marlin dip; a marvelous steamed fish in coconut-flavored cream sauce; tender pepper steak; and a revolving array of spicy jerk chicken, beef, pork, and fish.

Calabash Bay, Treasure Beach. ⓒ **876/965-3000**. Reservations recommended for dinner only Dec–Apr. Main courses J$400–J$1,200 (US$6.40–US$19). AE, DISC, MC, V. Daily 7:30am–9:30pm.

Wild Onion JAMAICAN/INTERNATIONAL   Isolated, and in a spot within a 10-minute walk from Jake's Hotel, and within about a 4-minute walk from the seacoast, this is a simple, congenially battered low-rise building that's recognizable because of its exterior spectrum of psychedelic-inspired colors. Inside, within a mostly tangerine-colored interior, Richard Ebanks runs the kind of simple Jamaican bistro that attracts adventurous clients from Jake's and other haunts along the south coast. Don't expect anything approaching glamour: it simply isn't here. Instead, you'll get stiff drinks, lots of Jamaican color, and food that includes lobster, fish, or shrimp that's prepared any way you specify (broiled, grilled, boiled, etc.), and various preparations of chicken or beef as well. *Escoveitch* of fish is always popular. Live music is presented Thursday, Friday, Saturday, or Sunday, and on rare occasion, whenever the fame of a band merits it, there's a cover charge imposed after 9pm. If you're asking for directions, most locals remember this place by its former (i.e., original) name, South Jammin'.

Treasure Beach (a 10-min. walk from Jake's). ⓒ **876/965-3618**. Reservations not necessary. Main courses J$150–J$650 (US$2.40–US$10). AE, DC, MC, V. Daily 10am–10:30pm; bar remains open, sometimes with live music, till at least 2am.

BEACHES & OUTDOOR PURSUITS

Treasure Beach ⟨✦✦⟩ is a catchall name for four beaches: Frenchman's Bay, Great Pedro Bay, Billy's Bay, and Calabash Bay. Beaches here are either coral colored or of black sand. At times you can virtually have a beach to yourself. The sea is at its calmest in the morning, so this is the best time for snorkeling. Be cautious when swimming in the rough currents, however. The waves along here are moderate but good enough for bodysurfing. About 92m (300 ft.) offshore are beautiful coral reefs ideal for snorkeling.

The coastline between Treasure Beach and Lover's Leap (see below) is riddled with footpaths that make for ideal hiking. You can often secure a mountain bike at your hotel and can ride along this flat or hilly terrain, stopping perhaps at a small rum bar for a refreshment.

LOVER'S LEAP

Eleven kilometers (6¾ miles) east of Treasure Beach is **Lovers' Leap** ☆☆, Southfield, Yardley Chase (ⓒ 876/965-6634), the most dramatic and widely publicized attraction along Jamaica's South Coast. It commemorates the Romeo and Juliet story of two runaway slaves who leapt to their deaths hand in hand rather than be separated and returned to captivity. During the 1990s the Jamaican government erected an observation deck, meeting space, restaurant, bar, and gift shop at the site of the famous double suicide—the top of a 533m (1,750-ft.) cliff, one of the steepest on the South Coast. If you're adventurous, you can follow a rocky and meandering footpath down to the sea, though most visitors opt just to enjoy the view that sweeps out over the coastline from the open-air platform. It's open daily 10am to 6pm, charging J$200 (US$3.20) adults, J$100 (US$1.60) children for a view of the site, lighthouse, and amazing panoramas.

If you have time, you can continue east along the coast, following the signs to Milk River. You'll first pass a small nature reserve called **Alligator Hole,** which charges no admission and is open daily from 9am to 4pm. This is the Jamaican home of the endangered manatee, called a "sea cow." The best time to see these marvelous but shy creatures is in the late afternoon.

The road continues from Alligator Hole east for 3 more kilometers (1¾ miles) to the end of our coastal journey at **Milk River,** the site of a hot mineral spring.

Milk River Mineral Bath ☆, Milk River, Clarendon (ⓒ 876/902-4657; fax 876/986-4974), boasts some of the world's most radioactive mineral waters, recommended by some doctors for the treatment of arthritis, rheumatism, lumbago, neuralgia, sciatica, and liver disorders. The cost of a bath is J$200 (US$3.20) for adults and J$100 (US$1.60) for children 10 and under. Baths usually last about 15 minutes (it isn't good to remain too long in the waters). Use of the baths is free if you're staying at the Milk River Mineral Spa & Hotel—20 rooms (most with bathrooms, many with air-conditioning, TV, and phone) from $110 to $117 double—and the waters are changed after use by each bather. A restaurant offers fine Jamaican cuisine and health drinks in a relaxed old-world atmosphere.

⟨Finds⟩ Bammy with Your Fish Fry

Escaping dining rooms, you can relax on the beach just an hour east from Treasure Beach at the little fishing village of Alligator Pond. Once here, you'll see a thatched hut, **Little Ochi** (ⓒ 876/965-4449), which serves the best and freshest fish in the area. Your choice, of course, is based on the day's catch, brought in fresh by the fishermen that morning. Select your own fish and tell the chef how you want it cooked. A fish dinner costs around $10, and it comes with bammy (the local name for cassava bread) and a "festival" (translated as cornmeal cake). To carb out, rice and peas accompany all fish platters.

---

2 Mandeville ⭑

Called the "English Town" because of its lingering British influence, Mandeville lies on a plateau more than 600m (2,000 ft.) above the sea in the tropical highlands of Don Figuerero Mountains. Much cooler than the coastal resorts, it's a possible base from which to explore the South Coast.

VISITOR INFORMATION

There is no Jamaica Tourist Board office here. Get information from the **Central & South Tourism Committee** at the Astra Country Inn, on the western outskirts (© **876/962-9758,** 876/376-6176, or 876/450-3443), open daily 9am to 5pm.

FAST FACTS: Mandeville

Banks A branch of **National Commercial Bank** (© 876/962-2083) can be found at 9 Manchester Rd.; open Monday to Thursday 8:30am to 3pm, Friday 8:30am to 4pm.

Hospital The town's major hospital, **Mandeville Hospital,** Hargreaves Avenue (© 876/962-2067), is the best medical center in the Central Highlands of Jamaica.

Internet Access The **Internet Café** at Manchester Shopping Centre (© 876/961-1829) is the largest in Jamaica, boasting 20 computers and charging J$200 (US$3.20) per half-hour. It is open Monday to Thursday from 8:30am to 5pm, Friday 8:30am to 4pm.

Mail The **Mandeville Post Office,** South Racecourse (© 876/962-3229), is open Monday to Friday 8am to 5pm. To mail packages, it's more efficient to use **Airpak Express,** 11 Caledonia Rd. (© 876/962-5101). Include "Jamaica, W.I." in all island addresses. At press time for this edition, the island had no zip codes, despite efforts that had been made throughout 2005 to inaugurate them within the Jamaican postal system.

Pharmacy The most convenient drugstore is the **Caledonia Mall Pharmacy,** Shop G5, Caledonia Road (© 876/962-0038), open Monday to Friday 8am to 5:30pm, Saturday 8am to 5pm.

Safety The police station, 8 Parkerson Rd. (© 876/962-2250), is on the north side of the central village green. Of all Jamaica's cities, Mandeville is the safest; still, take all the usual precautions.

Travel Agencies The best one is **Sterling Travel,** Caledonia Plaza (© 876/962-2203), open Monday to Friday 8:30am to 4:30pm.

WHERE TO STAY

Golf View Hotel   This hotel won't win any prizes for architectural finesse—it looks like a hospital. But despite its shortcomings, it's one of the best-maintained and most efficiently managed hotels in the area. It's a motel-like property with a small pool that's found in an unattractive courtyard. We'd give the Mandeville Hotel (see below) higher

ACCOMMODATIONS ■
Golf View Hotel **1**
Mandevile Hotel **3**

DINING ◆
Bloomfield
    Great House **5**
The New Den **2**
International Chinese
    Restaurant **4**

Church
Golf Course
Information
Post Office

marks, though it too is a bit spartan. About half of the rooms here overlook the verdant fairways of the local golf course (Manchester Country Club); others front a swimming pool and a banal courtyard. Rooms are outfitted motel-style with relatively comfortable furnishings. About a third of them have air-conditioning, and each is equipped with a shower-tub combination bathroom.

5½ Caledonia Rd, Mandeville. ☎ 876/962-4477. Fax 876/962-5640. www.thegolfviewhotel.com. 51 units. Year-round $55–$75 double; $75 1-bedroom suite; starting $80 2-bedroom suite. AE, DISC, MC, V. **Amenities:** Restaurant; bar; pool; airport transfers; business center; laundry service; rooms for those w/limited mobility. *In room:* A/C (in some units), ceiling fan, TV, iron.

Mandeville Hotel   This ornate hotel dates from 1875, once housing part of the British military garrison. In the 1970s the original hotel was replaced with a modern structure. There's a spacious lounge and good food and service. Bedrooms range in size from small to spacious, furnished with Jamaican styling, often including a four-poster bed and mahogany furniture. Bathrooms are old-fashioned but tidily maintained, each with a shower and tub. There are attractive gardens, plus golf and tennis at the nearby Manchester Country Club.

There is no pretension to the food at all; it's simple, homemade fare. From the dining room, you'll have a view of the pool and the green hills of central Jamaica.

4 Hotel St. (P.O. Box 78), Mandeville. ✆ 876/962-2460. Fax 876/962-0700. www.mandevillehoteljamaica.com. 29 units. Year-round $65–$125 double, $180–$210 apt. AE, MC, V. **Amenities:** Restaurant; bar; pool; limited room service; laundry service; rooms for those w/limited mobility. *In room:* TV, kitchenette (in 1 unit), fridge, coffeemaker.

WHERE TO DINE

Bloomfield Great House ✦✦ INTERNATIONAL   This is the only restaurant in town that's viewed as a destination in its own right. Serving excellent food in an intricately restored setting of historic interest, it's a hangout for the town's expatriate Australians, Brits, Americans, and Scandinavians. Surrounded by 2 hectares (5 acres) of landscaping, it's perched on a hilltop about .4km (¼ mile) south of the town's commercial core, in a verdant residential neighborhood of upscale private homes. Start off with a drink in the cozy mahogany-trimmed pub before dining on the rambling veranda (with views that sweep out over the town), or a high-ceilinged dining room with colonial-style trim and moldings. Superb menu items include charbroiled filet mignon with sherry sauce and crispy onions, and a delicious version of jumbo shrimp stuffed with jalapeño pepper, wrapped in bacon, and served with barbecue sauce. The pastas are house-made. New menu items include the house specialty, a seafood stew, chock full of shrimp, calamari, and fish in a spicy tomato sauce, known as "Neptune's Delight." Reef and Beef (beer-battered shrimp with filet mignon); chicken Cordon Bleu, and an all-Jamaican version of roasted oxtail with beans are other temptations.

8 Perth Rd. ✆ 876/962-7130. Reservations recommended for dinner. Main courses J$600–J$1,800 (US$9.60–US$29). AE, MC, V. Mon–Sat noon–10pm.

International Chinese Restaurant ASIAN   This is a good place if you're seeking some change-of-pace dining; you can eat well and inexpensively here. Some of the Chinese dishes have been given a Jamaican dash of flavor: a baked seafood medley comes with shredded coconut. Other dishes could be served at your favorite hometown Chinese eatery, such as chicken with cashew nuts. Try the special fried rice served with a combination of meats that include lobster, chicken, beef, and shrimp, all laced together with flavorful, extra-black soy sauce.

117 Manchester Rd. ✆ 876/962-1252. Reservations not necessary. Main courses J$300–J$1,670 (US$4.80–US$27). MC, V. Mon–Fri noon–9pm; Sat noon–9:30pm; Sun noon–8pm.

The New Den ✦ JAMAICAN   One of Mandeville's more venerated old favorites, this restaurant is installed in a century-old setting that was once a family home. You dine in what were the occupants' former bedrooms in a setting of wood and wicker furnishings, with an old rustic feeling. You can eat inside or outdoors. The chefs know their pots and pans, and turn out a savory cuisine including well-prepared grilled curry chicken, a steak kabob (with onions, pineapple, and peppers), and both jerk chicken and pork. Fish and chips appears often. The most famous dishes here include grilled fish and meats. Barbecued chicken is wonderful. The house specialty is the

---

Impressions

When you have troubles, don't cry—remember rum is standing by.

—Old Jamaican saying

famous mixed grill, wherein diners select their choice of three different grilled meats or fish from anything listed on the menu. A fine and decent place; not as posh as Bloomfield, but with a charm that's very appealing.

35 Caledonia Rd. ⓒ **876/962-3603**. Reservations recommended. Main courses J$300–J$1,500 (US$4.80–US$24). MC, V. Mon–Sat noon–9pm.

DISCOVERING THE TOWN

Mandeville sprawls across hills, but its historic core is easy to walk. The town centers around **Cecil Charlton Park** ⚘, named for a former mayor. The Mandeville Courthouse stands on the northern tier of this plaza. Built of cut limestone in 1816 in Georgian style, it has an unusual double staircase and is graced with Doric columns.

Adjoining the courthouse is the **Rectory**—the oldest structure in town, completed in 1820. Throughout its long history, it was both a tavern and a hotel before reverting to its current status as a private residence. On the south side of the square rises **St. Mark's Church,** also established in 1820. It's worth a look inside for its timbered clerestory. The graveyard is filled with tombs of British soldiers who died in a yellow-fever epidemic.

Shopping in the town is a pleasure, whether in the old center or in a modern complex such as **Grove Court.** The market in the center of town teems with life, particularly on weekends when country folk ride into town on their weekly visits. It's open Monday to Saturday 9am to 4pm.

A private garden in the area worth visiting is **Mrs. Stephenson's Garden** ⚘, 25 New Green Rd. (ⓒ **876/962-2328**), one of the most beautiful and well maintained in the area. An artist, Carmen Stephenson, still supervises this flamboyant "secret garden" herself. Call ahead for an appointment. The cost is a well-spent $3.

EXPLORING THE AREA

The **Manchester Country Club,** Brumalia Road (ⓒ **876/962-2403**), is Jamaica's oldest golf course. It's been expanded from 9 to 18 holes. Beautiful vistas unfold from 661m (2,201 ft.) above sea level. Greens fees are J$1,500 (US$24), with caddy fees running J$1,000 (US$16). The course has a clubhouse, and this is also one of the best places in central Jamaica to play tennis.

If you like coffee, visit the **Jamaican Standard Products Company** ⚘ (ⓒ **876/963-4211**), 3km (1¾ miles) north of Mandeville in Williamsfield. Call Monday to Friday about free tours. The factory, which has a wonderful aroma, exports mainly to Japan; it packages Blue Mountain coffee beans and its own "High Mountain" coffee. The factory also turns out spices and sauces. Call from 8am to 5pm. Tours begin at any time during the day if a guide is available.

Ocho Rios & Runaway Bay

Situated on Jamaica's northeast coast, the resort areas of **Port Antonio** (see chapter 8), **Runaway Bay,** and **Ocho Rios** helped to launch large-scale tourism in Jamaica. Known for its abundant rainfall, verdant landscapes, rolling hills, and jagged estuaries, this region was once the preferred hangout for Noël Coward, Errol Flynn, and a host of British and American literati. Ian Fleming, creator of the James Bond spy thrillers, lived at Goldeneye near Ocho Rios.

Some 31km (19 miles) west lies its chief rival, the resort of **Runaway Bay**—more secluded than Ocho Rios, and without the vendors or cruise ship arrivals. There's no real town here; it's mainly just a beachfront strip of hotels.

Just 8km (5 miles) to the west of Runaway Beach is **Discovery Bay,** whose name refers to the belief that Columbus first landed here in 1494.

A 2-hour drive east from Montego Bay, **Ocho Rios** was once a small banana and fishing port, but tourism long ago became its leading industry. Now Jamaica's cruise ship capital, the bay is dominated by an ore terminal and hotels with sandy beaches fringed by palm trees. The place is fine for a lazy beach vacation, but it's definitely not for anyone seeking a remote hideaway.

Ocho Rios is far lusher than Montego Bay, and many of its resort hotels boast private sandy beaches. On the other hand, golfing and nightlife are better in Montego Bay; if you want hedonism, head for Negril. Ocho Rios? It's more tranquil (some say blander) than either of them.

1 Ocho Rios

ORIENTATION

VISITOR INFORMATION　The local office of the **Jamaica Tourist Board** is at Office #3 in the Ocean Villa Plaza on Main Street (✆ **876/974-2582**). It is open Monday to Friday 8:30am to 4:30pm.

THE TOWN LAYOUT　Ocho Rios is hardly a place you can explore on foot, except for its inner core. Most of its uncontrolled development lies to the east of the center. The actual town stretches some 6km (3¾ miles) between Dunn's River Falls to the west and White River to the east. Connecting these far corners is the A3, often called Main Street. Mercifully, this traffic-clogged road bypasses the congested heart of town; curved like a snake, Main Street borders Turtle Bay with its beach. In the very center of town stands a handy-as-a-landmark clock tower. Main Street and Da Costa Drive meet at this point.

If you'd like to explore this northern part of Jamaica in more depth, especially by car, purchase the big fold-out map called *Ocho Rios and Beyond,* sold at all news kiosks in the center of town.

GETTING AROUND   It is not really necessary to rent a car in Ocho Rios. Taxis will make pickups when called to hotels. Taxis are governed by **JUTA** (© 876/974-2292). In the center of town, they are plentiful in the parking lot adjacent to Ocean Village Plaza. You can also hire a taxi from **Maxi Tours** (© 876/974-2971), which operates from premises directly across the highway from Sandals Ocho Rios.

There is no bus service within Ocho Rios.

SPECIAL EVENTS   The Caribbean's most important jazz festival is the weeklong **Ocho Rios Jazz Festival,** held at various venues during the second week in June. Big names like the Jimmy Smith Trio appear here. Although Jamaica is primarily associated with reggae music, it has also contributed great jazz artists to the world, including Bertie King on saxophone and Jiver Hutchinson on trumpet. For more details and information, contact the Ocho Rios Jazz Festival (© **866/649-2137** or 323/857-5358; www.ochoriosjazz.com).

FAST FACTS: Ocho Rios

Banks   The most convenient bank is **Scotiabank,** Main Street (© 876/974-2311), open Monday, Thursday, and Friday 8:15am to 4pm, and Tuesday and Wednesday 8:15am to 3pm. It has foreign exchange facilities and an ATM.

Bookstores   The best is **Everybody's Bookshop,** Shop 44 in Ocean Village Plaza (© 876/974-2932), open Monday to Saturday 9am to 5:30pm.

Emergencies   Call police or report a fire by dialing © 119. The police station (© 876/974-2533 for routine calls) is off Da Costa Drive, east of the clock tower.

Laundry   If your hotel doesn't have facilities, use **The Laundry Market** (© 876/974-5519), on Main Street, east of the center at the turnoff for Shaw Park. Hours are Monday to Saturday 9am to 6pm.

Library   The **Ocho Rios Public Library** is at Milford Road (© 876/974-2588), open Monday to Friday 9am to 5pm and Saturday 9am to 1pm.

Mail   The main **Ocho Rios Post Office** is on Main Street (© 876/974-2526), and it's open Monday to Friday 8am to 5pm. You can send faxes or telegrams from here, too. The post office is crowded and not as efficient as it should be; many visitors send important mail via UPS. The local office is at **Airpak Express,** Shop 9, Ocean Village Shopping Centre (© 876/974-0910). Hours are Monday to Friday 8am to 5pm. Include "Jamaica, W.I." in all island addresses. At press time for this edition, the island had no zip codes, despite efforts that had been made throughout 2005 to inaugurate them within the Jamaican postal system.

Medical Services   There is no hospital in Ocho Rios; the nearest is **St. Ann's Bay Hospital** (© 876/972-0150), 11km (6¾ miles) west. The **Central Medical Laboratory** (© 876/974-2614), at Shop #14 in the Carib Arcade on Main Street, in the center of town, offers basic services Monday to Friday 8am to 4:30pm, Saturday 9am to noon. So does **Medi-Rays,** at Shops #9–10, in the Carib Arcade on Main Street (© 876/974-6251), open Monday and Friday 8am to 6pm, Tuesday to Thursday 8am to 5pm, and Saturday 8:30am to 12:30pm.

Pharmacies   The most central pharmacy is **Ocho Rios Pharmacy,** Shop 27 in Ocean Village Plaza (© 876/974-2398), open Monday to Saturday 9am to 8pm

and Sunday 9am to 7pm. Another good one nearby is **Pine Grove Pharmacy,** in Simmons Plaza (© **876/974-2023**), open Monday to Saturday 9am to 8pm, Sunday 10am to 3pm.

Travel Agencies The most reliable travel agent is **Trafalgar Travel Ltd.,** Shop #2 in Soni's Place, 12 Main St. (© **876/974-9270**), open Monday to Friday 8:30am to 4:30pm and Saturday 9am to 12:30pm.

WHERE TO STAY

Note that all-inclusive resorts, where guests prepay one price for all lodgings, meals, entertainment, and often drinks, are listed separately below (p. 162). Most would fall into the Expensive or Very Expensive categories. Also, many properties, such as Beaches and Sandals, can be reached via toll-free numbers. Otherwise, use a good travel agent.

VERY EXPENSIVE

Jamaica Inn 🐠🐠   Built in 1950, and painted a shade of blue-violet that was specially named by the paint company that manufactures it, the gracious and elegant Jamaica Inn consists of a series of long, low two-story buildings set in a U-shape near the sea, 2km (1¼ miles) east of town. It's an elegant anachronism, a true retro hotel in the most upscale sense of the word, and has remained little changed in 4 decades, avoiding the glitter of all-inclusives like Sandals. Sir Winston Churchill came here frequently during the 1950s to paint—the suite named after him is a repository of many legends: Noël Coward, arriving with Katharine Hepburn or Claudette Colbert, was a regular, bashing out melodies on the piano in the bar, and Errol Flynn, Ian Fleming, and scads of quietly wealthy and otherwise reclusive socialites from both the U.K. and the U.S. used to drop in from time to time. In 2005, this time-honored grande dame upgraded many of its rooms and suites, adding postmodern minimalist touches to some of its more upscale suites, while retaining Sir Winston Churchill's suite basically the way it was when he checked in here.

Today, Jamaica Inn retains its pedigree as one of the genuinely elegant but low-key resorts, sticking to a way of life that many clients adore. Don't expect access to TV in your room; in keeping with the Inn's origins, they simply are not here. In lieu of that, guests are likely to be reading, playing croquet, or chatting with other guests in the plushly comfortable bar and library. And don't expect scads of children underfoot, either. In winter, children under 12 aren't allowed, and the rest of the year, children under 10 aren't allowed. Clients today are likely to include CEOs and well-placed business personalities; movers and shakers from, say, the Aspen or Sundance film festivals; or perhaps, supermodel and super-personality Kate Moss.

Lovely patios open onto the lawns, and the bedrooms are reached along garden paths. Guest rooms are English colonial in their appointments and very spacious, with mahogany two-poster beds, quality carved-wood period pieces, and balustraded balconies opening onto views of the sea. Bathrooms are elegant and roomy, gleaming with marble vanities, combination shower/tubs, robes, and deluxe toiletries. One of the genuinely appealing aspects to accommodations here involves very large open-sided verandas. They're large in even the cheapest units, and in the more upscale lodgings, they're big enough to be defined as sprawling living rooms in their own right,

Ocho Rios

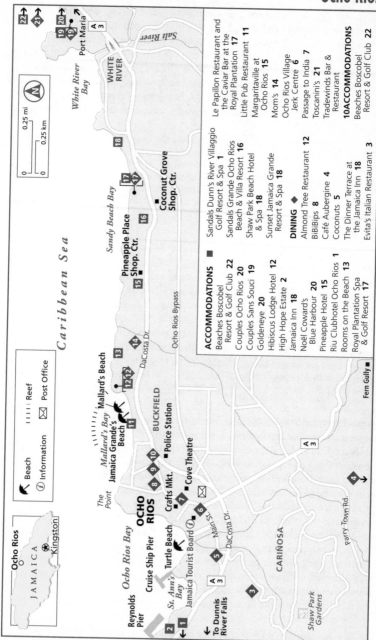

ACCOMMODATIONS ■

Beaches Boscobel
Resort & Golf Club **22**
Couples Ocho Rios **20**
Couples Sans Souci **19**
Goldeneye **20**
Hibiscus Lodge Hotel **12**
High Hope Estate **2**
Jamaica Inn **18**
Noël Coward's
Blue Harbour **20**
Pineapple Hotel **15**
Riu Clubhotel Ocho Rios **1**
Rooms on the Beach **13**
Royal Plantation Spa
& Golf Resort **17**

Sandals Dunn's River Villaggio
Golf Resort & Spa **1**
Sandals Grande Ocho Rios
Beach & Villa Resort **16**
Shaw Park Beach Hotel
& Spa **18**
Sunset Jamaica Grande
Resort & Spa **18**

DINING ◆

Almond Tree Restaurant **12**
BiBiBips **8**
Café Aubergine **4**
Coconuts **5**
The Dinner Terrace at
the Jamaica Inn **18**
Evita's Italian Restaurant **3**

Le Papillon Restaurant and
the Caviar Bar at the
Royal Plantation **17**
Little Pub Restaurant **11**
Margaritaville at
Ocho Rios **15**
Mom's **14**
Ocho Rios Village
Jerk Centre **6**
Passage to India **7**
Toscanini's **21**
Tradewinds Bar &
Restaurant

10ACCOMMODATIONS

Beaches Boscobel
Resort & Golf Club **22**

replete with plushly upholstered sofas, armchairs, and writing tables like you'd have expected in an indoor hotel suite. The beach is a wide, champagne-colored strip; close to the shore, the sea is almost too clear to make snorkeling an adventure, but farther out it's rewarding. The European-trained chef prepares both refined international and Jamaican dishes that are served in rituals as elegant and formal as anything in the Caribbean. The emphasis is on cuisine that uses fresh local produce. Men must wear a collared shirt with long trousers at night, but during February, when the clientele here mostly derives from England, most of the men voluntarily opt to wear jackets, usually without ties.

Main St. (P.O. Box 1), Ocho Rios. ✆ **800/837-4608** in the U.S., or 876/974-2514. Fax 876/974-2449. www.jamaicainn.com. 47 units. Winter $500–$750 double, from $780 suite for 2; off season $240–$370 double, from $370 suite for 2. MAP (breakfast & dinner) $90 extra per person per day, FAP (breakfast, lunch & dinner) $110 extra per person per day. Ten-night minimum stay required over Christmas. AE, MC, V. Children age 12 and under (in winter), and 10 and under (in off season) not accepted. **Amenities:** Restaurant; 2 bars; pool; 4 tennis courts; exercise room; 24-hr. limited room service; babysitting; laundry service; nonsmoking rooms; rooms for those w/limited mobility; kayaking; Sunfish sailing. *In room:* A/C, ceiling fan, TV, dataport, iron, safe.

MODERATE

Hibiscus Lodge Hotel *Value*   This intimate little inn offers more value for your money than any other resort in Ocho Rios. Perched precariously on a cliff along the shore near the Ocho Rios Mall, it has character and charm—and the golden sands of Mahogany Beach lie a 3- to 4-minute walk away. Medium-size bedrooms, either doubles or triples, have small, shower-only bathrooms, ceiling fans, and verandas opening onto the sea. After a day spent in a pool suspended over the cliffs, or lounging on the large sun deck, guests can enjoy a drink in the swinging bar (where chairs and settees swing from ropes overhead) or a meal at the Almond Tree (p. 169).

83 Main St. (P.O. Box 52), Ocho Rios. ✆ 876/974-2676. Fax 876/974-1874. www.hibiscusjamaica.com. 26 units. Winter $140 double, $184 triple; off season $129 double, $165 triple. Rates include breakfast. AE, MC, V. **Amenities:** Restaurant; bar; pool; tennis court; Jacuzzi; limited room service; laundry service; rooms for those w/limited mobility. *In room:* A/C, TV, hair dryer, iron/board, safe.

High Hope Estate *⌖*   Because this hotel is so intimate, whether you like it will depend on whether you click with the owner and the other guests. Basically, it's an upscale private home in the style of the British colonial world at its most rarefied that accepts paying guests. It was built in 1961 for a socially prominent heiress, Kitty Spence, granddaughter of prairie-state populist William Jennings Bryan, and later served as the home and laboratory of a horticulturist who successfully bred 560 varieties of flowering hibiscus. Dennis Rappaport is today's congenial owner. The estate's 16 hectares (40 acres), set 165m (550 ft.) above the coast and 11km (6¾ miles) west of Ocho Rios, thrive with flowering plants as well as memories of such luminaries as Noël Coward, who used to play the grand piano that graces one of the public areas. There are absolutely no planned activities here. Bedrooms are a delight—spacious, well thought out, and exceedingly comfortable. The excellent bathrooms have shower/tub combinations. The staff is on hand to help supervise children, maintain the property, and prepare meals for anyone who gives advance notice

The nearest beach is a 10-minute ride away.

Box 11, St. Ann's Bay, near Ocho Rios. ✆ 876/972-2277. Fax 876/972-1607. www.highhopeestate.com. 5 units. Year-round $95–$165 double. Rates include breakfast. MC, V. **Amenities:** Restaurant; pool; limited room service; babysitting; laundry service; nonsmoking rooms; rooms for those w/limited mobility; TV room. *In room:* Ceiling fan, cable TV (on request), minibar, coffeemaker, hair dryer, CD player.

INEXPENSIVE

Pineapple Hotel *(Kids)*   Next door to the Pineapple Place Shopping Centre, this pale-orange-and-green-painted hotel offers very basic accommodations at bargain prices. Expect no frills; stay only if you can't afford the high prices of Ocho Rios and plan to spend little time in your room. The tropically decorated white-walled accommodations include private bathrooms with showers, tile floors, and air-conditioning, but if you want to make a phone call, you must do it from the front desk. TVs are available in some rooms. Watersports can be arranged at the front desk; and there's a swimming pool on the premises. For a seaside romp, try Turtle Beach, a short walk away.

Pineapple Place (P.O. Box 263), Ocho Rios. (C) **876/974-2727.** Fax 876/974-9073. 20 units. Year-round $60 double. Children 11 and under stay free in parent's room. AE, MC, V. **Amenities:** Pool; watersports; kids camp. *In room:* A/C, TV, iron, safe, no phone.

Rooms on the Beach *(Value)*   Originally built in the 1970s, and reincarnated after a massive renovation, this comfortable and unpretentious hotel offers good value from a location within the shadow of its mammoth all-inclusive neighbor, the Sunset Jamaica Grande Resort & Spa, in the heart of Ocho Rios. Designed in an L-shaped format that embraces a wide courtyard terrace and a pool with its own swim-up bar, it opens directly onto a desirable stretch of Mallard's Beach. Views from its social center (i.e., its pool terrace) incorporate the arrivals and departures of some of the world's largest and flashiest cruise ships. Bedrooms are comfortable and practical, without a lot of extra frills, but well located and within a short walk of the dining and drinking options that proliferate within downtown Ocho Rios. Each has mahogany furniture, a tiled floor, and oversized, full-length windows that slide to the side in ways that imitate a sliding patio door. Under separate management, there's a likable restaurant with tables that spill onto the pool terrace, serving a "fusion-based" mix of Asian and Jamaican food. Although this place is not marketed as an all-inclusive resort, and although it's much less well-accessorized than any of the other members of the Super-Club chain, it's nonetheless included in the list of SuperClub's member hotels, mostly for the purposes of its marketing programs.

Main St. (P.O. Box 280), Ocho Rios. (C) **800/467-8737** or 876/974-6632. Fax 876/516-1544. www.roomsresorts.com. 99 units. Winter $94–$99 double, $103 junior suite; $110 family room; off season $89–$92 double, $99 junior suite, $110 family room. Children aged 2–13 $13 each. Rates include breakfast and greens fees at any golf course operated and maintained by SuperClubs. AE, DC, MC, V. **Amenities:** Pool bar; pool; golf privileges, w/no charge, at the Super-Clubs Runaway Golf Club; fitness center; watersports; Internet stations; coin-operated laundry facilities. *In room:* A/C, TV, beverage maker, hair dryer, safe.

NEARBY PLACES TO STAY

Noël Coward's Blue Harbour *(★) (Finds)*   This 1950s-era retreat, 24km (15 miles) east of Ocho Rios, was once owned by Coward, who entertained the rich and famous of his day here. Coward dubbed the place—his first Jamaica retreat—"Coward's Folly." Today the compound is rented whole or in part to paying guests who appreciate its funky nostalgia. The compound can comfortably accommodate 10 to 12 guests, though up to 18 could squeeze in, if needed. The main house is the Villa Grande, with two bedrooms and two bathrooms with shower, plus a kitchen, dining room, and terrace. Villa Rose, a guesthouse, contains two large bedrooms, and the smaller Villa Chica is a one-bedroom, one-bathroom cottage once favored by Marlene Dietrich and Katharine Hepburn. Meals—Jamaican, vegetarian, and international—are cooked by a friendly, helpful staff. All three of the villas share a single kitchen, and all meals are

Noël's "Folly"

Arriving in Jamaica in 1944, the brilliant English playwright, songwriter, raconteur, and actor Noël Coward discovered his dream island.

He returned in 1948 and rented Goldeneye from his friend Ian Fleming, the real-life spy who later created the James Bond character at this estate. During this stopover, Coward found a "magical spot" 16km (10 miles) down the coast at St. Mary's. The land was once owned by Sir Henry Morgan, the notorious buccaneer who had built a small fortress on the property so he could spy on any stray galleon entering local waters. It was here that Coward began construction on what he called his "folly"—**Blue Harbour**, which can be rented today (see above).

Once settled in, Coward sent out invitations to his "bloody loved ones." They included Laurence Olivier, Vivien Leigh, Alfred Lunt, Lynn Fontane, Errol Flynn, Katharine Hepburn, Mary Martin, Claudette Colbert, and John Gielgud, among others. Some stayed an entire month.

Blue Harbour became so popular on the North Coast cocktail circuit that in 1956 Coward fled it and built **Firefly** on a panoramic nearby hilltop, which still stands today much as he left it (p. 177). Coward lived at Firefly with his longtime companion, Graham Payn.

In 1965 the Queen Mother came to visit Coward, who prepared a lobster mousse for her only to have it melt in the hot sun. He quickly rushed to the kitchen and opened a can of split-pea soup. She found it "divine"—perhaps because Coward had hastily laced it with sherry.

Sir Winston Churchill, who also loved Jamaica, visited Coward several times at Firefly. He told the playwright: "An Englishman has an inalienable right to live wherever he chooses."

Coward died at Firefly and is buried on the grounds. You can still see his plain, flat white marble gravestone, which is inscribed simply: "Sir Noël Coward, born December 16, 1899, died March 26, 1973."

served at predesignated hours within a communal dining room. In some cases, the entire compound is rented out by a single party, shutting out other guests.

North Coast Rd. (P.O. Box 50), Port Maria, St. Mary. ℰ 876/725-0289 or 505/586-1244 (Questa, NM). Fax 505/586-1087. www.blueharb.com. 3 villas. Year-round $170 double; $1,190 weekly. Rates include meals but no drinks. No credit cards. On the North Coast Rd. (A4), 129km (80 miles) west of Montego Bay and 97km (60 miles) north of Kingston. **Amenities:** Dining room; pool; limited room service; in-room massage; babysitting; laundry service. *In room:* TV, kitchenette, minibar, iron/board, safe.

ALL-INCLUSIVE RESORTS

More so than any resort in Jamaica, Ocho Rios is now firmly in the all-inclusive resort camp. Many of the older and more established inns have been swallowed up by the Sandals umbrella, reborn as all-inclusives with names like "Beaches."

Not for independent or frugal types, these all-inclusives—where things can feel scheduled and formulaic—are nevertheless the best, most luxurious lodgings at Ocho Rios (with an exception or two). Most are quite expensive as a result. The following

resorts all include your room, drinks, and meals, plus often many activities, in the price. Seek detailed clarification of what's included when booking.

Beaches Boscobel Resort & Golf Club ★ Kids

Sixteen kilometers (10 miles) east of Ocho Rios on a beach, in an isolated spot that's many miles from any other hotel or any other population center, this resort looks new again, thanks to an $18-million renovation in 2004, which was followed with a $4.5-million renovation in 2006. Managed by the Sandals chain, it's specifically designed for families with children. Bedrooms are surprisingly large, and as such, are easily suitable for up to four family members at a time. Each is designed as a split level, with a slight difference in elevation between the "sleeping" and "living" areas of each accommodation. Each is furnished with deliberately understated, rather bland-looking furniture that's virtually indestructible. Each comes with a good-size private bathroom with tub/shower combination. Unless you have children of your own, or unless you simply adore children in general, think carefully before coming to this resort, since the venues are very clearly and deliberately configured as family-friendly—in some cases, even family-obsessed. Positioned at strategic intervals throughout the place are costumed replicas of characters from *Sesame Street,* including the Cookie Monster (with whom you and/or your children can go biking); Zoe (with whom you can dance); Elmo (who will read stories geared for—you guessed it—children); and Grover (with whom you can explore). Invariably, adults seem to enjoy these diversions as much as their kids, but unless you're caught up in the child-rearing cycle, you might find all of this just a bit too cute. If you need to get away from it all, remember that guests within this resort can play free at the nearby Sandals golf course.

Boscobel Beach (P.O. Box 63), Ocho Rios. ✆ 888/BEACHES or 876/975-7777. Fax 876/975-7622. www.beaches.com. 224 units. Year-round $280–$320 per person in a double. $80 per child (2–16). Children 1 and under free. Rates are all-inclusive. AE, MC, V. **Amenities:** 5 restaurants; 7 bars; 3 pools; nearby golf; 4 lit tennis courts; spa and fitness center; 3 Jacuzzis; full program of watersports (including kayaks, scuba, and windsurfing); Kids Camp program; game center; pool tables; limited room service; babysitting; rooms for those w/limited mobility; dance club; teen disco; beach volleyball; kiddie pool; petting zoo. *In room:* A/C, TV, coffeemaker, hair dryer, safe.

Couples Ocho Rios ★

This place is noticeably a bit less animated and raucous, and just a bit classier and perhaps a bit less glittery and flashy, than its counterparts within Sandals. Most of the clients here are married, and many are on their honeymoons. Everything is in pairs, even the chairs at night by the moon-drenched beach. Some guests slip away from the resort, which is an 18-minute drive (8km/5 miles) east of town, to Couples's private island to bask in the buff. (A shuttle boat transports visitors offshore to this beautiful little island with a fine sandy beach, a bar, and a pool. Security guards keep the gawkers from bothering guests here.)

The bedrooms have either a king-size bed or two doubles, pleasantly traditional furnishings, and a patio fronting either the sea or the mountains. Good-size bathrooms have a shower/tub combination. For a chain all-inclusive, the cuisine is above average.

Tower Isle, Rte. A3 (P.O. Box 330), Ocho Rios. ✆ 800/268-7537 in the U.S., or 876/975-4271. Fax 876/975-4439. www.couples.com. 207 units. Winter $535–$673 double, $696–$911 suite; off season $493–$546 double, $653–$783 suite. Rates are per couple, per night, and include all meals, drinks, and activities. AE, DISC, MC, V. The hotel usually accepts bookings for a minimum of any 3 nights of the week, though most guests book by the week. AE, DISC, MC, V. Children under 18 not accepted. **Amenities:** 5 restaurants; 4 bars; pool; golf; 4 tennis courts; health club and spa; 4 Jacuzzis; sauna; bike rental; Internet room; room service (breakfast only); nonsmoking rooms; rooms for those w/limited mobility; squash courts; yoga; kayaking; sailing; scuba diving; snorkeling; water-skiing; windsurfing; horseback riding. *In room:* A/C, TV, dataport, beverage maker, hair dryer, iron, safe.

Couples Sans Souci ✦✦✦   Positioned beside the coastal road about 3km (1.8m) east from the center of Ocho Rios, this is the most recent incarnation of a compound of buildings that were originally conceived, at the time of their construction, as an interconnected, medium-rise cluster of apartments and time shares. Today, painted a tasteful shade of coffee-with-cream, and after many different incarnations under many different management teams, it's operated as a member of Couples. What does that mean? Its rates are slightly lower than the roughly equivalent tariffs charged at its biggest competitor, the Sandals chain. (Couples markets its product a bit less aggressively than Sandals, and consequently, its rates tend to be a bit less expensive.) It's maintained as a couples-only resort, employing as part of their corporate vision a full time "Director of Romance." Most of the clients here are married, and many are on their honeymoons. Everything is arranged in pairs, even the chairs at night by the moon-drenched beach. There's a separate clothing-optional beach, a mineral bath big enough for an elephant, and a labyrinth of catwalks and bridges stretching over rocky chasms filled with surging water. Frankly, the building's architecture, although adapted since its initial construction into a format conducive to fun, sand, beach holidays, and the tropics, evokes a discreetly isolated apartment building that you might have found in any warm-weather (or for that matter, cold-weather) climate in the world.

Each unit features a veranda or patio, copies of Chippendale furniture, plush upholstery, and subdued colonial elegance. Some contain Jacuzzis. Accommodations range from rather standard bedrooms to vast suites with large living and dining areas, plus kitchens. Deluxe touches include glazed tile floors, luxurious beds, and marble bathrooms with whirlpool tubs.

Rte. A3 (P.O. Box 103), Ocho Rios. 📞 **800/268-7537** or 876/994-1206. Fax 876/994-1544. www.couples.com. 148 units. Winter $590–$1,000 double; off season $538–$850 double. Rates are all-inclusive. AE, DISC, MC, V. No children under 16. **Amenities:** 3 restaurants; 5 bars; 4 pools; golf; 2 lit tennis courts; health club and spa; 2 Jacuzzis; sauna; 24-hr. room service; laundry service; dry cleaning; nonsmoking rooms; rooms for those w/limited mobility; kayaks; sailing; scuba diving; snorkeling; water-skiing; windsurfing. *In room:* A/C, TV, minibar, beverage maker, hair dryer, iron, safe.

Goldeneye ✦✦   Few hotels in the world manage to be so luxurious and yet so appealingly informal as this intimate retreat. It's centered around the villa where the most famous secret agent in the world, James Bond (007), was created in 1952 by then-owner Ian Fleming. Fleming built the imposing but simple main house in 1946, and wrote each of the 13 original James Bond books there. In the early 1990s, music-publisher-turned-hotelier Chris Blackwell bought and restored the by-then dilapidated property to its original modernist dignity. Fleming's original desk remains, and the oversize Indonesian furniture is enhanced with memorabilia from what became the most famous spy movies in the world. The three-bedroom main house is usually only rented as a whole for extended house parties, often to rock stars and other celebs.

You're more likely to rent one of the four additional villas that were built in harmony with nature, on the surrounding property. Each evokes a tropical version of a billionaire's summer camp in Maine, thanks to a juxtaposition of indoor and outdoor spaces, sofas, and well-chosen decorative pieces. Each unit has a fully equipped kitchen. All drinks, food, and most activities are included in the price. The cuisine features some Jamaican favorites as well as international dishes.

There's a pool on the premises, but it's reserved for occupants of the main house. Masonry paths lead to a nearby beach.

Oracabessa, St. Mary. 📞 **800/688-7678** in the U.S., or 876/975-3354. Fax 876/975-3620. www.islandoutpost.com/goldeneye. 5 villas. Winter $950 1-bedroom villa, $1,150 2-bedroom villa, $1,350 3-bedroom villa, $3,800 Ian Fleming

house; off season $750 1-bedroom villa, $950 2-bedroom villa, $1,150 3-bedroom villa, $2,800 Ian Fleming house. Rates include all meals, drinks, and activities. AE, DISC, MC, V. **Amenities:** Restaurant; bar; watersports; limited room service; babysitting; laundry service; nonsmoking rooms; rooms for those w/limited mobility. *In room:* A/C, TV, dataport, kitchenette, minibar, coffeemaker, iron, safe.

Riu Clubhotel Ocho Rios ⓖ ✓*Value*   Set immediately adjacent to the sea, about a 3km (2-mile) drive along the coastal road west of the center, this sprawling member of the Spain-based all-inclusive hotel chain opened in 2005. Larger than any other hotel in town, and painted in tones of rose-violet that evoke a jungle orchid, it's big, bold, and ready, willing, and able to offer deeply discounted promotional prices that have many large-scale competitors deeply worried. The soaring open-air heart of the resort, near the bustling reception area, evokes the late-19th-century, with decorative touches that might have been inspired by the decors of the Spanish court during the 1890s, particularly the sinuous pink-and-brown stencils that snake and wind their way across the vaulted ceilings.

Everywhere you look at this high-volume, high-energy resort, you'll have views of the sea and the many organized activities presented by the staff. Accommodations lie within a pair of horseshoe-shaped wings, each with between four and six stories. One wing is exclusively devoted to conventional rooms, the other exclusively to suites, each of them facing the sands of Mammee Bay Beach. Accommodations are surprisingly *luxe,* each with private balconies or verandas, marble floors, and mostly mahogany furniture configured into vaguely neoclassical, Roman-revival patterns. Throughout the day and evening, lots of activities are offered, one of the best-attended of which involves dance lessons that focus on merengue, salsa, and bachata.

Mammee Bay, Ocho Rios. ⓒ **888/666-8816** or 876/972-2200. Fax 876/972-2203. www.riu.com. 837 units. Winter $288–$318 double, $346 junior suite; off season $226–$238 double, $290 junior suite. AE, DC, MC, V. **Amenities:** 7 restaurants; 7 bars; 2 swimming pools plus a shallow pool reserved for children; tennis courts; exercise rooms w/health club; children's programs; car rental; salon; live entertainment; disco; casino; aerobic classes; waterpolo; volleyball; petanque courts; ping pong; sailboats; windsurfing; snorkeling; kayaking; horseback riding. *In room:* A/C, ceiling fan, cable TV, minibar, safe.

Royal Plantation Spa & Golf Resort ⓖⓖⓖ   This stately inn, the town's foremost rival of the also-recommended Jamaica Inn, positioned 2km (1¼ mile) east of the town center, is marketed as the most upscale and most luxurious member of the Sandals chain in Jamaica. Its decor evokes the antebellum American South meets baroque Europe, thanks to an elegant and gracefully symmetrical Neoclassical entrance portico, spike-shaped Mediterranean cypresses, lavish use of patterned marble laid out into marquetry-inspired patterns, a series of terraces that seem to cascade in graduated and artfully landscaped ripples to the sea, strategically positioned gazebos jutting on either piers or rocky headlands into the sea, and exotic orchids positioned strategically whenever a sight line might even hint at being boring. There's a definite aura of drama, flashiness, and romance in the air here; a conscious response to the deliberately understated decor of, say, the also very posh Jamaica Inn.

Staff is hip, articulate, and urbanized, used to lavishing perks and extra services upon a clientele that might otherwise have felt at home within an upscale casino hotel in Las Vegas. A complete renovation has brought major improvements to the rooms and public areas and added a full-service Five-Star Diamond European spa. Gone are the tropical floral patterns of yesteryear: In its place are high-Victorian furnishings in the public areas (possibly the most upscale great house looks of any hotel in Jamaica), and in the suites, a Mediterranean theme of soothing earth tones mixed with lots of mahogany, and a traditional sense of old-time British glamour.

Management here provides a lot for guests to do, including the availability of painting classes from locally famous Jamaican artists, cigar-rolling classes, and every Thursday, cooking classes. Each of the accommodations is configured as a suite, each opening onto an ocean view. Bedrooms are handsomely equipped with scads of mahogany and marble, with such extras as plush cotton robes, your choice of four different styles of pillows, the daily *New York Times*, fax service, Internet connections, CD players, and the like. Guests have full exchange privileges with the two other Sandals resorts in the area. The cuisine is far superior to that at the other Sandals properties. (The resort's lead restaurant, Le Papillon, is recommended separately in "Where to Dine," below.) The atmosphere is less rowdy, and management has added some additional gewgaws and gimmicks that include the only caviar-and-champagne bar in Jamaica, perhaps in the entire Caribbean. An unusual perk to a stay of any length here includes the gratis transfer, in a private car, to and from the airport at Ocho Rios. Expect a clientele that's a bit older and more prosperous, and persons under 18 aren't admitted. *Note:* Stays are sold here based on an EP plan, but 70% or more of the clients here opt to pay a supplement for all-inclusive plan whereby most food, drinks, and sports programs are included as part of an agreed-upon package.

Main St., Ocho Rios. ⓒ 888/48ROYAL or 876/974-5601. Fax 876/974-5912. www.royalplantation.com. 77 units. Winter $450–$1,450 double; off season $320–$1,025 double. Supplement of $160 per person per day buys all meals, most drinks, all minibar fees, complimentary greens fees at a nearby golf course, plus transfers, unlimited access to scuba and other watersports, AE, DC, DISC, MC, V. **Amenities:** 3 restaurants; bar; golf at nearby Sandals; full-service spa; 24-hr. room service; glass-bottom boat; scuba diving, *In room:* A/C, cable TV, VCR, dataport, minibar, safe.

Sandals Dunn's River Villaggio Golf Resort & Spa ✪

Since its $24-million redesign and radical upgrade in 2005, this Sandals is better than ever. During its redesign, it wasn't afraid to go theme-ish: The venue is unabashedly Italian, with public areas that suggest an interconnected series of Tuscan piazzas, staff uniforms that evoke the Italian Renaissance, and a deeply entrenched commitment to eco-sensitive harmony at a beachfront setting of undeniable beauty. An immersion in the aesthetics of Italy is almost nonstop. Jugglers and mime artists add performance-artist spontaneity, and frequent bouts of live entertainment include Jamaican guitarists singing island folk songs or Italian singers performing arias from *bel canto* operas. Italian ice creams are served with gusto from the *gelateria*, with the cost of these treats invariably included as part of the resort's all-inclusive format. The bedrooms are upscale, appealing, and plush. Each has touches of stained glass and mahogany furniture. Accommodations are scattered among the six-story main building, two lanai buildings, and a five-story west wing. Extras include spacious balconies, walk-in closets, king-size beds, and shower/tub combinations. As at all Sandals resorts, only couples are allowed inside, and—unlike in former years—same-sex couples are now welcome, albeit not necessarily common. Set on the beachfront between Ocho Rios and St. Ann's Bay, the resort is very sports-oriented. It occupies 10 well-landscaped hectares (25 acres), offering attractively furnished and often quite spacious accommodations. Before retreating to the disco or enjoying the nightly entertainment, guests can choose among several dining options, selecting from an array of restaurants that attempt variety in lieu of first-rate cuisine. The Marco Polo serves international food within a venue of fabric-covered walls and rosewood furniture, Ristorante Colombo serves Caribbean specialties, Il Capitano offers Italian cuisine, and Kimonos serves teppanyaki-style Japanese cuisine and sushi.

North Coast Hwy. (P.O. Box 51), Ocho Rios. ⓒ 800/SANDALS in the U.S. and Canada, or 876/972-1610. Fax 876/972-1611. www.sandals.com. 250 units. Winter $350–$425 per person double, $450–$740 per person suite; off

season $335–$390 per person double, $425–$740 per person suite. Rates are all-inclusive. Minimum stay of 2 nights. AE, DISC, MC, V. No one under 18 allowed. **Amenities:** 5 restaurants; 4 bars; 2 pools; shuttle to a nearby 18-hole golf course; pitch-and-putt golf course; 4 tennis courts; health club and spa; 3 Jacuzzis; saunas; steam rooms; full array of watersports, scuba is included in the all-inclusive price; limited room service (in suites only); laundry service; non-smoking rooms; rooms for those w/limited mobility. *In room:* A/C, cable TV, iron, safe.

Sandals Grande Ocho Rios Beach & Villa Resort ✦

This resort opening onto a good sandy beach attracts a mix of unmarried and married couples, including honeymooners. At times the place seems like a summer camp for grown-ups (and some who didn't quite grow up). This is the most low-key of the Sandals properties, and also—at least in terms of acreage—the largest, with special care expended on landscaping. To help guests navigate their way across the sometimes steeply inclined terrain, a flotilla of 27 minivans shuttle their way across the sprawling acreage 24 hours a day. And in light of the fact that about half of the resort is terraced into a steep hillside, guests appreciate the rides. Is it romantic? Most guests think so.

Sprawling across 18 carefully landscaped hectares (44 acres), 2km (1¼ miles) west of the town center, it offers comfortably furnished rooms with either ocean or garden views. A large percentage of accommodations here (about 72 in all) are configured as hillside-hugging cottage units, a legacy of the recent expansion onto territory originally conceived as the Ciboney Resort. All units are renovated and upgraded, are reasonably large, with king-size, four-poster mahogany beds, armoires, and armchairs imported from Indonesia, and good-size bathrooms with shower/tub combinations. Nightly theme parties and live entertainment take place at scattered venues throughout this sprawling resort, sometimes (but not always) within a modern amphitheater. An unusual feature of the resort is an open-air disco. The resort's main dining room is Bayside. Other offerings include Valentino's, which serves Italian food; the Reef Terrace, which serves grilled meats and Tex-Mex cuisine, and a more recent addition, set directly on the waterfront, the Arizona, focusing on sizzling good steaks and Lone Star ribs.

Main St. (P.O. Box 771), Ocho Rios. ✆ **800/SANDALS** in the U.S. and Canada, or 876/974-5691. Fax 876/974-5700. www.sandals.com. 525 units. Winter $310–$370 per person double, from $405 per person suite; off season $300–$360 per person double, from $395 per person suite. Rates are all-inclusive. 2-night minimum stay required. AE, DC, DISC, MC, V. No one under 16 allowed. **Amenities:** 9 restaurants; 9 bars; 6 outdoor communal pools plus an additional 90 semi-private pools; 4 tennis courts; 2 fitness centers; 2 self-contained spas; 9 Jacuzzis; 4 saunas; watersports; room service in suites only; massage; babysitting; laundry service; nonsmoking rooms; rooms for those w/limited mobility. *In room:* A/C, ceiling fans, TV, dataport.

Shaw Park Beach Hotel & Spa ✦ *Value*

This is one of the genuinely respectable oldtime hotels of Ocho Rios, the one most often selected by local churches or charity organizations as a site of their meetings and conventions. The original opened in 1955 long before the slicker, glossier (or more naked) resorts of town. After years of decay, it's been newly restored and redesigned, although touches of its former dowdiness remain. It still is imbued with such a traditional Jamaican format you might find it endearing. There are even vague hints of old-fashioned British/Jamaican hospitality from the colonial era.

The hotel lies on a private white-sand beach about 457m (1,500-feet) long, opening onto Cutlass Bay and bordered on the east by White River. Almond trees, palms, and lush tropical plants adorn the 8.9-hectare (22-acre) gardens. All the midsize accommodations are well appointed and attractively furnished with soft tropical hues. These rooms and suites are housed in three low-rise buildings. You dine alfresco on the Palm Terrace or else more elegantly in the Palm Room Gourmet Restaurant, enjoying a first-rate Jamaican and international cuisine.

Cutlass Bay (P.O. Box 17), Ocho Rios. ℂ 800/377-1126 or 876/974-2552. Fax 876/974-5042. www.shawparkbeach hotel.com. 94 units. Winter $250–$280 double, $1,150 2-bedroom suite; off season $230–$250 double, $700 2-bedroom suite. Rates are all-inclusive. AE, DC, MC, V. **Amenities:** 3 restaurants; 3 bars; pool; 2 tennis courts; fitness center; spa; watersports; limited room service; babysitting; dry cleaning/laundry; nightclub. *In room:* A/C, TV, hair dryer, safe.

Sunset Jamaica Grande Resort & Spa ★ *Kids*   This is one of the largest hotels in Jamaica, a blockbuster all-inclusive that originated as a pair of high-rise beachfront properties in the 1970s, and which endured a series of radical makeovers under various owners (one of which included the Jamaican government) during the years that followed. In 2005, it reopened after the most radical of its many reincarnations under the supervision of a locally owned chain, the Sunset Group, which poured many millions of dollars into a dramatic and well-conceived overhaul. The result is hugely appealing—a Jamaica-inspired cluster of waterfalls, serpentine and lagoon-shaped swimming pools, majestic staircases that seem to get photographed as part of the many wedding parties conducted here, and a carload of Disney-inspired theatrics that unify its scattered elements into a coherent and well-organized whole. Even many locals, who otherwise aren't particularly interested in resort hotels, have applauded the stylish transformation of what had been an underappreciated white elephant into one of the most dramatic all-inclusive hotels in Jamaica.

There is much here that genuinely impresses: Set closer to the cruise ship docks than any other hotel in town, and painted in two vivid tones of canary yellow, it's impossible to miss. It boasts more beachfront (in this case, along Mallard's Beach) than any other hotel in Ocho Rios, and a comfortably rambling series of high-ceilinged, open-sided public rooms that are often filled with members of tour or conference groups. There are spa facilities, a choice of restaurants that's wide enough to keep even the most jaded diners from getting bored, a high-energy sense of fun that might remind you of the best aspects of Atlantic City, and a very large pavilion that's devoted exclusively to the amusement of adults and the care, feeding, and maintenance of children of all ages. Buffet restaurants here overflow with bounty, and as a change of pace, there are also restaurants devoted to Italian, Jamaican, Asian, and International cuisine. Best of all (at least for the parents of the many children who come here), it choreographs the best children's programs in Ocho Rios, carefully dividing participants into three different age-specific clusters (2–9; 10–13, and early teens) for child-minding throughout the day and early evening (all without extra cost). Bedrooms are tasteful, well-upholstered, up-to-date, with tropical-inspired fabrics, crown moldings, tiled floors, and mostly mahogany and rattan furniture. Each opens onto a private balcony, and contains a midsized private bathroom with tub and shower. There's even a disco (Jamaica'N Me Crazy) that, despite its usually being off-limits to non-residents, can be a lot of fun.

Main St. (P.O. Box 100), Ocho Rios, St. Ann. ℂ 800/243-1707 or 876/974-2200. Fax 876/974-2289. www.sunset jamaicagrande.com. 730 units. Winter $350–$410 double, $590 1-bedroom suite for 2; off season $300–$340 double, $500 1-bedroom suite for 2. Rates are all-inclusive. Non-residents can use the facilities, dine, and drink if they buy a day pass, priced at $60 per person, and valid from 7am to 6pm. AE, DC, MC, V. **Amenities:** 7 restaurants; 8 bars; 5 pools; 2 tennis courts; gym/health club; spa; whirlpools; saunas; watersports; children's program; a business center w/10 available Internet stations , limited room service; babysitting; laundry service; rooms for those w/limited mobility; disco; casino (slot machines only). *In room:* A/C, TV, dataport, minibar (in suites), coffeemaker, hair dryer, iron, safe.

WHERE TO DINE

Because nearly all the major hotels in Ocho Rios have gone all-inclusive, smaller, independent restaurants are struggling to survive.

VERY EXPENSIVE

The Dinner Terrace at The Jamaica Inn ★★ CONTINENTAL/CARIBBEAN

The timeless and discreetly upscale dining presentations at the Jamaica Inn seem to have endured better than many of this hotel's counterparts. There is, quite simply, nothing more upscale and dignified in town. Dinners, consequently, take on aspects of earlier, more graceful eras when guests actually gathered in the elegant, wood-paneled bar area, or on the moonlit terrace, for pre-dinner drinks before migrating into an open-sided (or, weather permitting, an open-air) dining room that's steeped in formal and undeniably upscale service rituals—the kind of venue where Sir Winston Churchill could (and frequently did) get in touch with colonial Jamaican posh. The menu changes nightly, and non-residents who opt to dine here are expected to reserve a table in advance. In 2004, age-old rules were modernized, allowing men to abandon their jackets and neckties in favor of well-groomed shirts with collars, and long pants, during the dinner hour.

Main St. © 876/974-2514. Reservations required. Fixed-price 5-course menu $65, w/no drinks. Daily 7:30–9pm.

Le Papillon Restaurant and the Caviar Bar at the Royal Plantation ★★

CONTINENTAL   This is the most aggressively upscale restaurant, with the most "fussed-over" cuisine, in Ocho Rios. It's marketed by the Sandals chain as the most prestigious dining option within any of their branches in Jamaica, and unlike most other members of the Sandals chain, this one is open to visitors who phone in advance for a reservation. The venue works hard to impress, and in most cases succeeds, albeit with an occasionally somewhat heavy-handed emphasis on its own glamour. It's located on the upper floor of what looks like a great house on steroids, whose neoclassical symmetry opens into a breathtaking decor that rivals some of the museums of Europe. At the top, past a bevy of formally dressed guardians, you'll find the only caviar-and-champagne bar in the Caribbean. (That's right: don't ask for a Red Stripe, at least not here...) Small jars of caviar are opened like holy relics—dispensed with pomp, fanfare, and ceremony in service rituals that include the necessary condiments—as part of rituals that can be delightful and fun or a wee bit pretentious, depending on your point of view. Frankly, we usually bypass the caviar bar here, opting instead for a seat in the artfully decorated Le Papillon. Here, amid cut-velvet wallpaper imported from France, within a room that evokes oceans of good taste, you'll enjoy formal meals with superb cuisine. Begin, perhaps, with roasted quail with an apple compote and black-pepper glaze; or tiger shrimp prepared three different ways (tempura, Cajun sauté, and jerk-style); move on to Caribbean-style lobster soup with black-pepper rum and crème fraîche. Main courses include a rock lobster spring roll; sea scallops on a skewer served with angel-hair pasta; parmesan-flavored grouper; a confit of duck with tamarind glaze and apple chutney; and one of the most upscale versions of surf and turf anywhere.

In the Royal Plantation, Main Street. © 876/974-5601. Reservations required. In Caviar Bar, 1 oz jar of Osetra costs $145–$190; a 4.4 oz jar costs $365. Champagne $120–$220 per bottle, $65 for a half-bottle. In Le Papillon, main courses $38–$50. AE, DC, MC, V. Tues–Sun 7–10pm.

MODERATE

Almond Tree Restaurant JAMAICAN/CONTINENTAL   The Almond Tree is a

two-tiered patio restaurant with a tree growing through the roof. Lobster Thermidor is the tastiest item on the menu, but we also like the "Annie Palmer" (steak that's flambéed with brandy and served with a peppercorn sauce), and the scallops with white

wine, cream, cheese, and mussels. Other excellent choices are the roast suckling pig, medallions of beef, and a fondue bourguignon. Jamaican plantation rice is a local specialty. The wine list offers a variety of vintages, including Spanish and Jamaican. Have a cocktail in the unique "swinging bar"—with swinging chairs, that is.

In the Hibiscus Lodge Hotel, 83 Main St. © 876/974-2813. Reservations recommended for dinner. Main courses $14–$31. AE, MC, V. Daily 7:30–10:30am, noon–2:30pm, and 6–9:30pm.

Café Aubergine 🍴🍴 *Finds* FRENCH/ITALIAN

This most intriguing restaurant, 18km (11 miles) south of Ocho Rios (and a 40-min. drive), is an offbeat adventure. European-trained chef Neville Anderson has converted an 18th-century tavern into a restaurant serving food as good as (or better than) that in the best restaurants of Ocho Rios.

You're welcomed inside a gingerbread-trim house with cascading pink and red flowers. On our last visit the cook was roasting half a cow. The dishes would pass muster on the Left Bank: sautéed breast of chicken in a lemon caper sauce over a bed of linguine or grilled lamb chops with a honey mustard sauce, for instance. We're also fond of baked crab with white wine (seasoned with fresh herbs) and the smoked marlin with pineapple sorbet.

Moneague. © 876/973-0527. Reservations recommended. Main courses J$850–J$1,950 (US$14–US$31). DC, MC, V. Wed–Sun noon–8:30pm (last seating at 8:30pm).

Coconuts JAMAICAN/INTERNATIONAL

When cruise ships are moored in front of the Ocho Rios piers, a series of iron gates seem mysteriously to get unlocked, and disembarking passengers can stroll, unimpeded, from the ship's gangways along the water's edge to access this likable dining and drinking venue. Be warned, however, that the moment the cruise ships depart, gates along the waterfront seem to slam mysteriously shut, requiring access via the conventional city streets and roads. Regardless, this restaurant enjoys a reputation among local office workers, many of them long-established groups of women, as a suitable place to hang out with friends after work, chugging down a series of rum-based, party-colored cocktails, and perhaps rounding off the experience with a plate or two of food. It's not a bad idea, since items are flavorful and imaginative. Examples include surf and turf; Thai-style snapper filet; tamarind-glazed shrimp; and stewed fish in brown sauce. There are also burgers, Cajun-blackened fish filets, fajitas, filet mignons, oxtail soups, jerk chicken, and club sandwiches. A pair of English-colonial gazebos, jutting out into the harbor, provide visual distraction and touches of class.

On the street level of the Fisherman's Point Hotel, Turtle Beach Road. © 876/795-0064. Reservations not necessary. Burgers, sandwiches, and salads $5.50–$7; main courses $6.50–$30. AE, DC, DISC, MC, V. Daily 11am–10pm.

Evita's Italian Restaurant 🍴 ITALIAN

A 5-minute drive south of the commercial heart of Ocho Rios, in a hillside residential neighborhood that enjoys a panoramic view over the harbor and beachfronts, this is one of the most fun restaurants along the north coast of Jamaica. Its soul and artistic flair come from Eva Myers, the convivial former owner of some of the most legendary bars of Montego Bay, who established her culinary headquarters in this green-and-white gingerbread Jamaican house in 1990. An outdoor terrace adds additional seating and enhanced views. More than half the menu is devoted to pastas, including almost every variety known to northern and southern Italy. The fish dishes are excellent—especially the snapper stuffed with crabmeat and the lobster and scampi in a buttery white cream sauce. Italian (or other) wines by the bottle might accompany your main course.

Eden Bower Rd. ⓒ **876/974-2333.** Reservations recommended. Main courses $12–$23. AE, MC, V. Daily 11am–11pm.

Little Pub Restaurant JAMAICAN/INTERNATIONAL   Located in the center of town, within a redbrick courtyard with a fishpond and waterfall, this simple pub is a local dining staple. No one will mind if you drop in just for a drink, but if you want dinner, proceed to one of the linen-covered tables topped with cut flowers and candles. We're fond of the barbecued chicken and grilled kingfish, but you might like snapper or fresh lobster.

59 Main St. ⓒ **876/974-2324.** Reservations recommended. Main courses $14–$30. MC, V. Daily 7am–10:30pm.

Margaritaville at Ocho Rios 𝘒𝘪𝘥𝘴 JAMAICAN   Positioned immediately adjacent to the cruise ship docks, it attracts more business than any other establishment within the shopping mall that contains it, thanks to pulsating music and an almost constant atmosphere of irreverent fun. Sure, it contains a series of bars, and lots of emphasis on food that's designed to taste fabulous with jello shots, Red Stripe beer, and tropical drinks. It also contains a theme-based shopping boutique (T-shirts, among others, celebrate "Jamaica Mistaica's"), and a venue for ongoing fun whose emphasis changes throughout the course of the day and night. Within an environment that's big enough for 450 diners at a time, it manages to appeal to both families with children and to singles on the make. Depending on your tastes, you'll either think this place is the most fun in town, or else flee toward other, calmer, venues. Attractions include a rooftop whirlpool tub, a 30m-long (100-ft.) water slide, and a freshwater pool, along with three bars and a Trading Post gift shop. The decor is rustic and appealingly battered West Indian, with an Afro-Cuban aura. There's dancing here—reggae disco-style—at night. Of course, in its role as a dive inspired by a Jimmy Buffett song, expect tropical margaritas, Caribbean daiquiris, and spiked lemonade, those delectable "Cheeseburgers in Paradise," conch chowder, Jamaican-style jerk chili; "I will never love another Caesar" salads, "Ex-patriated" American chicken; coconut shrimp, and 9-ounce filet mignons with Madeira sauce.

In the Island Village Shopping Center, Turtle Beach Rd. (at the cruise ship docks). ⓒ **876/675-8976.** Main courses $12–$18; burgers and salads $7–$11. AE, MC, V. Daily 8am–11pm; bar open nightly to 4:30am.

Toscanini's ITALIAN   The chef (P.G. Ricci) and headwaiter (his sister, Lella Ricci) are co-owners. Both hail from Parma, Italy, and London. Coming from a long line of restaurateurs, they bring style and a continental sophistication to their food service and preparation. The restaurant occupies the airy and gracious street level of a 19th-century stone pavilion whose upper floors function as an upscale art gallery. The menu offers many classic Italian dishes, supplemented by ever-changing specials, depending on what's fresh at the market. The best of the many specialties include spaghetti with lobster penne all' ortolana (vegetarian pasta with goat cheese and herbs); crespelle (oven-baked crepes with chopped callaloo and cheese); and local catch of the day with Acqua Pazza sauce (roasted tomatoes, fish reduction, white wine, and herbs). There's an ongoing strong emphasis on fresh fish and shellfish, especially lobster. The chef also caters to vegetarians. All this good food is backed up by a fine wine list.

In Harmony Hall, Tower Isles on the North Coast Highway (Rte. A3), 6km (3¾ miles) east of Ocho Rios. ⓒ **876/975-4785.** Reservations recommended. Main courses $9.50–$26; pasta dishes $12–$19. AE, MC, V. Tues–Sun noon–2pm and 7–10:30pm. Closed 1 week in June and 1 week in Sept.

Tradewinds Bar & Restaurant JAMAICAN/INTERNATIONAL It's cost-conscious, it's warm, and at its best it can even be cozy. A long bar that prefaces its dining room, all within a dark, vaguely nautical decor beneath a palm-frond-covered ceiling. If you opt for a meal here, you won't be alone: Anthony Hopkins, Steven Seagal, members of Kool and the Gang, Queen Latifah, and Jamaican singer Sean Paul (of Reggaeton) have preceded you. Dinners may include jerk chicken quesadillas; bruschetta with fresh basil and garlic; deep-fried conch strips with tartar sauce; grilled lobster; surf and turf; and a combination platter piled high with lobster, fresh shrimp, deep-fried conch, and calamari. All main courses come with vegetables and either rice, fries, or garlic mashed potatoes. Lunches are simpler, focusing on burgers, sandwiches, and salads.

47 Main St. ℭ **876/974-2433.** Reservations not necessary. Lunch platters $7–$10; dinner main courses $17–$28. AE, DC, MC, V. Mon–Sat 9am–10pm.

INEXPENSIVE

BiBiBips INTERNATIONAL/JAMAICAN Set in the main tourist strip of Ocho Rios, this restaurant (whose name is the owner's nickname) occupies a sprawling open-air compound of porches and verandas. Lots of single folks come just to hang out at the bar. Drinks and flirtations sometimes segue into dinner at the adjacent restaurant, where well-prepared menu items include Red Stripe shrimp, which is deep-fried in a beer-based batter; coconut-curried chicken; vegetarian Rasta Pasta; and a combination Creole-style seafood platter. Lunches are a bit simpler, focusing mostly on sandwiches, salads, and an especially delicious jerk chicken burger. There's live entertainment, usually some kind of rap or reggae band, every Friday, Saturday, and Sunday beginning at 8pm.

93 Main St. ℭ **876/974-7483.** Reservations not necessary. Lunch main courses $7–$23; dinner main courses $10–$30. AE, MC, V. Daily 11am–5:30pm and 6pm–2am.

Mom's JAMAICAN Crammed into a mishmash of oddly interconnected cement buildings in the most densely populated downtown sections of Ocho Rios, this ultra-simple restaurant has thrived here since 1983, when it was established by a local matriarch (Mrs. Boyd) that everybody refers to as "Mom." Don't expect glamour: the venue has cement walls, battered furniture, a color palette of cream and lime green that could use some touchups, and a staff, mostly supervised by Mrs. Boyd's daughters, who on bad days can appear very very glum. But with the assumption that you might arrive on a day when everybody's relatively cheerful, you might just have a merry old time getting lowdown with this place and actually sampling their food. No alcohol is ever served, but all-natural drinks include carrot, sorrel, soursop, passionfruit, and june plum juice. Food items are as straightforward and generic as the tenets of West Indian cuisine allows, but include basic preparations of fish, chicken, pork, oxtail, chicken-studded chop suey, and several kinds of stew. Frankly, the sheer fame of this place surprises us: It's at its best when Mom is actually on the premises.

7 Evelyn St. ℭ **876/974-2811.** Reservations not accepted. Main courses J$300–J$400 (US$4.80–US$6.40). No credit cards. Mon–Sat 8am–10pm.

Ocho Rios Village Jerk Centre ⭐ *Finds* JAMAICAN At this open-air restaurant, you can get the best jerk dishes along this part of the coast. When only a frosty Red Stripe beer can quench your thirst and your stomach is growling for the fiery taste of Jamaican jerk seasonings, head here—and don't dress up. Don't expect anything fancy: It's the food that counts, and you'll find fresh daily specials posted on a chalkboard menu on the wall. The dishes are hot and spicy, but not *too* hot; hot spices are presented on the side for those who want to go truly Jamaican. The barbecued ribs are

especially good, and fresh fish is a delight, perfectly grilled—try the red snapper. Vegetarian dishes are also available on request, and if you don't drink beer, you can wash it all down with natural fruit juices.

Da Costa Dr. ℂ **876/974-2549.** Reservations not accepted. Jerk pork $3.50 ¼ lb., $10 1 lb.; whole jerk chicken $14. MC, V. Daily 10am–11pm.

Passage to India ✦ INDOCHINESE   This is the most visible and most desirable Indian restaurant in northern Jamaica, one of the preferred favorites of the expatriate British and American communities living along Jamaica's North Coast. Set on the second floor of a busy shopping mall in the center of town, it's airy, cosmopolitan, and sophisticated, featuring some of the most creative and interesting Indian dishes we've ever seen. Menu items are surprisingly imaginative: shrimp prepared either in the spicy Szechuan style or with ginger; tandoori-style filet mignon; a "Passage to India" sizzler, where chunks of your choice of meats are prepared on a hot griddle set directly on your table; Goanese-style shrimp or chicken curry; Punjabi-style chicken Pakora (accompanied with split peas and tamarind sauce); Goanese chicken curry; boneless chicken with garlic, ginger, capiscum (an Indian form of cayenne pepper), and spices; mutton roasted with spices and hot pepper, and lobster vindaloo. Many diners opt to begin their experience here within the bar in back, outfitted in the Moghul style, like something from a Pasha's tent.

In Soni's Plaza, 50 Main St. ℂ **876/795-3182.** Reservations not necessary. Main courses J$655–J$1,500 (US$10–US$24). AE, DC, MC, V. Mon 10am–3pm; Tues–Sun 11:30am–10pm.

HITTING THE BEACH

The most idyllic sands are at the often-overcrowded **Mallard's Beach,** in the center of Ocho Rios, and are shared by hotel guests and cruise ship passengers. Locals may steer you to the white sands of **Turtle Beach** in the center, between the Renaissance Jamaica Grande and Club Jamaica. It's smaller, more desirable, and not as overcrowded as Mallard's.

The most frequented (and to be avoided when cruise ships are in port) is **Dunn's River Beach,** located below the famous falls. Another great spot is **Jamaica Grande's Beach,** which is open to the public. Parasailing is a favorite sport here.

Many exhibitionist couples check into the famous but pricey **Couples Resort,** which is known for its private au naturel island.

Our favorite is none of the above. We always follow the trail of 007 and head for **James Bond Beach** (ℂ **876/726-1630**), east of Ocho Rios at Oracabessa Beach. Entrepreneur Chris Blackwell reopened writer Ian Fleming's former home, Goldeneye. For $5 adults, $3 children, non-guests enjoy it any day except Monday.

Puerto Seco Beach lies on the eastern side of Discovery Bay, just an 8km (5-mile) drive west of Runaway Bay. On the far western side of the bay is its major attraction, Columbus Park Museum (see later in this chapter). Jamaicans who live in the hills nearby flock here on Sundays for a jivin' good time. The smoke from jerk chicken and a few ganja smokers fills the air, as do the sounds of Bob Marley and all his dozens of reggae imitators.

SPORTS & OUTDOOR PURSUITS

RAFTING ON THE WHITE RIVER   You can arrange to go river rafting down the White River to the east of Ocho Rios, a 45-minute drift that takes you down the largest river in the area. The trip is one of the finer ways to spend a day in Ocho Rios

when you tire of the beach. You glide along the banks of the river on a 9m (30-ft.) bamboo raft built for two, experiencing the rapids and looking at the lush growth. Halfway down the river you stop at the Jungle Bar for lunch and reggae music. The cost is $50 per person, including the services of a guide. To reach the site, head east from Ocho Rios to the White River Bridge, a distance of 5km (3 miles). Rafting is possible daily from 8:30am to 4:30pm. Call ℂ 876/974-2527 for more information.

PLAYING WITH DOLPHINS One of the most-visited attractions in Ocho Rios, **Dolphin Cove,** North Coast Highway (ℂ **876/974-5335;** www.dolphincovejamaica. com), attracts thousands of participants from cruise ships every month. Nestled among the seafronting rocks and low cliffs of a location 1.6km (1 mile) west of the center of Ocho Rios is an eco-sensitive series of stone and wire marine pens that are the home to about 16 dolphins. Each of them was caught, usually in fishing nets, off the coast of Mexico, and brought here after months of testing and training at enormous expense, for the amusement of their human counterparts. The headquarters of the venue is a 1950s, lemon-colored villa that functioned for years as the private home of the attraction's Jamaica-born owners, the Burrowes family. Check the photos in the building's entrance. At press time, two pens (soon to be expanded to incorporate several more) contain colonies of apparently happy and healthy dolphins that cavort, jump in the air, and swallow fish (mostly mackerel and herring imported from the cold waters of Canada) on a schedule that's noted below. Know in advance, however, that there's a lot more on-site than just a view of some sea mammals. The entire 2.8-hectare (7-acre) site has been configured as a self-contained beach and entertainment center that can and often does shelter and amuse cruise ship passengers throughout their ship's stopover in Ocho Rios. Snorkeling and swimming are available from a narrow beachfront. Immediately adjacent is a waterfall cascading directly into the sea from the Chico River. A restaurant features a lunchtime buffet, served daily from noon to 3pm, costing $12 per person. There is also transport in a glass-bottomed boat (rides cost $15 per person for a 30-minute float over the reefs). You have unlimited access to nature trails that meander through a jungle landscape that has been enhanced with the presence of caged birds, caged iguanas, and large yellow boa constrictors held in check by their handlers.

If the idea of swimming with the dolphins appeals to you, you should reserve a place in advance, participate in a 30-minute orientation lecture, put on a life preserver, and then get ready to pet, play with, and in some cases, get pushed or pulled around the watery pen by a well-trained marine mammal.

Dolphin shows are presented daily at 9:30am, 11:30am, 1:30pm, and 3:30pm. General admission to the compound costs $19 per person. Enhancements to the general admission cost are noted as follows, and in every case, includes general admission to the compound: "Touch the Dolphins" from a seat on the pier costs $45 per person; a one-on-one encounter in the water with a dolphin goes for $99 per person; and a two-on-two encounter whereby one swimmer will be pulled along the surface of the water while he/she holds their dorsal fins costs $175 per person. No children under 8 are allowed in the water with the dolphins.

GOLF **SuperClubs Runaway Golf Club,** at Runaway Bay near Ocho Rios on the North Coast (ℂ **876/973-7319**), charges no fee to guests who stay at any Super-Clubs. For nonguests, the price is $80 year-round. Carts cost $35 for 18 holes, club rentals are $14 for 18 holes.

Sandals Golf & Country Club ❄ (© **876/975-0119**), a 15-minute ride from the center of the resort, is a 5,944m (19,500-ft.) course known for its panoramic scenery. Rolling terrain, lush vegetation, and flowers and fruit trees dominate the 48-hectare (120-acre) course; a putting green and driving range are available as well. Sandals guests play free; nonguests pay $70 for 9 holes or $100 for 18 holes.

HORSEBACK RIDING   Renegade Stables, Galina, Oracabessa (© **876/994-0135**), is a stable that's home to about 14 horses, half of which are available for riding lessons. A trail ride lasting between 60 and 90 minutes costs about $50 per person and incorporates equestrian jaunts along both forest trails and beaches.

TENNIS   Sandals Grande Ocho Rios Beach & Villa Resort, Main Street, Ocho Rios (© **876/974-1027**), focuses more on tennis than any other resort in the area. It offers three clay-surface and three hard-surface courts, all lit for night play. Guests play free, day or night, but nonguests must call and make arrangements with the manager. Nonguests can purchase a day pass for $85 per person. The resort also sponsors twice-a-day clinics for both beginners and advanced players. Frequent guest tournaments are also staged, including handicapped doubles and mixed doubles.

EXPLORING THE AREA

A scenic drive south of Ocho Rios along Route A3 will take you inland through **Fern Gully** ❄, a lush gorge. This was originally a riverbed, but now the main road winds up some 210m (700 ft.) among a profusion of wild ferns, a tall rainforest, hardwood trees, and lianas. There are hundreds of varieties of ferns, and roadside stands offer fruits and vegetables, carved-wood souvenirs, and basketwork. The road runs for about 6km (3¾ miles). At Moneague, a small town, the A1 continues south into the interior of Jamaica, but the same route number (A1) also heads back north along a different route from the A3 you just took south. This A1 northerly road lies to the west of the A1 southern route to Moneague. If you take this A1 north, you'll come to the coast on the north shore again.

Heading up A1 north, you'll pass the ruins of **Edinburgh Castle** lying 13km (8 miles) southwest of Claremont, the major town on the route back (but of no tourist interest). These ruins—not worth a detour but of passing interest if you're driving by—are a local curiosity.

This 1763 lair was the former abode of one of Jamaica's most famous murderers, a Scot named Lewis Hutchinson, who used to shoot passersby and toss their bodies into a deep pit. At his so-called "castle," really a two-story house, Hutchinson invited his victims inside to wine and dine them before murdering and then robbing them.

The authorities got wind of his activities. Although he tried to escape by canoe, Hutchinson was captured and hanged at Spanish Town on March 16, 1773. Evidently proud of his achievements (evidence of at least 43 bodies was found), he left 100 British pounds and instructions for a memorial to be built in his honor. It never was.

These castle ruins can be viewed on the northern outskirts of the village of Bensonton, near the Bensonton Health Club.

Back on the A1 northern route again, you can drive to the coast, coming to it at **St. Ann's Bay,** the site of the first Spanish settlement on the island, where you can see the **statue of Christopher Columbus,** cast in his hometown of Genoa and erected near St. Ann's Hospital on the west side of town, close to the coast road. There are a number of Georgian buildings in the town—the **Court House** near the parish church, built in 1866, is the most interesting.

An Homage to Reggae

Looking for ways to deepen your appreciation of Jamaica's pre-eminent musical form? Consider a tour through what might be the grooviest museum in the world: **Reggae Explosion** (aka The Reggae Hall of Fame), which functions as a subdivision of the Island Village Shopping Center, Turtle River Road (© 876/ 675-8902). Owned and operated by Christopher Blackwell, the hotel/film/music mogul who's credited with having originally discovered reggae superstar Bob Marley, it's a combination museum/public relations tool for Marley and the Jamaican music industry as a whole—a party-colored temple to the greatness of the art form. Within a high-ceilinged decor that's mostly black but highlighted with Day-Glo colors, you'll follow on a route designated by captions that outline the history of Jamaican music. (According to the wall charts, it started with mento in the 1940s; moved on to ska after the independence of Jamaica from Britain in 1962; and evolved after 1966 into movements that included RockSteady, Roots, and several other groups that eventually led to reggae.)

Once you get used to the shadows and immediate sense of chaos reigning here, the place can be a lot of fun. There's a replica of a party-colored Jamaican rum shack near the entrance, a 1950s-era jukebox, lots of portraits and illustrations of reggae greats, and a bevy of what might be the hippest tour guides in Jamaica. By all means, head upstairs to the second floor of this museum, marveling at the pictorial history of the evolution of Jamaican music as you ascend, past tributes to stars such as Marley, Jimmy Cliff, Alton Ellis, and Lee Scratch-Perry (a music producer who won a Grammy award in 2003). There are also replicas from Abyssinian Coptic churches portraying Haile Selassie, videos of the 1996 cult movie *Dance Hall Queen,* and—highly unusual—a dancing platform where hearing-inpaired people can feel the amplified vibrations of reggae music. The museum is open Monday to Friday from 9am to 5pm, Saturday from 9am to 10pm. Admission costs $7 per person.

THE MAJOR ATTRACTIONS

Brimmer Hall Estate   Some 34km (21 miles) east of Ocho Rios, in the hills 3km (1¾ miles) from Port Maria, this 1817 estate is an ideal place to spend a day. You can swim in the pool and sample a wide variety of brews and concoctions. The Plantation Tour Eating House offers typical Jamaican dishes for lunch, and there's a souvenir shop with a good selection of ceramics, art, straw goods, woodcarvings, rums, liqueurs, and cigars. All this is on a working plantation where you're driven around in a tractor-drawn jitney to see the tropical fruit trees and coffee plants; the knowledgeable guides will explain the various processes necessary to produce the fine fruits of the island. This is a far more interesting experience than the trip to Croydon Plantation in Montego Bay, so if you're visiting both resorts and have time for only one plantation, make it Brimmer Hall.

Port Maria, St. Mary's. © 876/994-2309. Call 3 days in advance. Tours $18. Tours Mon–Fri 9am–4pm.

Coyaba Gardens and Museum, and Mahoe Falls   Two kilometers (1¼ miles) south from the center of Ocho Rios, at an elevation of 126m (420 ft.), this exuberantly landscaped park and museum were built on the grounds of a historic farm (the

Shaw Park Plantation) that dates back to the earliest days of Britain's colonial age in Jamaica. Components of the site include a low-slung, small-scale compound of museum buildings, each with its own veranda and each facing a flagstone-covered courtyard. Exhibits feature a collection of artifacts from the Arawak, Spanish, and colonial English settlements in the area. In 2005, management upgraded a labyrinth of masonry paths, steps, and walkways that descend from the gardens into the tropical forest and hug the edges of a stream (the Millford River) that splashes down, in a series of rapids and waterfalls, from significant elevations above. There's even a wide spot in the stream that visitors can use as a "swimming hole" if they're so inclined. Overall, the site is conceived as a sedate, eco-sensitive, and charming alternative to the rowdier theme-centered venues that proliferate in Ocho Rios. As such, the compound is visited by church groups, school groups, and by older or more sedate cruise ship passengers, who appreciate this exposure to Jamaican flora, fauna, and natural beauty. The word *coyaba* comes from the Arawak name for paradise.

Shaw Park Rd. ℂ **876/974-6235.** Admission to the garden $5, admission to the garden and the trails leading to the river walks and waterfalls $10; half-price for children 12 and under. Daily 8am–6pm. Take the Fern Gully–Kingston Road, turn left at St. John's Anglican Church, and follow the signs to Coyaba, just .4km (¼ mile) farther.

Cranbrook Flower Forest & Riverhead Adventure Trail ☆

Centered on a much-restored water mill built by a British planter 200-odd years ago, this 53-hectare (130-acre) commercial nursery welcomes visitors on guided tours of its formal lawns, fountains, lakes, and ponds. If you're a devoted botanist, you'll appreciate the diversity of plants. Within a greenhouse, you'll see thousands of flourishing orchids and anthuriums (many shipped as cut flowers to the U.S.). Horseback riding is also available here, costing $30 for 2-hour trail rides.

Laughland's P.O. Box 8, Llandovery, near St. Ann's Bay. ℂ **876/770-8071.** Admission $10, $5 children under 12. Daily 9am–5pm. From the center of Ocho Rios, take A1 west to the Chukka Cove turnoff, a distance of 29km (18 miles).

Dunn's River Falls *Overrated*

For a fee, you can relax on the beach or climb with a guide to the top of the 546m (600-ft.) falls. You can splash in the waters at the bottom of the falls or drop into the cool pools higher up between the cascades of water. The beach restaurant provides lackluster snacks and drinks, and dressing rooms are available. If you're planning to climb the falls, wear sneakers or sport sandals to protect your feet from the sharp rocks and to prevent slipping.

Climbing the falls with the crowds is a chance to experience some 183m (610 ft.) of cold but clear mountain water. In contrast to the heat swirling around you, the splashing water hitting your face and bare legs is cooling on a hot day. The problem here is slipping and falling, especially if you're joined to a chain of hands linking body to body. In spite of the slight danger, there seem to be few accidents. The falls aren't exactly a wilderness experience, with all the tour buses carrying cruise ship passengers here. The place is always overrun.

Rte. A3. ℂ **876/974-4767.** Admission $15 adults, $12 children 2–11, free for children under 2. Daily 8:30am–5pm (7am–5pm on cruise ship arrival days). From the center of Ocho Rios, head west along Rte. A3.

Firefly ☆

This vacation retreat was the home of Sir Noël Coward and his longtime companion, Graham Payn, who, as executor of Coward's estate, donated it to the Jamaica National Heritage Trust. The recently restored house is more or less as it was on the day Sir Noël died in 1973. His Hawaiian-print shirts still hang in the closet of his austere bedroom, with its mahogany four-poster bed. The library contains a collection of his books, and the living room is warm and comfortable, with big armchairs

and two grand pianos (where he composed several famous tunes). Guests stayed at Blue Harbour, a villa closer to Port Maria; they included Evelyn Waugh, Winston Churchill, Errol Flynn, Lord Laurence Olivier, Vivien Leigh, Claudette Colbert, Katharine Hepburn, Mary Martin, and the Queen Mother. Paintings by the noted playwright/actor/author/composer adorn the walls. An open patio looks out over the pool and the sea. Across the lawn, Sir Noël is buried under a simple white marble gravestone.

Grants Town, in St. Mary, 32km (20 miles) east of Ocho Rios above Port Maria. ℂ 876/725-0920. Admission $10. Children under 12 $5. Mon–Thurs and Sat 9am–5pm.

Green Grotto Caves ✦ ⓚⁱᵈˢ   Formed of coastal limestone, these caves were a haven for runaway slaves and pirates. The mammoth cave is full of rock formations, stalagmites, and stalactites, and has a roof of "ceiling pockets." The grotto is filled with numerous chambers and light holes, but its most dramatic feature is eerie Grotto Lake, a subterranean lake occupying its bowels.

Just off main coastal road (A3), 3km (1¾ miles) from Discovery Bay and 4km (2½ miles) west of Runaway Bay. ℂ 876/973-2841. Admission $20 adults, $10 children 4–12. Daily 9am–4pm.

Harmony Hall   This two-story stone and clapboard-sided pavilion originated late in the 19th century as the centerpiece of a once-thriving pimento plantation. Laboriously restored, and loaded with nostalgia and charm, it's the focal point of an art gallery (upstairs) and restaurant (Toscanini's, on street level—it's separately recommended in "Where to Dine," earlier in this chapter) that showcases one of the region's best assortment of contemporary Jamaican paintings and to a lesser degree, sculptures. Among them are works by some of the leading names in the Jamaican art world, including George Rodney, Graham Davis, Susan Shirley, PJ Stewart, and Jonna Brasch. Original paintings within this gallery range in price from $100 to $5,000.

There's also, added as something of an afterthought, a tasteful array of arts, crafts, and gift items. Among them are body oils and lotions, soaps, and candles, many of which contain natural additives harvested in Jamaica.

Tower Isles on Rte. A3, 6km (3¾ miles) east of Ocho Rios. ℂ 876/975-4222. www.harmonyhall.com. Free admission. Gallery daily 10am–6pm.

Island Village and Island Village Shopping Center ✦   The opening in 2002 of this exotic-looking cluster of shops, restaurants, bars, movie theaters, and reggae-themed attractions represents one of the largest private investments in the history of Ocho Rios. Scattered over 2 hectares (4 acres) on a beachfront within a few steps of the city's cruise ship terminal is a replica of an idealized Jamaican village, complete with elaborate gingerbread, hundreds of feet of boardwalk, and a medley of psychedelic colors that glow, rainbow-style, in the streaming sunlight. It's not without its own theme-park, Disney-ish overtones: They include **soundstages** strategically scattered within the sightlines of **bars** that serve the kind of high-octane cocktails that could fuel a heavily loaded jetliner from here to Kingston. Music and hotel impresario Christopher Blackwell, who takes credit for the "discovery" and marketing of Bob Marley, is half-owner of this venture—thus you won't find any shame here about emphasizing reggae as both a lifestyle and an artistic venue.

Within the compound you'll find about 35 **shops** selling clothing, books, souvenirs, "reggae wear," and Bob Marley memorabilia; and four or five restaurants and bars. These include everything from a branch of **Margaritaville,** a theme-ish offspring

of the Jimmy Buffett song where drinks splish splash throughout the day and night; and other eateries specializing in fast-food versions of Jamaican curries and jerk chicken or pork. There's even a movie theater and an audiovisual art gallery/minimuseum, **Reggae Explosion,** celebrating in audiovisual form the evolution of reggae from a local art to music recognized the world over. With the exception of Reggae Explosion, which is separately recommended, and the movie theaters, entrance to most aspects of the compound is free.

Small-scale reggae presentations occur spontaneously, often when a cruise ship is in port, and large-scale **blockbuster concerts** are scheduled about once a month, and are usually attended by hundreds, or even thousands. Except when there's a world-class concert—usually when there's no cruise ship in port—there's no admission charged for entrance to the compound, but an alert security staff ensures that "panhandlers, pickpockets, and lowlifes" (at least those residing in Jamaica) are kept off the premises. Since its opening, the place has welcomed more than a thousand visitors a day.

Island Village, Turtle Beach Rd. Complex open daily 9am–midnight. No central switchboard. Each establishment has its own phone.

Prospect Plantation

Beginning in 1936, this was a working plantation producing pimentos, allspice, and limes, all of it held together by its Scotland-born owner, Sir Harold Mitchell, who died in 1983. Since his death, its 405 hectares (1,000 acres) have been maintained as an eco-sensitive destination for tour groups, who climb into jitneys for 90-minute jaunts through the rolling highlands of its fertile terrain. If you opt to come here, you won't be alone: Some of the trees on the property bear signs indicating that they were planted by, among others, Winston Churchill, Henry Kissinger, Charlie Chaplin, Pierre Trudeau, Noël Coward, Edward Heath, and (incongruously) movie star Drew Barrymore. The sprawling property passes through several different climate zones; takes you high enough for sweeping views out toward the point where Christopher Columbus was shipwrecked for more than a year during his fourth visit to the new world in the 1500s; passes a colony of (caged) African ostriches; and meanders through fields devoted, respectively, to sugar cane, coffee, and chocolate. Within semi-private compounds on the property is a semi-military boy's academy. (Prospect Academy, established as a philanthropic act in 1956 by Sir Harold Mitchell, maintains one of the most stringent academic curriculums in Jamaica.) There is also the gracefully proportioned Prospect Chapel, a non-denominational church fashioned from limestone and timber derived from the acreage nearby. A visit to this property is an educational, relaxing, and enjoyable experience. You'll learn about and see pimento (allspice), bananas, cassava, sugar cane, coffee, cocoa, coconut, pineapple, and the famous *leucaena* ("Tree of Life"). You'll even see Jamaica's first hydroelectric plant, imported from Canada in 1939 by the plantation's founder, and sample some of the exotic fruit and drinks at the big, tipi-shaped bar and gift shop near each tour's point of origin.

Horseback riding is available on three scenic trails at Prospect and, depending on the venue, last from 1 to 2¼ hours. Advance bookings at least an hour in advance are necessary.

Rte. A3, 5km (3 miles) east of Ocho Rios, in St. Ann. © 876/994-1058. Jitney tours, w/each jitney carrying up to 35 passengers, last for 90 min. each and cost $27 for adults, $20 for children 12 and under; 1-hr. horseback rides $58, 90-min. horseback tours $65 each. Tours Mon–Sat at 10:30am, 2pm, and 3:30pm.

Sun Valley Plantation   A real working plantation—not one gussied up as a tourist attraction—is reached by taking the A3 from Ocho Rios toward the coastal town of Oracabessa. The plantation is in the hamlet of Crescent on the B13, lying 5km (3 miles) south of Oracabessa and 29km (18 miles) from Ocho Rios. Nolly and Lorna Binns, the plantation owners, take visitors on a guided tour of the property.

Crescent, near Oracabessa. ⓒ **876/995-3075.** Admission $12. Tours on the hr. daily 9:30am–2pm.

ORGANIZED TOURS

Caribic Vacations, 1310 Providence Dr., Ironshore Estate, White Sands Beach (ⓒ **876/953-9878**), is the market leader. They offer a tour of Ocho Rios including Fern Gully, Dunn's River Falls, and a visit to Coyaba Museum, with shopping time scheduled in the center of Ocho Rios. The tour lasts 5 to 6 hours, costing $35 per person.

Blue Mountain Tours, 121 Main St. (ⓒ **876/974-7075**), runs guided downhill bicycle tours of Jamaica's Blue Mountains. The cost is $93 per person, including transfers to the site, breakfast, and lunch. The single-gear bikes are woefully inadequate, however, for the terrain.

SHOPPING

For many, Ocho Rios with its relatively aggressive vendors provides an introduction to Jamaica-style shopping. After surviving the ordeal, some visitors may vow never to go shopping again. Literally hundreds of Jamaicans pour into Ocho Rios to peddle

---

The Potter's Art

The largest and most visible art pottery in Jamaica is found at **Wassi Art,** Bougainvillea Drive, Great Pond (ⓒ **876/974-5044;** www.wassiart.com). This enterprise is often cited for its entrepreneurial courage by the country's growing core of independent business owners. Established in 1990, it developed from a personal hobby of one of its owners, Theresa Lee, an amateur potter. Today, with her husband Robert, she employs at least 50 artisans and workers in a small-scale beehive of energy about 4km (2½ miles) north of the center of Ocho Rios. They turn out wonderful pottery. You'll reach the place via a winding and impossibly rutted road.

Tours of the factory (Mon–Sat 9am–5pm) are free, last about 15 minutes, and include a brief session trying to throw a pot on an electric potter's wheel. Don't expect a high-tech operation here, as virtually every aspect of the manufacturing process, including the digging, hauling, and processing of the Blue Mountain clay, is done the old-fashioned way—by hand. All glazes used in the process are nontoxic and FDA approved.

The finished pottery comes in colors that range from the earth- and forest-toned to the bright iridescent patterns reminiscent of Jamaican music and spice. Prices of objects range from $5 to $2,000, and anything you buy can be shipped by Federal Express. There's a cafe on the premises (try their meat-stuffed patties for an insight into what a Jamaican worker's lunch might include). Part of your experience here includes dialogues with talented artisans hailing from both Jamaica and Cuba.

items to cruise ship passengers and other visitors. Police precedent has done a lot to suppress too-aggressive behavior from shopkeepers, but in the past, something approaching pandemonium has greeted many an unwary shopper, who must also be prepared for some fierce haggling and some often unwelcome breaches of privacy. Every vendor asks too much at first, which gives them the leeway to "negotiate" until the price reaches a more realistic level. Is shopping fun in Ocho Rios? A resounding no. Do cruise ship passengers and land visitors indulge in it anyway? A decided yes.

In general, the shopping is better in Montego Bay, and crafts items tend to be just a bit cheaper. But if you're not going there, wander the Ocho Rios crafts markets, knowing in advance that much of the merchandise is repetitive.

SHOPPING CENTERS & MALLS   There are a number of shopping plazas in Ocho Rios. We've listed them because they're here, not because we heartily recommend them. Newer ones include the **New Ocho Rios Plaza,** in the center of town, with some 60 shops; opposite is the **Taj Mahal Mall,** with 26 duty-free stores. **Island Plaza** is another major shopping complex, as is the **Mutual Security Plaza** with some 30 shops.

Ocean Village Shopping Centre (© 876/974-2683) is one of the originals, with numerous boutiques, food stores, a bank, sundries purveyors, travel agencies, service facilities, and what have you. The **Ocho Rios Pharmacy** (© 876/974-2398) sells most proprietary brands, perfumes, and suntan lotions, among its many wares. Nearby is the major competitor of Ocean Village, the **Coconut Grove Shopping Plaza,** which is linked by walkways and shrubs. The merchandise here consists mainly of local craft items, and this center is often overrun with cruise-ship passengers. Ocean Village is slightly bigger and more upscale, and we prefer it.

Just east of Ocho Rios, the **Pineapple Place Shopping Centre** is a collection of shops in cedar-shingle-roofed cottages set amid tropical flowers.

The **Ocho Rios Craft Park** has 135 stalls. A vendor will weave a hat or a basket while you wait, or you can buy a ready-made hat, hamper, handbag, place mats, or lampshade. Other stands stock hand-embroidered goods and will make small items while you wait. Woodcarvers work on bowls, ashtrays, statues, and cups.

Island Plaza, right in the heart of Ocho Rios, has some of the best Jamaican art, all paintings by local artists. You can also purchase local handmade crafts (be prepared to haggle), carvings, ceramics, kitchenware, and the inevitable T-shirts.

SPECIALTY SHOPS   **Swiss Stores,** in the Ocean Village Shopping Centre (© 876/974-2519), sells jewelry and all the big names in Swiss watches. The Rolex watches here are real, not those fakes touted by hustlers on the streets.

One of the best bets for shopping is **Soni's Plaza,** 50 Main St., the address of all the shops recommended below. **Casa de Oro** (© 876/974-5392) specializes in duty-free watches, fine jewelry, and classic perfumes. **Gem Palace** (© 876/974-2850) is the place to go for diamond solitaires, tennis bracelets, and 14-karat gold chains. **Mohan's** (© 876/974-9270) offers one of the best selections of 14-karat and 18-karat gold chains, rings, bracelets, and earrings. **Soni's** (© 876/974-2303) focuses strictly on souvenirs from coffee mugs to T-shirts. **Taj Gift Centre** (© 876/974-9268) has a little bit of everything: Blue Mountain coffee, film, cigars, and hand-embroidered linen tablecloths. For something different, look for Jamaican jewelry made from hematite, a mountain stone. **Diamonds Duty Free Fine Jewelry** (© 876/974-6455) beats most competition with its name-brand watches, and jewelry.

The Coffee Museum and Café lies immediately upstairs from the Ocean's 11 Watering Hole, Lot # 6, Fisherman's Point Row (© **876/974-6896**). This is the closest thing to a Seattle-style coffee shop in Ocho Rios. Surprisingly well-accessorized, with a theme that involves the production, processing, and marketing of Jamaican coffee, it's airy, bright and divided into sections devoted to a cafe, a gift shop, and a museum. In the cafe, bagels cost $2; sandwiches cost $2.50 to $5, and steaming cups of espresso go for $2.50 each. The gift shop sells coffee mugs, coffee memorabilia, and vacuum-packed foil bags filled with Jamaica's finest coffee. The museum—worth a 5-minute walkthrough—encapsulates, through carefully worded captions and its collection of coffee-industry artifacts, the nuts and bolts of Jamaica's other most distinctive cash crop, coffee. The venue is open daily from 8:30am until between 8 and 10pm, depending on business. This shop contains five Internet stations, which anyone is free to use without charge.

We're always on the lookout for art galleries, so in lieu of schlepping out to Harmony Hall (where the selection of Jamaican paintings is broader and better), **Tallawah Arts,** in the Island Village Shopping Center (© **876/675-8789**), offers a small-scale collection of work by relatively minor artists that might suffice your gift-giving needs. Paintings, depending on their size, range from $15 to $140. The shop is open daily from 8am to 6pm.

After stamping into virtually every shop within this bustling shopping center, our considered opinion is that **Hemp Heaven,** in the Island Village Shopping Center (© **876/675-8969**), is its most interesting and creative shop. It only stocks items made from or related to hemp, which—in case you didn't know—is the fibrous stalk of the marijuana plant. Most of the objects were made in Jamaica, and manage to include hemp in some way that's beneficial to the object's texture, longevity, or healing powers. Inventories include bags; hats; T-shirts (45% cotton, 55% hemp) that, contrary to what you might have thought, are soft and not at all scratchy; hair oil; lotions; candles; massage creams; gift items that usually relate to Jamaica; and more. Garments here are durable, pre-shrunk, and despite their funky designs, they're sold and promoted with a sense of Jamaican nationalism and good fun.

Bookland, in the Island Village Shopping Centre (© **876/675-8791**), is a carefully maintained bookstore with a collection of books that cover various aspects of the Caribbean (ornithological, botanical, or whatever). There are also detailed maps of Jamaica and books that might distract you during off-moments aboard a Caribbean cruise. It's open Monday to Saturday from 9am to 5pm or, if ships are in port, until as late as 8pm. Regardless of whether ships are in port, it remains open every Thursday until 7pm.

OCHO RIOS AFTER DARK

It can be a strange and quirky place, Ocho Rios after dark. Dominated more than any other town in Jamaica by the cruise ship industry, its population swells during the day with foreign visitors, most of whom ship out just before dark, leaving the locals to fend, romantically speaking, for themselves. The result is a quirky set of nightclubs that range from the raw to the very very raw. Here, below, is a selection of some of the tamer choices. Those that we considered too edgy (but visited anyway), we deliberately didn't include. Nor, alas, did we include a detailed description of a club that we've enjoyed in the past, Jamaica'N Me Crazy, within the **Sunset Jamaica Grande Resort & Spa.** Despite its hot music and allure, it lies within an all-inclusive resort, with all the attendant difficulties for a non-resident to talk his or her way inside.

An alternative and somewhat more sanitized way to spend the early part of an evening involves signing up for a sunset cruise before dinner. Sunsets in this part of the world often evoke the color of peach melba. In operation since 1986, and one of the largest sailboat companies on the island, the best cruises are offered by **Heave-Ho Charters,** 180 Main St. ((© 876/974-5367). These early evening cruises cost $55 per person.

The **Sports Bar** at the Little Pub Restaurant (see "Where to Dine," earlier in this chapter) is open daily from 10am to 3am and benefitted from a radical overhaul early in 2006.

Amnesia As stated above, there are wilder, edgier, and scarier nightlife venues in Ocho Rios, but we're uncomfortable recommending them. This, therefore, is as edgy as we want to get, with the full understanding that the place can get wild, edgy, and scary—once you get used to the long line at check-in, the weapons check from the security-conscious staff, and the long process of maneuvering your way past a bevy of sullen and often surly off-duty police officers to get inside. Once you cross those hurdles, however, and climb to the top of an open-air concrete staircase that seems to carry the fumes of car exhaust with you, you can have a perfectly marvelous time grooving with locals to some of the most danceable reggae, hip-hop, r&b, and soca in town. Expect a mostly orange decor, Rasta-inspired murals, a sprawling bar area, lots of Jamaican locals, both male and scantily clad female, plus a very visible minority of horny British chicks with their (blonde) hair arranged into Rasta-inspired braids. At the top of a very short flight of stairs up from the bar, you'll find a large dance floor bathed in day-glo ultraviolet lighting. The place has managed to survive, despite the fickle fingers of fashion, since 1989. Admission costs J$300 (US$4.80), Red Stripes cost an additional J$180 (US$2.90) each. It's open nightly from 9pm to 4am. 70 Main St. (© 876/904-2633.

Ocean's 11 Popular with a widely divergent crowd of Europeans, Jamaicans, and Americans, it operates from a unpretentious-looking opening in a building that overlooks a boardwalk-style waterfront pier. There's a collection of aluminum-tube chairs placed near tables, directly on the dock, but the genuine extroverts usually opt for a seat directly at the bar, where they gossip and kibbutz for hours as the evening progresses. Open daily from 8am till midnight, it charges American-style prices (from $8.50 to $10 each) for daiquiris and for drinks with names that include Jamaica Me Crazy and Fire in the Hole. Our favorite night? Tuesdays, when some of the town's least likely candidates step up to the microphone for karaoke beginning at 9pm. Immediately upstairs from Ocean's 11 is Ocho Rios' most appealing coffee shop and Internet station, the Ocean's 11 Coffee Museum and Internet Cafe. For more on this coffee museum, refer to the "Shopping" section of this chapter. Watering Hole, Lot #6, Fisherman's Point Row. (© 876/974-6896.

Silks Disco Most of the clients who come to groove at this disco are Jamaican, albeit a relatively upscale crowd of party-makers, many of whom are regulars. It's located one floor below lobby level of the also-recommended hotel, a long-established resort that has been around since virtually anyone can remember. Expect a somewhat claustrophobic venue of dark varnished walls, a scattering of low-stakes slot machines, a busy bar area, and very few of the mostly U.S. clientele you're likely to see within more expensive all-inclusive hotels. Admission to this place costs $35 per person, but will include all the drinks you want. It's open nightly from 9pm to 1am. Cutlass Bay, in the Shaw Park Hotel. (© 876/974-2552.

Tips Jamaica Evaluates Its Jerks

Jamaicans, and especially professional drivers, are passionately committed to publicizing the virtues of whatever out-of-the-way stall or kiosk that serves—in their opinion—the country's best jerk pork and chicken. Debates rage in bars and on beaches, but one site that gets consistently good reviews from jerk aficionados is **Blueberry Hill** (*©* **876/403-5308**), which is located on the coastal road about .8km (½ mile) east of the North Shore community of Buff Bay, midway between Port Antonio and Ocho Rios. (It's near the junction of the North Shore Coastal Highway with one of the roughest roads in the Third World—the one that runs over the Blue Mountains back to Kingston.)

Don't expect a palace. Established in 1980 and within shouting distance of less-famous jerk stalls that have cropped up like clones, it's little more than a roadside lean-to, built from concrete blocks that are caked with the carbonization of years of the slow-cooking jerk process. It serves only jerk pork, jerk chicken, and on rare occasions, jerk fish. You"ll be asked in advance if you want a quarter-pound or a half-pound portion. (We always allocate a half-pound portion per person.) It will be presented on paper plates, wrapped in aluminum foil, and accompanied by slices of brown bread from the local supermarket, served with no pretense at all from its original plastic bag. If you take a slice, it will cost J$5 (US8¢) extra. Pork, fish, or chicken are all priced the same: J$250 (US$4) for a half-pound; and around J$150 (US$2.40) for a quarter-pound.

There's no dining room. With a sometimes engaging sense of conviviality (and at other times, in abject, sullen silence), clients collect their bounty in aluminum-foil wrappers, and eat with their fingers while standing beside the road, or perhaps sitting on a battered makeshift stool. Red Stripe beer and Ting (something akin to Sprite) are the drinks of choice. Overall, it's unpretentious, delicious, friendly, and fun, and it's open daily from 10am to 10pm.

Don't think for a moment that there aren't dozens of other jerk stands with reputations deeply entrenched throughout Jamaica. A much-respected competitor, located on the coastal highway (they call it "Main Street") 1.6km (1 mile) east of the center of Discovery Bay, is **Mackie's Jerk Center and Bar** (*©* **876/973-9450**). The roadside venue is a party-colored cluster of open-air verandas, one of which is circular and contains an area reserved for serious drinking 'round about twilight time. It's a tried-and-true destination for minibuses, loaded with foreign visitors, who stop for its toilet facilities, and who sometimes get the first exposures of their lives to the phenomenon known as jerk. It's open daily from 9am to 11pm. Prices are equivalent to those charged at Blueberry Hill (see above). "Festival bread" (deep fried cornmeal dough sprinkled with sugar) is fatteningly delicious and can be ordered separately. No credit cards accepted.

Any jerk stand in Jamaica will accept U.S. dollars, but know in advance that it usually works out to be just a bit cheaper for you, based on unfavorable exchange rates at the jerk stands, to pay for your meal in Jamaican, rather than in U.S. dollars. Why? Because jerk entrepreneurs, while very skilled at the culinary nuances of jerk cuisine, don't view themselves as bankers, and tend to charge not-very-favorable rates on the U.S.-to-Jamaican exchange rates.

Strawberry's   If you opt to drop into this three-tiered bar, restaurant, and nightspot, you might—to your surprise—recognize one of the door attendants from your hotel hanging out during his off hours. It's a three-in-one kind of spot, where most of the money is generated at the street-level sports bar (open daily from noon to midnight.) Also on site is a restaurant (open daily from 7am–11pm), with very ethnic local food priced at J$220 to J$750 (US$3.50–US$12 per platter), and an upstairs disco that's open only Friday to Sunday from 8pm till 2am. Decor throughout is beige and surprisingly drab, in a town that seems to love flashy Creole colors. If you opt to come here, please drop any residual beliefs that the staff will treat you with the same deference they'd pay you, say, during their work day in an all-inclusive hotel. But for a fast beer or two, and an insight into how the city drops all of its touristic pretenses after dark, it's a worthy choice. There's no cover charge, ever, but a Red Stripe will cost around J$85 (US$1.35). 6 James Avenue. ✆ **876/898-1091.**

2 Runaway Bay ✦

Once a mere satellite of Ocho Rios, Runaway Bay, 16km (10 miles) west of Ocho Rios, has become a destination in its own right, with white-sand beaches that are much less crowded than those in Ocho Rios.

Since you're so far removed from the action such as it is in Ocho Rios, you stay at Runaway Bay mainly if you're interested in hanging out at a particular resort. It is especially recommended for those who want to escape from the hordes descending on Ocho Rios, where cruise ship crowds and aggressive vendors can intrude on your solitude.

This part of Jamaica's North Coast has several distinctions: It was the first part of the island seen by Columbus, the site of the first Spanish settlement on the island, and the point of departure of the last Spaniards leaving Jamaica following their defeat by the British.

WHERE TO STAY & DINE

Runaway Bay offers several unusual accommodations, as well as all-inclusive resorts and notable bargains.

MODERATE

Runaway Bay H.E.A.R.T. Hotel ✦ *Value*   This place wins hands-down as the bargain of the North Coast. One of Jamaica's few training and service institutions, the club and its adjacent academy are operated by the government to provide a high level of training for young Jamaicans interested in the hotel trade. The helpful staff of both professionals and trainees offers the finest service of any hotel in the area. Runaway lies a 30-minute drive east of Paradise Beach and a 5-minute drive to Cardiff Hall Beach. Free shuttles are offered only to Cardiff Hall.

⌒ *Fun Fact* **Nude Nuptials**

At the Hedonism III resort (p. 187), couples who want to see what they're getting before they tie the knot can be married in their birthday suits. Instead of a gown and a tuxedo, suntan lotion is recommended so that any body parts, already exposed, might not become overexposed, at least to the sun. After the "I do's" are said, the happy couple can head for the honeymoon suite at this adults-only all-inclusive.

The good-size rooms are bright and airy. Bathrooms have generous shelf space and shower stalls. The accommodations open onto private balconies with views of well-manicured tropical gardens or vistas of the bay and golf course. Guests enjoy having a drink in the piano bar (ever had a cucumber daiquiri?) before heading for the dining room, the Cardiff Hall Restaurant, which serves well-prepared Jamaican and Continental dishes. Be warned in advance that although you might enjoy, for the first day or two, the lack of jadedness and enthusiasm of the staff-in-training, there isn't a lot to do here other than the venues you create for yourself, and you might get bored. Frankly, we prefer this place for just a few days, but definitely not for an entire extended vacation.

Picketts Ave. (P.O. Box 98), Runaway Bay, St. Ann. © 876/973-2671. Fax 876/973-4704. www.runawayheart.com.jm. 56 units. Year-round $149 double. Rates include breakfast and dinner. AE, DISC, MC, V. **Amenities:** Restaurant; bar; pool; gym; limited room service; nonsmoking rooms; rooms for those w/limited mobility. *In room:* A/C, TV, kitchenette, hair dryer, iron, safe.

ALL-INCLUSIVE RESORTS

The following hotels fold the cost of lodgings, meals, drinks, and most activities into one price.

Breezes Runaway Bay 🏄 (Kids)   This stylish resort is an all-inclusive that was artfully and deliberately conceived as a fun and lively place for couples with older children. Its clubhouse is approached by passing through a park filled with tropical trees and shrubbery. The lobby is the best re-creation of the South Seas on Jamaica, with hanging wicker chairs and totemic columns. There's a minijungle with hammocks and a nearby nude beach, in addition to the lovely stretch of sandy beach right out front. The resort, which lies 3km (1¾ miles) east of Paradise Beach and just next door to the town's second best beach, Cardiff Hall, contains 10 hectares (25 acres) that incorporate its own golf course. Its position happens to be astride some of the best scuba diving in Jamaica, lying immediately off the end of the deepwater Cayman trench. Scuba, water-skiing, and golf are all included as part of the all-inclusive price at this resort. Those virtues are offset by the fact that the decor is a bit "aesthetically challenged" and run-down. The overall impression is that of a boxy, low-rise resort that's a bit in need of an overhaul, but permeated with exceptionally good value for anyone interested in otherwise expensive sports such as scuba or golf.

Live music emanates from the stylish Terrace every evening at 7pm, and a nightclub offers live shows 6 nights a week at 10pm. Dine either in the beach-side restaurant or in the more formal Italian restaurant, Pastafari, which is the best. The resort's Starlight Grill has also expanded its menu to include a vegetarian cuisine.

P.O. Box 58 (10km/6¼ miles west of Ocho Rios), Runaway Bay. © 800/GO-SUPER in the U.S., or 876/973-4820. Fax 876/973-6390. www.superclubs.com. 234 units. Winter $319–$562 double; off season $308–$525 double. Rates include all meals, drinks, and activities. AE, DC, DISC, MC, V. No children under age 14. **Amenities:** 4 restaurants; 4 bars; pool; golf; 4 tennis courts; fitness center; 3 Jacuzzis; biking; limited room service; laundry service; nonsmoking rooms; rooms for those w/limited mobility; basketball; cricket; squash; dive shop; kayaking; sailing; scuba diving; snorkeling; water-skiing; windsurfing. *In room:* A/C, TV, minibar (in some), beverage maker, hair dryer, iron, safe.

FDR (Franklyn D. Resort) (Kids)   Located on Route A1, 27km (17 miles) west of Ocho Rios, FDR is an all-inclusive that's the number-one choice if you're traveling with children. FDR lies 3km (1¾ miles) east of Paradise Beach and about .4km (¼ mile) east of Cardiff Hall Beach. Its own no-name beach stretches for about 182m (600 ft.), a mixture of stone and sand. The resort, named after its Jamaican-born owner and developer, Franklyn David Rance, is on 2 hectares (6 acres) of flat, sandy land dotted with flowering shrubs and trees, on the main seaside highway. Each of the Mediterranean-inspired

buildings has a terra-cotta roof, a loggia or an outdoor terrace, Spanish marble in the bathrooms, a kitchenette, and a personal attendant (called a vacation nanny), who cooks, cleans, and cares for children. Although neither the narrow beach nor the modest pools are the most desirable on the island, and most rooms lack a sea view, many visitors appreciate the spacious units and the resort's wholehearted concern for kids.

Two restaurants on the property serve free wine with lunch and dinner (and offer special children's meals), and a piano bar provides music every evening. There's live music nightly.

Main St. (P.O. Box 201), Runaway Bay, St. Ann. ✆ 888/FDR-KIDS in the U.S., or 876/973-4592. Fax 876/973-4600. www.fdrholidays.com. 76 units. Winter $610–$680 double; off season $480–$540 double. Rates are all-inclusive. Children age 5 and under stay free in parent's suite. Children 6–15 $50 extra each. AE, MC, V. **Amenities:** 3 restaurants; 3 bars; 2 pools; tennis court; health club; Jacuzzi; bikes; children's center; free babysitting (9:30am–4:45pm); laundry service; nonsmoking rooms; Internet cafe; disco; dive shop; kayaks; scuba diving; snorkeling; windsurfing. *In room:* A/C, ceiling fan, TV, kitchen.

Grand Lido Braco ☞

Established in 1995, this is one of the most historically evocative all-inclusive resorts in Jamaica, mimicking as it does the design and layout of a 19th-century, fretwork-studded colonial English village in the tropics. It lies beside a prime stretch of sandy, 319m (1,050-ft.) beachfront. Set on 34 hectares (85 acres) of land near Buena Vista, a 15-minute drive west of Runaway Bay, it's a re-creation of a 19th-century Jamaican Victorian village, with charming gingerbread architecture. A copy of a courthouse is the site for after-dark bouts of live entertainment, and benches line the borders of the town square, where artisans display their handiwork. The old Jamaica that's portrayed here is a rather sanitized, Disney-esque version. Yet this is not a place for children; it is a primarily adult retreat.

Accommodations are in 12 blocks of three-story buildings, each trimmed in colonial-style gingerbread and filled with wicker furniture. Each of the spacious units has a private patio or veranda and faces the ocean; blocks one through six are closer to the beachfront, and blocks five and six face a strip of sand designated as a "clothing-optional" area. Beds are very comfortable, with fine linen; the bathrooms are well maintained and have showers. Of the accommodations, a relatively high number of them (73 in all) are suites.

Separate dining areas serve tasty Jamaican cuisine, pizza and pasta, and blander international fare; the Piacere Restaurant offers upscale dinners and has a dress code. For variety, Munahana serves Japanese sushi and teppanyaki cuisine. Golfers especially appreciate the fact that greens fees are included in the rates. Patrons can use, without extra charge, either a 9-hole golf course immediately on-site, or either of two 18-hole golf courses within a reasonably close transfer.

Rio Bueno, Trelawny, Jamaica. ✆ 877/GO-SUPER in the U.S., or 876/954-0000. Fax 876/954-0020 or 876/954-0021. www.superclubs.com. 230 units. Winter $678–$1,366 double; off season $398–$1,182 double. Rates include all meals, drinks, airport transfers, and activities. AE, DC, DISC, MC, V. Children under age 16 not accepted. **Amenities:** 5 restaurants; 8 bars; 2 pools; 9-hole golf course; 3 tennis courts; health club and spa; 4 Jacuzzis; sauna; steam room; bikes; business center; 24-hr. room service; laundry service; dry cleaning; disco; squash; kayaks; scuba diving; snorkeling; Sunfish sailboats; water-skiing; windsurfing. *In room:* A/C, TV, beverage maker, hair dryer, iron.

Hedonism III ☞

Following a chain format established in Negril, this latest beachfront Hedonism bills itself as a "truly active (and slightly wicked!) vacation." Though this branch of Hedonism isn't as rowdy and raunchy as the Negril branch, and it utterly lacks the Negril branch's long-established self-image as an early outpost of defiantly extroverted sexual liberation—it's a little more serene and isolated from the action in town—it's still for the serious party person who likes to drink all night, hang out at the beach all day, and go wild at those toga parties. Set on 6 hectares (15 acres)

of landscaped gardens on the eastern end of Runaway Bay, it features a Jamaican-Georgian motif of clapboard-sided colonial buildings gussied up with gables, fretwork, verandas with elaborate balustrades, and a strong sense of symmetry along both parallel and perpendicular lines. Hedonism III has its own private, slightly rocky beach stretching for some 182m (600 ft.)—part of it is often nude. It lies a 15-minute drive east of Paradise Beach and a 10-minute walk west of Cardiff Hall Beach.

Bedrooms—with ocean views from all rooms—are roomy and freshly decorated, with Jamaica's first-ever block of "swim-up" rooms. All swim-up rooms feature large marble tub-and-shower bathrooms with Jacuzzis and CD players. Single guests are paired up with a roommate of the same sex, or have to pay a single supplement.

The food is quite decent—everything from Italian to Japanese to Jamaican. There is even a disco with a four-story water slide! The resort also offers Jamaica's only circus workshop that features a flying trapeze, juggling, a trampoline "clinic," and various unicycle and bike-balancing acts. It's presented Monday to Saturday.

Runaway Bay. ℂ 877/GO-SUPER in the U.S., or 876/973-4100. Fax 876/973-5402. www.superclubs.com. 225 units. Winter $427–$698 double; off season $308–$690 double. Rates include all meals, drinks, and activities. AE, DC, DISC, MC, V. No children under age 18. **Amenities:** 5 restaurants; 6 bars; 3 large pools; 3 tennis courts; fitness center; 3 Jacuzzis; sauna; game room; 24-hr. room service; nonsmoking rooms; rooms for those w/limited mobility; disco; basketball court; ice-skating rink; rock-climbing; volleyball; kayaks; sailing; scuba diving; snorkeling; water-skiing; windsurfing. *In room:* A/C, TV, dataport, beverage maker, hair dryer, iron, safe.

SPORTS & OUTDOOR PURSUITS

BEACHES & WATERSPORTS The two best beaches at Runaway Bay are **Paradise Beach** and **Cardiff Hall Public Beach.** Both wide, white-sand strips are clean and well maintained—ideal spots for a picnic. If you're staying in Ocho Rios and want to escape the crowds, come here. You don't get a lot of facilities, however, so you'd better bring along whatever you need.

The waters are calm almost all year. Prevailing trade winds will keep you cool in the mornings and late afternoon. Because there are no lifeguards, be especially careful if you're with children.

Runaway Bay offers some of the best **snorkeling** in Jamaica. The reefs are close to shore and extremely lively with marine life, including enormous schools of tropical fish such as blue chromis, triggerfish, small skate rays, and snapper. You can also go diving. **Jamaica Dive Center,** at the Club Ambiance resort (ℂ **876/973-4845**), has as its slogan: "We Be Divin'." The dive facility takes you to one of several protected reefs where the currents aren't dangerous, and where fishing boats are required to stay at least 82m (600 ft.) away from divers and snorkelers. The dive outfitter offers everything from one-tank dives to six-boat packages. All equipment needed can be rented on-site. A one-tank dive costs $42, a two-tank dive costs $75.

GOLF **SuperClubs Runaway Golf Club** (ℂ **876/973-7319**) charges no admission for guests staying at any of Jamaica's affiliated SuperClubs. For nonguests, the price is $80 year-round. Any player can rent carts for $35 for 18 holes; clubs are $14 for 18 holes.

HORSEBACK RIDING Jamaica's most complete equestrian center is the **Chukka Caribbean Adventures,** at Richmond Llandovery, St. Ann (ℂ **876/972-2506;** www.chukkacaribbean.com), less than 6km (3¾ miles) east of Runaway Bay. If you opt for an equestrian experience here, don't expect a demure and sedate experience in a penned-in riding rink. The shortest ride they offer lasts for 3 hours, and carries you and your mount along a combination of forest trails and beachfront, and culminates with a ride through the surf. The per person cost of $67 includes refreshments. Polo

A Tribute to Bob Marley

Reggae fans from all over the world visit the little hamlet of Nine Mile to pay their respects at the **Bob Marley Centre & Mausoleum** (© 876/995-1763), which is open daily from 9:30am to 6:30pm, charging an admission of $12. Neither the hours of opening nor the price is writ in stone.

The village where Marley grew up and where he was buried has the unusual name of Nine Mile. It's a group of ramshackle farms, stray goats, and chickens.

You can go inside Marley's two-room shanty, filled with family memorabilia, including photographs. Marley lived here from the ages of 6 to 13. Adjoining the shack is the so-called mausoleum in which Marley was buried. He shares the gravesite with his half-brother, who was gunned down by police in Miami during a drug bust.

On-site is a vegetarian restaurant and a little shop selling Marley tapes.

The big event of the year here is Marley's birthday each February 6. Reggae fans descend on Nine Mile to listen to concerts. The performer's son, Ziggy Marley, also a reggae star, often appears to entertain.

To reach the pilgrimage site, take the B3 from Ocho Rios south to Brown's Town, a distance of 39km (24 miles). From there continue south to Alexandria for 10km (6¼ miles). Once at Alexandria, turn east (signposted ALVA), going for another 15km (9¼ miles) until you arrive at the hamlet of Nine Mile of Marley fame.

lessons are also available, costing $50 for 30 minutes. A more recent feature is a mountain-and-sea adventure on a bike (90% of which is downhill). The 2½-hour bike ride, priced at $65, ends with a swim and some snorkeling.

EXPLORING THE AREA

Columbus Park Museum ⋒, on Queens Highway, Discovery Bay (© 876/973-2135), is a large, open area between the main coast road and the sea at Discovery Bay. Just pull off the road and walk among the fantastic collection of exhibits; admission is free. There's everything from a canoe made from a solid piece of cottonwood (the way Arawaks did it more than 5 centuries ago) to a stone cross that was originally placed on the Barrett Estate (14km/8¾ miles east of Montego Bay) by Edward Barrett, brother of poet Elizabeth Barrett Browning. You'll see a tally, used to count bananas carried on men's heads from plantation to ship, as well as a planter's strongbox with a weighted lead base to prevent its theft. Other items are 18th-century cannons, a Spanish water cooler and calcifier, a fish pot made from bamboo, a corn husker, and a water wheel. Pimento trees, from which allspice is produced, dominate the park, which is open daily from 8am to 4pm (admission is free).

You can also visit the **Seville Great House,** Heritage Park (© 876/972-2191). Built in 1745 by the British, it contains a collection of artifacts once used by everybody from the Amerindians to African slaves. In all, you're treated to an exhibit of 5 centuries' worth of Jamaican history. Modest for a great house, it has wattle-and-daub construction. A small theater presents a 15-minute historical film about the house. It's open daily from 9am to 5pm; admission is $4.

Port Antonio

From Ocho Rios, drive east along Highway A4/A3, which takes you through some sleepy fishing villages, including Port Maria, until you reach **Port Antonio.** Situated on the coast just north of the Blue Mountains, the town is surrounded by some of the most rugged and beautiful scenery in Jamaica. Many visitors prefer to visit the mountains and highlands from a base here, rather than starting in Kingston, to avoid the capital's urban sprawl.

This is the parish of Portland. It's the rainiest, greenest parish in Jamaica, known for its many rivers and waterfalls. Once the cradle of Jamaican tourism, the region has since been eclipsed by Montego Bay, Ocho Rios, and Negril. It remains a preferred hideaway, however, for a chic and elegant crowd that comes for a handful of posh hotels.

Port Antonio itself is a verdant and sleepy seaport 97km (60 miles) northeast of Kingston. You may have seen it in the Hollywood film *Cocktail* (still talked about here as if it were shot yesterday). Here you can still catch a glimpse of the Jamaica of old. This small, bustling town is like many in Jamaica: clean though ramshackle, its sidewalks surrounding a market filled with vendors, tin-roofed shacks compete with old Georgian and modern brick and concrete buildings. Locals busily shop, talk, and laugh, while others sit and play dominoes (loudly banging the pieces on the table, which is very much part of the game).

Go to the colorful markets to browse for local craftworks, spices, and fruits—or just to listen to conversations, negotiations, and the news of the day.

Navy Island and the long-gone Titchfield Hotel were owned for a short time by film star Errol Flynn, who was much loved and admired by Jamaicans and totally integrated into his community. Locals still talk of Flynn in Port Antonio, especially the men, who speak of his legendary womanizing and drinking in almost reverent tones.

We find Port Antonio an elite retreat, a virtual Shangri-La when compared to busier Ocho Rios or Montego Bay. It also has some of the finest beaches in Jamaica, and has long been a center for some of the Caribbean's best deep-sea fishing. Some of the most expensive yachts sailing the Caribbean can be seen here with the opening of the first-class **Port Antonio Marina** ⫝̸⫝̸. It's a good place to go to get away from it all.

COMPARING RESORTS

Unlike Montego Bay, Negril, and Ocho Rios, less visited and much more remote Port Antonio is an elite retreat—long a favorite of visiting celebrities such as Bette Davis, Ginger Rogers, Harrison Ford, and Denzel Washington.

Although much of Jamaica is overbuilt, Port Antonio lies in a relatively undeveloped area. As one local vendor put it, "Ocho Rios attracts the tourist; we attract the traveler."

> **Fun Fact** **Hyperbole Through the Ages**
>
> The first "tourist," Christopher Columbus, called Port Antonio "the fairest land mine eyes have ever seen." The American poet Ella Wheeler Wilcox (1855–1919) perhaps had imbibed one too many rum punches when she exclaimed that "Port Antonio is the most exquisite place on earth." And what did swashbuckler Errol Flynn have to say? "Port Antonio is more beautiful than any woman I've ever seen."

The area's white-sand beaches are among the island's finest and least crowded. Only a few resorts here can be described as upmarket; most of this region is a haven for the frugal traveler seeking modest digs. Port Antonio lacks the all-inclusive megaresorts of Ocho Rios or Mo Bay; if that's what you need, head elsewhere. The same goes for shopping, nightlife, and deluxe dining: If they're absolutely essential to your vacation, hit the road. And if you like to run naked on the beach, your hair in braids, Negril is more your speed. Port Antonio, quite frankly, is perhaps the most staid of the major Jamaican resort towns. It's also generally acknowledged as the home base of the least aggressive, most low-key, and most restrained, street vendors.

Most mainstream beach-going, sun-loving Americans tend to gravitate to Mo Bay, Ocho Rios, and Negril (in that order). In Port Antonio, by contrast, you're much more likely to encounter eco-sensitive and "adventurous" European visitors, especially from Germany and Holland, and a handful of Americans interested in botany, bird watching, environmental issues, nature hikes, and eco-exploring.

You can link up with other resorts or attractions on day trips while staying here. Port Antonio is within easy driving distance of Ocho Rios; the Blue Mountains and John Crow Mountains are at the town's southern edge.

Hoteliers in Port Antonio know the area may never be as chic as it was in the 1950s or the early 1960s. Still, they are preparing for stiff competition in the 21st century with a push to attract a new type of traveler, the upmarket, eco-sensitive traveler who wants to explore the natural beauty of the island—especially that mountain scenery to the south of Port Antonio. If you love nature, there may be no better place in Jamaica to base yourself.

And if a movie star still sneaks into town on occasion to chill out, well, that's okay with the locals, too.

1 Orientation

GETTING THERE BY PLANE If you're going to Ocho Rios first, you'll fly into the **Donald Sangster Airport** in Montego Bay (see "Orientation" in chapter 4) or the **Norman Manley International Airport** in Kingston (see "Orientation" in chapter 9). Some hotels, particularly the larger resorts, will arrange for airport transfers. Be sure to ask when you book. You can also fly to Port Antonio's small airport, booking your connection through **International Air Link** (© **888/AIR-LINK** or 876/940-6660; www.intlairlink.com). This local airport, **Ken Jones Aerodrome** (© **876/913-3173**), lies 10km (6¼ miles) west of the center of Port Antonio, and several taxis always meet arriving planes to take you where you want to go along the northeast coastline. There are no more direct flights from the Kingston airports into Port Antonio. The only way

Bligh, the Bounty & the Breadfruit

The true story of the HMS *Bounty* and its mutinous crew is the stuff of legend and film—and if you're renting videos, by the way, the Clark Gable/Charles Laughton 1930s version is far better than the 1984 Mel Gibson/Anthony Hopkins disappointment. But we digress.

Though a rich, fertile land, Jamaica in its early days did not grow enough food to support itself. Supplies were shipped down from what later became the United States, but vessels stopped sailing during the American Revolution, leading to starvation on the island. In London, Captain William Bligh was ordered to sail to Tahiti in command of the HMS *Bounty*, collect a hold of starchy, bland-tasting breadfruit, and then carry it onward to feed the Jamaicans.

The *Bounty* sailed from London in 1787, rounding Cape Horn. In Tahiti breadfruit plants were duly collected. On the way back, however, the crew—led by Fletcher Christian—mutinied in protest of Bligh's harsh command. Bligh and some of his most loyal men were set adrift in the middle of the Pacific, as Christian—now the captain—sailed for Ascension Island.

Somehow Bligh survived and returned to London. He was found not guilty of wrongdoing, was made captain of the HMS *Providence*, and set sail once again to fulfill his breadfruit mission. The *Providence* sailed from London in 1791; Bligh returned to Tahiti, securing more breadfruit plants, and finally did reach the island of Jamaica in February of 1793.

The plants were sent to a little spa at Bath with its botanical gardens, where they flourished and became an important food staple on the then-starving island. If there's a statue or memorial to Bligh's remarkable persistence, though, we haven't seen it.

to reach Port Antonio from Kingston by air is to fly across the country to Montego Bay, board a separate flight, then fly back across the country to Port Antonio (it takes hours).

BY BUS   The bus from Montego Bay costs $25 one-way. We recommend the private company **Tour Wise** (© **876/979-1027**), whose bus will drop you off at your hotel. The trip takes about 5 hours.

BY RENTAL CAR OR TAXI   You can rent a car in Montego Bay for the 216km (134-mile) drive east along the A1. The highway becomes the A3 and then the A4 before it reaches Port Antonio. Figure on at least 5 hours to make this drive safely. Expect some rough going, as the road is traffic-clogged in many spots and broken up with horrendous potholes in others. (Jamaican officials promise an improvement in this highway, probably during the lifetime of this edition.) You also must compete with bikes, goats, pedestrian traffic (within the towns), and the like. Even though it's at times tedious, it does provide the opportunity of seeing a roadside view of down-home, down-scale Jamaica for a bit. A private taxi will charge between $240 and $280 for the one-way transit between Montego Bay and Port Antonio—a dauntingly high fee.

A private taxi between Kingston and Port Antonio charges around $120 each way, and the drive takes less than 2 hours. Therefore, if Port Antonio is your final destination within Jamaica, it's more convenient and cheaper to fly into Kingston.

Officially sanctioned **JUTA taxis** (📞 **876/927-4534**), found at both the Montego Bay and Kingston airports, will take you over land to Port Antonio.

VISITOR INFORMATION

The local office of the **Jamaica Tourist Board** is on the second floor of City Centre Plaza (📞 **876/993-3051**), at the west end of Harbour Street in the center of town. Hours are Monday to Friday 8:30am to 4:30pm and Saturday 9am to 1pm. If you want information about Jamaica in general (i.e., information that's not necessarily related to tourism), go to the **Jamaican Information Service,** 23 Harbour St. (📞 **876/ 993-2630**), which maintains the same hours.

THE TOWN LAYOUT

Separated by the Titchfield Peninsula, the heart of Port Antonio lies between two harbors. Divided only by a narrow channel, the privately owned Navy Island, still called "Errol Flynn's Island" by some old-timers, lies just offshore.

There are no clever names here, only literal ones. The western part is called West Harbour; the eastern bay is known as East Harbour. West Palm Avenue is the major avenue running at the southern tier of West Harbour. The larger East Harbour is bordered by Allan Avenue going east.

The town center is crisscrossed by three main roads—Gideon Avenue, Harbour Street, and William Street—each running parallel to the others. Linking up with Harbour Street, Fort George Street rises uphill along the Titchfield Peninsula. West and Harbour streets converge at a clock tower, flanked by the courthouse and the post office.

The center of Port Antonio is easy to traverse on foot, although if you get lost, asking directions can be frustrating (or amusing): Townsfolk often defy mapmakers, calling streets or roads by local nicknames. Allan Avenue, for example—which begins at the junction with Harbour Street, near Christ Church—is locally called "Folly Road" for some reason we can't discern.

GETTING AROUND   Bus transportation here is a disaster. If you don't have a private car, use a taxi. **JUTA** (📞 **876/993-2684**) runs a fleet of station wagons and minivans around the area. A typical charge, say from the heart of Port Antonio to San San Beach or the Blue Lagoon, is $15 to $20. If you're being taken to the beach and want to spend some time there before returning, you can even arrange with a driver to be picked up at a certain time.

Minibuses operate throughout the town on erratic schedules and can be waved down. They are far cheaper, costing only $2 per person. "Robot" or shared cabs are also plentiful, but some of these are illegal, and some of them aren't adequately insured. Know in advance that vehicles with red license plates are usually insured and authorized to carry paying passengers.

FACT FACTS: **Port Antonio**

Banks   The largest and most convenient banks include **Scotiabank,** 3 Harbour St. (📞 876/933-2523), **RBTT Jamaica Ltd.,** 28 Harbour St. (📞 876/993-9755), and

First International Caribbean Bank, on West Street (© 876/993-2785), and are all open Monday to Thursday 9am to 2pm, Friday 9am to 4pm.

Libraries To catch up on your reading, or for access to a handful of Internet-accessible computer stations, head for the **Portland Parish Library,** Lower Fort George Street (© 876/993-2793), open Monday to Friday 9am to 6pm, Saturday 9am to 4pm.

Mail The **Port Antonio Post Office,** Harbour Street (© 876/993-2158), lies in the exact center of town by the clock. Include "Jamaica, W.I." in all island addresses. The island has no zip codes, although at press time for this edition, discussions were under way about assigning zip codes to each of the various districts of Jamaica. Depending on the local bureaucracies, these new zip codes may or may not be in effect during the lifetime of this edition.

Medical Services The hospital is the **Port Antonio Hospital** (© 876/993-2646), which lies south of West Harbour on Naylor's Hill.

Pharmacies A trio of pharmacies is found in the center of town. They are **A&E Pharmacy,** Port Antonio Square (© 876/993-9348), open Monday to Wednesday, Friday, and Saturday 9am to 6pm, Thursday 9am to 2pm; **The City Plaza Pharmacy** on Harbour Street (© 876/993-2620), open Monday to Wednesday, Friday, and Saturday 9am to 6pm, Thursday 9am to 2pm; and **Square Deal Pharmacy,** 11 West St. (© 876/993-3629), open Monday to Saturday 9am to 6pm.

Safety Generally speaking, Port Antonio is a safer destination than Montego Bay, Negril, or Ocho Rios—and much safer than Kingston. When shopping the Musgrave Market, however, pay special attention to your wallet or purse. The narrow little streets of Port Antonio, with their bad lighting at night, also invite muggers. Wander there at your own risk.

Travel Agencies The best travel agency here is **Trafalgar Travel,** 2–6 Harbour St. (© 876/993-2645), open Monday to Friday 8:30am to 4:30pm, Saturday 10am to 1pm.

2 Where to Stay

In spite of the charms of Port Antonio, it is currently suffering from somewhat of a lack of business—resort clients are drawn to the more famous Negril, Ocho Rios, and Montego Bay resorts. Many of the hotels below are thus having to fill empty rooms with low-cost tour groups originating in anywhere from Italy to Canada. This, in turn, is causing a major (and unfortunate) deterioration in the physical condition of some of the properties, which no longer seem to be maintained in a state-of-the-art condition.

If you're booking your own accommodations in Port Antonio, check out the information that's available through the website (www.go-jam.com) of the **Port Antonio Guesthouse Association & Friends.** Another useful web address is www.portantonio travel.com.

Traveling frugally? The restaurant **San San Tropez** (p. 202) rents six plain but very affordable rooms.

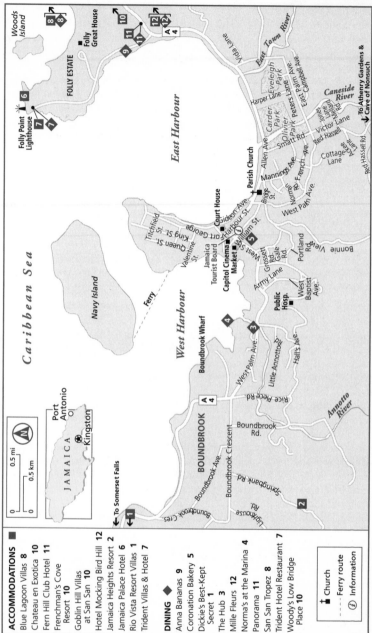

Port Antonio

Woods Island

Caribbean Sea

JAMAICA
Port Antonio
Kingston

0   0.5 mi
0   0.5 km

N

To Somerset Falls

Navy Island

West Harbour

East Harbour

Ferry

Folly Point Lighthouse
Folly Great House
Folly
FOLLY ESTATE

East Town River

Caneside River

To Athenry Gardens & Cave of Nonsuch

Eveleigh Park
Harper Lane
Carder Park
Olivier
Allen Ave.
Manning Ave.
Smatt Rd.
R. French Rd.
Norman Ave.
West Palm Ave.
Cottage Lane
Red Hassell
Victor Lane
Jones Lane
Metfield Lane
Red Hassell Rd.
East Palm Ave.
Park Peters Lane
East Palm Ave.
Campbell Ave.

Parish Church
Court House
Gideon Ave.
Harbour St.
Fort George
King St.
Queen St.
Titchfield St.
Valentine St.
Jamaica Tourist Board
Capitol Cinema
Market
William St.
West St.
Briggs St.
Gresett Rd.
Gale Rd.
Portland Rd.
Bonnie View
Army Lane
Public Hosp.
West Baptist Ave.

Boundbrook Wharf

BOUNDBROOK
Boundbrook Rd.
Boundbrook Ave.
Boundbrook Crescent
Boundbrook Cres.
Springbank Rd.
Lighthouse Rd.
Rice Piece Rd.
West Palm Ave.
Little Annotto
Halls Ave.
Annotto River

Vidal Lane

ACCOMMODATIONS ■
Blue Lagoon Villas **8**
Chateau en Exotica **10**
Fern Hill Club Hotel **11**
Frenchman's Cove Resort **10**
Goblin Hill Villas at San San **10**
Hotel Mocking Bird Hill **12**
Jamaica Heights Resort **2**
Jamaica Palace Hotel **6**
Rio Vista Resort Villas **1**
Trident Villas & Hotel **7**

DINING ◆
Anna Bananas **9**
Coronation Bakery **5**
Dickie's Best-Kept Secret **1**
The Hub **3**
Mille Fleurs **12**
Norma's at the Marina **4**
Panorama **11**
San San Tropez **8**
Trident Hotel Restaurant **7**
Woody's Low Bridge Place **10**

✝ Church
■ Ferry route
ⓘ Information

VERY EXPENSIVE

Blue Lagoon Villas 🜲🜲🜲   This complex of villas is often favored by discreetly wealthy residents of the U.S., who come to this resort just as they did in decades past. This is one of the most exclusive resorts in the Port Antonio area, a pocket of low-key posh that evokes the luxury of the late 1950s. Each of the elegantly decorated private villas comes with its own chef, housekeeper, and butler. Villas contain two, three, or four bedrooms, and are each only a 2-minute walk from the Blue Lagoon. Bedrooms are the most stylish in Port Antonio, with an emphasis on privacy and seclusion. All open onto panoramic views of the sea, and all are very spacious, with luxurious tub/shower combination bathrooms. Because the resort attracts lots of media types, each villa has a TV, VCR, and entertainment center with CD player—not to mention both indoor and outdoor dining areas, sun decks with luxe chaise lounges, and a full kitchen. These are among the most frequently photographed villas in the Caribbean, having appeared in the pages of such magazines as *Town & Country* and *Gourmet*. Note, however, that you can rent them only by the week, not the night. Nonguests may dine at the hotel's Blue Lagoon Restaurant.

The Blue Lagoon, Fairy Hill, Port Antonio. © **800/237-3237** or 876/993-8491. Fax 876/993-7792. www.bluelagoon villas.com. 13 villas. Winter $7,500 2-bedroom villa, $8,500 3-bedroom villa, from $9,500 4-bedroom villa; off season $6,500 2-bedroom villa, $7,500 3-bedroom villa, from $8,500 4-bedroom villa. Rates are by the week and include breakfast and pickup at the airport. MC, V. **Amenities:** Restaurant; massage; laundry service; chef; housekeeper; butler; kayaks. *In room:* A/C, TV, kitchen, private bar, safe.

Chateau en Exotica 🜲🜲 *Finds*   If you want the honeymoon retreat of all time, or else want to slip away for an illicit week, consider this oasis near San San Beach and the Blue Lagoon. It is the ultimate fantasy retreat. It's small and exclusive, standing on a 2-hectare (5-acre) private estate. On the *Million Dollar Player* show, the estate was twice chosen as the grand-prize destination. Even Jamaica's usually reserved *Daily Gleaner* has acclaimed the property as "a dream house, a place of serenity"—and so it is. Many feature films or TV shows have used the setting as a backdrop, including *Lifestyles of the Rich and Famous*. Its crystal-clear, rainbow-tiled, and fountain-fresh swimming pool is reason enough to check in. In the courtyard is a spa with thermo hydra jets and miniwaterfalls. A second spacious heated spa is set in a secluded garden gazebo hideaway. The living quarters are spacious and beautifully furnished with a certain elegance and much comfort. Breakfast in bed is a daily option. You've also got your own butler and nanny (housekeeper being the more politically correct term).

Lavish dinners can be arranged in the tented dining room, with a white-gloved butler in attendance at the candlelit setting. You can also dine alfresco by the pool with lighted Tiki torches. The tropical setting is one of fruit trees and lavish flora, with fountains and fish ponds.

San San Estate, Port Antonio. ©/fax **561/793-7257**. www.iwms.com/exotica. 3 units. Winter $495 double, $595 for 3–6 guests; off season $395 double, $495 for 3–6 guests. No credit cards. **Amenities:** Dining room; pool; 2 whirlpools; 2 spas; 5 complimentary boats; free bicycles; limited room service; babysitting; laundry service; basketball court. *In room:* A/C, TV, fridge, hair dryer, safe, Jacuzzi.

Trident Villas & Hotel 🜲🜲   This luxury hideaway is located on Allan Avenue, on the coast stretching northeast of town toward Frenchman's Cove. Designed like a British colonial compound of white-sided buildings with cedar-shingle roofs, it sits regally above jagged coral cliffs with a seaside panorama. The hotel's main building is furnished with antiques and cooled by sea breezes. Your accommodations will be a studio cottage or tower, reached by a path through the gardens. In the cottages, a large

bedroom with ample sitting area opens onto a private patio with a sea view. All units have ceiling fans, plenty of storage space, and tasteful Jamaican antiques and colorful chintzes. Beds are most comfortable, while bathrooms have combination shower/tubs. Despite major renovations to the place in the wake of Hurricane Ivan's devastation in 2004, maintenance on some of the exteriors of this place has fallen off, giving to some visitors the impression of an elegant grand piano that's just slightly out of tune. Service, however, is attentive, old-fashioned, and white-gloved, evoking Jamaica the way it was during the heyday years of the 1950s, and bedroom areas look good and well maintained. Trident has a horseshoe-shaped sandy beach cove at one end of its grounds, which is accessible by a path that meanders along a landscaped terrain. It's a strip of muddy bottomed seafront that's not as appealing as a dip in the hotel pool. That pool is positioned near a graceful gazebo and sits above jagged rocks where the surf crashes and churns most of the day.

Men are required to wear jackets and ties at dinner, which is a multi-course, excellent fixed-price meal; if you have dietary restrictions, make your requirements known early.

Rte. A4 (P.O. Box 119), Port Antonio. ⓒ 876/993-2602. Fax 876/993-2960. www.tridentvillas.netfirms.com. 27 units. Winter $120–$180 double, $180 1-bedroom villa; $360 2-bedroom villa; off season $120 double, $150–$180 1-bedroom villa, $240 2-bedroom villa. MAP $48 extra per person per day. AE, MC, V. **Amenities:** Restaurant; bar; pool; limited room service; massage; babysitting; laundry service; rooms for those w/limited mobility; croquet; deep-sea fishing; scuba diving; snorkeling. *In room:* A/C, minibar, beverage maker, hair dryer, safe.

EXPENSIVE

Frenchman's Cove Resort 🅡 *Kids*   Lying 8km (5 miles) east of the center of Port Antonio, this once world-famous resort is the most retro-elegant in town, with simple but very large villas that are comfortable, sprawling, and eminently suitable for extended families with children. The 18-hectare (45-acre) private estate opens onto a sheltered white-sand beach, one of the most idyllic along the northern coast of Jamaica, that's bisected with its own freshwater running stream. Although there's a charming beachfront restaurant on site, featuring mostly Jamaican food, many visitors opt to prepare most of their meals within their lodgings, giving the place an atmosphere something like that of a sprawling and verdant bed and breakfast. Accommodations include regular doubles and suites within the resort's central core, called "The Great House," as well as one-, two-, or three-bedroom villas spread across a sea-bordering cliff in parklike grounds. Each accommodation, regardless of its size, is attractively furnished but in a durable minimalist style that's vaguely inspired by the Caribbean tropics, usually with a combination of wicker and dark wood, with large walls of glass that are screened and louvered. Most of the villas evoke small-scale Jamaican-style stone-and-timber cottages, often with bathrooms that feature sunken showers. The large three-bedroom villa (no. 18) was once occupied by Queen Elizabeth and her family in the 1970s, a decade that was the heyday of this resort. Today, in a format that's considerably calmer, quieter, and less flamboyant than it was during its glory years, it's owned by Granger Watson, an investor from Texas. One of our favorite accommodations is villa no. 7, nestled on cliffs in the midst of rainforest shrubbery with a clear view of the beach below. On the way to the beach, you can pick a few oranges to go with your lunch.

Frenchman's Cove (P.O. Box 101), Port Antonio. ⓒ 876/993-7270. Fax 876/993-7404. www.frenchmans-cove-resort.com. 12 units, 18 villas. Year-round $90 double, $100 suite, $130 1-bedroom villa, $175 2-bedroom villa, $200 3-bedroom villa. Rates include continental breakfast. MC, V. **Amenities:** Beachfront grill-style restaurant; 2 bars; babysitting; laundry service; rooms for those w/limited mobility. *In room:* A/C, fridge (in villas), beverage maker (in villas), iron, phone in Great House rooms only.

Goblin Hill Villas at San San ⚑ This green and sunny hillside—once said to shelter goblins—is now filled with Georgian-style vacation homes within a neighborhood to the northeast of Port Antonio known as San San Estate. The pool is surrounded by a vine-laced arbor, which lies just a stone's throw from an almost impenetrable forest. A long flight of steps leads down to the crescent-shaped sands of San San Beach. This beach is now private, but guests of the hotel receive a pass. Everything has the aura of having last been redesigned in the 1970s, but the resort is still comfortable, albeit just a bit faded and dated. The accommodations are town house–style; some have ceiling fans and king-size beds (some have twin beds), but none have phones and overall, there's a lingering suspicion of the dowdiness of yesteryear. Accommodations are roomy and filled with handmade pinewood furniture, each with a split-level living and dining area with a fully equipped kitchen. All units have well-maintained bathrooms with shower-tub combinations. Housekeepers prepare and serve meals and attend to chores within each individual villa. Some residual damage from the hurricane of 2004 is still visible, but overall, the resort is up, running, and competent. Know in advance that there's no working restaurant on-site, a fact that places special emphasis on guests preparing, usually with the assistance of the housekeepers, meals within their individual accommodations.

San San (P.O. Box 26), Port Antonio. ✆ **800/472-1148** or 876/925-8108. Fax 876/925-6248. www.goblinhill.com. 28 units. Winter $125–$195 1-bedroom villa, $205–$265 2-bedroom villa; off season $115–$165 1-bedroom villa, $170–$195 2-bedroom villa. AE, MC, V. **Amenities:** Bar; pool; 2 tennis courts; car rental; limited room service; babysitting; laundry service; nonsmoking rooms. *In room:* A/C, ceiling fan, TV, kitchen, fridge, beverage maker (in some), no phone.

MODERATE

Fern Hill Club Hotel Airy and panoramic but showing signs of wear, and accessible via one of the most dismayingly potholed and badly maintained access roads in Jamaica (locally, they refer to it as "adventurous"), Fern Hill occupies 8 forested hectares (20 acres) high above the coastline, attracting a primarily German, British, and Canadian tour-group clientele, as well as many vacationing Jamaican families. The nearest beach is San San, a deeply rutted 10-minute drive east of the hotel. There's no shuttle but the reception desk can arrange for a taxi to take you there. This is a far less elegant choice than its main competitor, Goblin Hill (see above), though you can almost always get cheaper rates here. Technically classified as a private club, it's comprised of a colonial-style clubhouse and three outlying villas, plus a comfortable annex at the bottom of the hill. The accommodations come in a wide range of configurations, including standard rooms, junior suites, spa suites, and villas with cooking facilities. All units are highly private and attract many honeymooners.

See "Where to Dine," below, for a review of the hotel restaurant, Panorama, which offers a standard international menu.

Mile Gully Rd., San San (P.O. Box 100), Port Antonio. ✆ **876/993-7375.** Fax 876/993-7373. 31 units. Year-round $140 1-bedroom villa, $252 2-bedroom villa. MC, V. Drive east along Allan Ave. and watch for the signs. **Amenities:** Restaurant; bar; 3 pools; tennis court; laundry service. *In room:* A/C, TV, kitchenette (in villas), iron, safe.

Hotel Mocking Bird Hill ⚑ A 10km (6¼ mile) drive east of Port Antonio, this charming, homey, and well-maintained inn competes effectively with hotels and resorts that are larger, grander, and sometimes, much more pretentious. In 1993, two imaginative women transformed the place into a blue-and-white enclave of good taste, reasonable prices, and ecological consciousness. Set about 180m (590 ft.) above the

coastline on a hillside laden with tropical plants, within a 5-minute drive from French-man's Cove Beach, the hotel attracts a clientele of mostly European visitors who revel in the artsy and ecologically alert setting. The accommodations are simple but taste-ful and at their best, understatedly elegant, with neatly kept shower-only bathrooms, balconies or verandas, spinning ceiling fans, mosquito netting, and views that sweep over the rainforest down to the sea. Much of the establishment's interior, including its separately recommended restaurant (Mille Fleurs—see "Where to Dine," later in this chapter), is decorated with artworks, many executed by Barbara Walker, one of the own-ers. There are massage options available on-site, as well as day hikes and classes in paint-ing and drawing. If that doesn't tempt you, you can just relax and enjoy a herbal massage or the views that sweep out over the Blue Mountains and the Jamaican coastline.

Mocking Bird Hill (P.O. Box 254), North Coast Hwy., east of Port Antonio. $\textcircled{C}$ 876/993-7267. Fax 876/993-7133. www.hotelmockingbirdhill.com. 10 units. Winter $245–$295 double; off season $155–$195 double. AE, MC, V. **Amenities:** Restaurant; bar; pool; Internet access; limited room service; laundry service; nonsmoking rooms; rooms for those w/limited mobility. In room: Ceiling fans, beverage maker, hair dryer, safe, no phone.

Jamaica Palace Hotel ⚜   This stately mansion, originally conceived as a shopping center but skillfully adapted, after carloads of architectural changes, into a palatial hotel, rises from a hillock that's the centerpiece of 2 tropically landscaped hectares (5 acres) of verdant land.. It's usually cited as the best-maintained hotel in Port Antonio, the ambitious and hard-won by-product of a German-Iraqi couple that, in its way, represents one of the most sophisticated and cosmopolitan collaborations in town. The public rooms are filled with European furnishings and art, including a 2m (6-ft.) Baccarat crystal candelabrum, lavish art objects, heroic/monumental paintings, fine carpets, and a pair of Italian ebony-and-ivory chairs from the 15th century. Outside, the Palace offers white-marble columns, sun-filled patios and balconies, and an unusual 35m (114-ft.) pool shaped—much to the delight of local nationalists—like an aerial view of Jamaica itself. All but a handful of the accommodations are large, with 4m (13-ft.) ceilings and oversize marble bathrooms with tub and shower. Even the handful that are smaller are comfortably appointed. Suites are especially opulent, each furnished with a luxurious but quirky collection ("The Habsburgs meet Jamaica") with crystal chandeliers, Persian rugs, and original works of art. All units have excellent beds, often sleigh beds. Both Continental and Jamaican food are served in the main dining room, with its lighted "water wall" sculpted from Jamaican cave stones. Frankly, the only drawback to this place is that it's not on the beach, but a free shuttle will take you to one of the best sandy beaches in the area, Frenchman's Cove Beach. There is also a poolside cafe with barbecue, live dance and calypso bands, and a boutique. Expect goodly percentages of clients here from *Mittel Europa* and fre-quent, sometimes ironic, references to Old Europe.

Williamsfield (8km/5 miles east of Port Antonio; P.O. Box 277). $\textcircled{C}$ 876/993-7720. Fax 876/993-7759. www.jamaica-palacehotel.com. 80 units. Winter $150–$170 double, $190–$350 suite; off season $130–$150 double, $190–$310 suite. AE, MC, V. **Amenities:** 2 restaurants; bar; pool; free beach shuttle; limited room service; babysitting; laundry service; nonsmoking rooms; rooms for those w/limited mobility. In room: A/C, TV, safe.

Rio Vista Resort Villas ⚜⚜ (Finds   Featured several years ago as part of a photo lay-out within *Condé Nast Traveler,* and popular with folk who want to be far from "the madding crowds" and bustle of an urban area, this place is ideal for a honeymoon, a luxurious vacation, or perhaps an off-the-record weekend with an illicit lover. Posi-tioned about 6km (3¾ miles) west of Port Antonio (most of the other competing luxe

---

> **Fun Fact Enter the Dragon**
>
> The all-inclusive resort chain of **Sandals** (© 800/SANDALS; www.sandals.com) has acquired the 22-hectare (55-acre) **Dragon Bay Beach Resort** and is turning it into another one of their properties, which already exist in profusion elsewhere on the island, especially in Montego Bay, Negril, and Ocho Rios. The property will open onto Dragon Bay Beach, a little cove to the east of the more famous Blue Lagoon, 11km (7 miles) east of Port Antonio. This was the backdrop for the Tom Cruise bomb, *Cocktail*. Remember when he performed gymnastics with a liquor bottle? That is, if you bothered to catch the flick at all. Stay tuned for future developments.

---

properties lie to the east), Rio Vista is only 3km (1¾ miles) from the little local airstrip, and nestled between the Rio Grande and the Caribbean Sea. On a 4-hectare (10-acre) estate planted with tropical fruits, it offers handsomely furnished one- and two-bedroom cottages, plus a honeymoon villa with a river view. The setting is a garden of flowers, spices, and sweet-smelling herbs. Rooms have vaulted wooden ceilings and well-maintained tiled bathrooms, each with a shower, and spectacular views that sweep out over the river and tropical rainforest. A housekeeper services each cottage and can assist with meals. Candlelit dinners can be arranged. Air-conditioning in summer costs $10 extra.

St. Margarets Bay (P.O. Box 4). © **876/993-5444.** Fax 876/993-5445. www.riovistajamaica.com. 5 villas. Year-round $120 1-bedroom villa, $140 2-bedroom villa. Children 12 and under stay free in parent's room. MC, V. **Amenities:** Restaurant; bar; pool; rafting; limited room service; massage; laundry service; nonsmoking rooms. *In room:* A/C, TV, dataport, kitchen, beverage maker.

INEXPENSIVE

Jamaica Heights Resort 𝄢 *Finds*   The funkiest, most amusing, and hippest guesthouse in town might be full of rock stars from Düsseldorf or up-and-coming filmmakers cranking out tomorrow's indie fave. The very worldly owner, Helmut Steiner, former professor of literature and philosophy in Berlin, and his wife, Charmaine, maintain this affordable but sophisticated retreat. It's set at the top of a rutted and very steep series of roads. The resort is not on a beach but provides transportation to two of the finest beach strips of sand at Port Antonio, Frenchman's Cove and San San.

Scattered amid the wedge-shaped 3-hectare (7½-acre) property are a half-dozen buildings, each white-walled with shutters, gazebos, climbing vines, and a pavilion for meditating over views of the forested terrain that cascades down to Port Antonio's harbor. The garden sports exotic palms, a stream with its own waterfalls, the most elegant Ping-Pong pavilion in the world, and dozens of botanical oddities from around the world. The minimalist accommodations are spotlessly clean. Each has a four-poster bed and funky lighting fixtures, plus tub/shower combination bathrooms. Doors can be opened or closed to create suites with between two and four bedrooms.

Spring Bank Rd., Port Antonio. © **876/993-3305.** Fax 876/993-3563. www.jamaicaheights.net. 8 units. Year-round $75–$105 double. No credit cards. **Amenities:** Restaurant; pool; watersports; laundry service; nonsmoking rooms. *In room:* Ceiling fan, beverage maker, no phone.

3 Where to Dine

Norma's at the Marina &&& JAMAICAN/CONTINENTAL   This is the newest branch of an upscale, Jamaica-wide restaurant chain made famous by a Jamaica-born, Florida-trained matriarch (Norma Shirley), who has been the subject of more publicity in the culinary press than any equivalent entrepreneur in Jamaica. Established in 2005, the restaurant sprawls between two oversized gazebos that mark either end of a brick-floored beachside terrace inside the fenced-in compound of the Port Antonio marina. Your meal might be served outdoors, on the above-mentioned terrace, or one floor above ground level, within a high-ceilinged, mahogany-trimmed dining room that's open to the breezes on two sides. Menu items are elegant and flavorful, representing the best of modern and creative Jamaican cuisine, and include crab back salad, elegant slices of smoked marlin, a "reggae salad" studded with sautéed shrimp, several different versions of grilled fish, teriyaki-flavored rib-eye steak, wood-smoked pork riblets with a tamarind-flavored honey sauce, pan-seared butterfish filets, and grilled lobster with lime-flavored herb butter.

At the Port Antonio Marina. (©) **876/993-9510.** Reservations recommended for dinner, not necessary for lunch. Main courses J$700–J$1,200 (US$11–US$19). MC, V. Tues–Sat 10am–10pm; Sun noon–8pm.

The Green Gold of Port Antonio

The Spanish didn't do Jamaica much good, but they did leave a botanical legacy: the banana. From the Canary Islands, their colony off the western coast of Africa, they introduced the banana to Jamaica in 1520. It had nearly the same impact that introducing the tomato had on Italy: Banana trees took to Jamaican soil at once, even better than in their native land.

At first the Caucasian residents of Jamaica refused to eat the banana, considering it fit only for animals or slaves. Nonetheless, the banana saved many an impoverished family from starvation.

In 1873 Captain Lorenzo Dow Baker of Massachusetts loaded some bananas on his ship to take back to New England. They were an instant success there, and the future of the banana was secured, as orders came in for more and more of this tasty fruit. The Boston Fruit Company rushed to Port Antonio and began establishing banana plantations and hiring the descendants of slaves as its low-paid workers.

In time, bananas became known as "green gold." They could be picked green and would ripen in the ships carrying them back to New England.

By 1905 Captain Baker had erected the Titchfield Hotel, Jamaica's first bona-fide hotel, and began hauling in tourists. Some of the wealthiest people in America, including J. P. Morgan, came to visit at this Jamaican playground—and it all began with the banana.

In the 1920s, however, a banana blight arrived from Central America, eventually destroying Port Antonio's banana crops. The local economy collapsed, and it has never really bounced back since, except for the tourism boom that hit—briefly—during the 1960s.

Trident Hotel Restaurant ♛ INTERNATIONAL/JAMAICAN   The elegant Trident Hotel Restaurant serves meals that evoke the Jamaica of the 1950s. The cuisine is always prepared with first-class ingredients, though the British-colonial setting, the sense of romance, and the white-glove service are generally more memorable than the food. The high-pitched wooden roof set on white stone walls holds several ceiling fans that gently stir the air. The antique tables are set with old china, English silver, and Port Royal pewter. The formally dressed waiters will help you choose your wine and whisper the name of each course as they serve it. The five-course dinner menu changes daily but may include a Jamaican salad, mahi mahi with mayonnaise-and-mustard sauce, steak with broccoli and sautéed potatoes, and for dessert, peach melba and Blue Mountain coffee with Tia Maria, a Jamaican liqueur.

In Trident Villas & Hotel, Rte. A4. ✆ **876/993-2602**. Reservations required. Jackets required for men. Fixed-price dinner $48. AE, MC, V. Daily 7:30–9:30pm. Head east on Allan Ave.

MODERATE

Panorama INTERNATIONAL/JAMAICAN   One of the most reliable dining spots in Port Antonio offers a sweeping view of the rugged coastline, with great sunsets. Specialties include jerk chicken, jerk pork, grilled lobster, and Creole fish. Depending on who's in the kitchen, the food here can be quite satisfactory, though once in a while, especially off season, the cuisine might be a bit of a letdown. The club also offers entertainment, with a calypso band during the week. Be warned in advance that the road leading up into the hills toward this place is sometimes cited as the worst-maintained access road in town.

In the Fern Hill Club Hotel, Mile Gully Rd. ✆ **876/993-7374**. Reservations recommended. Main courses $8–$10 lunch, $10–$25 dinner. AE, DISC, MC, V. Daily 7:30am–10pm. Head east on Allan Ave.

San San Tropez ♛ ITALIAN   In 1994 Milan-born Fabio Favalli bought a well-located villa that had originally been conceived as the staff quarters for an upscale resort (Frenchman's Cove) that was devastated and bankrupted in the late 1980s by a hurricane. Since then, the villa has earned a well-deserved reputation as a provenance for superb Italian food. This is served at lunch and dinner, conducted in either an indoor dining room (its decor emulates that of an ancient Roman villa) or at candlelit tables beside the swimming pool. Menu items include well-prepared homemade pastas, especially linguine "Blue Lagoon" (with shellfish), lasagna, or spaghetti served either with carbonara or bolognese sauce. Any of these could be followed by portions of very fresh fish, grilled and seasoned with Italian and Jamaican herbs, and a medley of refreshing desserts. Other good choices include the staples of Italian cuisine, chicken or veal parmigiana, and osso buco.

On-site are six suites, each with ceiling fans, cable TV, air-conditioning, and a separate living room and bedroom. Depending on the season, they cost from $94 to $136, double occupancy, with breakfast included.

On San San Bay. ✆ **876/993-7213**. Reservations recommended. Pizzas $10–$17; main courses $14–$20. AE, MC, V. Daily noon–4pm and 6–9:30pm.

INEXPENSIVE

Anna Bananas JAMAICAN   Architecturally, the building that contains this open-air seafront restaurant features little more than a wooden deck with a soaring roof. There aren't even any walls to prevent storms or rain from penetrating the inside, but in light of how relaxed the place is, most clients don't seem to care. Painted a bright shade of yellow and named after the childhood nickname of the owners' daughter

(who hated bananas), it was established in the late 1990s by a consortium of Texan and Jamaican entrepreneurs. By the mid-2000s, all vestiges of the original Texans had vanished, leaving the place a purely Jamaican venue. Menu items, as described on a chalkboard, include cheese sandwiches, tender savory oxtail, fried fish or chicken, BLT sandwiches with avocado, and platters of zesty jerk chicken and pork (on weekends). Drinks are wide-ranging and frothy.

7 Folly Rd. Ⓒ 876/715-6533. Reservations not accepted. Main courses J$300–J$1,000 (US$4.80–US$16). AE, DC, MC, V. Daily 7am–10:30pm.

Coronation Bakery ✸ (Finds) The best bread in town emerges, steaming, from the ovens at this bakery, a landmark that the late William Chung established in June of 1953. Owned today by his son Cyril, it's set in the heart of Port Antonio, in a 70-year-old all-wood house whose carved columns and graceful lattices support an old-fashioned zinc-roofed veranda on the second floor. Inside, for a picnic or to take back to your villa, you can buy fresh loaves of hard-crusted sourdough, perhaps with the intention of smearing it with the guava jelly that's available at any local supermarket. They also make fresh cocoa buns, a savory version of cornbread, a peppery version of Jamaican patties (dough envelopes filled with minced and heavily peppered meat), and old-fashioned "sugar buns" flavored with Jamaican allspice and nutmeg. Especially interesting are the bulla cakes, a fast-baked, unleavened bread that used to be a cheap staple for agrarian workers laboring away in the sugarcane fields. Many years ago, they were fast-baked at high temperatures (as a means of saving fuel) with very little sugar, whatever flour the homeowner had on-hand, and a small amount of bacon grease or lard. Even today they're known for their prolonged shelf life in hot, humid climes. They sell here for about a dime each; locals maintain they're best consumed with a thick slice of cheese, perhaps as part of a picnic at the beach.

18 West St. Ⓒ 876/993-2110. Reservations not accepted. Loaf of bread J$75–J$100 (US$1.20–US$1.60) each; pastries from J$6 (US10¢). No credit cards. Mon–Sat 8am–8pm.

Dickie's Best-Kept Secret ✸ (Finds) JAMAICAN It's the most unusual dining option in Port Antonio, and perhaps in Jamaica. Unconventional and entirely dependent on the whims and imagination of its owner, Dickie (Alvin) Butler, it occupies a small but charming, virtually unmarked, faux-Victorian cottage set at a bend in the coastal highway at Bryan's Bay, about 1.5km (1 mile) west of Port Antonio. Don't come here expecting anything ordinary: Meals must be ordered in advance since supplies are brought in only according to the guests who have pre-booked on any given evening. The premises, at least from the outside, looks like a tropical version of the kind of Victorian cottage that might have nurtured the Brontë sisters in 19th-century England, until you realize that the gables, the cornices, and the casement windows are purely decorative, cleverly fashioned out of wire, steel mesh, and sheet metal. You'll immediately descend into a pair of crazed-angled dining rooms loaded with a surrealistic combination of High Victorian English and Jamaican Rastafarian accessories. Dinner unfolds with bemused humor, something like a High Tea in the Cotswolds on psychedelics. Some of the most massive stone foundations in the neighborhood, all of them visible from the cozy and claustrophobic dining rooms, keep the building from crashing off the cliff into the sea. Local wits claim that the view from the toilets here is the most panoramic in and around Port Antonio, and after checking them out, we entirely agree. Depending on what you ordered, in advance, you and your party will enjoy that pivot around well-flavored main courses of chicken, fish, or lobster.

If you opt for a meal here (we refer to it as "a Jamaican experience that just happens to include dinner"), you won't be alone. Clients as diverse as Winnie Mandela, relatives of the Presidents Bush, some high-placed executives from Paramount Studios, and restaurant critics from *The Jamaica Observer* magazine will have been there before you. Dickie (i.e. Alvin) performed dinner service, it's widely rumored, for Queen Elizabeth II during her stay, early in the 1970s, at Frenchman's Cove Resort, when both Dickie and The Queen were a lot younger. Alas, if the idea of a meal within Dickie's orbit appeals to you, hurry, since the Jamaica Department of Highways and Dickie are feuding, presently, over Jamaica's stated intention of widening the coastal highway. If the government's wishes prevail, Dickie's and its stacks of newspaper clippings and guest books will be shoved into the sea, alas, all in the name of progress. Dickie's very handsome son, incidentally, who may or may not be helping with the dinner service at the time of your arrival, is Dennis Wickliffe Butler.

On the East Coast Hwy., in Bryan's Bay. ℂ 876/809-6276. Reservations required. Full dinners $20–$28 per person. No credit cards. Daily 5–11pm.

The Hub *(Finds* JAMAICAN   Set within a cement-sided, relatively nondescript building just east of the town center, and identified by one of the most obscure and difficult-to-spot signs in Port Antonio, this is an intensely local eatery that incorporates a workaday bar area (Red Stripe being the after-work drink of choice), a battered dining room, and a front veranda with rickety tables and chairs. Don't expect luxury—that ain't what you'll get here. The venue is way, way off the beaten tourist track, and therein, if you're adventurous with a sense of humor, lies its rough-edged charm. Lloyd Bentley, the long-time owner, maintains a sense of humor about his restaurant's lack of a view. (Originally built as a food distribution warehouse, it overlooks a parking lot and a side yard of the now-defunct local railroad. And when the wind blows in from a certain direction, there's just a whiff or two from a local barnyard too.) But in a town loaded with seafront panoramas, local electricians, carpenters, and construction workers identify this place as their "regular." Menu items are fresh-made and flavorful, featuring a tried-and-true blend of such dishes as pork chops, three different preparations of chicken (including a version in brown-stew sauce), curried goat, steamed fish, oxtail, and stewed peas with rice.

2 West Palm Ave. ℂ 876/715-6943. Reservations not accepted. Main courses J$150–J$600 (US$2.40–US$9.60). No credit cards. Mon–Sat 8:30am–midnight; Sun noon–8pm.

Woody's Low Bridge Place *☆ (Finds* JAMAICAN   No one leaves Woody's without generating memories (about cuisine, about Jamaica, and about life in general) that remain in place long after your check is paid. Port Antonio's most famous counter-culture dining shack occupies a party-colored clapboard-and-concrete roadside compound in Drapers, a nearby suburb, about a 10-minute drive from the center. You'll place your food order at an open window in the main building, and then consume it within a circular open-sided pavilion with a tee-pee-shaped roof. Local hotel owners insist that their vegetarian burgers (made from chopped callaloo, bok choy, and cabbage, first steamed, then fried) are the best in Jamaica; and scads of European clients have photographed every square inch of the place. But despite the torrents of approval for this rustic and down-home Jamaican eatery, Woody (Papa Woody) Cousins and his wife Cherry exude a folksy and friendly allure that is as timeless as the appeal of the food itself.

Our favorite spot is the cozy inside bar, where rum punch costs from J$70 to J$150 (US$1.10–US$2.40), Red Stripe costs J$80 (US$1.30), and Rastafarian-inspired artwork

and painted slogans include, "It's nice to be important, but it's more important to be nice. Therefore, just be nice."

What's a low bridge, and why was this place named after one? It results from the low-hung doorways that require taller visitors to stoop a bit before entering. Miss Cherry cooks and serves the savory food, dispensing wisdom and cheer; Woody mixes drinks, serves food, and if you're lucky, will sing. Don't imagine that the full menu will automatically be available after around 4pm: Although it will probably be open as a bar, dinners need to be pre-ordered in advance. Menu items include burgers; "run down fish" (catch of the day prepared with coconut); "Jamaica Jamaica" chicken that's either curried, jerked, barbecued, and/or brown-stewed; and steak with fried green peppers. Main courses, as part of the price, are preceded with a meatless creamy soup "built" from eight local vegetables, and accompanied with rolls, rice, "festivals" (deep-fried dough), yams, and sweet potatoes. Coconut cake with ice cream is a yummy dessert. The non-alcoholic ginger beer here, by the way, is entirely homemade.

Drapers. © 876/993-7888. Reservations not necessary for breakfast and lunch, reservations required for dinner. Lunch platters J$170–J$300 (US$2.70–US$4.80); dinner platters J$650–J$800 (US$10–US$13). No credit cards. Daily 10am–10pm.

A NEARBY PLACE TO DINE

Mille Fleurs ✸✸ CARIBBEAN   This restaurant is terraced into a verdant hillside about 180m (600 ft.) above sea level with sweeping views over the Jamaican coastline and the faraway harbor of Port Antonio. Sheltered from the frequent rains, but open on the side for maximum access to cooling breezes, it features candlelit dinners, well-prepared food, and lots of New Age charm. Overseeing it all are two of the most cosmopolitan and sophisticated hoteliers in Port Antonio, Jamaican-born Barbara Walker, a talented painter and sculptor with years of culinary training in France and Switzerland, and Shireen Aga, an India-born hotelier with extensive experience in the hospitality industry in Germany. Lunches include sandwiches, salads, grilled-fish platters, and soups. At night, you might feast on fresh lobster or locally raised duck served with passionfruit sauce. Smoked marlin is a savory beginning, and on special occasions, you're likely to see roasted goose with sorrel sauce on the menu. The restaurant has been praised by *Gourmet* magazine for its dishes. You may want to try a superb version of orange and carrot soup, chicken with coriander and lime sauce, and jerk-spiced meatballs topped with grilled bananas and rum sauce, and the fish with spicy mango-shrimp sauce is a specialty. Breads and most jams are made on the premises. At least two dishes on the menu every day and every night are vegetarian, and dietary restrictions of all kinds are catered to and acknowledged.

In the Hotel Mocking Bird Hill, North Coast Hwy. © 876/993-7267. Reservations recommended. Lunch platters $9–$30; dinner main courses $21–$40. AE, MC, V. Daily 8:30–10:30am, noon–2pm, and 7–9:30pm.

4 Beaches & Outdoor Pursuits

BEACHES

Although local waters can be turbulent at times, and it rains a lot, the white-sand beaches in and around Port Antonio put it on the tourist map. Invariably, they are far less crowded than those of Montego Bay and Ocho Rios. The best of these white sandy strips follow.

JAMAICAN REEF BEACH   Set on the northern periphery of town, this short, sanitized, and usually very clean strip of sand lies on the northern coast of the Titchfield

Peninsula. Its premises were incorporated into the fenced-in premises of the Port Antonio Marina early in the millennium. As such, it's now the beach most often visited by cruise ship passengers who find themselves in Port Antonio for a day and who aren't interested in negotiating taxi or minibus passage to beaches that are farther afield. No longer a bonafide public beach, and considerably cleaner than it was in years past, its edges are now flanked with such upscale establishments as the dining terrace of Norma's at the Marina. As such, its sands have become for the most part decorative—the kind of watery stretch that's best admired from a dining table or a barstool. Of course, if you happen to be dining at Norma's, and if, between the salad course and the main course, you want to throw yourself into the water for a fast bout of exercise and/or exhibitionism, no one will object—including the other diners, if you just agree not to splash them.

FRENCHMAN'S COVE ☜   Back in the 1960s you might have seen Richard Burton and Elizabeth Taylor recovering from the night-before's hangover, sprawled on the sands of the beach in this cove, 8km (5 miles) east of the center of Port Antonio. During those heady days, celebrities who included the Queen of England flocked to the chic Frenchman's Cove Resort, still occupying its scenic spot on a windswept headland. Actually, this is a rather small and narrow beach whose beauty derives from a sandy bottom, and from clean fresh waters that flow into the sea from a freshwater stream flanked with lush gardens. (Nutrients flowing into the sea from that stream contribute to the rich underwater life in the waters offshore.) It costs J$200 (US$3.20) to enter daily from 9am to 5pm. There are showers on the beach to wash away the sand, and at least one beachfront barbecue restaurant serving Red Stripe, rum drinks, jerk chicken, and grilled fish.

SAN SAN BEACH   Not as tidily kept as Frenchman's Cove (maintenance along its length has actually deteriorated in the past decade or so), San San is a private beach that's both longer and narrower than its more fashionable neighbor. Its sands are sometimes frequented by wealthy owners of palatial second homes built along a small nearby peninsula known as Alligator Head.

Guests who check into such hotels as The Jamaica Palace, Goblin Hill, and Fern Hill (see "Where to Stay," earlier in this chapter) can use this beach for free, and it's open to anyone else willing to shell out $8 between 10am and 4pm. The little island you see offshore goes by various names that include Woods Island, Pellow Island, and—because of having once been bought by the Aga Khan for his wife, Princess Nina—"Princess Island." Many visitors swim to the islet from San San Beach; if you try it, beware of the potentially painful colonies of spiny sea urchins as you step ashore. The island also has a good reef for snorkeling.

WINNIFRED BEACH   This is not the name of your spinster aunt, but a strip of sand described by a local hotel executive as "the best example in the country of a Jamaican public beach." Clean and well maintained, and dotted with vendors selling jerk food, it lies just to the east of Dragon Bay Beach, en route to Boston Bay Beach (see below), within about a 25-minute drive from the center of Port Antonio. The half-moon-shaped strip of sand attracts more islanders than foreign visitors, and as such, provides a sometimes-charming spectacle of contemporary Jamaican life. Yes, there's a colony of vendors selling souvenirs and crafts items, but they're generally acknowledged for being less aggressive and a lot more laid-back than the occasionally obnoxious vendors you're likely to encounter in, say, Ocho Rios. Offshore is a dramatic

(Fun Fact) The Blue Lagoon

Remember 14-year-old Brooke Shields, way back before she became a star on TV and Broadway? She made the film *The Blue Lagoon* playing a teen cast-away who swam naked with now-forgotten Christopher Atkins. Although the film was actually shot on an isolated atoll in the South Pacific, it has, correctly or incorrectly, been associated ever since with this idyllic spot in Jamaica. Films whose footage partially derive from the surrounding landscape include selected scenes from *Cocktail* (featuring early Tom Cruise) and *Club Paradise*.

Lying about 2km (1¼ miles) east of San San Beach, the Blue Lagoon ℛℛℛ is not on a beach. But when you see these beautiful waters, you'll forget all about sands and take the plunge. The lagoon isn't always cerulean blue: Throughout the day, reflections can turn it jade or sapphire. Once we noticed a rainy sky turning it a shade of mauve. The water is 56m (185 ft.) deep at its deepest point, although the Arawak Indians believed it was bottomless. It was once the lair of the pirate Tom Mallard, when it was called Mallard's Hole—before the name was changed to something more romantic, that is.

Tales spin about the Blue Lagoon. One concerns Errol Flynn, who is said to have dived to the bottom of the lagoon aided only by snorkeling gear. Some say he did it once; others maintain he performed this feat every day. That's dubious, but it *is* true that Robin Moore, author of *The French Connection,* once owned most of the land opening onto the lagoon.

Islanders also maintain that if you swim in the lagoon with your mouth open, drinking in the water, it will "turn a man into a bull." Hundreds of people make this claim about the aphrodisiac powers of these waters. "In America," a caretaker told us, "men take Viagra. Here all we need is one cup from the Blue Lagoon, and we're fit as a fiddle all night."

On-site is a small restaurant with changing rooms, along with a little mineral spring bath. Many visitors flock here for a Saturday night bash, when live reggae is played.

During the day someone at one of the little makeshift kiosks is on-hand to rent you a paddleboat or snorkeling equipment. The Blue Lagoon teems with marine life, including schools of rainbow-hued fish, and even on occasion a squid gliding by and, less welcome, a barracuda giving you the fish eye.

This beauty spot, one of the finest on the island, is open daily from 9am to 10pm, charging an admission of $4. Call ℂ **876/993-7791** for more information.

reef of living coral teeming with marine life, attracting snorkelers to this beach, which has toilet facilities (none of which are particularly clean or well maintained) and changing rooms. During the day a boatman or two will, if you negotiate the price in advance, take you out on a bamboo raft or one of their small craft to a secluded little beach just around the headland; escape with a loved one if you find Winnifred too crowded. No admission fee is charged for access to this famed and much-respected public beach. Technically, the address of this beach is "Fairy Hill," but even if the

The Jerk Center of the Universe

Boston Bay Beach is the most famous jerk center in Jamaica, with at least a half-dozen smoky barbecue pits lining the potholed road that accesses the beach. Locals suggest that the jerk is as good as it gets here, in Portland Parish, where the culinary form originally developed. According to local traditions, Maroons (escaped slaves) living in the nearby hills of what is now known as Portland Parish were skilled at killing wild boar. Trading fresh-killed pork for spices from British or Jamaican merchants, they elevated the art of seasoning and slow-cooking pork, and later, chicken, fish, or whatever, over green pimiento wood into the art form as it's known today. According to Jamaican aficionados, Portland Parish is still the home of the best jerk food in the world. Sometimes residents of Kingston drive all the way up here just to stock up on these tasty, carefully seasoned bits of slow-cooked meat.

The jerk sauce is made from little rounds of crenellated red and yellow peppers grown in the countryside. After sampling one of these sauces, you'll surely agree that your favorite Texas red-hot sauce tastes like a cool glass of V8; the hot sauce is so hot that many visitors claim it's hallucinogenic. You can also purchase cans of the sauce from various vendors.

More adventurous jerk fans go for the pig or goat heads, cow feet, or chitterlings. All parts of the animal are cooked here—and, really, after enough of that hot sauce, you won't know what you're eating anyway.

All the stands are good, but if hard-pressed to name our favorite jerk stand here, we'd give our vote to Mickey's, which occupies a painted concrete shell on the left, the first of the jerk stands you'll see as you navigate your way along the bumpy and potholed road leading towards the beach. You'll recognize the place by the rows of wooden skewers cooking pork and chicken over huge barbecue pits. Fish is also smoked here. You can also order "sides" of roast baked yams or roasted breadfruit.

The downing of this peppery food will give you a reason "to put out the fire," as the locals say, and that means downing one Red Stripe beer after another.

locals don't recognize that nomenclature; virtually everyone in and around Port Antonio will know how to direct you there.

BOSTON BAY BEACH   Another public beach, Boston Bay is more famous for its jerk-pork stands (see the nearby box, "The Jerk Center of the Universe") than it is for its sands. Lying 18km (11 miles) east of Port Antonio, and .8km (½ mile) to the east of Winnifred Beach, it is a strand of golden sands opening onto turquoise waters that aren't always tranquil. Hidden away on a secluded cove, this beach was once owned by the writer Robin Moore. You'll find lots of picnic tables where you can enjoy your recently purchased lunch of jerk pork, chicken, or whatever. Ironically, despite the fact that proponents of windsurfing sometimes cite Boston Bay Beach as potentially the best beach in Jamaica for the pursuit of this sport, it never really caught on here, and is practiced far less frequently than you'd have expected, given the favorable conditions.

DEEP-SEA FISHING

Northern Jamaican waters are world-renowned for their game fish, including dolphin fish (mahimahi), wahoo, blue and white marlin, sailfish, tarpon, barracuda, and bonito. The Port Antonio International Marlin Tournament is held at Port Antonio every September or October, depending on the phases of the moon (and presumably, the migration patterns of the marlin) for that particular year. Most major hotels from Port Antonio to Montego Bay have deep-sea-fishing facilities, and there are many charter boats. For more information on this loosely organized annual event, contact the Sir Henry Morgan Angling Association, c/o Dr. Ronald Duquesnay (© 876/909-8819; or e-mail him at RonDQ@mail.infochan.com). Additional information about this fishing tournament can be downloaded from www.TheMarinaatPortAntonio.com.

Nadine, a 12m-long (40-ft.) **sportfishing boat** (© 876/993-3209 or 876/909-9552) with a tournament rig is available for charter rental. Designed for up to six passengers at a time, it charges $925 per half-day or $1,650 per full day, with crew, bait, tackle, and soft drinks included. It docks at Port Antonio's Marina, off West Palm Avenue, in the center of town. Call Captain Paul, or a member of his crew (see phone numbers above) for bookings.

GOLF

Port Antonio may never rival Montego Bay as a golfing mecca, but the 9-hole **San San Golf Course & Bird Sanctuary** (© 876/993-7645) lies 6km (3¾ miles) east of San San Beach. A course existed here in Port Antonio's heyday in the 1960s. In 1998 the course was reopened. Its setting offers dramatic scenery, with a backdrop of lush vegetation on one side and the ocean on the other. A round of 9 holes costs $50. You can also play the course twice for $70. Caddies cost $12, with pull carts going for $5. Clubs are rented at the pro shop for $10. Birders often flock to the area to see the many species here.

HIKING

The Rio Grande Valley (see "Exploring the Area," below) is one of the lushest places in the Caribbean to go on hiking jaunts. Hiking trails often follow paths blazed decades ago by hunters seeking wild pigs.

If you're not a serious hiker and want only an easy preview of this luxuriant valley, you can take the 30-minute hike to the **Scatter Waterfalls** from Berridale, 10km (6¼ miles) southwest of Port Antonio. Here bamboo rafts will transport you across the Rio Grande, where you can walk to the falls in about 20 minutes. There you'll find pools for cooling off and a little bar serving fresh tropical punches.

Most other hikes are far more strenuous. One of the most difficult is the 19km (12-mile), 2-day hike to **Nanny Town,** named after Queen Nanny, the Amazon-like warrior goddess of the Maroons. One of the most remote places in all of Jamaica, this was the legendary hideout of the Maroons in the 1700s, who came here to escape from the British and went undiscovered for years. A campsite can be found along the Makunnu River. This hike is only for the seriously in-shape and valiantly stout of heart who are intrigued by, rather than daunted by, some of the roughest terrain within the Blue Mountains.

Less difficult is the 5-hour hike to **Watch Hill,** a former lookout point for the Maroons. You'll pass miles of banana groves and the decaying ruins of an 18th-century sugar plantation. This hike is graded moderate.

Our favorite trail is the 6km (3.75-mile), 7-hour **White River Falls** ✦ hike starting at Millbank, a hamlet south of the Maroon stronghold of Moore Town (see "Exploring the Area," below). Know before you embark on this hike that the drive from Port Antonio to the debut of the hiking trail, because of horribly maintained roads, will require up to 2 bone-bruising hours of transit time, each way. This hike takes you along the White River, and you can also go upstream to the Seven Falls. After a swim in the first one or two falls, you may decide not to press on, as the going gets rough and the trail is slippery. If you're lucky, you'll see colonies of the rare swallowtail butterfly. These beautiful insects are enormous, and make for one of the most memorable sights nature has to offer in Jamaica.

Shorter and easier hikes in the Lower River Valley can also be arranged, including a 4-hour hike, rated medium grade, along the **Darley Trail.**

One final trail, also difficult, is the 7-hour, 11km (6.75-mile) **Guava River Trail,** starting in the hamlet of Bellevue. The trail goes along the Guava River in the heart of the Blue Mountains. You can swim in the river and continue upstream until you come to some hot springs.

The best and most professional outfitter for arranging tours is listed in the "Eco-Cultural Tours" box, on p. 212.

SNORKELING & SCUBA DIVING

At a depth range of 24 to 27m (80–90 ft.), **Alligator Long** is one of the most visited dive sites east of Port Antonio. Advanced divers come here. Divers go along a narrow coral ridge 9m (30 ft.) high and peppered with sea fans, sponges such as the azure vase sponge, soft gorgonians, and many coral heads. Marine life includes the pork fish and several species of hamlets (the indigo hamlet, for example). You'll see squirrelfish darting about, along with stingrays, triggerfish, and spadefish.

The best outfitter, **Lady Godiva's Dive Shop,** lies within the Port Antonio Marina (© **876/428-3437** or 876/335-2663), 11km (6¾ miles) from Port Antonio. Full dive equipment is available. Technically, you can snorkel off most of the beaches in Port Antonio, but you're likely to see much more further offshore. The best spot is at Winnifred Beach on the other side of Dragon Bay. The reef is extremely active and full of a lot of exciting marine life. Lady Godiva offers two excursions daily to this spot for $25 per person including snorkeling equipment for the day.

RAFTING

Although it's not exactly adventurous (it's a tame and safe outing), rafting the Rio Grande is the best rafting experience on the island, and the most fun. Rafting started on the river as a means of transporting bananas from plantations to waiting freighters. In 1871 a Yankee skipper named Lorenzo Dow Baker decided that a seat on one of the rafts was better than walking, but it was not until actor Errol Flynn arrived that the rafts became popular as a tourist attraction. Flynn used to hire the rafts for his friends, and he encouraged the rafters to race down the Rio Grande against one another, betting on winners. Now that bananas are transported by road, the raft skipper makes perhaps one or two trips a day down the waterway. If you want to take a trip, contact **The Rio Grande Experience,** Berrydale (© **876/993-5778**).

The rafts, some 10m (33 ft.) long and only 2m (6 ft.) wide, are propelled by stout bamboo poles. There's a raised double seat about two-thirds of the way back. The skipper stands in the front, trousers rolled up to his knees, the water washing his feet, and guides the craft down the lively river, about 13km (8 miles) between steep hills covered with coconut palms, banana plantations, and flowers, through limestone cliffs pitted

---

Fun Fact **How *Not* to Raft a River**

Local legend tells of the day the noted author Truman Capote visited to try rafting the Rio Grande. He'd had a brief, abortive affair in New York with Errol Flynn, who had invited him down to Port Antonio. Like Flynn, Capote was a heavy drinker.

As though playing a part in some madcap comedy, Capote's unfortunate raft tipped over right in the middle of the river, and it was all local guides could do to rescue the drunken author. They still chuckle about it today.

---

with caves, through the "Tunnel of Love," a narrow cleft in the rocks, and then on to wider, gentler water.

Trips last 2 to 2½ hours and are offered from 9am to 4pm daily at a cost of $55 per raft, which holds two passengers. A fully insured driver will take you in your rented car to the starting point at Berrydale, where you board your raft. If you feel like it, take a picnic lunch, but bring enough for the skipper, too, who will regale you with lively stories of life on the river.

5 Exploring the Area

You need spend no more than an hour touring the center of raffish Port Antonio—there's not that much to see. Another hour can be spent visiting the markets (see "Shopping," later in this chapter). After that, it's either back to your resort to lie on the beach or, if you're adventurous, you can drive along the coast or dip into the hinterlands south of Port Antonio.

The newest major improvement to the infrastructure of Port Antonio, the **Port Antonio Marina** (© **876/993-3209**), opened in stages beginning in 2003. It takes the form of a fenced-in compound dotted with shops, gazebos, and waterfront diversions specifically built with cruise ship passengers in mind. At press time, there was dock and wharf space for small and medium-sized cruise ships, berths for up to 32 private yachts, a restaurant (Norma's at the Marina; see "Where to Dine," earlier in this chapter), a scattering of lawns and ornamental gazebos, an outdoor swimming pool reserved for use by yacht owners and cruise ship passengers, and a very limited handful of boutiques. Completed in 2005 at an overall cost of $50 million, and with ambitions of filling up some of its empty storefronts during the lifetime of this edition, its aim was to increase the visibility of Port Antonio as a colorful option for cruise ship stopovers.

A STROLL THROUGH PORT ANTONIO

The **Central Square** of Port Antonio is dominated by an old clock tower (though no one remembers when it was last in working order). It stands in front of the two-story **Port Antonio Courthouse,** constructed in the 1890s in the Georgian style. The cast-iron balcony adorning it was a gift from a foundry in Glasgow, Scotland. This is also the site of the post office, the busiest place in town besides the market.

You, too, can join the shoppers here by going across the street and into the **Village of St. George Shopping Mall,** perhaps the strangest, most bastardized bit of architecture in all of Jamaica. Local wits cite it as the only place in the Caribbean where you can see a mishmash of 5 centuries of European architecture crammed into one surreal and jumbled 5-minute overview.

From the square, walk north along Harbour Street, which will become Fort George Street as it takes you to the tiny **Titchfield Peninsula,** a spit of land that separates the town's East Harbour from West Harbour. At the end of the peninsula, you'll come to Titchfield High School, erected on the grounds of **Fort George** by the British. The old cannons and some decaying walls of the former fort can still be seen. To defend West Harbour, the British erected the fort here in 1729, with walls 3m (10 ft.) thick. A total of 22 cannons were turned toward the sea against a possible invasion.

Along Fort George Street once stood the **Titchfield Hotel,** the first bonafide hotel in Jamaica, bought during its declining years, and managed badly, by Errol Flynn. After a disastrous fire, it was demolished, but in its heyday during the early 20th century, with around 400 rooms, it was the most fashionable hotel in the West Indies, drawing the likes of Rudyard Kipling and William Randolph Hearst.

Continue down Fort George Street until it empties into Harbour Street. Walk southeast on this street until you come to **Christ Church** (© **876/993-2600**), a red-brick Anglican church that is vaguely Romanesque in architecture. The church dates from 1840 and was designed by Annesley Voysey, who adorned it with a large stained-glass window and wooden pews. At the turn-of-the-20th century, the Boston Fruit Company—growing rich on the bananas being shipped out of Port Antonio—donated the church's eagle lectern.

Leaving the church, you can walk back up Harbour Street, cutting west at the intersection with West Street. As you walk down this street, on your right you will see the Port Antonio Market (it's also known as the **Musgrave Farmer's Market**), the most famous market for foodstuffs in northeast Jamaica. Most of what you'll see from the front side involves fruits and vegetables, but buried deep along its back side you'll also find a battered handful of outlets selling locally made crafts.

If you continue past this market, West Street becomes West Palm Avenue. **Boundbrook Wharf** is immediately to the west. Back when bananas were more important to the local economy than they are now, Boundbrook Wharf was the busiest loading dock in the West Indies. It inspired a cheerful song about the backbreaking labor required to keep the industry afloat (see the nearby box, "Loading Dem Bananas on

Eco-Cultural Tours

Some of the most devoted naturalists in Port Antonio are associated with the Hotel Mocking Bird Hill, which has carved a niche for itself among like-minded clients since the day it was established. The entity here that has laboriously researched every possible eco-sensitive excursion in eastern Jamaica is **Jamaica Explorations,** in the Hotel Mocking Bird Hill, North Coast Highway, Port Antonio (© **876/993-7267**). They're experts in everything to do with bird watching, butterfly chasing, Maroon history and culture, waterfall climbing, river-rafting, beach appreciation, spa treatments, art lessons, papermaking classes, homestays, Jamaican culture, and all kinds of air, land, and watersports. Even if you're not a client of Mocking Bird Hill, don't overlook these ladies and their encyclopedic knowledge of their district: Their expertise and devotion to the subject is encyclopedic.

Dat Barge"). Today, however, loading machines have replaced the sweaty, hard-working laborers of yesteryear.

From the marina or the wharf, you can walk east, retracing your steps back to Central Square where your walk began. Taxis are found here waiting to take you where you want to go next.

If a guided tour of Port Antonio appeals to you, consider the offerings of **Joanna's Port Antonio Tours** (**②** **876/831-8424** or 876/859-3758). They're conducted by the well-intentioned and endlessly well-informed Joanna Hart, whose "interpretive" tours of the city are loaded with the kind of jewel-like, sometimes gossipy anecdotes that bring the town and its checkered history to life. During most of the week, Joanna is associated in some way with the administration of Goblin Hill Villas (separately recommended in "Where to Stay," earlier in this chapter). Tours usually last about 2 hours and cost from around $35 per person.

EAST OF PORT ANTONIO ★★

The coast east of Port Antonio wins our beauty contest for one of the most beautiful shorelines in the Caribbean, and most definitely in Jamaica. There's a nostalgic aura to it, too, as if it yearns to return to the glamorous 1950s and 1960s when celebrities haunted its coves and villas much more often than they do today.

If some of the coast looks like a movie set, know that more films have been shot here than anywhere else in the Caribbean—none of them really very good, however.

The northeastern coastline of Jamaica is sometimes called "Errol Flynn country" because the actor created a plantation along its shore. The A4 highway goes by the **Errol Flynn Estates** at Fair Prospect and Priestman's River. Flynn's aging, elegant widow, the film star of the 1950s, Patrice Wymore Flynn, still lives here on these 809 hectares (2,000 acres) of pastureland and coconut groves.

The first stopover is at:

THE FOLLY GREAT HOUSE   Come here only if you don't have a lot to do that day, and expect to see a roofless structure with weeds growing up through the foundations. Perhaps it'll inspire you to write a Gothic novel. This house was built in 1905 by Arthur Mitchell, an American millionaire, for his wife Annie—the daughter of Charles Tiffany (founder of the famous New York jewelry store). In one of the most outrageous frauds in the history of the Jamaican construction industry, seawater was used in the concrete mixtures of its foundations and in the mortar, and the house began to collapse only 11 years after the couple moved in. Because of the beautiful location, it's easy to see what a fine great house it must have been.

The desecrated ruins lie on Folly Peninsula in the East Harbour, right on the outskirts of Port Antonio. For decades, broken bottles and graffiti marred the elegant dimensions of the Gilded Age mansion that rose from this site. But during the lifetime of this edition, plans will be activated for the designation of these ruins as a protected, patrolled, and cleaned-up national historic site, with the hint that some degree of rebuilding would transform the ruins into a more recognizable shadow of its former grandeur. Nothing has been fully defined or predetermined, but if you plan a detour to view this ruined folly, contact the Port Antonio branch of the Jamaican Tourist Board (**②** **876/993-3051** or 876/993-2665) in advance of your visit for visiting hours, venues, prices, and details.

If you drive out to the end of Folly Peninsula, you'll see the **Folly Point Lighthouse,** which makes a good spot for a picnic overlooking Woods Island or Monkey Island (among its other names), where Mitchell briefly maintained a colony of monkeys.

TURTLE CRAWLE BAY   At a bend in the sea-fronting road, 3km (1¾ miles) east of Port Antonio, you'll blink and then blink again. Your eyes aren't deceiving you. On a headland jutting out into the sea stands the lavishly ornate **Trident Castle** ✦, all gleaming white and looking like something Walt Disney might have created as part of a tropical version of an Alpine dream. Locals sometimes call it "Folly II" (after The Folly Great House; see above), because the *faux* castle lay unfinished for many years for lack of money.

Originally this Austrian baroque fantasy with its rococo stonework was the creation, during the 1970s and 1980s, of Baroness Fahmi, at the time Port Antonio's most flamboyant resident. She sold it to the architect, Earl Levy, scion of one of the most prominent Jamaican families. Their long-standing feud has often provided fodder for the press; Levy, who had his own architectural ideas, is now in charge and allowed scenes from *Clara's Heart* to be shot at the castle. That wasn't its only starring role. Remember *The Mighty Quinn,* starring Denzel Washington? Mimi Rogers, a "hotel guest" in the film, seduced Denzel here.

Regrettably, the castle is not open to the public—unless you want to rent it, that is. It is indeed possible to book the entire castle as part of a family (or group) vacation package. The manager of the adjacent Trident Hotel will have full details.

The baroness struck back by erecting the faux-Greek Revival Jamaica Palace in 1989, on the eastern shore of Turtle Crawle Bay. Her palace, standing almost in defiance of Trident Castle, was used as a backdrop for *Playmates in Paradise,* bringing in those lecherous boys from *Playboy* magazine in pursuit of "bunnies." Her hotel is now a rival of Levy's Trident Hotel. Both of these hotels, incidentally, are recommended in "Where to Stay," earlier in this chapter.

LONG BAY   From Boston Bay Beach, the A4 highway continues its southeasterly descent along the coast until it reaches Long Bay and its mile-long "half moon" of pale sandy beach. The expression "the deep blue sea" could be used to describe the waters offshore. The distance is 8km (5 miles) from Boston Bay, about a 40-minute drive eastward from Port Antonio. Regrettably, there are dangerous, sometimes life-threatening undertows along the length of this beach, coupled with strong, sometimes overpowering surf. But although its waters are dangerous, it's ideal for a picnic, thanks to the presence of strategically positioned stands selling jerk pork, jerk chicken, and bottled beer. Many locals still make their living from the sea, and their fishing boats, evocative of canoes, can be seen along the shore. You can usually persuade one of these fishermen, for a fee to be negotiated, to haul you out into the bay for an impromptu tour.

In recent years, Long Bay has become something of a destination for frugal travelers, especially backpackers. In winter we've sometimes encountered young backpackers experiencing Jamaica on the cheap. Surprisingly, despite constant winds, windsurfing hasn't really caught on along the length of this or along the length of any of the other beaches within the neighborhood. Chalk it up, perhaps, to developments to come in future years.

⎛Fun Fact   **Loading Dem Bananas on Dat Barge**

"Work all night for a drink of rum, daylight come and me wanna go home." Everyone knows that simple song, "Day O." Boundbrook Wharf (see above) inspired it; the time-tested tune about backbreaking labor aboard a banana boat is still played and sung throughout the Caribbean—and elsewhere.

Caribbean Sea

Turtle
Crawle
Bay

Port Antonio   ○ Drapers   Zion Hill
                                 Beach
                Fairy Hill ○   Boston
                                 Beach
■ Athenny Gardens and Boston Bay ○
  Cave of Nonsuch
○ Fellowship   Castle   ○ Priestman's River
■ Rio Grande   Mountain ▲
  Valley   Long Bay
PORTLAND   Beach
               Windsor Forest ○
                              ○ Long Bay

○ Moore Town

  ○ Comfort
    Castle
                                        ○ Manchioneal
SURREY   ■ Reach
                           Falls   Innis Bay
Dinner Time   Beach
        ▲   ▲ Macca Sucker
ST. THOMAS   ○ Hectors River

MANCHIONEAL   Eleven kilometers (6¾ miles) from the coast along the A4 from Long Bay, you come to the sea town of Manchioneal, the most venomously named of any town in Jamaica. The fishing village is named for the poisonous manchineel tree (a different spelling from the town). Most of those dangerous trees have been cut down, but the name remains. This tree is still found throughout the Caribbean, often near beaches. Any innocent who has sought shelter under it in a rainstorm can testify to its poisonous acid—that is, if they are still around.

The small fishing village drowses in the hot sun against the backdrop of a scallop-shaped bay of sapphire blue waters. The sandy beach here is wide, and many lobster fishermen sail out in their boats from the village. For lunch you can patronize one of the little jerk shacks along the shore. One of the savory delicacies sold here is roast conch, which is spicily seasoned and delectable (as long as you don't mind its slightly rubbery consistency).

Manchioneal has a reputation for being the least friendly town along the northern coast. Under no circumstances should you take someone's picture without asking their permission, which is rarely granted. Locals are very suspicious of foreigners. "Why?" we asked one of the vendors along the shore. "We figure you're up to no good or you wouldn't be here," he enigmatically replied.

(Fun Fact) Bush Medicine

Have a headache? Forget aspirin as you travel through the Rio Grande Valley; bush medicine is still commonly practiced here. You can take a "headache-no-more" powder, made from the cowfoot leaf, and chances are your headache will go away—though we're not doctors and can't give medical advice, some of this medicine actually does seem to work. One elderly woman told our party that the cowfoot leaf powder "not only cure the headache, but take care of your piles [hemorrhoids] too." The jury's still out on that one.

The best retreat from Manchioneal is to head inland for 3km (1¾ miles) until you come to **Reach Falls** ୧୧, one of the most beautiful spots in all of Jamaica. For years the Jamaica Tourist Board featured Reach Falls in its brochures advertising their island. But few people ever came here because it is so remote.

All that changed after the release of the film *Cocktail.* Tom Cruise and his film girl-friend indulged in some aquatic hanky-panky beneath these waterfalls, and soon the falls were on every local's and visitor's itinerary, attracting tour buses from as far away as Ocho Rios.

There's usually someone on-site trying to extract money from you, often $4, though it could be less. You're allowed to go into the falls, fed by Driver's River, to cool off. No one objects if you drop your swimsuit here and flaunt your wares, either. The cascades tumble over tiers of limestone into a pool that has the color of a jade ring. Ironically, and much to the confusion of many island visitors, access to the falls is "officially" closed, but locals as well as visitors usually manage to access the site anyway.

If you want to take a hike for .8km (½ mile) up the river, with its lush foliage, you'll come to **Mandingo Cave.** The cave has a whirlpool and can be explored, but be warned: It has quite deep pools, and isn't completely safe.

RIO GRANDE VALLEY   One of the lushest and most dramatic valleys in the Caribbean lies directly south of Port Antonio. The river itself is fed from drainage from the John Crow Mountains, creating luxuriant growth along with waterfalls, a tropical rainforest, and roaring rivers. Among its beauty spots are Nonsuch Caves and the Athenry Gardens.

Most visitors flock here to go rafting on the Rio Grande (see "Beaches & Outdoor Pursuits," earlier in this chapter). For the serious adventurer, this country invites deeper exploration, especially those willing to hike through it and put up with some hardships along the way.

For some recommended hikes, see "Hiking," also under "Beaches & Outdoor Pursuits," earlier in this chapter.

The Rio Grande Valley is also the home of the Windward Maroons, a formerly hostile, warlike people who fought the British and refused to become docile slaves. They believed in freedom or death. The descendants of these once-fierce people still live in the area, practicing bush medicine and following ancient rites little changed from the days when their ancestors lived in Africa.

It is recommended that you always explore this valley in the company of an experienced guide. If you'd like to discuss a number of tour options, you can consult a specialist. See the box, "Eco-Cultural Tours," on p. 212.

The Windward Maroons

Known often as the Blue Mountain Maroons, the Windward Maroons fled into the hills to escape slavery and British soldiers who were hunting them down during the late 17th and early 18th centuries. In the remote high-altitude hinterlands of Jamaica, they survived for years before the British found and destroyed their settlements.

The descendants of those Maroons live in the Rio Grande Valley today, although their young men and women have a tendency to drift off to seek a better life in Kingston once they grow up.

It wasn't until 1739 that Quao, the Blue Mountain Maroon leader, bowed to Cudjoe, the Maroon leader in the west of Jamaica, and signed a peace treaty with the British, granting the Maroons some form of autonomy and independence, which they still enjoy today.

The most legendary of the Maroons was Queen Nanny, although not much is known about her. She was said to possess magical powers. According to tall tales, she kept a cauldron bubbling day and night without benefit of fire, to boil alive any British soldier who tracked her down.

At the Maroon center of Moore Town (see below), the locals are still staunchly independent and still suspicious of foreigners.

MOORE TOWN Eighteen kilometers (11 miles) south of Port Antonio, a long-forgotten world unfolds. This is the largest surviving village of the Windward Maroons, who held off British soldiers for years, refusing enslavement.

Moore Town consists of just one dirt road running along the Wildcane River. It was founded in 1739 when the peace treaty with the British was signed (see box above); a Council of Maroons, with 24 members, is the governing body. The council is led by a "colonel." If he's spotted and pointed out by your guide, you should ask him permission to visit the town, which is usually granted. Of course, you don't have to ask permission, but it's considered polite to do so, in recognition of the community's sovereignty.

At the southern end of town lies **Bump Grave,** the burial site of Queen Nanny, the fierce leader of the Windward Maroons (see box above). The grave is inevitably marked with flying flags and often with fresh flowers from the Blue Mountains.

The traditional dances and ceremonies here, imported directly from Africa, have changed little over the years. They include the Kromanti Drum Dance, its name that of an infamous slave market on Africa's Ivory Coast. Sometimes the Maroon dancers continue for hours in a ritual of communication with ancestral spirits, climaxing with the sacrifice of an animal. These ceremonies are not open to the public, however—the Maroons, in general, still seem very distrustful of outsiders, and toting a camera into their inner enclaves isn't recommended.

Directly south of Moore Town is another little hamlet, **Cornwell Barracks,** yet another Maroon settlement.

WEST OF PORT ANTONIO

With far less attractions than the east of Port Antonio, the western coastline is worth a day of your time if you can spare it.

As you leave Port Antonio heading west along Route A4, you come first to:

ST MARGARET'S BAY   At this point the Rio Grande empties into the ocean, 8km (5 miles) from Port Antonio. The river rushes under an iron bridge, built in 1890, on its way to the sea.

HOPE BAY   This fishing town, with its unattractive beach of grayish sand, need not occupy much of your time. There are some jerk stands, tropical punch bars, and several crafts shops hawking their wares, but not much else.

The adventurous should instead head south along a secondary road, where it's easy to spot several places to go swimming on the upper reaches of the fast-flowing and aptly named Swift River. South of Hope Bay, a beautiful drive takes you through lush valleys surrounded by mountains and groves of bananas and cocoa.

Watch for an unusual drink served at roadside stands called a "chocolate tea ball." The bartender grates a cocoa ball into a mixture of hot water and milk, then adds a shot of rum—a kind of local toddy.

There's a hamlet called Swift River where you can cross a tiny bridge over the river and follow it to some intoxicatingly cool, deep pools good for swimming.

At a point just over 3km (approx. 2 miles) from Hope Bay on the A4 highway, you come to:

SOMERSET FALLS   Here, the waters of the Daniels River pour down a deep gorge through a rainforest, with waterfalls and foaming cascades. You can take a short ride in a rowboat or put-put motorboat to the hidden falls. A stop on the daily Grand Jamaica Tour from Ocho Rios, this is one of Jamaica's most historic sites; the falls were used by the Spanish before the British captured the island. At the falls, you can change into a swimsuit and enjoy the deep rock pools. You can also buy sandwiches, light meals, soft drinks, beer, and liquor at the snack bar. The guided tour includes the gondola ride and a visit to both a cave and a freshwater fish farm. On certain days, the site is likely to be overrun with camera-toting tourists. Expect a manicured, somewhat sanitized landscape punctuated for the tourist trade with caged birds and a scattering of kiosks devoted to the sale of trinkets, souvenirs, and rum-based drinks. For $7, tours are conducted daily from 9am to 5pm.

En route to Buff Bay you can stop off at a fairly good beach of golden sand at **Orange Bay** for a quick dip.

The A4 highway then continues into:

BUFF BAY   This little seafront hamlet is where farmers from the Blue Mountains bring their produce to market. If you're not really interested in a walk through this market, continue for another 16km (10 miles) or so along the A4 highway to:

ANNOTTO BAY   This town's heyday has come and gone. Back in the 19th century it was a center for banana exports. It owed its success to a Scottish doctor, John Pringle (1848–1923), who came here, purchased 18th-century sugar plantations going to ruin, and converted them into banana plantations, which became a quick cash crop.

The banana business went belly-up, as did the sugar factory—the town's chief employer. Hurricane Gilbert in 1988 almost completely killed Annotto, yet it struggles on. Nothing much remains of the British-built Fort George that guarded the harbor, however.

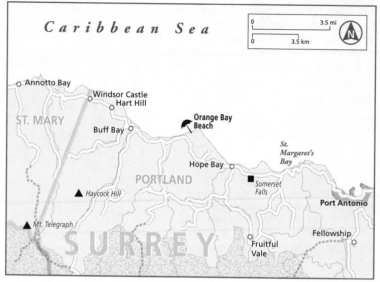

From Annotto, continue along Route 4 until you come to A3 cutting south. Follow this route along the Wag River Valley until you come to:

CASTLETON BOTANICAL GARDENS ✿ Midway between Kingston and Annotto Bay, this is one of the most remote botanical gardens in the West Indies. The gardens grow lushly here because of heavy mountain rains on the western periphery of the Blue Mountains.

On 6 luxuriant hectares (15 acres) you'll see mahogany trees, tree ferns, teak, calabash, cannonball trees, coffee, ebony, cocoa, azaleas—you name it. Nothing is state of the art, however. You are out in the wilderness in "unknown Jamaica" if you visit here.

Begun in 1862 with plants shipped from England's Kew Gardens, these botanical gardens are far more accessible than the once-famous ones at Bath. The gardens are known for introducing many trees to Jamaica, including the Poinciana. The gardens aren't what they used to be, after nature and lack of care have taken their toll. But they still make for a fascinating visit.

The flora is mammoth, including the junglelike ferns. In 1897 some 180 species of palms were planted here, some of whose "children" still survive. On the banks of the river, under a big shady tree, a picnic table awaits you. You might be offered a fruit to taste, perhaps the exotic African velvet apple. This is also a habitat of the streamer tail hummingbird (called a doctor bird), the national bird of Jamaica. We've also seen the tiny bee hummingbird here, one of the smallest birds on the planet.

The gardens (no phone) are open daily from 9am to 5pm; admission is free but tips are appreciated.

ORGANIZED TOURS

Valley Hikes, from a base on Harbour Street, in Port Antonio (© **876/993-3881**), arranges well-choreographed hikes through the Rio Grande Valley. The hikes are conducted in a lush area between the Blue Mountains and the John Crow Mountains,

with experienced local guides. Many different variations on the tours, ranging from 2 hours to 2 days, are available, one of the most popular and best being a 2-hour waterfall tour priced at $35 per person. A 6.5km (4-mile) hike into the Blue Mountains, seeking its flora and fauna, can also be arranged.

Attractions Link, 229 Harbour St., Unit #10, in Port Antonio (© 876/993-2102 or 876/873-4808; www.attractionslink.com), also offers well-conceived exposures to the Jamaican wild. It offers one of the best bus tours into the Blue Mountains, with a visit to a coffee plantation and a picnic in Hollywell National Park at 1,518m (5,060 ft.) above sea level. Including lunch, the cost is $75 per person.

Another excursion, this one scheduled from 9am to 3:30pm, takes you to Reach Falls and Long Bay Beach, east of Port Antonio and along the coast, where you can go for a dip. (Beware of the undercurrents on this beach!) Go with someone else who loves and enjoys a cooling dip: The cost is $30 per person.

Attractions Link also offers a **Tour of a Maroon Village,** which, if enough participants have signed up, includes a visit to Nanny Waterfall and insights into the mysterious Maroon subculture, or at least what's left of it. When available, it's scheduled for a departure from your hotel at 8:30am, a return to your hotel around 5pm, and an exposure to some of the most isolated villages in the region. The cost, per person, is $65.

One of our personal favorites is the company's **Butterfly and Birdwatching Tour,** which, because of the feeding habits of Jamaican fauna, requires an early-morning departure at 5am, with a return to your hotel before noon on the same day, following excursions deep into Sherwood Forest, and the Reach Falls area of the Blue Mountains. Tours are accompanied with a trained and licensed ornithologist, and cost $85 per person. Sightings will usually include the Jamaican crow, the scavenging John Crow, the Jamaican streamer tail hummingbird (the country's national bird), the (nocturnal) Jamaican owl, and a host of rare orchids and other plants.

6 Shopping

Port Antonio is not a shopping bazaar like Montego Bay and Ocho Rios. Most activity centers around **Musgrave Market** ⊛, on West Street, in the center of town. This is one of our favorite markets in all of Jamaica. It evokes a movie set on which the director is about to call, "Lights, camera, action!" The most active market day is Saturday. To see the market at its most frenzied, go any day of the week from 8am to noon.

The sprawling **Fort George Village Shopping Arcade,** which opened in 1997 to immediate denunciations, is not a mirage. What would that architectural critic, Prince Charles, think? To call it an architectural monstrosity would be too kind; this three-floor structure looks like some of the world's major architectural ideas, thrown into a blender—baroque, English Tudor, French Gothic, with hints of Syria and Iraq thrown in for spice—and spat out. In theory, at least, the arcade was designed to represent various architectures from around the world.

Regardless of what you think of its design, the arcade is fun for a shopping jaunt, thanks to outlets for jewelry, antiques/junk, CDs, computers, and more. Many of the shops found no one willing to sign a lease. The market can be seen in the center of town across from the courthouse, en route to Titchfield Hill.

On Harbour Street, you'll come to the **City Centre Plaza,** but it's rather dull. As for its crafts, we've seen better. Still, it might come in handy for souvenirs and those

---

Fun Fact **Better Than What the Snake Gave Eve**

If you want to taste one of the most luscious fruits grown in the West Indies, go into Musgrave Market and ask one of the fruit-and-vegetable vendors to sell you a juicy ripe plum called a "June." Some of the old-timers refer to the fruit as "Jew." After you bite into this succulent fruit, which locals will tell you came from the Garden of Eden, you'll become addicted to it.

---

things visitors always need: postcards for the ones you left behind, suntan lotion, and that Nora Roberts paperback for the beach.

If you've already perused the shopping possibilities of the native markets, you might scout out the craft and gift stores of the resort hotels.

At the **Gallery Carriacou** ✿, on the grounds of Hotel Mocking Bird Hill, on Mocking Bird Hill (© **876/993-7267**), you can view the sensuous and evocative paintings and sculptures of Barbara Walker, who is one of the partners in the hotel. Her works, and those of other noted Jamaican artists, make up the finest collection of art for sale in the area. Walker also conducts classes, on request, in sculpture and painting.

At the **Port Antonio Marina,** you'll find space for up to 32 different shops and boutiques, even though only some of those spaces will be occupied by the time of your visit. The most appealing of the lot is **Things Jamaican** (© **876/715-5347**), where gift items, fashion accessories, and housewares—each made in or pertaining to Jamaica—are lined up for easy-on-the-eyes shopping. The selection, alas, is disappointingly small, but each item is carefully chosen for its representation of Jamaica's British Colonial age and its enduring appeal.

7 Port Antonio After Dark

Go at your own risk to the infamous **Roof Club,** 11 West St. (no phone). The most crowded and animated nightclub in Port Antonio, it lies one floor above street level in a boxy-looking industrial building in the heart of town. Inside, the venue is earthy, raunchy, crowded, and boozy, with enough secondhand ganja smoke to get virtually anyone high. Recorded (and more rarely, live) reggae and soca music blares at high volumes—so loud, in fact, that first-timers might not immediately understand the blandishments of other clients, male and female, to buy them a drink.

Expect a neo-psychedelic decor of mirrors, UV lighting, and free-form Day-Glo artwork. A visit here is not for the squeamish or the faint-hearted, and it's a good idea to come with a friend and/or ally. Try to stay relatively sober, keep your wits about you, and enjoy the slow-moving gyrations of ordinary folks who—sometimes with the help of a spliff or two—get involved in the beat of the music and groove accordingly. Beers cost from $3 to $4 each. It's open nightly from around 6pm, but most of the genuine hanging out and crowding happens after 11pm, especially from Thursday through Sunday.

Its leading competitor is **Baldi's Bar & Grill,** in the Town Talk Building, 4 Harbour St. at the corner of Fort George St. (© **876/715-6773**). To reach it, you'll have to climb to the third floor of a sturdy cement building in the heart of town. There, a party-colored neoclassical balustrade keeps drinkers and diners from falling off a "high-altitude" dining-and-drinking area that's otherwise open and exposed to sea

breezes on all sides. It's open daily from 10am till "very late." Beer and mixed drinks cost from J$140 to J$200 (US$2.25–US$3.20). Menu items in the grill area are Jamaican and international, but most people just come here to drink and flirt.

Less formalized and much more free-form would involve a hike along Port Antonio's eastern waterfront, Folly Road, known locally as the town's "Folly Strip." Here, a battered and mud-splattered row of rum shacks and jerk stands, each painted long ago in once-bright colors, play recorded music and try to show a foreign visitor a good time. A culinary "highlight" of the Folly Strip is **Oliver's Vegetarian Restaurant** (no phone), whose presentation might be nominally a bit more solid than some of its neighbors. At any of the shacks along the strip, expect to pay between J$70 and J$100 (US$1.10–US$1.60) for a Red Stripe beer. If you opt for a visit to this strip, we recommend that you wrap up your evening by around 10pm.

The **Tree Bar,** on the grounds of Goblin Hill Villas at San San (© **876/925-8108**), stands high on a hill commanding a panoramic view of 4 hectares (12 acres). The aptly named bar is wrapped around huge ficus trees, whose mammoth aerial roots dangle over the drinking area. Giant-leafed pothos vines climb down the trunks. It's the sort of eco-adventure place that should prove increasingly popular.

Kingston & the Blue Mountains

Kingston, the largest English-speaking city in the Caribbean, is the capital of Jamaica and its cultural, industrial, and financial center. It's home to more than 660,000 people, including those living on the plains between the Blue Mountains and the sea. The buildings here are a mixture of modern, graceful, old, and just plain ramshackle. The bustling port is evocative of one in Africa, with a natural harbor that's among the largest in the world. The University of the West Indies has its campus on the edge of the city.

Few other cities in the Caribbean carry as many negative connotations as Kingston, thanks to widely publicized reports of violent crime, congestion, bad roads, and difficult-to-decipher traffic signs. But it is also here that you find Jamaica at its most urban and confident, most witty and exciting, most challenging. No other place in Jamaica offers so many bars, clubs, or cultural outlets. And no other place in Jamaica has such a concentration of creative artists and opinions.

We've carefully screened the recommendations contained within this guidebook, eliminating any that lie within the most dangerous neighborhoods. Keep an open mind about Kingston—it can be a lot of fun if you keep your guard up, but it isn't for the faint of heart.

When you've had enough of the city, escape to the **Blue Mountains** at the northern edge of the city. There is no more beautiful mountain chain in the West Indies. The hills are at their most stunning and evocative when a blue mist hovers over them. The Blue Mountains are most famously associated with a celebrated coffee bean, but they're also full of trails, rivers, waterfalls, bird life, fruit, and even marijuana.

Don't expect superhighways: The roads are terrible. Luckily, the best way to appreciate this amazing scenery is by foot—though only if you're very fit.

1 Orientation

ARRIVING BY PLANE   International arrivals are at **Norman Manley International Airport,** while domestic flights—say, from Montego Bay—fly into the smaller **Tinson Pen Airport.**

Norman Manley Airport lies 27km (17 miles) southeast of the center of Kingston. Guard your luggage carefully, as there have been many reports of theft—sometimes involving baggage handlers.

GETTING FROM THE AIRPORTS INTO THE CITY   If you're driving in a rented car, do not stop even if someone is flagging you down. That person appearing to be in distress might actually be an armed robber.

The best way to get into town is aboard an officially sanctioned **JUTA** taxi (© 876/ 957-4536). The cost of a ride is about $22 from Norman Manley airport, $14 from Tinson Pen airport.

VISITOR INFORMATION   The main office of the **Jamaica Tourist Board** is at 64 Knutsford Blvd. (© **876/929-9200**), open Monday to Friday 8:30am to 4:30pm.

CITY LAYOUT

Downtown Kingston is the historic core, rising just north of the waterfront and harbor. The "main street" is **King Street,** heading north from the water to the Parade. King Street begins at **Ocean Boulevard** and runs north to **Sir William Grant Park.**

Parallel to Ocean Boulevard run two more arteries—**Port Royal Street** and **Harbour Street,** bordered by North and South Parade.

GETTING AROUND   Driving around Kingston is a journey into hysteria. The public bus transportation is horrendous, and foreigners are often pickpocketed. Thus, the taxi is the most reliable form of transportation. Official taxis with red license plates fall under the **JUTA** umbrella, the government-sanctioned taxi agency (© **876/957-4536**). Your hotel will call one (unless one is parked out front). Taxis meet arriving planes, and are also plentiful in the shopping district.

Fares are charged per car, not per passenger. Because most taxis aren't metered, tell the driver where you are going and agree on the rate before getting in. Make sure you and the cabbie agree on which dollars you are talking about—American or Jamaican.

FAST FACTS: Kingston

Banks   The best and most convenient bank is **Scotiabank,** at Duke and Royal streets (© **876/922-1000**), open Monday to Friday 8am to 5pm. Another convenient choice is **Citibank,** 63–67 Knutsford Blvd. (© **876/926-3270**), open Monday to Thursday 9am to 2pm and Friday 9am to 3pm.

Bookstores   There are no great bookstores in all of Kingston, but if you want some light reading, try **Bookland,** 53 Knutsford Blvd. (© **876/926-4035**), open Monday to Friday 9am to 6pm and Saturday 10am to 5pm.

Internet Access   In Kingston you can generally use your hotel phone line to get online with a laptop. Otherwise, you can go to **Hilton Kingston Jamaica Cyber,** 77 Knutsford Blvd. (© **876/926-5430**), open daily 7am to 10pm, charging $7.50 per hour. Six computers are available.

Mail   The main **Kingston Post Office** is at South Camp Road (© **876/922-9430**), open Monday to Friday 8am to 5pm. Keeping the same hours is another branch at 115 Hope Rd. (© **876/927-7258**). Many savvy visitors skip the inefficient postal systems in Jamaica and deal directly with **FedEx** at 40 Half Way Tree Rd. (© **876/960-9192**), open Monday to Friday 9am to 5pm and Saturday 9am to noon. Another option for fast service is **DHL,** 60 Knutsford Blvd. (© **888/CALL-DHL**), open Monday to Friday 8:30am to 5pm and Saturday 9am to 1pm. Include "Jamaica, W.I." in all island addresses. The island has no zip codes, although at press time, discussions about assigning zip codes to each of the various districts of Jamaica were ongoing. Depending on local bureaucracies, new zip codes may or may not be in effect during the lifetime of this edition.

Medical Services   Most of the medical facilities of Jamaica are found in Kingston. A private facility that's best for visitors is **Medical Associates Hospital,** 18 Tangerine Place (© **876/926-1400**), with an emergency ambulance service as

well. Another well-regarded medical facility in Kingston is **Saint Joseph's Hospital,** 22 Deanery Rd. (② **876/928-4955**). **St. John's Ambulance,** 2E Camp Rd. (② **876/926-7656**), offers ambulance service in Kingston. The **Deluxe Ambulance Service,** 54 Molynes Rd. (② **876/923-7415**), is on 24-hour call.

Pharmacies The most convenient in New Kingston (where virtually everybody stays) is **Moodies Pharmacy** in the New Kingston Shopping Centre at 30 Dominica Dr. (② **876/926-4174**), open Monday to Saturday 8:30am to 7pm. There's another good pharmacy, the **Manor Park Pharmacy,** 186 Constant Spring Rd. (② **876/924-1424**), open daily 8:30am to 10:30pm.

Safety Kingston is the most dangerous city in the Caribbean. Take more precautions here than you would elsewhere. The major problem facing most foreigners is mugging: Robbery is commonplace.

New Kingston is the safest place to be. The downtown area is far more dangerous—in fact, some Jamaican taxi drivers have refused to take us there on business. Two readers from Kansas City wrote that their car broke down in downtown Kingston. They locked it and went to get help—and by the time they returned, their luggage and all their possessions had been stolen. The car was also completely stripped, from the radio down to the tires.

The downtown is not without its attractions, but should be visited carefully, and almost never at night. Some of the most dangerous districts, Six Miles and Riverton City, should be avoided at all times. Finally, if you hear Kingstonians talking about what parts of their city they won't go to, take heed.

Travel Agents The best one is **Great Vacations,** New Kingston Shopping Centre, 30 Dominica Dr. (② **876/929-6290**), open Monday to Friday 7am to 7pm and Saturday 10am to 2pm. It is the local representative of Thomas Cook.

2 Where to Stay

The best accommodation, Strawberry Hill, and the reason many people visit the Kingston area in the first place, is not in the city but within the Blue Mountains. All leading hotels in security-conscious Kingston have guards.

EXPENSIVE

Hilton Kingston Hotel ☞   This imposing mass of pink stucco pierced with oversize sheets of tinted glass is an almost peas-in-the-pod version of the Pegasus (see below): If you were to wake up in the middle of the night at either hotel, it would take a minute to discern which hotel you're sleeping in. The main core of the hotel is an 18-floor tower, containing 190 of the guest rooms. The remainder of the units lie within the two-story lanai wing, where rooms have balconies and windows that actually open onto views of the surrounding cityscape and/or the pool area. Rooms in the lanai wing are a bit cheaper than those in the central tower, and have a decor that's just a bit older. In 2006, the hotel was undergoing a complete refurbishment, accentuating designs that manage to mix an English colonial theme with Jamaica-inspired touches of bright colors and jungle-tropical patterns. Bathrooms are tiled and modern looking, with all the contemporary comforts. On site are four restaurants, the most elaborate of which is the Palm Court Restaurant. Less formal dining is available in the Terrace Cafe.

Kingston Area

ATTRACTIONS ●
Bob Marley Museum **20**
Devon House **15**
Gordon House **31**
Headquarters House **31**
Hope Botanical Gardens & Zoo **25**
Institute of Jamaica **32**
Jamaica House **17**
The Jewish Synagogue **30**
King's House **18**
Mico College **3**
National Arena **28**
National Gallery **33**
National Heroes Park **2**
National Library **32**
National Museum **32**
National Stadium **27**
St. Andrews Scots Kirk **14**
St. William Grant Park **1**
University of the West Indies **26**

ACCOMMODATIONS ■
Altamont Court Hotel **11**
The Courtleigh **8**
Hotel Four Seasons **10**
Indies Hotel **13**
The Jamaica Pegasus **5**
Hilton Kingston Hotel **7**
Strawberry Hill **24**
Terra Nova All-Suite Hotel **16**

DINING ◆
Akbar **29**
Alexander's **8**
Boon Hill Oasis **19**
Chelsea Jerk Centre **9**
The Columbus Restaurant **5**
Heather's **4**
The Hot Pot **6**
Indies Pub and Grill **12**
Jade Garden **21**
Norma's on the Terrace **15**
Palm Court **7**
Redbones the Blues Café **22**
The Restaurant at the
   Hotel Four Seasons **10**
Strawberry Hill **24**
Thai Gardens **29**
The Upper Crust (Guilt Trip) **23**

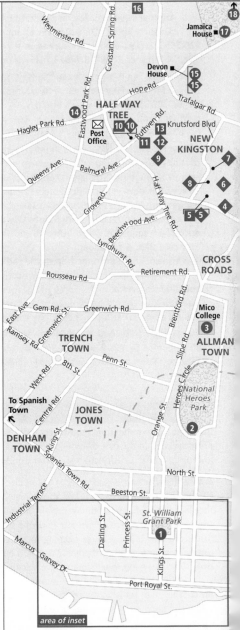

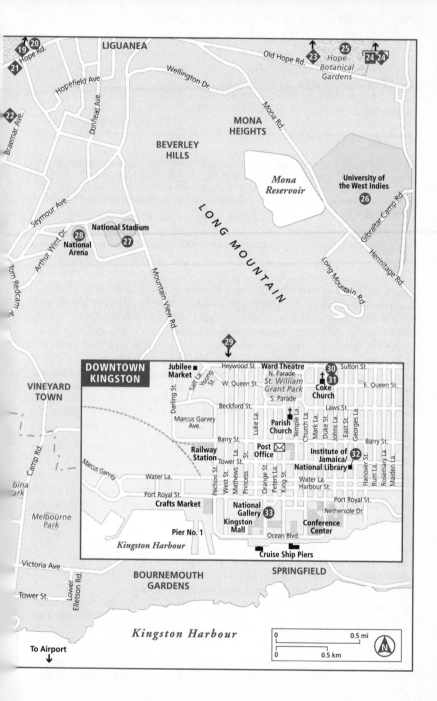

A Calypso Lament

Oh, I'm sad to say, farewell today,
I'll be back to Kingston town bay,
My heart is down, my thoughts are spinning around,
Because the girl I love is here in Kingston town.

—Jamaica farewell

77 Knutsford Blvd. (P.O. Box 112), Kingston 5. ✆ **876/926-5430.** Fax 876/929-7439. www.hilton.com. 303 units. Year-round $140–$230 double, from $345 suite. Children under 12 stay free in parent's room. AE, DC, MC, V. Free parking. In the center of New Kingston. **Amenities:** 4 restaurants; 2 bars; nightclub; pool; 2 tennis courts; gym; sauna; business center; limited room service; laundry service/dry cleaning; nonsmoking rooms; rooms for those w/limited mobility. *In room:* A/C, TV, dataport, hair dryer, safe.

The Jamaica Pegasus ✦   A favorite with business travelers, the Jamaica Pegasus barely outclasses its nearest rival, the Hilton. It's located in the banking area of Kingston, which is also a fine residential area. After a major renovation, the hotel is now better than ever and is the site of many conventions and social events. The hotel combines British style with Jamaican warmth, arranging watersports and sightseeing. Each of the well-furnished bedrooms is of moderate size and contains bathrooms with combination tubs and showers and balconies opening onto mountain, sea, or cityscapes. The decorating, in dark tones, often brown, makes you yearn for the lighter pastel look of most Caribbean hotel bedrooms. Several floors of luxuriously appointed suites form the Knutsford Club, which offers special executive services.

81 Knutsford Blvd., Kingston 5. ✆ **876/926-3690.** Fax 876/929-5855. www.jamaicapegasus.com. 300 units. Year-round $120–$150 double; $230 junior suite; $530 royal suite. AE, DC, DISC, MC, V. **Amenities:** 3 restaurants; 2 bars; pool; 2 tennis courts; fitness center; 24-hr. business center; 24-hr. room service; laundry service; dry cleaning; non-smoking rooms; jogging trail; rooms for those w/limited mobility. *In room:* A/C, TV, dataport, minibar, hair dryer, safe.

MODERATE

The Courtleigh ✦✦   We often prefer the Courtleigh to the Hilton or Pegasus because it's a warmer, friendlier place, and has a more personal atmosphere. The prices are affordable as well. The six-floor hotel is the filling in the "sandwich" between the Hilton and the Pegasus, standing at the core of the business district. The well-furnished bedrooms live up to the standards of its two neighbors. We like the mahogany furnishings, evocative of the West Indies, and always request one of the units with a four-poster bed. The suites are particularly notable here, including such extras as big desks, two TVs, a dining table, a kitchenette, and a walk-in closet. Each comes with a midsize, tiled private bathroom with a tub/shower combination. The rectangular pool is often a rendezvous for business clients, and Alexander's (p. 231), the hotel restaurant, is worth a visit even if you're not a guest.

85 Knutsford Blvd., Kingston 5. ✆ **876/929-9000.** Fax 876/926-7744. www.courtleigh.com. 127 units. Year-round $145 double; $192–$398 suite. AE, DISC, MC, V. Rates include continental breakfast. **Amenities:** Restaurant; 2 bars; pool; gym; limited room service; laundry service/dry cleaning; coin-operated laundry; nonsmoking rooms; rooms for those w/limited mobility. *In room:* A/C, TV, dataport, kitchenette (in some units), coffeemaker, hair dryer, iron, safe.

Terra Nova All-Suite Hotel ✦ *Finds*   This house is on the western edge of New Kingston, near West Kings House Road. Built in 1924 for a young bride, it was converted into a hotel in 1959. At one time it was the family home of the well-known

hotelier and Island Records mogul Chris Blackwell. Set in 1 hectare (2½ acres) of gardens with a backdrop of greenery and mountains, it's now one of the best small Jamaican hotels, although the rooms are rather basic and not at all suited for those who want a resort ambience. Most of the bedrooms are in a new wing. All units have neatly kept bathrooms with shower units.

17 Waterloo Rd., Kingston 10. ℂ 876/926-2211. Fax 876/929-4933. www.terranovajamaica.com. 35 units. Year-round $145–$280 double. AE, MC, V. **Amenities:** 2 restaurants; coffee shop; 2 bars; pool; fitness center; limited room service; nonsmoking rooms; rooms for those w/limited mobility. *In room:* A/C, TV, dataport, minibar (in some), beverage maker, hair dryer, iron, safe.

INEXPENSIVE

Altamont Court Hotel   This hotel offers a less-expensive alternative to larger competitors such as the Hilton. It might remind you of a motel, thanks to exterior hallways and furniture like you might expect within a well-kept roadside inn in Florida. The staff here is less alert and well informed than you might hope for, but rooms are comfortable and there's a sense of well-ordered decency and thrift. Each of the rooms has either two double beds or one king-size bed, and all units contain a small private bathroom with tub/shower combination. The hotel's most alluring feature is its large swimming pool.

1–5 Altamont Terrace, New Kingston, Kingston 5. ℂ 876/929-4497. Fax 876/929-2118. www.altamontcourt.com. 58 units. Year-round $110 double; $140–$160 suite. AE, DC, MC, V. **Amenities:** Restaurant; bar; pool; Jacuzzi; limited room service; babysitting; laundry service/dry cleaning; nonsmoking rooms; rooms for those w/limited mobility. *In room:* A/C, TV, dataport, coffeemaker, hair dryer, safe.

Hotel Four Seasons *Kids* *Value*   Small-scale, well maintained, and respectable, this is one of the most appealing hotels in Kingston, thanks to a sophisticated design that combines a once-private home with a rambling series of modern wings, courtyards, gardens, and fountains. Rooms are cozy and comfortable, but the spiritual core of the place is the Elizabethan-inspired bar and restaurant (see "Where to Dine," below). Owned by two German sisters, this place enjoys something approaching cult status in Germany. Guest rooms evoke the furnishings of a well-maintained, upscale motel, and are usually decorated in wicker or plantation-style furniture. Most rooms have French doors opening onto private balconies or patios, overlooking either the garden or the pool. Each unit comes with a small private bathroom. Oh, and don't be confused by the name: It has absolutely no association with the big Four Seasons hotel chain.

18 Ruthven Rd. (near Halfway Tree Rd.), Kingston 10. ℂ 876/929-7655. Fax 876/929-5964. 76 units. Year-round $76–$90 double. AE, DC, MC, V. **Amenities:** Restaurant; 2 bars; pool; gym; limited room service; laundry service/dry cleaning; nonsmoking rooms. *In room:* A/C, TV, dataport, fridge (in some units), iron, safe.

Indies Hotel   On a small side street in the heart of New Kingston, opening onto a flower garden, this half-timbered building with double gables features a small reception area decorated with potted plants. The adequate and reasonably comfortable bedrooms, restaurant, and bar are grouped around a patio. Each unit is furnished with a small bathroom with a shower. There's a friendly atmosphere and good-quality budget meals. The fish and chips are good, and they also bake pizzas, serve steak with all the trimmings, and sometimes cook lobster thermidor.

5 Holborn Rd., Kingston 10. ℂ 876/926-2952. Fax 876/926-2879. http://indieshotel.com. 15 units. Year-round $64–$67 double; $81 triple. AE, MC, V. Near the intersection of Trafalgar Rd. **Amenities:** Restaurant; bar; limited room service; laundry service; dry cleaning. *In room:* A/C, TV, iron, safe.

3 Where to Dine

Kingston has a good range of places to eat, whether you're seeking stately meals in plantation houses, hotel buffets, or fast-food shops.

EXPENSIVE

The Columbus Restaurant 🏵 ITALIAN   The finest Italian cuisine in Jamaica is served at this hotel restaurant, a favorite with business travelers. The elegantly furnished restaurant offers good service and quality ingredients. Chefs tempt you with penne pasta with chicken, vegetables, and a white-wine sauce, and tender and flavorful sautéed beef loin with a spicy sauce. Another specialty that's a worthy dish is breast of chicken sautéed with herbs and spices, glacé, and ham and cheese. Members of Kingston's fashionable set often come here for a festive occasion, which is made all the more so if they order the Amaretto cheesecake.

In the Jamaica Pegasus Hotel, 81 Knutsford Blvd. ℂ **876/926-3690.** Reservations required. Main courses J$550–J$1,275 (US$8.80–US$20). AE, MC, V. Daily 24 hrs. In New Kingston, off Oxford Rd.

Norma's on the Terrace 🏵🏵 JAMAICAN/INTERNATIONAL   This is the creation of Jamaica's most famous businesswoman, Norma Shirley, purveyor of food to stylish audiences as far away as Miami. It's housed beneath the wide porticos of the gallery surrounding Kingston's most famous monument, Devon House. Ms. Shirley has taken the old, woefully dusty gardens and transformed them into something you'd find on a manicured English estate. Menus change with the season, but usually reflect Ms. Shirley's penchant for creative adaptations of her native Jamaican cuisine. Stellar examples include Jamaican chowder with crabmeat, shrimp, conch, and lobster; grilled whole red snapper encrusted with herbs and served with a thyme-and-caper sauce; and grilled smoked pork loin in a teriyaki/ginger sauce, served with caramelized apples.

In Devon House, 26 Hope Rd. ℂ **876/968-5488.** Reservations recommended. Main courses $15–$40. AE, DISC, MC, V. Mon–Sat 10am–10pm.

Palm Court 🏵 INTERNATIONAL   One of the best hotel restaurants in New Kingston is this one, on the Kingston Hilton's mezzanine floor. In a formal, intimate setting, you can dine on a refined cuisine beneath paintings by prominent Kingston artists. The chef's specialty is "Port Royal," a plate of snapper, salmon, jumbo shrimp, and lobster sautéed just right in a white-wine sauce before being served with a saffron sauce. Snapper often appears as a separate main course in either a butter sauce or a sauce sprinkled with slivered almonds. Imported meats, such as a rack of lamb or steaks from the United States, are also served here.

In the Kingston Hilton, 77 Knutsford Blvd. ℂ **876/926-5430.** Reservations recommended. Main courses J$750–J$3,400 (US$12–US$54). AE, DC, MC, V. Mon–Fri noon–10:30pm; Sat 6:30–10:30pm.

Redbones the Blues Café 🏵🏵 *Finds* JAMAICAN   The name alone lured us to this elegant place, which is the only restaurant in Kingston with cuisine as good as Norma's on the Terrace. All aglow in yellow and peach hues, Redbones is in a former Spanish colonial house. You're greeted with pictures of jazz greats on the wall, everybody from Billie Holiday to Louis Armstrong. A cozy bar, its ceiling studded with records, is installed in someone's former bedroom. Owners Evan and Betsy Williams give standard Jamaican dishes a new twist. Ask for "bammy," a cassava dish crowned with sautéed shrimp, or a platter of stuffed crab backs, a delectable selection on a tri-color salad. A

spinach callaloo with cream cheese is encased in a divine strudel. Seafood pasta is laden with shrimp, lobster, and salmon in a creamy coconut sauce. The best item on the menu is spicy lamb chops in a guava glaze. Live jazz or something is always going on.

21 Braemar Ave. 🕐 876/978-6091. Reservations required. Main courses J$800–J$2,000 (US$13–US$32). AE, MC, V. Mon–Fri noon–11pm; Sat 3pm–midnight.

MODERATE

Alexander's JAMAICAN/INTERNATIONAL   This is the showplace dining room of one of Kingston's top hotels, and as such, it often attracts business meetings, government delegations, and international travelers who appreciate its good service and culinary savvy. Within a setting inspired by the Jamaican sugar plantations of the 1800s, with muted tropical colors and a view that overlooks the hotel's swimming pool, you can order such starters as smoked marlin or Caribbean crab backs, then move to sirloin steaks; medallions of beef with grilled tomatoes; or filets of pork with brandy, mustard, and cream sauce. After dinner, consider a drink in the hotel's bar, Mingles.

In the Courtleigh Hotel, 85 Knutsford Blvd. 🕐 876/968-6339. Reservations recommended. Lunch main courses J$385–J$620 (US$6.15–US$9.90); dinner main courses J$460–J$1,200 (US$7.35–US$19). AE, DISC, MC, V. Mon–Fri 6:30–10am, noon–3pm, and 6–10:30pm; Sat and Sun 6:30–11am, noon–4pm, and 6–11pm.

Jade Garden ✦ CHINESE   The best Chinese restaurant in Kingston, Jade Garden serves well-prepared food in an elegant, formal setting. Chow mein and chop suey dishes are here, but ignore them to concentrate on the more challenging offerings. Beef with oyster sauce is delectable, as is the pork with ham choy. For unusual flavors, try Pi Paw bean curd with chopped Chinese sausage, shrimp, black mushrooms, and water chestnuts. Also excellent is Subgum War Bar, a combination of meats sautéed with Chinese vegetables and served on a sizzling-hot platter. Deep-fried prawns stuffed with prawn mousse and served in a garlic-butter sauce are excellent as well.

106 Hope Rd., in Sovereign Centre. 🕐 876/978-3476. Reservations recommended. Main courses J$600–J$3,600 (US$9.60–US$58). AE, MC, V. Daily noon–10pm. North of the town center, west of National Stadium.

The Restaurant at the Hotel Four Seasons *Value* GERMAN/JAMAICAN/INTERNATIONAL   This hotel restaurant (see "Where to Stay," above) offers one of the most consistently reliable luncheon buffets in Jamaica. It's supervised by a pair of hardworking East German–born sisters whose unfailing standards have made it a staple on the capital's restaurant scene. Menu items are freshly made and succulent, with everything from Jamaican pepper-pot soup to goulash, jerk chicken or pork, schnitzels and sauerbraten, and roulades of pork or veal.

18 Ruthven Rd. 🕐 876/929-7655. Reservations recommended. Fixed-price buffet lunch J$750 (US$12); lunch and dinner main courses J$480–J$1,600 (US$7.70–$US26). AE, MC, V. Daily noon–3pm and 6–10pm. Near Half Way Tree Rd.

A Call to Action

You're gonna lively up yourself and don't be no drag,
You're gonna lively up yourself because reggae is another bag.
You lively up yourself and don't say no,
You're gonna lively up yourself 'cause I said so.

—Bob Marley, "Lively Up Yourself"

INEXPENSIVE

Akbar *Finds* NORTHERN INDIAN This is the best Indian restaurant in Kingston. It consists of four dining rooms, each outfitted in earth tones with touches of mint green. Don't overlook the possibility of a meal in the Moghul-style garden, within earshot of a splashing fountain. Menu items are rich with the seasonings of the East, with seafood, vegetarian, lamb, beef, and chicken dishes, as well as a selection of exotic breads. Specific and stellar examples include Chicken Moghlai cooked in cream sauce with nuts and egg butter; mutton in a spicy sauce; and beef Akbar—one of the most justifiably popular house specialties, skewered and flavored with herbs.

11 Holborn Rd. ① **876/926-3480**. Reservations recommended. Main courses J$595–J$1,200 (US$9.50–US$19). AE, MC, V. Daily noon–4pm and 6–11pm.

Boon Hall Oasis *Finds* JAMAICAN Down a series of pathways and steps carved into a remote hillside outside the city, this place serves Sunday brunch only beneath galvanized metal roofs in a series of dining pavilions, all within a garden. Well-prepared menu items include filet of red snapper with brown sauce or a vinegar-based *escoveitch* (marinated fish); three different preparations of shrimp (including one flambéed in honey-flavored rum sauce); and three different preparations of chicken. Art exhibitions and poetry readings sometimes take place here.

Stony Hill, St. Andrew. ① **876/942-3064**. Reservations recommended. Sun brunch J$1,000 (US$16). MC, V. Sun 11am–3pm (last order). Take a taxi from Kingston, or turn on Seaview Rd. (opposite Petcom Gas Station—Stony Hill Sq.). Take the 3rd left onto Airy Castle Rd., then look out for the signs pointing to Boon Hall Oasis.

Chelsea Jerk Centre *Value* JAMAICAN This is the city's most popular purveyor of jerked meats. Set in a low-slung angular concrete building, it offers food to take out or eat in a comfortably battered dining area. Although no formal appetizers are served, you might order a side portion of what the scrawled-on chalkboard refers to as "festival" (fried cornmeal dumplings). The best bargain is Chelsea's Special: rice, peas, and vegetables, plus jerked pork or chicken. Remember to order the various components of your meal at different kiosks in the huge hall; oxtail, stewed fish, and beer are also available.

7 Chelsea Ave. ① **876/926-6322**. Reservations not accepted. Jerk half-chicken J$360 (US$5.75); .5kg (1 lb.) jerk pork J$640 (US$10). MC, V. Mon–Thurs 10am–10pm; Fri–Sat 10am–1am; Sun noon–10pm. Near the New Kingston Shopping Centre.

Heather's JAMAICAN/SYRIAN Loud, convivial, and sometimes boisterous, this establishment combines a popular singles bar with a somewhat more sedate restaurant. There's a massive mango tree thrusting its way skyward through a hole in the roof. Tasty menu items include grilled fish kabobs, sweet-and-sour fish, Cajun-style blackened fish, Heather's crab cakes, and Heather's special shrimp.

9 Haining Rd., New Kingston. ① **876/926-2826**. Reservations recommended. Main courses J$600–J$1,425 (US$9.60–US$23). AE, DC, MC, V. Mon–Sat noon–4pm and 5pm–midnight.

The Hot Pot JAMAICAN Set within a short walk of both the Pegasus and Hilton hotels, this is a simple local restaurant with an animated crowd of regulars and straightforward, unfussy cuisine. Within a green-and-white interior, near a view of a modest garden, you can drink Red Stripe beer or rum drinks. The chefs are so good you'll want to hire them to cook for you, especially after you've tasted their garlic chicken, their ackee with salt fish, and their sweet-and-sour fish. The place stays open throughout the day, serving breakfast, lunch, and dinner without interruption. The

food is what you'd be served in a typical Jamaican home—nothing fancy, but satisfy-ing and filling—and the prices are astonishingly low.

2 Altamont Terrace. ℂ 876/929-3906. Reservations not accepted. Main courses J$300–J$555 (US$4.80–US$8.90). AE, MC, V. Mon–Sat 7am–8pm, Sun 7pm–midnight.

Indies Pub and Grill JAMAICAN   Indies, an informal neighborhood restaurant across the street from the Indies Hotel, was designed around a garden terrace. You can also dine in the inner rooms, haphazardly but pleasantly decorated with caribou horns, tortoise shells, half-timbered walls, an aquarium sometimes stocked with baby sharks, and even a Canadian moose head. There's a full sandwich menu at lunchtime. In the evening you can enjoy grilled lobster, fish and chips, barbecued chicken or pork, chicken Kiev, or roast beef. It's a little better than standard pub grub. Pizza is a specialty. A bottle of Red Stripe, the Jamaican national beer, is the beverage of choice.

8 Holborn Rd. (in New Kingston, off Hope Rd.). ℂ **876/920-5913**. Reservations not accepted. Main courses J$400–J$1,255 (US$6.40–US$20); pizzas J$410–J$1,450 (US$6.55–US$23). DISC, MC, V. Mon–Fri 11am–midnight; Sat 11am–1am.

Thai Gardens 🎖 *Finds* THAI   The chefs here come directly from Bangkok, and the flavors are authentic, achieved with imported ingredients. The place is filled with arti-facts sent over from Thailand. We recommend it as a change of pace when you've had too much Jamaican cuisine. Specialties include fried noodles with Thai shrimp wrapped in an eggshell, and steamed snapper served with chili-laced lemon sauce.

10 Holborn Rd. ℂ **876/906-3237**. Reservations recommended. Main courses J$695–J$1,595 (US$11–US$26). Daily noon–4pm and 6–11pm.

The Upper Crust (Guilt Trip) JAMAICAN/INTERNATIONAL   About 2km (1¼ mile) north of New Kingston, this open-air restaurant originated as a small-scale pas-try shop that eventually expanded into a neighborhood institution. In addition to the pastries, which are made on the premises and displayed behind a glass-fronted case, menu items include crab-back salads, curried snapper, jerk chicken lasagna, grilled lamb chops with ratatouille, and an especially good grilled filet of snapper with dried-pepper shrimp in a curry sauce.

20 Barbican Rd., Liguanea. ℂ **876/977-5130**. Lunch main courses J$350–J$1,150 (US$5.60–US$18); dinner main courses J$650–J$1,250 (US$10–US$20). MC, V. Daily noon–3pm and 6–11pm.

4 Beaches & Other Outdoor Pursuits

BEACHES   You don't really come to Kingston for beaches, but there are some here. To the southwest of the sprawling city are the black-sanded **Hellshire Beach, Gun-boat Beach,** and **Fort Clarence.** These beaches are very popular with the locals on weekends, and all have changing rooms, heavy security, and numerous food stands. The reggae concerts at Fort Clarence are legendary on the island.

Just past Fort Clarence, the fisherman's beach at **Naggo Head** is an even hipper des-tination, or so Kingston beach buffs claim. After a swim in the refreshing waters, opt for one of the food stands selling "fry fish" and bammy (cassava bread).

The closest beach to the city is **Lime Cay** 🎖, a little island on the outskirts of Kingston Harbour, reached by a short boat ride from Morgan's Harbour at Port Royal. This is one of the best spots we've found in Kingston for a picnic. Weekend cookouts are commonplace, and the swimming is good in unpolluted waters. To get a boat ride to the beach, check with the reception desk at Morgan's Harbour Hotel (p. 242).

CRICKET   This is the national pastime of Jamaica. The best cricket games are played in Kingston at **Sabina Park** on South Camp Road. For information about matches, contact the tourist office (see "Orientation," earlier in this chapter).

GOLF   Caymanas Golf Course, Spanish Town (© 876/922-3386), lies 10km (6¼ miles) west of Kingston and is open to the general public. This is an 18-hole, par-70, 6,855-yard course. Golfers praise this course for its elevated tees and its uphill shots. It costs $41 for a round of golf here on weekdays, $47 on weekends, plus $23 for the cart rental, and another $15 for the club rental.

A course closer to town, **Constant Spring** at Constant Spring (© 876/924-1610), dates from the 1920s. A mentor of Robert Trent Jones, Sr., Stanley Thompson, laid out this par-70, 6,196-yard, 18-hole golf course at the foot of the Blue Mountains. A round costs J$2,000 (US$32) on weekdays, J$2,500 (US$40) on weekends, and club rentals are available. There's also a small pro shop, restaurant, and bar.

SCUBA DIVING   Some of the best-known dive sites in the area include **Windward Edge,** with a depth range of 21 to 27m (70–90 ft.). Reached after a 30-minute boat ride, this site lies 11km (6¼ miles) outside of Kingston Cays. There are great photo opportunities here.

Suitable for all levels of divers, the *Cayman Trader* wreck has a depth range of 9 to 15m (30–50 ft.). A Norwegian cargo ship, the *Trader* caught on fire in 1977. It was later towed to this site and sunk. The wreck is scattered over a large area. Another stunning wreck that an outfitter can take you to is the *Texas,* a U.S. Navy ship that went down in 1944. Advanced divers seek out this site, at a depth of 30m (100 ft.). It is particularly known to divers for its stunning black coral.

TENNIS   The best tennis courts are at two hotels in New Kingston. **The Jamaica Pegasus,** 81 Knutsford Blvd. (© 876/926-3690), offers two hard-surface courts, each lit for night play. Courts are open to the public, costing $15 per hour during the day or night. Two hard-surface courts are also at the **Hilton Kingston Hotel,** 77 Knutsford Blvd. (© 876/926-5430), charging $10 during the day or $13 at night. These courts are also open to nonguests.

5 Seeing the Sights

Even if you're staying at Ocho Rios or Port Antonio, you may want to visit Kingston, Port Royal, and Spanish Town to sightsee.

IN TOWN

The most important art collection in Jamaica is housed at the **National Gallery** ★★, Roy West Building, Kingston Mall (© 876/922-1561). This gallery is a showcase for the nation's most talented artists. On the ground floor you're greeted with the controversial bronze statue of the late Bob Marley, the reggae great. A work by Christopher Gonzalez, the statue originally was meant to stand in Celebrity Park, but aroused opposition among Marley fans, who felt it portrayed their hero in an unflattering light. You be the art critic here.

The Edna Manley College of the Visual and Performing Arts is best highlighted by Edna Manley, a well-known sculptor who was married to Norman Manley, the former prime minister. She was also the mother of another prime minister, Michael Manley. Locals refer to her as the "Barbara Bush of Jamaica." She died in 1976 at the age of 86. One of her most celebrated sculptures is *Ghetto Mother,* located in the main lobby.

Also attracting a lot of attention locally are the mahogany figurines and other works by Mallica Reynolds, better known as Kapo. His religious themes have made him a household word in Kingston. Some art critics have called his sculpture "the work of a modern genius."

Entrance is $1.50 for adults and $1 for children. Hours are Tuesday to Thursday 10am to 5pm, Friday 10am to 4pm, and Saturday 10am to 3pm. You'll better understand what you're seeing if you hire a guide, costing J$800 (US$13) for a tour.

One of the major attractions, **Devon House** *⚘*, 26 Hope Rd. (*©* **876/929-6602**), was built in 1881 by George Stiebel, a Jamaican who made his fortune mining in Latin America—becoming one of the first black millionaires in the Caribbean. A striking classical building, the house has been restored to its original beauty by the Jamaican National Trust. The grounds contain crafts shops, boutiques, two restaurants, shops that sell the best ice cream in Jamaica (in exotic fruit flavors), and a bakery and pastry shop with Jamaican puddings and desserts. Admission to the main house is $5; hours are Monday to Saturday from 9:30am to 5pm. Admission to shops and restaurants is free.

At the **Hope Botanical Gardens & Zoo** *⚘⚘*, Hope Road (*©* **876/927-1257**), you can visit a Jamaican Shangri-La, a 93-hectare (230-acre) plot of beauty and the largest botanical garden in the West Indies. It is adjacent to the Mona campus of the University of the West Indies. The "Hope" in the name comes from Richard Hope, a British Army commander who lived here in the mid–17th century. After the grime of downtown Kingston, it's a lovely place for a tranquil stroll; attractions include a cactus garden, sago palms, an orchid house, various greenhouses, an ornamental pond, and a "forest garden," with an aviary for the "birdie" in you. There's also a little zoo on-site.

Admission to the gardens themselves is free, and they are open daily from 6am to 6pm. Admission to the zoo, however, costs J$50 (US80¢) for adults and J$30 (US50¢) for children aged 3 to 11. The zoo is open Monday to Thursday 10am to 5pm; Friday 10am to 4pm; and Saturday and Sunday 10am to 6pm. On site is the Ashanti restaurant, a strictly vegetarian restaurant, serving lunch and dinner daily, using only organically grown ingredients. To reach these gardens from the commercial center of Kingston, take bus nos. 61, 66, or 78.

Between Old Hope and Mona roads, on the eastern outskirts, a short distance from the Botanical Gardens, is the **University of the West Indies** *⚘* (*©* **876/927-1660**), built in 1948 on the Mona Sugar Estate. Ruins of old mills, storehouses, and aqueducts are juxtaposed with modern buildings on what must be the most beautifully situated campus in the world. The chapel, an old sugar-factory building, was transported stone by stone from Trelawny and rebuilt. The remains of the original sugar factory here are well preserved and give a good idea of how sugar was made in slave days. Organized tours are available. You are also allowed to stroll around the campus Monday to Saturday from 9am to 5pm. You must see the Public Relations office first.

The **National Library of Jamaica** at the Institute of Jamaica, 12 East St. (*©* **876/967-1526**), a storehouse of the history, culture, and traditions of Jamaica and the Caribbean, is the finest working library for West Indian studies in the world. It has the most comprehensive, up-to-date, and balanced collection of materials on the region, including books, newspapers, photographs, maps, and prints. It's open Monday to Thursday from 9am to 5pm, Friday from 9am to 4pm.

Bob Marley Museum, 56 Hope Rd. (*©* **876/927-9152**), is the most-visited sight in Kingston, but if you're not a Marley fan, it may not mean much to you. The clapboard

house with its garden and high surrounding wall was the famous reggae singer's home and recording studio until his death on May 11, 1981, in a Miami hospital. You can tour the house and view assorted Marley memorabilia, and you may even catch a glimpse of his children, who often visit the grounds. Hours are Monday to Saturday from 9:30am to 4pm. Admission is J$500 (US$8) for adults, J$200 (US$3.20) for children 4 to 18. It's reached by bus no. 70 or 75 from Halfway Tree, but take a cab to avoid the hassle of dealing with Kingston public transportation.

ORGANIZED TOURS

The best tours, the most personal, and the most comfortable are operated by **Island Car Rentals** (© **876/929-5875;** www.islandcarrentals.com), which will make arrangements to pick you up at your hotel. A minimum of two people is required for a tour. One of the most requested tours is the **Bob Marley & More tour,** taking in the Kingston sights associated with the reggae star. The cost is $48 per person. The rental agency also conducts a cultural and historic tour of the highlights of Kingston for $58 per person. For a tour of what's left of Port Royal, the charge is $54 per person.

6 Shopping

To protect you from the sun, covered arcades lead off King Street, but everywhere many people go about their business, including beggars and the inevitable peddlers who sidle up and offer "hot stuff, *mon*"—which frequently means highly polished brass lightly dipped in gold and fraudulently offered at high prices as real gold.

There is no more typical or evocative city market in all of Jamaica than **Jubilee Market,** overflowing onto Orange Street on the west side of the Parade (Sir William Grant Park), under a roof and in the heart of Kingston. This market was named to honor Queen Victoria's Jubilee. A haven for pickpockets, it is nonetheless filled with all the flamboyant color and drama of Jamaica. Virtually "everything is for sale," one vendor told us, "from Jamaican babies to the most exotic fruits to possessions of Bob Marley." All the Marley mementos are fake, of course.

Kingston Crafts Market, at the west end of Harbour Street (reached via Straw Ave., Drummer's Lane, or Cheapside), is a large, covered area of small stalls, selling all kinds of island crafts: wooden plates and bowls; pepper pots made from mahoe (the national wood of the island); straw hats, mats, and baskets; batik shirts; banners for wall decoration, inscribed with the Jamaican coat of arms; and wood masks with elaborately carved faces. You should bargain a bit and vendors will take something off the price, but not very much.

One of the most modern shopping centers in Jamaica, the **New Kingston Shopping Centre,** 30 Dominica Dr., is known for the range of merchandise rather than for a particular merchant. It's sleek and contemporary, centered around a Maya-style pyramid. This is where to head if you're looking for the highest quality goods, including local items that might not readily be available in your hometown.

The **Shops at Devon House,** 26 Hope Rd. (© **876/929-6602**), ring the borders of a 200-year-old courtyard once used by slaves and servants. It's one of the most beautiful and historic mansions on Jamaica. Four of the shops are operated by Things Jamaican (see below), a nationwide emporium dedicated to the enhancement of the country's handicrafts. Shops include the Cookery, offering island-made sauces and spices, and the Pottery, selling crockery and stoneware.

Things Jamaican, 26 Hope Rd. (© **876/926-1961**), is affiliated with the government and was set up to encourage the development of Jamaican Arts and Crafts. There is an array of products, including rums, liqueurs, jerk seasonings, and jellies such as orange pepper. Look for Busha Brown's fine Jamaica sauces, especially their spicy chutneys such as banana, and their spicy "love apple" sauce (it's actually tomato). Many items are carved from wood—not only sculptures, but salad bowls and trays as well. You'll also find hand-woven baskets and women's handbags made of bark (in Jamaica, these are known, unflatteringly, as "old lady bags").

Wassi Art Gallery and Collectibles, 26 Hope Rd. (© **876/906-5016**), is one of the most interesting shops in Devon House. All the merchandise is made by Wassi Art, a labor-intensive, low-tech Jamaican method. Look for functional, durable kitchenware prized by Jamaican homeowners for its eco-sensitive, earthy appeal. Anything you buy can be shipped home via FedEx. Items cost from $5 to $2,000.

Frame Centre Gallery, 10 Tangerine Place (© **876/926-4644**), is one of the most important art galleries in Jamaica. Its founder and guiding force, Guy McIntosh, is widely respected as a patron of the Jamaican arts. There are three viewing areas and more than 300 works.

The **Mutual Life Gallery,** Mutual Life Centre, 2 Oxford Rd. (© **876/929-4302**), is one of Jamaica's most prominent art galleries. This center offers an insight into the changing face of Jamaican art. The gallery's exhibitions are organized by Gilou Bauer, who encourages unknowns as well as showcasing established artists with flair. Exhibitions change once a month, but there are usually long-term exhibits as well. The gallery is a not-for-profit institution.

Tuff Gong Recording Studios, 220 Marcus Garvey Dr. (© **876/923-9383**), can be both a shopping expedition and an attraction. South of Denham Town, this is the headquarters of the late Bob Marley's family business. You might even run into his son, Ziggy Marley, coming out of a recording session; his Melody Makers have their headquarters here. Sometimes you can persuade someone to let you in for a tour. If not, settle for a visit to their gift shop, filled with reggae CDs and tapes, records, T-shirts, handicrafts, and other mementos. The studios can be visited as part of a brief and extremely informal tour that's conducted Monday to Friday 8:30am to 5pm for a cost of J$130 (US$2.10) per person.

Loaded with a wider variety of medications than any other pharmacy in Kingston, the **Dick Kinkead Pharmacy, Ltd.,** 72–76 Harbour St. (© **876/922-6525**), has been compared to a civic institution. Local residents sometimes head here for advice before seeing a doctor. All substances are made on the premises, including a medicinal toothpaste made from tropical roots and herbs called Chew Dent; it's made from chew stick *(gouania lupuliodes),* in the tradition of West Africans.

7 Kingston After Dark

Kingston offers a variety of nighttime entertainment. Most events are listed in the daily press, along with a host of other attractions, including colorful carnivals and festivals that are held island-wide throughout the year. In nearly all the after-dark establishments of Kingston, foreign visitors are only about 3% of those in attendance. Most Kingston places, except for the bars in first-class hotels, are patronized mainly by locals.

Caution: The city is very unsafe at night. Take taxis everywhere.

THE PERFORMING ARTS

Kingston is a leading cultural center of the West Indies. Notable theaters include **Ward Theatre** on North Parade Road ((© 876/922-0453), and the **Little Theatre** on Tom Redcam Drive near the National Stadium ((© 876/926-6129). Both stage local and imported plays and musicals, light opera, revues, Jamaican dance and choral groups, and pop concerts. Ticket prices vary. From downtown Kingston (Parade and Cross roads), buses 90A and 90B run here.

THE CLUB & BAR SCENE

Within the relatively sedate premises of one of Kingston's best-established hotels, **Mingles** (in the Courtleigh Hotel, 85 Knutsford Blvd.; © 876/929-9000) is a rich-looking—and richly popular—bar and disco. Sheathed with full-grained mahogany panels, with uniformed bartenders whose look might remind you of Jamaica during the era of Noël Coward, it's a clubby-looking but often rocking site known for a revolving combination of reggae, pop, soca (a danceable form of reggae), and Latino meringue. Folk here tend to flirt, talk, and gossip on Friday night, and dance, dance, dance on Saturday night. The bar is open Monday through Friday 5pm to midnight and Saturday 5pm to 3am. There is no cover charge except on Saturday, when it's J$200 (US$3.20).

One of the hottest new venues after dark is **Asylum,** 69 Knutsford Blvd. ((© 876/ 929- 4386), where the program changes nightly. Some nights are devoted only to reggae music, other nights to various contests, sometimes to the old hits of the 1970s and 1980s. A crowd, mainly of locals in their 20s or 30s, flocks here to enjoy the music, the dance, the entertainment, and even karaoke. It's very tropical and very happening, Tuesday to Sunday from 10pm to 4am, charging a cover ranging from J$300 to J$400 (US$4.80–US$6.40).

The open-air **Carlos Café,** 22 Belmont Rd. (© 876/926-4186), is all the rage with its flamingo-colored tones and Caribbean decor. There's a whimsical feel here, attracting a crowd of men and women in their 20s and 30s. You can also dine here—on Monday, crab is featured on the menu. On Friday it's a fish fry and karaoke. On any night something is happening, perhaps a show by Cuban salsa dancers. There's no cover, with a Red Stripe beer costing J$200 (US$3.20). Hours are Monday to Friday 5pm to 2am, Saturday 3pm to 2am.

8 Side Trips to Spanish Town & Port Royal

Historic Spanish Town and Port Royal can both be reached easily from Kingston and are well worth a visit.

SPANISH TOWN ✦

Spanish Town, some 16km (10 miles) west of Kingston, was the capital of Jamaica from 1662 to 1872 and was founded by the Spanish.

The English cathedral, surprisingly retaining its Spanish name, **San Jago de la Vega** ✦ (© 876/986-4405), was built in 1666 and rebuilt in 1712. Because the cathedral was built on the foundation and remains of the old Spanish church, it is half English, half Spanish, and shows two definite styles—one Romanesque, the other Gothic. It's one of the most interesting historical buildings in Jamaica. The black-and-white marble stones of the aisles are interspersed with ancient tombstones, and the walls are heavy with marble memorials that almost form a chronicle of Jamaica's history, dating back as far as 1662.

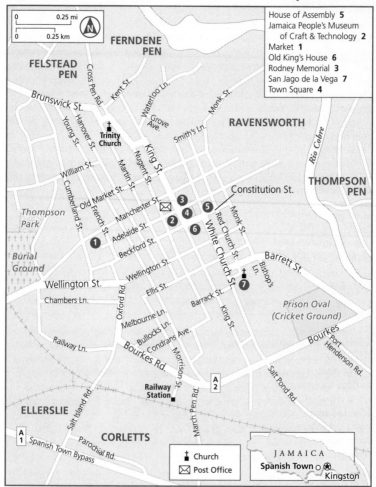

House of Assembly **5**
Jamaica People's Museum
of Craft & Technology **2**
Market **1**
Old King's House **6**
Rodney Memorial **3**
San Jago de la Vega **7**
Town Square **4**

FERNDENE
PEN

FELSTEAD
PEN

Cross Pen Rd.

Kent St.

Waterloo Ln.

Monk St.

RAVENSWORTH

Rio Cobre

Brunswick St.

Young St.

Hanover St.

Grove
Ave.

Smith's Ln.

King St.

Nugent St.

Trinity
Church

William St.

Martin St.

Old Market St.

Manchester St.

Constitution St.

THOMPSON
PEN

Thompson
Park

Cumberland St.

Old French St.

Adelaide St.

Beckford St.

White Church St.

Red Church St.

Monk St.

Burial
Ground

Wellington St.

Wellington St.

Ellis St.

Barrett St.

Bishop's
Ln.

Chambers Ln.

Oxford Rd.

Melbourne Ln.

Barrack St.

King St.

Prison Oval
(Cricket Ground)

Railway Ln.

Bullocks Ln.

Bourkes
Rd.

Condrans Ave.

Morrison St.

A
2

Bourkes
Port
Henderson Rd.

Salt Pond Rd.

Railway
Station

ELLERSLIE

Salt Island Rd.

CORLETTS

A
1

Spanish Town Bypass

Parochial Rd.

March Pen Rd.

✝ Church

✉ Post Office

JAMAICA

Spanish Town ○ ⊛
Kingston

After visiting the cathedral, walk 3 blocks north along White Church Street to Constitution Street and the **Town Square,** surrounded by graceful royal palms. On the west side is **Old King's House,** residence of Jamaica's British governors until 1872, when the capital was transferred to Kingston. It hosted many celebrated guests—among them Lord Nelson, Admiral Rodney, Captain Bligh of HMS *Bounty* fame, and King William IV. Gutted by fire in 1925, its facade has been restored.

Jamaica People's Museum of Craft & Technology, Old King's House, Constitution Square (✆ **876/907-0322**), is open Monday to Friday from 9:30am to 4:30pm. Admission is J$100 (US$1.60) for adults, J$40 (US65¢) for children. The garden contains examples of old farm machinery, an old water-mill wheel, a hand-turned sugar mill, a fire engine, and more. An outbuilding houses a museum of crafts and technology, together with a number of smaller agricultural implements. In the small

archaeological museum are old prints, models, and maps of the town's grid layout from the 1700s.

The streets around the old Town Square contain many fine Georgian town houses intermixed with tin-roofed shacks. Nearby is the **market,** so busy in the morning that you'll find it difficult, almost dangerous, to drive through. It does provide, however, a bustling scene of Jamaican life.

On the north side of the square is the **Rodney Memorial,** the most dramatic building on the square, commissioned by a grateful assembly to commemorate the 1782 victory of British admiral Baron George Rodney over a French fleet, saving the island from invasion.

The remaining side of the square, the east, contains the most attractive building, the **House of Assembly,** with a shady brick colonnade running the length of the ground floor, above which is a wooden-pillared balcony. This was the stormy center of the bitter debates of Jamaica's governing body. Now the ground floor is the parish library.

PORT ROYAL ✦
From West Beach Dock, Kingston, a ferry ride of 20 to 30 minutes will take you to Port Royal, subject of a hundred adventure novels that conjure up visions of swashbuckling

The Wickedest City on Earth

As the notorious pirate Henry Morgan made his way through the streets in the late 17th century, the prostitutes hustled customers, the rum flowed, and buccaneers were growing rich and sassy. The town was Port Royal, at the entrance to the world's seventh largest natural harbor. It was filled with drinking parlors, gambling dens, billiard rooms, brothels, and joints offering entertainment such as cock fights, target shoots, and bear baiting. Buccaneers not only got drunk—they fought duels and pursued "foul vices" after long months at sea. All this earned Port Royal the title of "The Wickedest City on Earth."

All this came to a thundering end on the hot morning of June 7, 1692. Without warning, a severe earthquake sunk most of the town, killing some 2,000 people. The skies turned copper over this once-vibrant pirate city. To this day it is known as the famous "Sunken City" of Port Royal.

Actually, the 1692 earthquake was only one of nine that descended upon Port Royal. The area was also struck by 16 of the worst hurricanes to hit the Caribbean, and three devastating fires ravaged the town. It's a wonder anything is still standing today.

Norman Manley International Airport shares the same thin peninsula with Port Royal, but otherwise, all is quiet in the town today. It's easy to conjure up images not only of Morgan but of another buccaneer, Roche Brasiliano, who liked to roast Spaniards alive. To celebrate, he'd break out a keg of wine on the streets of Port Royal; whether they wanted to or not, he forced passersby to have a drink with him at gunpoint.

What happened to Henry Morgan after piracy was outlawed here in 1681? He was knighted in England and sent back to arrest his old hell-raising mateys.

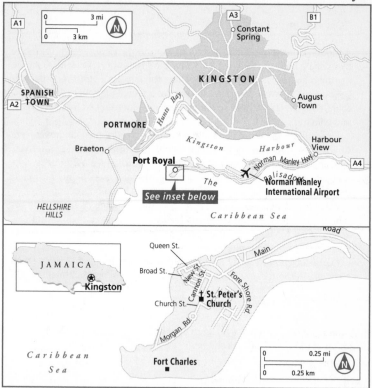

pirates, led by Henry Morgan, swilling grog in harbor taverns. This was once one of the largest trading centers of the New World, with a reputation for being the "wickedest city on earth." Blackbeard stopped here regularly on his Caribbean trips. But it all came to an end on June 7, 1692, when a third of the town disappeared underwater during a devastating earthquake.

Today Port Royal, derelict and rundown, is a small fishing village. Some 2,000 residents—and a lot of ghosts—live here. A seafaring tradition continues, and the town is famous for fresh seafood and quaint architecture. Once there were six forts here with a total of 145 guns; some of the guns remain today, but only Fort Charles still stands.

SEEING THE SIGHTS

As you drive along the Palisades, you arrive first at **St. Peter's Church.** It's usually closed, but you may persuade the caretaker, who lives opposite, to open it if you want to see the silver plate, said to be spoils captured by Henry Morgan from the cathedral in Panama. In the ill-kept graveyard is the tomb of Lewis Galdy, a Frenchman swallowed up and subsequently regurgitated by the 1692 earthquake.

Fort Charles (© 876/967-8438), the only one remaining of Port Royal's six forts, has withstood attack, earthquake, fire, and hurricane. Built in 1656 and later strengthened by Henry Morgan himself for his own purposes, the fort displays scale models of

Cays & Mangroves

Although close to the urban sprawl of Kingston, you can return to nature by taking a boat tour leaving from **Morgan's Harbour Hotel & Marina**. The nearby mangroves are a natural habitat for Jamaica's bird life, especially pelicans and frigates, which use the area as a breeding ground. Entirely surrounded by water, it is also an important haven for other water-loving birds and wildlife.

Close to Morgan's Harbour and the Kingston airport, the mangroves have survived hurricanes and earthquakes. Jamaican officials created a waterway, allowing small boats to enter. During this trip you can see oyster beds, fish-breeding grounds, and a wide assortment of mangroves, along with boat wrecks. If you're lucky, you may even spot a pod of dolphins.

After the mangroves you're taken on a tour of some of Jamaica's most famous cays, including Lime Cay and Maiden Cay. Close to them is Gun Cay, aptly named for the remains of cannons and large guns. Many a "bloody war" among notorious pirates was fought here.

Regrettably, there aren't any organized tours anymore, but the staff at Morgan's Harbour can generally hook you up with a local boatman.

ships from past eras. It's open daily from 9am to 5pm; admission is J$200 (US$3.20) for adults, J$100 (US$1.60) for children.

WHERE TO STAY

Morgan's Harbour Hotel & Marina   On the premises of this yachtie favorite is a 200-year-old redbrick building once used to melt pitch for His Majesty's navy, a swimming area defined by docks and buoys, and a series of wings whose eaves are accented with hints of gingerbread. Set on 9 hectares (22 acres) of flat and rocky seashore, the resort contains the largest marina in Kingston, plus a breezy waterfront restaurant and a popular bar (where ghost stories about the old Port Royal seem especially lurid as the liquor flows on Fri night). Longtime residents claim that the ghosts of soldiers killed by a long-ago earthquake are especially visible on hot and very calm days, when British formations seem to march out of the sea.

The well-furnished bedrooms are laid out in an 18th-century Chippendale-Jamaican style. Medium-size bathrooms are tidily maintained, each with a shower in the bathroom. The Buccaneer Scuba Club organizes dives to some of the 170-odd wrecks lying close to shore (see the nearby box, "Cays & Mangroves").

Port Royal, Kingston 1. ✆ 876/967-8030. Fax 876/967-8073. www.morgansharbour.com. 60 units. Year-round $140–$160 double; $250 suite. AE, MC, V. Take the public ferryboat that departs every 2 hr. from near Victoria Pier on Ocean Blvd.; many visitors arrive by car or taxi. **Amenities:** Restaurant; bar; 2 pools; limited room service; laundry service; nonsmoking rooms. *In room:* A/C, TV, dataport, minibar, beverage maker, hair dryer, iron.

WHERE TO DINE

Sir Henry Morgan's Restaurant INTERNATIONAL/JAMAICAN   This bar and restaurant offer guests panoramic views of Kingston Bay and the Blue Mountains. Except for the elegant lobster or seafood salad, lunch is a relatively simple affair. You

can order various sandwiches and desserts, along with a daily luncheon special—a traditional Jamaican dish. The catch of the day is steamed or fried. You get more of a choice at dinner; your best bet is either the fresh Jamaican lobster, which can be prepared in a number of ways—everything from thermidor to grilled with garlic butter. The traditional Jamaican pepper steak, with hot and sweet peppers, is excellent, as is the selection of homemade ice creams to finish your meal.

In Morgan's Harbour Hotel & Marina, Port Royal. © **876/967-8075.** Main courses J$400–J$1,500 (US$6.40–US$24). AE, DISC, MC, V. Daily 7am–10:30pm.

9 Exploring the Blue Mountains ⊁⊁⊁

Jamaica has some of the most varied and unusual topography in the Caribbean, including a mountain range laced with rough rivers, streams, and waterfalls. The 77,699-hectare (192,000-acre) **Blue Mountain–John Crow Mountain National Park** is maintained by the Jamaican government. The mountainsides are covered with coffee fields, producing a blended brew that's among the leading exports of Jamaica. But for the nature enthusiast, the mountains reveal an astonishingly complex series of ecosystems that change radically as you climb from sea level to fog-shrouded peaks.

The Blue Mountains, Jamaica's highest peaks, form a virtual botanical Garden of Eden. Steep and exhausting, and invariably hot and muggy, the trails and hikes are not as hazardous—or frightening—as, say, the Alpine peaks of Switzerland and Austria. The foothills of the Blue Mountains begin on the outskirts of Kingston.

To the east of the Blue Mountains, moving toward the sea, are the **John Crow Mountains** ⊁⊁, another vast area of scenic beauty, although the trails here are more overgrown than the more trodden paths of the Blue Mountains. The most dedicated hikers can go, in 3 days, from the Grand Ridge of the Blue Mountains to Port Antonio on the coast. But they need a machete to hack their way and blaze a trail.

GETTING AROUND   If you're not a hiker, the easiest way to tour the Blue Mountains is by car, although you'll miss the most remote or difficult-to-reach beauty spots. You can, however, get quite a dramatic preview via the road. The main route into the Blue Mountains is the B1, which begins on the western outskirts of Kingston. Follow signposts to the hamlet of The Cooperage, the gateway to the mountains.

Though improved, this narrow road is still difficult; landslides do occur during the rainy season. Many drivers prefer a four-wheel-drive vehicle. Also watch for oncoming trucks—the macho drivers won't give an inch. And remember that the last gas station (called "petrol" here) is on the outskirts of Papine, in northeast Kingston. You'll need to fill up there. Public transport in the mountains is hopelessly unreliable.

ORGANIZED TOURS

Cycling is a good option when touring the Blue Mountains. **Blue Mountain Bike Tours** (© **876/974-7075** in Kingston) offers all-downhill bike tours through the Blue Mountains—you peddle only about a half-dozen times on this several-mile trip. Visitors are driven to the highest navigable point, then cruise most of the way down. Lunch, snacks, and lots of information about coffee, local foliage, and history are provided. The cost is about $93 per person.

You can opt to head out alone into the Jamaican wilderness, but considering the dangers of such an undertaking, and a possible mugging you might encounter en route, it isn't advisable. A better bet involves engaging one of Kingston's best-known

specialists in eco-sensitive tours, **Sunventure Tours,** 30 Balmoral Ave., Kingston 10 (© **876/960-6685;** www.sunventuretours.com).

The staff offers lots of tour choices. The **Blue Mountain Sunrise Tour** involves a camp-style overnight in one of the most remote and inaccessible areas of Jamaica. For a fee of $75 to $120 per person, participants are retrieved at their Kingston hotels, driven to an isolated ranger station accessible only via four-wheel-drive vehicle, and guided on a two-stage hike that begins at 2pm. A simple mountaineer's supper is served at 6pm around a campfire; late, at 3am, climbers hike by moonlight and flash-light to a mountaintop aerie selected for its view of the sunrise. You stay aloft until around noon, then head back down to Kingston. There's also a shorter 4-hour trek offered, costing $25 to $30 per person.

HIKING

Most visitors come to the Blue Mountains for hiking. Because of rains, the worst months for hiking are May, June, September, and October. Of the more than 30 known trails in the Blue Mountains, only two-thirds are likely to be passable at any given time.

At no point do we recommend that you hike alone in the Blue Mountains. Weather conditions can change rapidly, and hiking maps are, in general, very poor; it is easy to lose your direction. Security is also a major concern for the unaccompanied hiker on the Kingston side of the mountains. A guide will not only clear an overgrown path for you, but may keep you out of harm's way. (To retain the services of a guide, ask at the tourist office.)

The most popular and scenic hike begins at **Whitfield Hall** ★★ (© **876/927-0986**), a high-altitude hostel and coffee estate about 10km (6¼ miles) north of the hamlet of Mavis Bank (see below). Reaching the summit of Blue Mountain Peak requires between 4 and 5 hours from here each way. You can also take much shorter hikes if you don't want to see everything. En route, hikers pass through acres of cof-fee plantations and forest, with temperatures cooler than one might expect and high humidity encouraging lush vegetation. Along the way, watch for bird life such as hum-mingbirds, many species of warblers, rufous-throated solitaires, yellow-bellied sap-suckers, and Greater Antillean pewees.

Dress in layers and bring bottled water. If you opt for a 2am departure to watch the sunrise from atop the peak, carry a flashlight as well. Sneakers are usually adequate, though many climbers bring hiking boots. Be aware that even during the "dry" season (Dec–Mar), rainfall is common; during the "rainy" season (the rest of the year), rain, fog, and mist are all frequent.

EXPLORING THE BLUE MOUNTAINS

IRISH TOWN   From the hamlet at Papine on the northern tier of Kingston, you can continue on the winding road north to Irish Town, going via **The Cooperage,** 3km (1¾ miles) to the north, a tiny hamlet taking its name from the Irish coopers who lived and worked here in the 19th century. They made wooden barrels to hold the Blue Mountain coffee that was transported to Kingston, where it was later shipped to the ports of New York, Boston, and London.

From here, you can continue north to Irish Town, also named for the coopers who lived here, or swing east toward Mavis Bank.

For this route, however, we'll continue north to Irish Town, home to Chris Black-well's magnificent **Strawberry Hill.** This is the premier place for food and lodging in

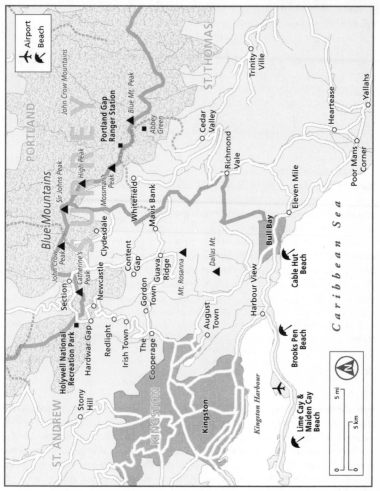

the Blue Mountains; Bob Marley was brought to this site to recover in 1976 after an attempt on his life by a gunman. In later years other visitors have included Mick Jagger and the Rolling Stones, and U2.

Nearby is a hamlet called **Redlight** that was once one of the most notorious villages in the West Indies, filled with whorehouses catering to the soldiers stationed in barracks at Newcastle.

After Redlight, the winding B1 takes you to:

NEWCASTLE   This village has one of the best views of Kingston from any vantage point in the Blue Mountains.

Towering over Newcastle is the 1,542m (5,060-ft.) **Catherine's Peak** ☆☆, named for Lady Catherine Long, the first woman to scale it—in 1760! It's the highest point

in the parish of St. Andrew. A little road off the B1 just north of here takes you to the summit, often shrouded in mist.

WHERE TO STAY

Strawberry Hill ★★ *Finds*   Music-industry-mogul-turned-hotelier-extraordinaire Chris Blackwell worked here to re-create an idealized version of Jamaica that he remembered from his childhood. The setting is a former coffee plantation in the Blue Mountains, on precariously sloping rainforest terrain 930m (3,100 ft.) above the sea. Views from its terraces overlook the capital's twinkling lights. Eco-sensitive and fully contained, it has its own power and water-purification system, a small-scale spa, and elaborate botanical gardens. One former guest described this exclusive resort as a "home away from home for five-star Robinson Crusoes." Maps and/or guides are provided for tours of nearby coffee plantations, hiking and mountain biking through the Blue Mountains, and tours by night or by day of the urban attractions of nearby Kingston.

Accommodations are lavishly nostalgic, draped in bougainvillea and Victorian-inspired gingerbread, and outfitted with gracious mahogany furniture like that of a 19th-century Jamaican great house. Local craftspeople fashioned the cottages and furnished them with canopied four-poster beds and louvered mahogany windows. The elegant bathrooms, each designed in an artfully old-fashioned motif, come with shower/tub combinations. The food served in the hotel's glamorous restaurant is good enough to draw foodies from throughout eastern Jamaica.

Irish Town, Blue Mountains. © 800/OUTPOST in the U.S., or 876/944-8400. Fax 876/944-8408. www.islandoutpost.com/strawberry_hill. 12 units. Year-round $670–$890 1-bedroom suite or deluxe studio; $799 deluxe villa; $775 2-bedroom villa. Rates include all meals. AE, DISC, MC, V. Guests are personally escorted to the hotel in a customized van or via a 7-min. helicopter ride. It's a 50-min. drive from the Kingston airport or 30 min. via mountain roads from the center of the city. **Amenities:** Restaurant; bar; pool; spa w/hydrotherapy facilities and massage; sauna; bike rental; limited room service; babysitting; laundry service; nonsmoking rooms; rooms for those w/limited mobility. *In room:* TV, kitchenette (in some), hair dryer, iron, safe.

WHERE TO DINE

Strawberry Hill ★★★ MODERN JAMAICAN   The most charming restaurant in the Jamaican capital involves a taxi ride up a meandering Blue Mountain road to the hotel of the same name (see "Where to Stay," above). Dining is within an interconnected series of catwalks, verandas, and gazebo-style pavilions that were meticulously re-created along 19th-century patterns. The delectable menu items change with the season, but are likely to include such Jamaican dishes as grilled shrimp with fresh cilantro, fresh grilled fish with jerk mango and sweet-pepper salsa, or rotis stuffed with curried goat and fresh herbs. It's called "new Jamaican cuisine," and it is. Sunday brunches are enduringly popular, thanks partly to a lavish array of more than 40 dishes, each arranged in a separate gazebo-like pavilion like a temple to fine gastronomy.

Irish Town, Blue Mountains. © 876/944-8400. Reservations recommended. Main courses $10–$24; fixed-price Sun brunch $40. AE, MC, V. Daily 8–10:30am, noon–3pm, and 6:30–10pm; Sun brunch 11:30am–2:30pm. From Kingston, drive 11km (6¾ miles) north, following Old Hope Rd. to the northern suburb of Papin. When you get to Papin, turn left onto Gordon Town Rd., cross a bridge, and turn left onto Newcastle Rd., where you go left. From there, follow the steep uphill road for another 11km (6¾ miles) along dramatic and winding mountain roads, following the signs to Strawberry Hill.

Three kilometers (1¾ miles) past Newcastle the road continues to:

HARDWAR GAP   This hamlet at the crest of Grand Ridge is a famous stopover point for those doing the tour of the Blue Mountains. Visitors drop by the restaurant described below for a welcome bite.

WHERE TO DINE

The Gap Cafe & Gift Shoppe ⸙ *(Finds)* JAMAICAN   The location is 1,260m (4,200 ft.) above sea level in the mountains overlooking Newcastle, with vistas of Kingston and the surrounding hills; Ian Fleming wrote parts of *Dr. No* in the house. The Blue Mountain coffee alone is worth the visit, and it's individually ground and brewed as you sit back taking in the scenery. You can also partake of curry or sautéed shrimp, and our favorite dish, pasta with jerk chicken. The chef is quite proud—and rightly so—of his crab backs, as well.

Main Rd., Hardwar Gap in the Blue Mountains, John Crow Mountain National Park. ⓒ **876/997-3032**. Main courses J$550–J$700 (US$8.80–US$11). AE, MC, V. Mon–Fri 10am–5pm; Sat–Sun 10am–6pm.

Just 183m (600 ft.) above the Gap Cafe you arrive at the:

HOLYWELL NATIONAL RECREATION PARK ⸙⸙   This 121-hectare (300-acre) park, part of the greater Blue Mountain park, is the end of the line for most visitors who want to have a glimpse of the Blue Mountains but don't want to venture forth on any arduous hikes into unknown terrain. If you brought the makings of a picnic lunch, it is also an ideal spot.

The enveloping forest covers **Oatley Mountain,** a sanctuary for wildlife, mainly tropical birds, which are seen in abundance here. For those who'd like short hikes to sample the mountain scenery without having to do much difficult hiking, this is the place to go. The main trails, and also the most scenic, have been outlined on bulletin boards in the area. The ranger station here (ⓒ **876/997-8044**) will provide more details, and perhaps a ranger may even accompany visitors on short hikes.

Our favorite is the 3km (1¾-mile) **Oatley Mountain Trail,** which goes into an almost junglelike interior. There are also lookout points where you can enjoy panoramic views. Another trail, the **Cascade Water Trail,** is only 2km (1¼ miles) or so and takes you to a beauty spot where you can plunge into the chilly waters to cool off.

The **Jamaican Conservation and Development Trust,** 29 Dunbarton Ave. in Kingston (ⓒ **876/960-2848**), rents a trio of cabins in the area for those who book in advance. Six people can fit comfortably into the bigger cabin, four overnighters in a smaller cabin. The cost of a cabin for the night ranges from J$2,750 to J$3,800 (US$44 to US$61). Tent sites are J$200 (US$3.20).

The cost of entering Holywell Park is $5 for adults and $2 for children ages 4 to 12. The park is open Tuesday to Sunday 10am to 6pm.

SECTION   After leaving Holywell, and after another 5km (3 miles), you arrive at the hamlet of **Section,** the heart of the coffee-growing district. The road to the left takes you all the way to the coast and Buff Bay if you're going on to Port Antonio (see chapter 8), a distance of 29km (18 miles).

Other than the gorgeous scenery, the attraction at Section is the **Old Tavern Coffee Estate** ⸙ (ⓒ **876/999-7070**). A British fellow, Alex Twyman, started this estate when he arrived some 3 decades ago; his coffee is the finest in the Blue Mountains. Caffeine aficionados pay $35 for a .5kg (1-lb.) bag, and it's worth it—ask Martha Stewart. Visitors are allowed to tour for free the 52 hillside hectares (130 acres) and learn more about coffee than they ever wanted to know. You should, however, call in advance. There's even a waterfall where you can take a dip.

Back at the Cooperage (see above), if you had driven north instead of east, you would arrive in the hamlet of:

GORDON TOWN   En route east to Gordon Town, you pass through the riverside village of **Industry.** In spite of its unattractive name, this is a good spot for river swimming. Gordon Town is the only settlement in the Blue Mountains that could be called an actual town. It takes its name from the Gordon Highlanders of Scotland, who were once billeted here.

There's little to see, but hikers come to take the winding **Gordon Town Trail** ⟨⟩ above Industry and Redlight until they reach the Sugar Loaf, at 2,100m (7,000 ft.). This 21km (13-mile) trail (called a "track" here) is one of the most scenic and rewarding in the Blue Mountains.

Continuing east from Gordon Town, the road takes you to the hamlet of **Guava Ridge,** from which you can head north for 5km (3 miles) to explore **Content Gap,** another center of coffee production. Many hikes are possible from here, including one that goes back to Gordon Town. There are only a few meager hostels and campsites for sleeping, however.

CLYDESDALE   This hamlet is filled with evocative memories, as it was once the site of a well-known coffee plantation that went belly-up in 1937. Today the Jamaica Forestry Department runs this lone commercial tree plantation in the Blue Mountains, with picnic spots and a waterhole where you can jump in buck-naked if you wish.

Towering over Clydesdale is the spectacular **Cinchona Botanical Gardens** ⟨⟩⟨⟩ at 1,500m (5,000 ft.). You can only go with a car about 2km (1¼ miles) from the gardens. You'll have to follow a signpost the rest of the way. The admission-free gardens keep no set hours, but it's best to show up any day of the week between 9am and 4pm. This 4-hectare (10-acre) site was once planted with cinchona trees for producing quinine used to treat malaria in the old days. The slopes are also covered with wild coffee plants. If a gardener is free, he might take you on a **Panoramic Walk** where he'll point out some of the rarer botanical species. A tip would be nice.

Hikers strike out from here for a 10km (6¼-mile) bit of trailblazing down to Mavis Bank (see below).

Back south at Guava Ridge, the road continues directly east and into:

MAVIS BANK   This mountain hamlet, in the Yallahs River Valley, is the last true settlement on the trail to the Blue Mountain Peak. If you're driving into the Blue Mountains, this is the end of the road for vehicles; there's a parking lot close to the police station. Some Land Rovers go beyond, but we find the roads disastrous.

There's one attraction in town worth a visit: the **Jablum Coffee Company** ⟨⟩ (© 876/ 977-8015), open for tours by appointment, costing $8. Hours are Monday to Friday 9 to 11am and 1 to 3pm. This century-old enterprise, one of the most famous coffee factories in Jamaica, produces from 75,000 bushels of Blue Mountain coffee a year. At the start of a tour you're offered a cup of the delectable brew, then led through the entire process of production "from the coffee bean to the steaming cup." This is very much a working factory, not something gussied up for visitors. Afterward, you may want to purchase some bags of coffee—it's far cheaper here than in Kingston.

ABBEY GREEN   Although some hikers begin at Mavis Bank, others prefer to go all the way to Abbey Green 8km (5 miles) to the northeast in order to begin their long trek to the Blue Mountain Peak. This is an almost magical part of Jamaica, some 1,350m (4,500 ft.) above sea level.

WHERE TO STAY

Whitfield Hall ⚔ One of the most isolated places in Jamaica, this hostel is located more than halfway up Blue Mountain. The main draw is the opportunity to see the mountains from a hill climber's point of view. Whitfield Hall is a coffee plantation dating from 1776, the last inhabited house from that colonial period. It provides basic accommodation for 30 guests in rooms containing two or more beds. Blankets and linens are provided, but personal items such as towels and soap are not. There is no official restaurant, but for a small fee all three meals can be provided. All water comes from a spring, and lighting is by kerosene pressure lamps called *tilleys*. A wood fire warms the hostel and its guests—it gets cold in the mountains at night. Most guests request a pickup in Kingston by the hostel's Land Rover, which costs $40 each way for up to six passengers; you can also drive yourself via Old Hope Road to the Kingston suburb of Papine, then to Gordon Town, turning right over the bridge near the police station and continuing into the hills another 16km (10 miles) to Mavis Bank.

c/o John Allgrove, 8 Armon Jones Crescent, Kingston 6. ☏ **876/927-0986.** 8 units (none w/bathroom), 1 2-bedroom cottage. Year-round J$950 (US$15) per person; J$4,250 (US$68) cottage for up to 4 occupants. No credit cards. *In room:* No phone.

BLUE MOUNTAIN PEAK ⚔⚔⚔ The ultimate goal of the adventurous hiker, this mountain, at 2,220m (7,400 ft.), is the tallest in Jamaica. The first time we visited, our Jamaican guide told us, "This is where God takes you when he wants a compliment about how wonderful he created the world." You wander into a lush Eden filled with orchids, bromeliads, ginger lilies, cheesebury, and lichens.

Many hikers prefer to come here very early to watch the sun rise. The climb from Abbey Green is about 13km (8 miles), and you'll need a guide to take this trail to the top. See "Organized Tours," earlier in this chapter, for details of a good tour company.

The first part of the trail, called Jacob's Ladder, is the most difficult. After walking for about 2 hours, a distance of more than 6km (3¾ miles), you come to the **Portland Gap Ranger Station.** It's wise to stop in and alert the ranger on duty that you're taking this trail. Leave your name and that of a contact person. At the station you'll find potable water, foul pit toilets, and a trio of basic cabins where you can crash on the floor for $10 a night. Bookings can be made with the **Jamaican Conservation and Development Trust,** 29 Dunbarton Ave. (☏ **876/960-2848**), in Kingston.

Beyond the ranger station, it's still another 5km or more (3 or more miles) to the panoramic peak. Some hikers give up when they reach aptly named **Lazy Man's Peak** at 2,100m (7,000 ft.). There's a good view of the main peak here. But if you're determined, it's another 30 minutes to reach the summit. There is no more spectacular panorama in all the West Indies: You feel you're standing at the top of the world.

The downside? You have to get back down that mountain—and return to civilization.

Appendix:
Jamaica in Depth

1 History 101

IN THE BEGINNING Jamaica was settled around 6000 B.C. by Stone Age people about whom little is known. They were displaced around A.D. 600 by the Arawak, who originated in northern South America (probably in the area of modern Guyana). Skillful fishers and crafters of pottery and bead items, they had copper-colored skin and lived in thatch-covered huts similar to those used in parts of Jamaica today. The Arawak made flint knives and spears tipped with sharks' teeth, but they never developed the bow and arrow. They lived mainly on a diet of fish and turtle steak. The Arawak were completely unprepared for the horrors brought by the Spanish conquest.

CRUEL COLONY In 1494, during his second voyage to the New World, Christopher Columbus visited Jamaica and claimed the island for the Spanish monarchy. Although he quickly departed to search for gold and treasure elsewhere, he returned accidentally in 1503 to 1504, when he was stranded with a group of Spanish sailors for many months off Jamaica's northern coastline while they repaired their worm-eaten ships.

Beginning in 1509, Spaniards from the nearby colony of Santo Domingo established two settlements on Jamaica: one in the north (Nueva Sevilla, later abandoned) in modern St. Ann Parish; and another in the south, San Jago de la Vega (St. James of the Plain), on the site of present-day Spanish Town. Pirates estimated the Arawak population in Jamaica at the time to be about 60,000.

In 1513 the first African slaves reached Jamaica, and in 1520 sugar cane cultivation was introduced. In the 1540s the Spanish Crown grudgingly offered the entire island to Columbus's family as a reward for his service to Spain. Columbus's descendants did nothing to develop the island's vast potential, however. Angered by the lack of immediate profit (abundantly available from gold and silver mines in Mexico and Peru), the Spanish colonists accomplished very little other than to wipe out the entire Arawak population. Forced into slavery, every last Arawak was either executed or died of disease, overwork, or malnutrition.

RAISING THE UNION JACK After 146 years as a badly and cruelly administered backwater of the Spanish Empire, Jamaica met with a change of fortune when a British armada arrived at Kingston Harbour in 1655. The fleet sailed on orders from Oliver Cromwell, but it had failed in its mission to conquer the well-fortified Spanish colony of Santo Domingo. Almost as an afterthought, it went on to Jamaica. Within a day, the Spaniards surrendered the whole island to the British, who allowed them to escape. Most of the Spaniards emigrated to nearby Cuba, although a handful remained secretly on the island's North Coast.

Six months later, British colonists arrived, but many died. In 1657 Spaniards based in Cuba initiated a last-ditch effort to recapture Jamaica. Two of the fiercest and biggest battles in Jamaican history pitted the Spanish against the British. The

defection from the Spanish army by some Maroons (escaped slaves and their descendants living in the Jamaican mountains) led to the permanent exit in 1660 of Spanish troops from Jamaica. Humiliated, these soldiers escaped to Cuba in canoes.

In 1661 the British began to colonize Jamaica in earnest. They appointed a governor directly responsible to the Crown, with orders to create a governing council elected by the colonists. All children born of British subjects in Jamaica became free citizens of England. Within 2 years the population of Jamaica had grown to more than 4,000. Hostilities between England and Spain continued, with skirmishes and raids by the British on Spanish colonies in Cuba and Central America.

EARTHQUAKES, FIRES & PROSPERITY British interest in Jamaica grew as opportunities for adding profit and territory increased. In 1687 Sir Hans Sloane, physician to powerful British aristocrats and namesake of London's Sloane Square, wrote two influential scholarly books on the geography, flora, fauna, and people of Jamaica. The volumes helped convince Britain to continue its investments in the island.

In 1690 a slave rebellion was crushed by the British, who executed its leaders. Some participants escaped to the mountains, where they joined the independent Maroons.

On June 7, 1692, just before noon, one of the most violent earthquakes in history struck the city of Port Royal. In less than 20 minutes the three shocks, ascending in intensity, caused the sea to recede and then rush back with terrible force, drowning the virtuous and wicked alike. Much of the city actually dropped into the sea. A handful of survivors attempted to rebuild parts of the city, but in 1704 a great fire destroyed every building except a stone-sided fort.

Although the centerpiece of Jamaica had disappeared, the countryside was fast becoming one of the world's great producers of sugar—mostly to sweeten the flood of tea being imported by Great Britain from Asia.

POWER STRUGGLES & EMANCIPATION The struggle for control of Jamaica intensified over the next 50 years as the island became one of the most profitable outposts of the British Empire, despite hurricanes, pirate raids, and slave rebellions. For ease of government, it was divided into 13 parishes, whose boundaries remain today.

Most troublesome for the British were the Maroons, who escaped control by fleeing into the mountains and forests. In 1734, in one of many dramatic battles, the British captured the Maroon stronghold of Nanny Town, destroying its buildings and killing many of its inhabitants.

Dateline

- ca. 6000 B.C. Indian groups settle Jamaica.
- ca. A.D. 600 Arawak Indians come to the island.
- 1494 Columbus visits Jamaica.
- 1503–1504 Columbus is stranded on the North Coast.
- 1509 Spain establishes colony at St. Ann's Bay.
- 1513 First enslaved Africans arrive.

- 1520 Sugar cane cultivation introduced.
- 1655 British troops overrun Jamaica.
- 1658 British repel Spanish invaders.
- 1661 Major British colonization begins.
- 1670 Hundreds of privateers given royal protection in Jamaica.
- 1692 Earthquake destroys Port Royal.

- 1739 Rebellious Maroons sign treaty with British.
- 1800 Census reveals huge majority of blacks in Jamaica.
- 1808 Slave trade abolished by Great Britain.
- 1838 Slavery ended.
- 1866 Jamaica becomes a British Crown Colony.
- 1930 Jamaicans push for autonomy.
- 1943 Bauxite mining begins.

(continued)

The survivors committed suicide by jumping off a cliff, preferring death to enslavement.

By 1739, however, both the British and the Maroons recognized the virtues of mutual cooperation, and signed a series of peace agreements. The Maroons were given tax-free land in different parts of the island and were allowed to govern themselves. In return, the Maroons also agreed to hunt down runaway slaves and return them to their masters.

By the time of the American Revolution, the population of Jamaica had reached almost 210,000, some 193,000 of whom were slaves. After 1776 it increased further as Loyalist residents of the United States moved south to Jamaica. An official census in 1800 revealed a Jamaican population of 300,000 blacks and 20,000 whites. This disparity was not lost upon either the powers in London or the leaders of the increasingly politicized blacks.

However, the boom times—dependent on a supply of slave labor—would not last. The importation of forced laborers from Africa was outlawed in 1807, and in 1838 slavery itself was made illegal in all British dependencies, including Jamaica. The sugar industry began to decline.

A MODERN AGE DAWNS Still, progress marched forward on other fronts, ushering in a more modern Jamaica less dependent on a plantation economy. Telegraph communication with Europe was established in 1869; nickel coins—guaranteed by the Bank of England—were issued for the first time. The educational system was improved, irrigation projects were initiated, and British tourism began to revive fortunes in the 1890s. A Lands Department was organized to sell government land to local farmers cheaply. Island teachers organized themselves into unions, and the railroad was extended to Jamaica's northeast tip at Port Antonio. New bridges and improved roads also helped open the island. Jamaican planters began investing heavily in the production of bananas.

On January 14, 1907, another great earthquake shattered much of Kingston, destroying or damaging nearly every building. More than 800 lives were lost, and total damage was estimated at £2 million. But Parliament and the Church of England spent massive funds to rebuild Kingston; the new street plan they created remains the basis for the city's layout to this day.

During World War I, Jamaica sent about 10,000 men to fight with British forces in Palestine, where they battled heroically against the Ottoman Empire. The war effort was complicated by hurricanes that devastated the island's banana crop, but progress was still made: In May

- **1944** Universal adult suffrage instituted.
- **1960s** Tourist industry grows.
- **1962** Jamaica achieves independence on August 6.
- **1970s** Bob Marley and reggae gain world fame.
- **1972** Michael Manley, a socialist, becomes prime minister.
- **1980** Edward Seaga, a moderate, succeeds Manley.
- **1980s** High unemployment spreads, though tourism thrives.
- **1988** Hurricane Gilbert devastates Jamaica.
- **1989** Manley, now moderate, returns to power.
- **1992** P. J. Patterson becomes prime minister.
- **1997** Patriarch Michael Manley dies; elections retain Patterson and People's National Party.
- **2001** Violence erupts in Kingston; 40 are killed.
- **2002** Queen Elizabeth's visit rekindles emotions about the British role in modern Jamaica.
- **2006** "Disaster Ship" arrives at Montego Bay.

Jamaica Natural

Jamaica and the rest of the Caribbean archipelago are summits of a submarine string of mountains, which in prehistoric times probably formed a land bridge between modern Mexico and Venezuela. Covering about 10,982 sq. km (4,240 sq. miles), the island is approximately the size of Connecticut, yet offers a diverse landscape. It is 235km (146 miles) long; its width ranges from 35 to 93km (22–58 miles).

Millions of years ago, volcanoes thrust up from the ocean floor, forming Jamaica's mountains, which reach to 2,221m (7,402 ft.) high (loftier than any along the eastern seaboard of North America). These mountains, located in an east-to-west line in central Jamaica, contain more than 120 rivers and many waterfalls, as well as thermal springs. In the high mountains of the east, the landscape features semitropical rainforest and copses of mist-covered pines. The mountains are bordered on the north and east by a narrow coastal plain fringed with beaches. The flat, arid southern coastline reminds visitors of African savanna or Indian plains, whereas the moist, fertile North Coast slopes steeply from hills down to excellent beaches. Much of Jamaica is underlain by limestone, dotted with dozens of caves that store large reservoirs of naturally filtered drinking water.

Almost everything grows in Jamaica, as proved by colonial British botanists who imported flowers and fruits from Asia, the Pacific, Africa, and Canada. The island contains unique orchids, ferns, bromeliads, and varieties of fruit, like the Bombay mango, that don't flourish elsewhere in the Western Hemisphere. Birds, insects, and other animals are also abundant.

Framing the capital of Kingston, the Blue Mountains dominate the eastern third of the island. This is the country's most panoramic area, and it's split by a network of paths, trails, and bad roads—a paradise for hikers. From this region comes Blue Mountain coffee, the most expensive in the world. Younger than the Blue Mountains, the John Crow Mountains rise at the northeastern end of the island. Only the most skilled mountain climbers or advanced hikers should attempt this rugged karstic terrain. It rains here almost daily, creating a rainforest effect.

Jamaica's longest river is called Black River, and it's bordered by marshes, swamps, and mangroves where bird and animal life, including reptiles, flourish. Black River, which is also the name of a small port, is in the southwestern section, lying east of Savanna-la-Mar and reached by Route A2.

1917, for instance, Jamaican women were given the right to vote.

In 1938 Alexander Bustamante organized Jamaica's first officially recognized labor union. At first imprisoned but later freed and knighted by the British, he is today regarded as the founder of modern Jamaica.

At the outbreak of World War II in 1939, Jamaica was placed under rigid control, as the governor set prices and censored the press, the telephones, the telegraph, and international mail. By 1943 many Jamaicans were moving north to the United States to work in munitions

factories. During that same year, bauxite, the raw material for aluminum, was mined for the first time in St. Ann Parish. The next year, a new constitution provided for universal adult suffrage.

FREEDOM ARRIVES   In 1957 Jamaica attained full internal self-government under a system based on well-established British models. Lengthy celebrations marked the event. Montego Bay airport opened 2 years later, and Kingston airport was expanded to handle the flood of visitors. Despite economic growth, however, large-scale emigration to Great Britain continued.

On August 6, 1962, Jamaica finally achieved its independence (though it still recognizes the British monarch as the formal head of state). Sir Alexander Bustamante, head of the Jamaica Labour Party (JLP), became the country's first prime minister. And the last British troops in Jamaica departed the island, officially ending a colonial era begun in 1655.

RECENT TIMES   In 1966 Haile Selassie I, emperor of Ethiopia, came to Jamaica on a 3-day state visit. The stay sparked national interest in the emperor's life, and as a result there was a notable increase in Jamaican converts to Rastafarianism, a religion that venerates the late emperor, known earlier as Ras Tafari (see "Rastafarianism," below). During the 1970s the popularity of Rastafarian musician Bob Marley and other Jamaican reggae performers spread worldwide, carving a place for Jamaica on the international music stage.

In 1972 Michael Manley, a trade unionist who headed the left-wing People's National Party (PNP), was sworn in for the first of what would eventually be several terms as prime minister. Jamaicans began arguing vehemently about whether

---

Fun Fact   Did You Know?

- Jamaica is the third largest of the 51 inhabited islands in the Caribbean—only Cuba and Hispaniola are bigger.
- Ackee, though cooked and used as a vegetable, is actually a fruit that is poisonous until it bursts open and its gases escape. It is part of Jamaica's national dish, ackee and salt fish.
- Blue Mountain coffee, grown on the slopes of Jamaica's loftiest mountain, is among the tastiest and most sought-after coffees in the world.
- From 1503 to 1504, Christopher Columbus spent about a year off the North Coast of Jamaica because his worm-eaten vessels weren't seaworthy.
- In the 17th century, the notorious privateer Henry Morgan presided over Jamaica's Port Royal, known as the "wickedest city on earth."
- On August 6, 1962, England's Princess Margaret and U.S. Vice President Lyndon B. Johnson watched as the British Union Jack was lowered and a new flag was raised as Jamaica attained independence. The new flag featured a gold cross on a black-and-green background.
- Rastafarians, a Jamaican religious group, venerate the late Ethiopian emperor, Haile Selassie.
- Some Jamaicans regard ganja (marijuana) as a sacred plant and testify to its healing power.

the nation should embrace socialism, and about its relationship with the United States. In 1977 Cuban President Fidel Castro paid a 6-day official visit, which led to a perception in Washington that Jamaican politics were increasingly shifting leftward.

Despite Manley's political prowess, Edward Seaga of the moderate JLP defeated him and became prime minister. Shortly afterward, Jamaica broke diplomatic ties with Cuba. Seaga's mandate was solidified during the 1983 elections. Seaga attempted to promote economic growth and cut inflation, but with little success. Unemployment rose, as did violent crime. Then, in September 1988, the island was devastated by Hurricane Gilbert, which destroyed 100,000 homes and affected a number of resort properties.

A more moderate Manley returned to power as prime minister in 1989, retiring in 1992 due to ill health; he was succeeded by Percival J. Patterson, also a moderate. In 1998 Patterson launched a crackdown on those who badgered tourists to buy or barter for drugs, sex, or merchandise. Jamaica also established night courts, making it possible for law-enforcement officers to appear in court without having to abandon their beats.

Still, in 2001 Jamaica saw yet another eruption of violence; gun battles between police and government opponents caused at least 40 deaths. To quell the violence, Patterson ordered out the entire Jamaican army of 3,000 soldiers. What sparked this violence wasn't clear.

In early 2002, the "queen of Jamaica"—Queen Elizabeth II—paid a royal visit. She came to show good will, but also stirred up controversy about why an independent nation still retained a European monarch as head of state—a throwback to colonialism that many still resented. For his part, Patterson assured Jamaicans he would work to create a national identity more distinct than ever from the former days of British rule.

Jamaica faced a dim financial year in 2003, with a budget deficit of about 11%. High interest rates kept inflation in the single figures but the Jamaican dollar weakened.

In March of 2006, the *Star Princess*, carrying 2,690 passengers and 1,123 crew members—and bound for its port of Montego Bay—caught fire. Before it was put out, 1 passenger was dead, 11 people were injured, and at least 100 staterooms scorched. Apparently, the fire was started by a cigarette. Once in port, inspectors noted that metal was twisted because of the intensity of the heat.

2 Jamaican Style

ART

The bulk of Jamaican artwork has been executed since 1940, when the yearning for independence and a sense of national destiny colored many aspects of the country's life. Whereas reggae, the national musical form, is strongly influenced by a subculture (the Rastafarians), Jamaican painting is much wider-ranging and diverse.

The most easily accessible Jamaican artwork is "yard art," which rises from the concrete, litter, and poverty of the island's cities. Punctuated with solid blocks of vivid color, and sometimes interspersed with graffiti, these murals are often viewed as an authentic reflection of the Jamaican soul. Subjects include political satire, naive (or intuitive) depictions of an artist's friends and family, idealized Jamaican landscapes, and kaleidoscopic visions of heaven and hell. Examples of yard art seem to increase, along with graffiti and political slogans, before each election. Predictably, however, a flood of uninspired woodcarvings, handicrafts,

and banal paintings have appeared in recent years because of worldwide commercial and sociological interest in yard art. *Caveat emptor.*

Jamaica's leading painters include Carl Abrahams, whose recurrent theme is the Last Supper; Barrington Watson, known for a romanticized, charming view of the Jamaican people; Eugene Hyde, one of the country's first modern abstract artists; and British-born Jonathan Routh, whose illustrations of Queen Victoria during elaborate state visits to Jamaica—none of which really occurred—provoke laughter as far away as London. Also noteworthy are Christopher Gonzalez, who won a commission from the Jamaican government for a statue of reggae superstar Bob Marley; David Boxer, one of the first Jamaican surrealists; and Osmond Watson, known for his sharp-angled and absorbing depictions of the human face.

ARCHITECTURE

The obsession of Jamaican planters with contemporary British taste helped create an architectural elegance rivaled by only a handful of other British colonies, notably Pennsylvania, Massachusetts, and Barbados. Although the island style began with an allegiance to Georgian models, concessions were made to the heat, humidity, bugs, hurricanes, and earthquakes of the tropics. Later, after Jamaica became recognized as the leading outpost of British military power and agrarian skill in the West Indies, Jamaican architectural principles spread to other parts of the Caribbean.

Georgian-type design, manifest in Jamaica's port facilities, Customs houses, and civic buildings, was most graceful in the island's many Great Houses. Intended as centerpieces for enormous sugar plantations, these buildings include some of the finest examples of domestic architecture in the West Indies. Among common design elements are wide verandas on at least two sides, balustrades, intricate fretwork, sophisticated applications of contrasting types of lattice, deep and sometimes ornate fascia boards, and a prevalence of pineapple-shaped finials above cornices and rooflines. The first floors of Jamaican buildings were usually elevated by low stilts or pilings to allow air to circulate. This prevented rot, cooled the ground floor, and helped keep insects, rodents, and scorpions out of living quarters.

Not all of Jamaica's 18th-century buildings were designed along Georgian lines. Smaller, less pretentious houses were built in styles appropriate to the income of the owners and the demands of the sites. Jamaican vernacular architectural style was developed by tenant farms and indentured servants, many from Scotland, and by the children of freed enslaved persons. These houses usually received the prevailing trade winds, and typically were angled to prevent smoke from the kitchen from blowing into living quarters. Known for the pleasing proportions of their inner spaces, the buildings continue to surprise contemporary architectural critics by their appropriate placement and convenient interior traffic patterns.

Since the end of World War II, architecture in Jamaica has followed two distinct variations on colonial themes. Banks, civic buildings, and commercial structures have generally been inspired by the thick walls, small windows, and massive dignity of the island's 18th- and 19th-century British forts. Hotels and private dwellings, on the other hand, typically trace their inspiration to the island's Great Houses or the unpretentious wooden cottages that still dot the landscape.

3 The Jamaican People & Their Culture

Jamaica's 2.5 million people form a spectrum of types that bespeak the island's heritage. Most Jamaicans are black, but there are also people of Chinese, Asian Indian, Middle Eastern, and European background. About 75% of the people are classified as black African, and about 15% as Afro-European.

Jamaicans are generally friendly, funny, opinionated, talented, and nearly impossible to forget. Their sense of humor is dry and understated, yet robust. National pride is specific—beating the British at cricket, winning gold medals in the Olympics, or attaining world boxing titles.

And Jamaica is more diverse than one might imagine. The British brought slaves from the west coast of Africa, notably the area of modern Ghana, who belonged to the Fanti and Ashanti ethnic groups. Others are descended from the Ibo and Yoruba people of present-day Nigeria. When the forced laborers were freed in 1838, most deserted the plantations and settled in the hills to cultivate small plots of land. They founded a peasantry that is still regarded as the backbone of Jamaica.

After slavery was abolished, the British brought in Chinese and East Indians to work the plantations. You can still see pockets of these immigrants here and there.

Jews are among the oldest residents of Jamaica. Jewish families have been here since the time of the earliest Spanish settlements. Though small in number (about 400), the Jewish community has been influential in government and commerce.

In 2003 the birthrate in Jamaica was about 17 per 1,000 persons; the death rate 5 per 1,000. Life expectancy at birth was 78 years for females, 76 years for males. There was a net out-migration of 6 persons per 1,000 inhabitants. The annual population growth rate was .61%.

RASTAFARIANISM

Although relatively small in number (there were about 14,000 firm adherents in the early 1980s), Rastafarians have had a wide-ranging influence on Jamaican culture. Their identifying dreadlocks (long, sometimes braided, hair) can be seen at virtually every level of society. In 2003, there were 265,000 Rastafarians.

Stressing the continuity of black African culture throughout history, Rastas believe in their direct spiritual descent from King Solomon's liaison with the Queen of Sheba. Rastafarianism, according to some, is based on an intuitive interpretation of history and scripture—sometimes with broad brush strokes—with special emphasis on the reading of Old Testament prophecies. Rastafarians stress contemplation, meditation, a willingness to work inwardly to the "I" (inner divinity), and an abstractly political bent.

Their beliefs are enhanced through sacramental rites of ganja (marijuana) smoking, Bible reading (with particular stress on references to Ethiopia), music, physical exercise, art, poetry, and cottage industries like handicrafts and broom making. Reggae music developed from Rasta circles has produced such international stars as the fervently religious Bob Marley. Jamaica's politicians, aware of the allure of Rastafarianism, often pay homage to its beliefs.

A male Rastafarian's beard is a sign of his pact with God (Jah or Jehovah), and his Bible is his source of knowledge. His dreadlocks are a symbol of his link with the Lion of Judah and Elect of God, the late Emperor of Ethiopia Haile Selassie, who, while a prince, was known as Ras Tafari (hence the religion's name). During the emperor's 1966 visit to Jamaica, more than 100,000 visitors greeted his airplane in something approaching religious ecstasy. The visit almost completely eclipsed Queen Elizabeth's a few months earlier.

Ganja

Marijuana use is the island's biggest open secret, and you'll no doubt encounter it during your vacation. (To be honest, it's the big draw for some visitors.) Vendors seem to hawk it at random, often through the chain-link fences surrounding popular resorts.

Ganja is viewed with differing degrees of severity in Jamaican society, but it's still officially illegal. We should warn you that being caught by the authorities with marijuana in your possession could lead to immediate imprisonment or deportation.

Marijuana and Jamaica have long endured a love-hate relationship. The plant was brought here by indentured servants from India in the mid–19th century. Revered by them as a medicinal and sacred plant, and referred to by the British as "Indian hemp," it quickly attracted the attention of the island's plantation owners because its use significantly reduced the productivity of those who ingested it. Legislation against its use quickly followed— not for moral or ethical reasons, but because it was bad for business.

During the 1930s the slow rise of Rastafarianism (whose adherents believe marijuana use is an essential part of their religion) and the occasional use of marijuana by U.S. bohemians, artists, and jazz musicians, led to growing exports of the plant to the United States. A massive increase in U.S. consumption occurred during the 1960s. Since the mid–1970s, after more stringent patrols were instituted along the U.S.–Mexico border, drug trafficking has slowed. Still, today between 75% and 95% of all marijuana grown in Jamaica is consumed in the United States.

Cultivation of the crop, when conducted on the typical large scale, is as meticulous and thorough as that of any horticulturist raising a prize species of tomato or rose. Seeds, sold illegally by the quart, must first be coaxed into seedlings in a greenhouse, then transplanted into fields at 60-centimeter (2-ft.) intervals. Popular lore claims that the most prolific seedlings are raised in Jamaica's red, bauxite-rich soil and nurtured with all-organic fertilizers such

LANGUAGE

The official language of Jamaica is English, but the unofficial language is a patois. Linguists and a handful of Jamaican novelists have recently transformed this oral language into written form, although for most Jamaicans it remains solely spoken—and richly nuanced. Experts say more than 90% of its vocabulary is derived from English, with the remaining words largely borrowed from African languages. There are also words taken from Spanish, Arawak, French, Chinese, Portuguese, and East Indian languages.

Although pronounced similar to standard English, the patois preserves many 17th- and 18th-century expressions in common use during the early British colonial settlement of Jamaica. This archaic and simplified structure, coupled with African accents and special intonation, can make the language difficult to understand. Some linguists consider it a separate language, whereas others view it as an alternate form of English. Some of the most interesting anecdotes and fables in the Caribbean are usually told in the

as bat dung or goat droppings. As the plants mature, tattered scarecrows, loud reggae music, fluttering strips of reel-to-reel recording tape, and sling-shots manned by local laborers are used to fend off the birds that feed on the seeds.

Even more feared than natural predators, however, are the Jamaican police. The constables periodically raid fields and destroy the crop by burn-ing it or spraying it with herbicide.

Marijuana plants reach maturity 5 to 6 months after transplanting, often with a height of about 3m (9½ ft.). Stalks and stems are then pressed for hash oil; leaves are dried for smoking, baking into pastries, or use in herbal teas. Most seeds are saved for the next planting.

Various types of ganja can be grown in a single field, each identified by names like McConey, Cotton, Burr, Bush, Goat's Horn, Lamb's Breath, and Mad. Bush and Mad are the least potent of the crop, while the strongest are acknowledged to be Lamb's Breath, Cotton, and Burr. The last three are mar-keted in the United States under the name *sinsemilla* (Spanish for "without seeds"). Rastafarians typically prefer specific types of marijuana, much the way a gastronome might prefer specific types of caviar or red wine. To each his own.

Smuggling the dried and packaged final product is disconcertingly effi-cient. A small plane lands at any of the country's hundreds of outlaw airstrips, which are sometimes disguised immediately before and after use by huts and shacks moved into place by crews of strong-armed men. The planes then whisk away the crop, much of it to Florida. Undoubtedly, in a country with chronically low wages and constant fear of unemployment, the temptation to accept bribes runs high among government officials in both high and low positions.

Despite its widespread presence, marijuana is illegal in Jamaica and drug-sniffing dogs are employed at all airports. Our advice? Don't end your vaca-tion in jail.

---

patois, so understanding its structure can add to your insight into Jamaican culture.

Proverbs and place names express some of the vitality of Jamaican language. For "Mind your own business," there is "Cock-roach no business in fowl-yard." For being corrupted by bad companions, "You lay wid dawg, you get wid fleas." And for the pretentious, "The higher monkey climb, the more him expose."

Both British and biblical place-names abound in Jamaica. Examples include Somerset and Siloah, Highgate and Horeb.

One also sees Arawak names like Lin-guanea, Spanish ones like Oracabessa, Scottish names like Rest-and-Be-Thank-ful, and entirely Jamaican names like Red Gal Ring.

A final note: The patois has been embellished and altered with the growth of Rastafarianism. Rastas have injected several grammatical concepts, one of the most apparent being the repeated use of "I"—a reminder of their reverence of Ras Tafari. "I" is almost always substituted for the pronoun "me." It is also substituted for

many prefixes or initial syllables. Thus, "all right," becomes "I're," "brethren" becomes "Idren," and "praises" becomes "Ises." The Rastafarian changes of Jamaica's patois are a recent phenomenon and have not always been adopted by non-Rastas.

FOLKLORE

Nothing shaped the modern culture of the Caribbean more than the arrival of slaves from various parts of Africa. They brought gods, beliefs, superstitions, and fears with them. Although later converted to Christianity, they kept their traditions vibrant in fairs and festivals. Jamaican cultural and social life revolved mostly around the church, which was instrumental in molding a sense of community. Storytellers helped maintain ties to the past for each new generation, since little was written down until the 20th century.

Some folk beliefs are expressed in music, notably in the lyrics of reggae. Others are expressed in rhythmic chanting, whose stresses and moods once accompanied both hard labor and dancing. Other beliefs can be found in fairy tales and legends about the island's slaves and their owners. The telling of oral narrations is a highly nuanced art form. Repetition and an inspired use of patois are important features.

Healing arts make use of Jamaican tradition, especially in the "balm yard," an herb-garden-cum-healing place where a mixture of religion and magic is applied by a doctor or "balmist" of either sex. Some medicines brewed, distilled, or fermented in the yard are derived from recipes handed down for many generations and can be effective against ailments ranging from infertility to skin disease. A balm yard is usually encircled by a half-dozen thatch-covered huts, which house supplicants (patients). Bright-red flags fly above each hut to chase away evil spirits. Ceremonies resembling revival meetings are held nightly, with a "mother" and a "father" urging the crowd to groan ecstatically and in

unison. The threat of damnation in hellfire may be mentioned as punishment for anyone who doesn't groan loudly enough or believe fervently enough. It is believed that prayer and supplications to Jesus and various good and evil spirits will help relieve the sick of their ailments.

The two most famous spirits of Jamaica are Obeah and the jumbie. Originating in the southern Caribbean, Obeah is a superstitious force that believers hold responsible for both good and evil. It is prudent not to tangle with this force, which might make trouble for you. Because of a long-established awareness of Obeah, and an unwillingness to tempt it with too positive an answer, a Jamaican is likely to answer "Not too bad" if asked about his or her health.

There's no agreement on the nature of a jumbie. It's been suggested that it is the spirit of a dead person that didn't go where it belonged. Some islanders, however, say that "they're the souls of live people, who live in the bodies of the dead." Jumbies are said to inhabit households and to possess equal capacities for good and evil. Most prominent are Mocko Jumbies, carnival stilt-walkers seen in parades.

One folk tradition that can while away hours of a Jamaican's time is reciting Anansi stories. A notorious trickster—with a distinctly Jamaican sense of humor—Anansi manipulates those around him and eventually acquires whatever spoils happen to be available. In one well-known story, Anansi steals sheep from a nearby plantation; in another, he pilfers half of every other person's plantain. Among the funniest are episodes in which Anansi exposes the indiscretions of an Anglican priest. Anansi's traits include a lisp, a potent sense of greed, and a tendency to be wicked.

These stories are sometimes funny, sometimes poignant, sometimes sexually suggestive. They often are parables, teaching a basic lesson about life. Each narrative

has a well-defined and often charming ending, which tends to be followed by an explosion of laughter from the storyteller. Several collections of Anansi stories have been published.

DANCE & DRAMA

A sense of drama and theatrics is innate to most Jamaicans, as shown in the easy laughter, irreverent humor, and loose-limbed style that are the island's pride and joy. In Kingston in particular, everyone is a star, if only for a moment, during one or another of any day's interpersonal exchanges.

The natural flair of Jamaicans has been channeled into many different drama and dance groups. One of the most visible is the **National Dance Theatre Company (NDTC),** whose goal is to assemble a body of dancers, actors, and singers to express and explore the Jamaican sense of stylized movement. Applauded by audiences around the world, the company offers abstract interpretations of the Jamaican experience, going far beyond the parameters of a purely folkloric dance troupe. Members are mostly volunteers (lawyers, secretaries, laborers, and nurses by day, highly motivated performers by night), and the troupe has usually refused to accept funds from the government. Among the troupe's most famous performers are Rex Nettleford, a dancer and cofounder, and Louise Bennett, pantomime artist, storyteller, and an early proponent of Jamaican patois as a literary language. Established in 1962, NDTC holds a season running from July to December, with most performances in August. It performs at several locations, so you'll need to inquire about where to attend on a particular day.

4 Calypso, Reggae & Rap: The Rhythms of Jamaica

Many people visit Jamaica just to hear its authentic **reggae.** Reggae is now known around the world and is recognized in the annual Grammy Awards run by the U.S. music industry.

The roots of Jamaica's unique reggae music can be found in an early form of Jamaican music called **mento.** This music was brought to the island by African slaves, who played it to help forget their anguish. Mento is reminiscent of the rhythm and blues that, in the mid–20th century, swept across North America. It is usually accompanied by hip-rolling dances known as dubbing, with highly suggestive lyrics to match. Famous Jamaican mento groups reaching their prime in the 1950s included the Ticklers and the Pork Chops Rhumba Box Band of Montego Bay.

In the late 1950s, Jamaican musicians combined boogie-woogie with rhythm and blues to form a short-lived but vibrant music named **ska.** Jamaican artists in this form included Don Drummond, Roland Alphanso, Lloyd Knibbs, Theophilus Beckford, and Cluet Johnson. The five often played together during a vital chapter in Jamaica's musical history. It was the politicization of ska by Rastafarians that led to the creation of reggae.

CALYPSO

No analysis of Jamaican music would be complete without the inclusion of Jamaican-born musician, actor, and political activist Harry Belafonte. Recognizable to more North American and British listeners than any other Jamaican singer in the 1950s and early 1960s, he became famous for his version of the island's unofficial anthem, "Jamaica Farewell," in which the singer leaves a little girl in Kingston Town. Although he worked in other musical forms, Belafonte is particularly known for his smooth and infectious calypsos. *Note:* Some purists in the crowd will point out that calypso is really a

product of Trinidad, but it remains very popular in Jamaica (and Barbados).

REGGAE

The heartbeat of Jamaica, reggae is the island's most distinctive musical form, as closely linked to Jamaica as soul is to Detroit, jazz to New Orleans, and blues to Chicago. The term *reggae* is best defined as "coming from the people." It is taken from a song written and performed in the late 1960s by Jamaica-born "Toots" Hibbert and the Maytals ("Do the Reggay").

With a beat some fans claim is narcotic, it has crossed political and racial lines and temporarily drained the hostilities of thousands of listeners, injecting a new kind of life into their pelvises, knees, fingertips, and buttocks. It has influenced the music of international stars such as the Rolling Stones, Eric Clapton, Paul Simon, the B-52s, Stevie Wonder, Elton John, and Third World, as well as lesser-known acts such as Black Uhuru, Chicago's Blue Riddim Band, and many rap groups. Most notably, it propelled onto the world scene a street-smart kid from Kingston named Bob Marley. Today the recording studios of Kingston, sometimes called "the Nashville of the Third World," churn out hundreds of reggae albums every year, many snapped up by danceaholics in Los Angeles, Italy, and Japan.

Reggae's earliest roots lie in the African musical tradition of mento. Later, the rhythms and body movements of mento were combined with an improvised interpretation of the then-fashionable French quadrille to create the distinctive hip-rolling and lower-body contact known as dubbing. Lyrics became increasingly suggestive (some say salacious) and playful as the musical form gained confidence and a body of devoted adherents.

In the 1950s calypso entered Jamaica from the southern Caribbean, especially Trinidad, while rhythm and blues and rock 'n' roll were imported from the United States. Both melded with mento into a danceable mixture that drew islanders into beer and dance halls throughout Jamaica. This music led to the powerful but short-lived form called ska, made famous by the Skatalites, who peaked in the mid–1960s. When their leader and trombonist, Don Drummond, became a highly politicized convert to Rastafarianism, other musicians followed and altered their rhythms to reflect the African drumbeats known as **kumina** and **burru.** This fertile musical tradition, when fused with ripening political movements around 1968, became reggae.

One of the most recent adaptations of reggae is **soca,** which is more upbeat and less political. Aficionados say that reggae makes you think, but soca makes you dance. The music is fun, infectious, and spontaneous—perfect for partying—and is often imbued with the humor and wry attitudes of Jamaican urban dwellers. Soca's most visible artists include Byron Lee and the Dragonaires. A skillful entrepreneur and organizer, Lee is the force behind the growing annual Jamaica Carnival (first week of April), which draws more than 15,000 foreign visitors to Kingston, Ocho Rios, and Montego Bay.

Leading early reggae musicians included Anton Ellis and Delroy Wilson. Later, Bob Marley and (to a lesser degree) Jimmy Cliff propelled reggae to world prominence. Marley's band, the Wailers, included his Kingston friends Peter MacIntosh (later known as Peter Tosh), Junior Brathwaite, and Bunny Livingston (now known as Bunny Wailer). Since the death of Marley in 1981, other famous reggae musicians have included his son Ziggy Marley, Roy Parkes, Winston "Yellowman" Foster, and Roy Shirley. Among noteworthy bands are Third World and The Mighty Diamonds.

RAP

After 1965 the influx of Jamaican immigrants to North America's ghettos had a

profound (and profitable) influence on popular music. Such Jamaican-born stars as Clive Campbell, combining the Jamaican gift for the spoken word with reggae rhythms and high electronic amplification, developed the roots of what eventually became known as rap. Taking on a street-smart adaptation of rhyming couplets, some of which were influenced by Jamaica's rich appreciation of word games and speech patterns, he organized street parties where the music of his groups—Cool DJ Herc, Nigger Twins, and the Herculords—was broadcast to thousands of listeners from van-mounted amplifiers.

Designed to electrify rather than soothe, and reflecting the restlessness of a new generation of Jamaicans bored with the sometimes mind-numbing rhythms of reggae, popular Jamaican music became less awestruck by Rastafarian dogmas, less Afro-centric, and more focused on the urban experiences of ghetto life in New York. Music became harder, simpler, more urban, and more conscious of profit-searching market trends. Dubbed dance-hall music, the sounds seemed inspired by the hard edge of the survival-related facts of life ("girls, guns, drugs, and crime") on urban streets.

One of the major exponents of the new form is Super Cat (William Maragh), who wears his hair cut short ("bald-head") in deliberate contrast to the dreadlocks sported by the disciples of Marley. The sounds are hard and spare, the lyrics as brutal and cruel as the ghetto that inspires them. Whereas Marley, during the peak of his reggae appeal, sold mainly to young whites, the new sounds appeal mostly to young black audiences who relate to the sense of raw danger evoked by dance-hall music's rhythms and lyrics. During some of Shabba Ranks's concerts, audiences in Jamaica have shown their approval by firing gunshots into the air— known locally as a "salute of honor."

RECOMMENDED RECORDINGS

Jamaica's culture is indicative of and certainly can be defined by its main musical export—reggae. The undisputed king of reggae, the late Bob Marley, popularized the genre, which is musically stylized by percussive guitar riffs and lyrically peppered with political and social activism.

Legend (Best of Bob Marley and the Wailers) (Tuff Gong/Island Records, 422846210-2) chronicles the late artist's body of work. Termed a poet and a prophet, Marley brought reggae into the American conscience and mainstream. The album features a collection of hits such as "Get Up, Stand Up," "Jamming," "One Love," and perhaps his biggest hit, "Stir It Up." *Legend* was released in 1984 and has already outsold such megahits as The Beatles' *Sgt. Pepper's Lonely Hearts Club Band,* and Pink Floyd's *Dark Side of the Moon.*

Honorary Citizen (Columbia/Legacy, C3H 65064), a three-CD boxed set, covers the career of Marley's contemporary, Peter Tosh, a reggae legend in his own right and also termed a poet, prophet, preacher, and philosopher. *Honorary Citizen* features the best of Tosh's work, including some unreleased and live tracks with artists such as Marley, Bunny Wailer (of the Wailers), Mick Jagger, and Keith Richards. Tracks include "Fire Fire," "Arise Blackman," and "Legalize It" (Columbia/Legacy, C3H 65064).

Liberation (Shanachie Records, 43059) by Bunny Wailer is another important album of the reggae movement. When *Newsweek* selected the three most important musicians in the Third World, Bunny Wailer was among them. He has controlled his artistic development, despite tragedies in his career, while avoiding any compromise of his vision.

One Love (Heartbeat Records, CDH111/112) by Bunny Wailer, Bob Marley, and Peter Tosh (Three Greats) offers the three

biggest legends of reggae together on one album—a "Three Tenors" of reggae. This compilation is the first chronological and definitive study of Bob Marley and the Wailers and Peter Tosh in their formative years. The music, the cornerstone of the ska era, includes previously unreleased alternate takes and rarely recorded Jamaican singers.

Ziggy Marley and the Melody Makers, Best of 1988–1993 (Virgin, 724384490821), spans the successful and ongoing career of one of Bob's many children. Ziggy is largely responsible for reggae's 1990s mainstream acceptance, penning such crossover hits as "One Bright Day," "Joy and Blues," and "Brothers and Sisters," which are contained in this collection. His debut album, *Conscious Party,* is still his best work.

Liberation—The Island Anthology (Island Records, 314518282-2) by Black Uhuru is a boxed set of collected works from the band's 1980s Island Records catalog. The 1980s were still dominated by the Marley sound, and Black Uhuru was the band that passed the reggae torch along to Ziggy Marley.

The Lee "Scratch" Perry Arkology (Island/Jamaica, 61524 3792) is another recent boxed set release of another "old skool" reggae artist from "back in the day." Covering Perry's entire career, it contains recordings from the many different bands he formed, as well as solo works, including two never-before-released tracks.

In Concert—Best of Jimmy Cliff (Reprise, 2256-2) is a recording with a legendary pedigree. Produced by legends Andrew Loog Oldham and Cliff, this album features Ernest Ranglin on lead guitar and Earl "Baga" Walker on bass. It includes the classic "Many Rivers to Cross" and "The Harder They Come."

Jah King Don (Mango/Island Records, 162539915-2) by Burning Spear is known for its strongly political lyrics. This record could serve as a definition for hard-core reggae. It includes "World Power" and "Land of My Birth."

Too Long in Slavery (Virgin, CDFL9011) is an album by one of Ziggy Marley's contemporaries, Culture. All songs were written and performed by J. Hill, K. Daley, and A. Walker.

The recordings by the Marleys, Tosh, and the Wailers are considered to be purist reggae, defined as such today because of reggae's splintering into many different forms, such as dance/house music and rap.

Best Sellers (Rykodisc Records, 20178) by Mikey Dread is a compilation album spanning the career of Dread, Jamaica's best-known DJ. With material ranging from 1979 to 1990, it was Dread (along with the band Maxi Priest) who ushered reggae into the new dance movement.

Many Moods of Moses (VP Records, VPCD1513-2) by Beenie Man is the latest release by an artist whose political lyrics maintain all the criteria for purist reggae, but he adds a dance beat heard only from the likes of Dread before the 1990s. Tracks from this album include "Who I Am (Zim Zamma)" and "Oysters and Conch."

Sawuri (Dom Records, CD 1067), the self-titled release by Sawuri, offers a Creole taste to the Jamaican sound. It features the Caribbean artists Marcel Komba and Georges Marie.

Militant (Ras Records, ML 81811-2), released by Andrew Bees, is a signal that the purist reggae will always remain en vogue in Jamaica. Tracks such as "Struggle and Strive," "Militant," and "Life in the Ghetto" evoke modern realizations of the same themes Marley, Tosh, and Wailer sang about in the past—except now with the mounting frustrations of citizens from a Third World society.

5 Jamaican Food & Drink

A visit to Jamaica doesn't mean a diet of just local cuisine. The island's eating establishments employ some of the best chefs in the Caribbean, hailing from the United States and Europe, and they can prepare a sumptuous meal of elegant French, Continental, and American dishes.

When dining in Jamaica, try some fish, which is often delectable, especially dolphin (the game fish, not the mammal), wahoo, yellowtail, grouper, and red snapper. These fish, when broiled with hot lime sauce as an accompaniment, may represent your most memorable island meals. Sweet-tasting Caribbean lobster is different from the Maine variety.

Elaborate buffets are often a feature at the major resort hotels. These buffets display a variety of local dishes along with other, more-standard fare, and they are almost always reasonably priced. Entertainment is often a reggae band. Even if you are not staying at a particular hotel, you can call on any given night and make a reservation to partake of a buffet.

Before booking a hotel, it's wise to have a clear understanding of what is included in the various meal plans offered.

To save money, many visitors prefer the Modified American Plan (MAP), which includes room, breakfast, and one main meal per day, nearly always dinner. The visitor is then free to take lunch somewhere else. If the hotel has a beach, guests often will order a light a la carte lunch at their hotel, which is added to the bill. The American Plan (AP), on the other hand, includes all three meals per day. Drinks, including wine, are usually extra.

If you want to eat your main meals outside the hotel, book a Continental Plan (CP), which includes only breakfast. To go one step further, choose the European Plan (EP), which includes no meals.

APPETIZERS

Except for soup, appetizers don't loom large in the Jamaican kitchen. The most popular appetizer is **stamp and go,** or salt-fish cakes. **Solomon Gundy** is made with pickled shad, herring, and mackerel, and seasoned with onions, hot peppers, and pimento berries. Many Jamaicans begin their meal by enjoying **plantain and banana chips** with their drinks.

The most famous soup, **pepper pot,** is an old Arawak recipe. It is often made with callaloo, okra, kale, pig's tail (or salt beef), coconut meat, yams, scallions, and hot peppers. Another favorite, **ackee soup,** is made from ackee (usually from a dozen ripe open pods), flavored with a shin of beef or a salted pig's tail. **Pumpkin soup** is seasoned with salted beef or a salted pig's tail. **Red-pea soup** is also delicious (note that it's actually made with red beans).

Tea in Jamaica can mean any nonalcoholic drink, and **fish tea,** a legacy of plantation days, is made with fish heads or bony fish, along with green bananas, tomatoes, scallions, hot peppers, and other spices.

MAIN COURSES & SIDE DISHES

Because Jamaica is an island, there is great emphasis on seafood, but many other tasty dishes are also offered. **Rock lobster** is a regular dish on every menu, presented grilled, thermidor, cold, or hot. **Salt fish and ackee** is the national dish, a mixture of salt cod and a brightly colored vegetable-like fruit that tastes something like scrambled eggs. *Escoveitch* (marinated fish) is usually fried and then simmered in vinegar with onions and peppers.

Among meat dishes, **curried mutton** and **goat** are popular, each highly seasoned and likely to affect your body temperature. **Jerk pork** is characteristic of rural areas, where it is barbecued slowly over wood fires until crisp and brown.

Apart from rice and peas (usually red beans), usually served as a sort of risotto with added onions, spices, and salt pork, some vegetables may be new to you. They include **breadfruit,** imported by Captain Bligh in 1723 when he arrived aboard HMS *Bounty;* **callaloo,** rather like spinach, used in pepper-pot soup (not to be confused with the stew of the same name); **cho-cho,** served boiled and buttered or stuffed; and **green bananas** and **plantains,** fried or boiled and served with almost everything. Then there is **pumpkin,** which goes into soup, as mentioned, or is served on the side, boiled and mashed with butter. **Sweet potatoes** are part of main courses, and there is also a sweet-potato pudding made with sugar and coconut milk, flavored with cinnamon, nutmeg, and vanilla.

You'll also come across intriguing **dip and fall back,** a salty stew with bananas and dumplings, and **rundown,** mackerel cooked in coconut milk and often eaten for breakfast. The really adventurous can try **manish water,** a soup made from goat offal and tripe said to increase virility. **Patties** (meat pies) are a staple snack; the best are sold in Montego Bay. Boiled corn, roast yams, roast salt fish, fried fish, soups, and fruits are available at roadside stands.

DRINKS

Tea, as mentioned above, is a word used in Jamaica to describe any nonalcoholic drink, a tradition dating back to plantation days. Fish tea (see "Appetizers," above) is often consumed as a refreshing pick-me-up and is sometimes sold along the side of the road. **Skyjuice** is a favorite Jamaican treat for a hot afternoon. It's sold by street vendors from not-always-sanitary carts. It consists of shaved ice with sugar-laden fruit syrup and is offered in small plastic bags with a straw. **Coconut water** is refreshing, especially when a roadside vendor chops the top off a fruit straight from a tree.

Rum punches are available everywhere, and the local beer is **Red Stripe.** The island produces many liqueurs, the most famous being **Tía María,** made from coffee beans. **Rumona** is another good one to bring back home with you. **Bellywash,** the local name for limeade, will supply the extra liquid you may need to counteract the tropical heat. **Blue Mountain coffee** is considered among the world's best coffees—it's also very expensive. Tea, cocoa, and milk are also usually available.

Index

See also Accommodations and Restaurant indexes, below.

FROMMER'S® COMPLETE TRAVEL GUIDES

Alaska
Amalfi Coast
American Southwest
Amsterdam
Argentina & Chile
Arizona
Atlanta
Australia
Austria
Bahamas
Barcelona
Beijing
Belgium, Holland & Luxembourg
Belize
Bermuda
Boston
Brazil
British Columbia & the Canadian
  Rockies
Brussels & Bruges
Budapest & the Best of Hungary
Buenos Aires
Calgary
California
Canada
Cancún, Cozumel & the Yucatán
Cape Cod, Nantucket & Martha's
  Vineyard
Caribbean
Caribbean Ports of Call
Carolinas & Georgia
Chicago
China
Colorado
Costa Rica
Croatia
Cuba
Denmark
Denver, Boulder & Colorado Springs
Edinburgh & Glasgow
England
Europe
Europe by Rail
Florence, Tuscany & Umbria

Florida
France
Germany
Greece
Greek Islands
Hawaii
Hong Kong
Honolulu, Waikiki & Oahu
India
Ireland
Israel
Italy
Jamaica
Japan
Kauai
Las Vegas
London
Los Angeles
Los Cabos & Baja
Madrid
Maine Coast
Maryland & Delaware
Maui
Mexico
Montana & Wyoming
Montréal & Québec City
Moscow & St. Petersburg
Munich & the Bavarian Alps
Nashville & Memphis
New England
Newfoundland & Labrador
New Mexico
New Orleans
New York City
New York State
New Zealand
Northern Italy
Norway
Nova Scotia, New Brunswick &
  Prince Edward Island
Oregon
Paris
Peru
Philadelphia & the Amish Country

Portugal
Prague & the Best of the Czech
  Republic
Provence & the Riviera
Puerto Rico
Rome
San Antonio & Austin
San Diego
San Francisco
Santa Fe, Taos & Albuquerque
Scandinavia
Scotland
Seattle
Seville, Granada & the Best of
  Andalusia
Shanghai
Sicily
Singapore & Malaysia
South Africa
South America
South Florida
South Pacific
Southeast Asia
Spain
Sweden
Switzerland
Tahiti & French Polynesia
Texas
Thailand
Tokyo
Toronto
Turkey
USA
Utah
Vancouver & Victoria
Vermont, New Hampshire & Maine
Vienna & the Danube Valley
Vietnam
Virgin Islands
Virginia
Walt Disney World® & Orlando
Washington, D.C.
Washington State

FROMMER'S® DAY BY DAY GUIDES

Amsterdam
Chicago
Florence & Tuscany

London
New York City
Paris

Rome
San Francisco
Venice

PAULINE FROMMER'S GUIDES! SEE MORE. SPEND LESS.

Hawaii

Italy

New York City

FROMMER'S® PORTABLE GUIDES

Acapulco, Ixtapa & Zihuatanejo
Amsterdam
Aruba
Australia's Great Barrier Reef
Bahamas
Big Island of Hawaii
Boston
California Wine Country
Cancún
Cayman Islands
Charleston
Chicago
Dominican Republic

Dublin
Florence
Las Vegas
Las Vegas for Non-Gamblers
London
Maui
Nantucket & Martha's Vineyard
New Orleans
New York City
Paris
Portland
Puerto Rico
Puerto Vallarta, Manzanillo &
  Guadalajara

Rio de Janeiro
San Diego
San Francisco
Savannah
St. Martin, Sint Maarten, Anguila &
  St. Bart's
Turks & Caicos
Vancouver
Venice
Virgin Islands
Washington, D.C.
Whistler

FROMMER'S® CRUISE GUIDES

Alaska Cruises & Ports of Call
Cruises & Ports of Call
European Cruises & Ports of Call

FROMMER'S® NATIONAL PARK GUIDES

Algonquin Provincial Park
Banff & Jasper
Grand Canyon

National Parks of the American West
Rocky Mountain
Yellowstone & Grand Teton

Yosemite and Sequoia & Kings
Canyon
Zion & Bryce Canyon

FROMMER'S® MEMORABLE WALKS

London
New York
Paris
Rome
San Francisco

FROMMER'S® WITH KIDS GUIDES

Chicago
Hawaii
Las Vegas
London

National Parks
New York City
San Francisco

Toronto
Walt Disney World® & Orlando
Washington, D.C.

SUZY GERSHMAN'S BORN TO SHOP GUIDES

France
Hong Kong, Shanghai & Beijing
Italy

London
New York

Paris
San Francisco

FROMMER'S® IRREVERENT GUIDES

Amsterdam
Boston
Chicago
Las Vegas

London
Los Angeles
Manhattan
Paris

Rome
San Francisco
Walt Disney World®
Washington, D.C.

FROMMER'S® BEST-LOVED DRIVING TOURS

Austria
Britain
California
France

Germany
Ireland
Italy
New England

Northern Italy
Scotland
Spain
Tuscany & Umbria

THE UNOFFICIAL GUIDES®

Adventure Travel in Alaska
Beyond Disney
California with Kids
Central Italy
Chicago
Cruises
Disneyland®
England
Florida
Florida with Kids

Hawaii
Ireland
Las Vegas
London
Maui
Mexico's Best Beach Resorts
Mini Mickey
New Orleans
New York City

Paris
San Francisco
South Florida including Miami &
the Keys
Walt Disney World®
Walt Disney World® for
Grown-ups
Walt Disney World® with Kids
Washington, D.C.

SPECIAL-INTEREST TITLES

Athens Past & Present
Best Places to Raise Your Family
Cities Ranked & Rated
500 Places to Take Your Kids Before They Grow Up
Frommer's Best Day Trips from London
Frommer's Best RV & Tent Campgrounds
in the U.S.A.

Frommer's Exploring America by RV
Frommer's NYC Free & Dirt Cheap
Frommer's Road Atlas Europe
Frommer's Road Atlas Ireland
Great Escapes From NYC Without Wheels
Retirement Places Rated

FROMMER'S® PHRASEFINDER DICTIONARY GUIDES

French
Italian
Spanish

THE NEW TRAVELOCITY GUARANTEE

EVERYTHING YOU BOOK WILL BE RIGHT, OR WE'LL WORK WITH OUR TRAVEL PARTNERS TO MAKE IT RIGHT, RIGHT AWAY.

To drive home the point, we're going to use the word "right" in every single sentence.

Let's get right to it. Right to the meat! Only Travelocity guarantees everything about your booking will be right, or we'll work with our travel partners to make it right, right away. Right on!

Here's a picture taken smack dab right in the middle of Antigua, where the guarantee also covers you.

The guarantee covers all but one of the items pictured to the right.

Now, you may be thinking, "Yeah, right, I'm so sure." That's OK; you have the right to remain skeptical. That is until we mention help is always right around the corner. Call us right off the bat, knowing that our customer service reps are there for you 24/7. Righting wrongs. Left and right.

For example, what if the ocean view you booked actually looks out at a downright ugly parking lot? You'd be right to call – we're there for you. And no one in their right mind would be pleased to learn the rental car place has closed and left them stranded. Call Travelocity and we'll help get you back on the right track.

Now if you're guessing there are some things we can't control, like the weather, well you're right. But we can help you with most things – to get all the details in righting,* visit **travelocity.com/guarantee**.

*Sorry, spelling things right is one of the few things not covered under the guarantee.

I'd give my right arm for a guarantee like this, although I'm glad I don't have to.

✱✱ travelocity

You'll never roam alone.

IF YOU BOOK IT, IT SHOULD BE THERE.

Only Travelocity guarantees it will be, or we'll work with our travel partners to make it right, right away. So if you're missing a balcony or anything else you booked, just call us 24/7. **1**-888-TRAVELOCITY.

travelocity

You'll never roam alor